T0215563

Troubleshooting Microsoft Teams

Enlisting the Right Approach and Tools in Teams for Mapping and Troubleshooting Issues

Balu N Ilag
Arun M Sabale

Apress®

Troubleshooting Microsoft Teams: Enlisting the Right Approach and Tools in Teams for Mapping and Troubleshooting Issues

Balu N Ilag
Tracy, CA, USA

Arun M Sabale
New Jersey, NJ, USA

ISBN-13 (pbk): 978-1-4842-8621-0
https://doi.org/10.1007/978-1-4842-8622-7

ISBN-13 (electronic): 978-1-4842-8622-7

Managing Director, Apress Media LLC: Welmoed Spahr
Acquisitions Editor: Smriti Srivastava
Development Editor: Laura Berendson
Coordinating Editor: Shrikant Vishwakarma
Copy Editor: Mary Behr

Cover designed by eStudioCalamar

Cover image designed by Freepik (www.freepik.com)

Distributed to the book trade worldwide by Springer Science+Business Media New York, 1 New York Plaza, Suite 4600, New York, NY 10004-1562, USA. Phone 1-800-SPRINGER, fax (201) 348-4505, e-mail orders-ny@ springer-sbm.com, or visit www.springeronline.com. Apress Media, LLC is a California LLC and the sole member (owner) is Springer Science + Business Media Finance Inc (SSBM Finance Inc). SSBM Finance Inc is a **Delaware** corporation.

For information on translations, please e-mail booktranslations@springernature.com; for reprint, paperback, or audio rights, please e-mail bookpermissions@springernature.com.

Apress titles may be purchased in bulk for academic, corporate, or promotional use. eBook versions and licenses are also available for most titles. For more information, reference our Print and eBook Bulk Sales web page at http://www.apress.com/bulk-sales.

Any source code or other supplementary material referenced by the author in this book is available to readers on GitHub (https://github.com/Apress). For more detailed information, please visit http://www.apress.com/source-code.

Printed on acid-free paper

This book is dedicated to my mother (Chandrabhaga) and father (Nivrutti), who is no more, but their blessing always support and motivate me.

I also dedicate this book to my wonderful wife (Vaishali) and lovely daughters (Chanda and Shravya), who always understand and support and stand by me during every struggle and all my successes.

—Balu N Ilag

Table of Contents

About the Authors

 **Balu N Ilag** is currently working as a unified communication and collaboration engineer. His role combines product support and customization, implementation, and strategic guidance for enterprise customers. He is fascinated with artificial intelligence and machine learning technology. Balu is a Microsoft Certified Trainer (MCT), a former Microsoft MVP (2013 – 2019), and a Microsoft Certified Solution Expert (MCSE) for communication. He is an author of *Understanding Microsoft Teams Administration* and *Introducing Microsoft Teams* and regularly writes blog posts and articles on Microsoft products.

Arun M Sabale is a Microsoft Certified Azure architect and a Microsoft Certified Modern Desktop Expert. He has written several blog posts on Azure services and automation, PowerShell, ARM, and Terraform. Arun has more than 12 years of experience in PowerShell automation and other Microsoft services like AD, DNS, DHCP, and VMM, and more than 6 years of experience with Azure infra design/deployment/automation, PowerShell, ARM, Terraform, and Azure DevOps. His current role is a combination of Azure design and development and automation.

About the Technical Reviewer

 **Vikas Sukhija** has more than 15 years of IT infrastructure experience with expertise in Microsoft technologies and IT automations. He is a blogger, architect, and Microsoft MVP and is known by the alias TechWizard. As an experienced professional, he works with clients in automating Microsoft Azure, Microsoft 365, and Amazon AWS cloud.

His community contributions can be found at
@Blog http://TechWizard.cloud
@Page www.facebook.com/TechWizard.cloud
@Twitter https://twitter.com/techwizardcloud
@Coderepo https://github.com/VikasSukhija

Acknowledgments

Much gratitude to all whose work, research, and content helped us write this book, especially Microsoft documentation and training sessions.

This would have been impossible without Microsoft's rich documentation and learning academy. I am always grateful to the Microsoft MVP and MCT community, who helped and guided me from time to time in this journey.

I am thankful for and lucky enough to get constant encouragement, support, and supervision from all teaching staff, Smriti Srivastava and Nirmal Selvaraj Rasiah, technical reviewer Vikas Sukhija, and editor Mark Powers, which helped us complete this project. Also, I would like to express our genuine esteem to all of the staff at Apress for their timely support.

Introduction

If you are a Microsoft Teams support engineer or administrator, this book will help you understand, recognize, capture, and resolve common issues by utilizing best practices, unique approaches, and advanced troubleshooting methods. This book covers troubleshooting topics as you prepare for Microsoft Exam MS-740: Troubleshooting Microsoft Teams.

This practical book provides a comprehensive overview of Microsoft Teams functionality, call quality troubleshooting, phone system (PSTN) connectivity troubleshooting, and best practices. Teams support engineers and administrators, including Unified Communication and Collaboration administrators, helpdesk engineers, and network administrators, will learn how to identify Teams sign-in issues, client connection issues, call quality issues, and phone system connectivity and call routing problems; troubleshoot the Teams service and functionality in a holistic fashion; and appropriately prioritize and utilize troubleshooting approaches.

Co-author Balu Ilag, a UC&C engineer and former Office Apps and Service MVP and Microsoft Certified Trainer (MCT), explains the tools available to help administrators troubleshoot network issues impacting Microsoft Teams call connectivity and quality. This book provides potential problems, a troubleshooting approach, and relevant tools mapping for troubleshooting. He has designed a unique approach and pattern that classifies the tools and the affected component to troubleshoot. This author has already written two books on Microsoft Teams. *Understand Microsoft Teams Administration* (https://link.springer.com/book/10.1007/978-1-4842-5875-0), focuses on administration aspects including configuring, customizing, and managing the Teams experience. *Introducing Microsoft Teams* (https://link.springer.com/book/10.1007/978-1-4842-3567-6) focuses on comprehending the new chat-based workspace in Microsoft 365. This book is more focused on Teams troubleshooting.

Co-author Arun Sabale, an Azure Architect, explains how to design a call quality dashboard to identify pain points and troubleshoot poor voice and video issues.

You will learn how to quickly diagnose Teams connectivity and quality problems and discover the root cause of any Teams issues. Troubleshooting approaches and techniques in this book are compatible with Microsoft Teams and all client application versions. They cover Teams service and phone systems specifically.

Readership

This book is for Microsoft Teams administrators, support engineers, helpdesk engineers, telecom, and network engineers.

We suppose you have a basic knowledge of Microsoft Teams from administration, support engineer, helpdesk engineer, or consultant experience and wish to add to your Teams troubleshooting skills. If so, this book is ideal for you. The ability to navigate and use basic Microsoft Teams commands is expected.

What Will You Learn?

This book covers potential issues and relevant tools for troubleshooting. In it, you will

- Learn about unique approaches and techniques to identify the problem, capture the diagnostic log, and analyze the log file.

- Explore what tools are available to help you troubleshoot network issues impacting a Teams workload.

- Learn about Teams management and troubleshooting aspects using PowerShell commands.

- Explore an author-designed new tool pattern that classifies the Teams components and tools that help in troubleshooting the issues.

- Detect poor audio/video calls and troubleshoot underline problems.

- Get a definitive guide to troubleshooting Teams connectivity and meeting reliability and quality issues.

- Learn and understand Microsoft Teams architecture, newly deployed features, signaling, media traffic, phone system connectivity, call routing, and policy assignment.

This book comprehensively addresses convergence and scalability and common concerns such as Team sign-in issues, client performance issues, update issues, meeting join topics, PSTN connectivity issues, call routing, and phone system issues. For every case, key concepts are presented, along with basic configuration, detailed troubleshooting methods, and clear illustrations. Whenever appropriate, Teams service and client behaviors are described and analyzed.

The two expert authors emphasize the Microsoft Teams-related issues you are most likely to encounter in real-world implementations, including problems that cause poor audio and video quality in meetings when users work remotely.

This book will help you prepare for Microsoft certification MS-740: Troubleshooting Microsoft Teams.

Chapter List

1. Microsoft Teams (troubleshooting) introduction: The Unified Communication and Collaboration (UC&C) presents organizations with unprecedented opportunities to unite a dispersed global workforce and increase productivity while reducing infrastructural costs and maximizing return on investment. Microsoft Teams is the most popular UC&C tool because it helps you easily connect naturally with chat, meet, call, and content sharing in real-time.

Teams is the platform for communications and collaboration within Microsoft 365, formerly Office 365. Teams brings chat, presence, one-to-one and group calls, meetings, collaboration, and application integration into a single experience. Users can share files and data, manage tasks, and collaborate on documents with people inside and outside your organization. Teams can simplify your work by integrating with the other apps and processes you use. This chapter provides a detailed introduction to Microsoft Teams and the phone system with troubleshooting information.

2. Microsoft Teams overview: This chapter provides the complete Teams overview, Teams Service architecture, Teams capabilities, Teams licensing, Teams client architecture, Teams phone system (calling plan, operator connect, and direct routing), Teams live events, and Teams user and service administrator through the Microsoft Teams admin center. After completing this chapter, you will know the Teams service and client architecture and how to manage and administer Teams. Also, this chapter identifies common Teams problems and explains how to approach troubleshooting Teams issues.

3. Microsoft Teams phone (voice) configuration and management: Teams brings together calling, meeting, chat collaboration, and apps to help users easily stay connected right in their workflow. Microsoft Teams provides calls (1:1 and group) and multiparty meetings with optimal audio/video quality. Apart from Voice over IP (VoIP) communication, Teams provides external calling (PSTN call) through a calling plan, operator connects, and Teams direct routing. The Teams (Microsoft 365) Phone System is Microsoft's technology for enabling call control and Private Branch Exchange (PBX) capabilities in the Microsoft 365 cloud with Microsoft Teams. In this chapter, you learn how to plan and configure the Microsoft Teams phone system (calling plan, operator connect, and Teams Direct routing with voice and emergency call routing policies and phone number management). Additionally, you learn how to configure Teams calling features such as group call, auto-attendant, and call queue. This chapter describes configuring Teams phone devices (Teams IP phone, CAP, Teams Room, and Teams Display).

4. Microsoft Teams client-side troubleshooting: Developing a systematic troubleshooting approach is essential in solving Teams problems. This chapter provides information about Microsoft Teams network configuration; collecting teams diagnostic logs and analysis process; diagnosing common Teams problems; troubleshooting issues with Teams apps (first- and third-party); troubleshooting problems with public and private channels; deploying and updating Teams client software; troubleshooting Teams client startup and configuration, troubleshooting audio and video devices; troubleshooting Teams desktop client performance issues; understanding and troubleshooting external (federation) access issues; enabling and troubleshooting Teams Guest access issues; and troubleshooting issues with interoperability with Skype for Business. This chapter is primarily focused on Teams' client issues and troubleshooting.

5. Troubleshoot Microsoft Teams call quality issues: Microsoft Teams is a cloud-only service that is constantly evolving to provide optimal call quality to end users. Microsoft Teams supports all communication needs across the spectrum in the hybrid workplace, from one-to-one meetings to virtual events. Additionally, people can join meetings with different kinds of clients. For example, users can attend sessions from regular phones by dialing into the meeting using audio conferencing.

This chapter provides detailed information to help you deliver an excellent call quality experience over your existing infrastructure. Additionally, this chapter covers different troubleshooting scenarios, including troubleshooting Teams meeting creation and recording issues, examining Teams content sharing and attendee access problems, Teams live events troubleshooting and management, and troubleshooting Teams messaging and reporting problems.

6. Troubleshoot Microsoft Teams phone system (calling plan and direct routing) issues: As a Teams admin, you are concerned with configuring and troubleshooting Microsoft Teams phone system problems. In this chapter, you learn how to deploy, configure, and maintain the Teams phone system. You learn how to troubleshoot any Teams' phone system direct routing and call plan issues; how to enable voice services for users to make and receive calls; and how to facilitate voice services using Teams Phone System with calling plans and facilitate voice services for users when direct routing is configured.

7. Real-world troubleshooting: This chapter emphasizes end-users' day-to-day problems while using Microsoft Teams. Teams' admin requires Teams client troubleshooting knowledge and service side troubleshooting knowledge. It should also be able to troubleshoot Teams' phone system direct routing and call plan issues. Readers will also learn how to enable voice services for users to make and receive calls. Additionally, they will learn how to facilitate voice services using the Teams Phone system with Calling plans and promoting voice services for users when Direct Routing is configured.

8. Teams quality dashboard for call quality troubleshooting: Microsoft Teams is a unified communication and collaboration tool that provides real-time conversation, presence, audio/video calls, meetings with desktop sharing, phone calls, and content sharing. These features are highly critical and require constant monitoring to ensure users get good call quality. This chapter provides detailed guidance on Microsoft Teams call monitoring using an in-built report. You also get an idea of how to create a PowerBI-based call quality dashboard.

CHAPTER 1

Microsoft Teams (Troubleshooting) Introduction

Currently, many organizations are experiencing a digital transformation. Companies see the advantages of employee engagement, better collaboration, clear communication, and working together towards a common goal, which ultimately helps boost an organization's overall performance. Microsoft Teams is a cloud-based communications platform that combines different services for communication and collaboration, such as chat, meetings, calling, files, and content sharing. Teams are tightly integrated into Microsoft 365 (formerly known as Office 365) and incorporate multiple workloads into a unified communication and collaboration system. In addition, Teams offers integration capabilities for other tools and third-party products.

Unified communication and collaboration (UC&C) technology has been recognized as an essential productivity enabler in firms. According to C. Rigg (2021) and a 2013 survey from ZK Research, 43 percent of firms use basic UC&C functionalities. Only 5 percent have implemented the complete solution that includes document sharing, chat, video conferencing, the voice-over-Internet protocol (VoIP), web conferencing, and email. The technology provides communication and collaboration tools that enable individuals to work from any point on the globe. This is a significant added value for firms, as it allows for flexibility, interoperability, efficiency, and productivity.

© Balu N Ilag and Arun M Sabale 2022
B. N. Ilag and A. M. Sabale, *Troubleshooting Microsoft Teams*, https://doi.org/10.1007/978-1-4842-8622-7_1

Unified Communication and Collaboration History

The foundation of the voice network started with the invention of the telephone by Alexander Graham Bell in 1876. Since then, the phone has become a staple in the communications industry and today remains one of the critical elements for business operations. The traditional telephone voice network consists of numerous circuit switches that make up the public switched telephone network (PSTN), which are used to make and maintain connections for the duration of a phone call. The PSTN has been around for an extended period and is considered reliable.

Today, VoIP is an emerging technology that has become a viable alternative in voice communications. In contrast to the traditional PSTN, the VoIP network is connectionless. In other words, a physical connection does not exist between the two endpoints. Instead, the VoIP network uses data packets and network routers to transfer data to and from each endpoint via the Internet. VoIP allows voice calls to be routed over existing data networks to avoid a separate voice network, thus reducing overhead. However, the VoIP communication network is less reliable than the PSTN network. It can be susceptible to voice latency and jitter.

Microsoft Unified Communication Product History

Microsoft has a long history of unified communication applications: Live Communications Server 2003, Live Communications Server 2005, Office Communicator 2007, Office Communication Server 2007 R2 in 2009, Microsoft Lync 2010, Lync Server 2013, Skype for Business 2015 and 2019, and then Microsoft Teams as the hub for unified communication and collaboration as a purely cloud service.

Why Is Teams So Popular?

In today's world, remote work has changed on how people work. It is essential to know how they adapt to change. People quickly thrive when they meet, collaborate, and stay in the flow of work with the full context, and this is where Microsoft Teams comes in. It's a digital workplace that brings people together, and organized teams achieve more no matter how and from where they work.

Teams helps users easily connect naturally with chat, meet, call, and content sharing in real time. Users can switch their devices easily from desktop to mobile or vice versa. Teams helps in collaborating with people the way they work. Information is always available to users; even if they miss a meeting, they can check recordings and transcripts. Microsoft Teams is also deeply integrated with applications to give full context in one place.

One report shows that 70% of workers want flexible remote work options to continue. The same survey also indicates that 65% of people want more in-person time with their teams. So, people want flexibility in when, where, and how they work. Also, most organizations are trying to adopt hybrid work.

Microsoft Teams helps you move to hybrid work with a successful transition. With Teams, you can chat, call, and meet from your digital workspace.

Teams meetings are more effective and engaging. In Microsoft Teams, a cameo in-speaker coach feature brings the connection back to the conference by helping the speaker read the virtual room and keep the listener engaged with energy and expression on the speaker's face as they present.

Teams' new integration with Apple Car Play helps users stay connected while driving. The front row helps even the playing field between those in the conference room and those participating online. All of this is instrumental to an organization's team thriving with hybrid work.

By design, Microsoft Teams is for organizations that want the cost and agility benefits of cloud-based chat, presence, audio/video call, content sharing, and meetings without sacrificing the business-class capabilities of on-premises applications. With Microsoft Teams, Microsoft deploys and maintains the required server infrastructure, and it handles ongoing maintenance, security updates, and upgrades. You as a customer can selectively enable a Teams subscription in a Microsoft 365 tenant. For Microsoft Teams troubleshooting, there are two main tools available: the Teams admin center and the Windows PowerShell command-line interface to manage settings specific to Teams.

Why Is Microsoft Teams Complex?

Teams is the platform for communications and collaboration within Microsoft 365, formerly known as Office 365. Teams brings chat, presence, one-to-one and group calls, meetings, collaboration, and application integration into a single experience. User can share files and data, manage tasks, and collaborate on documents with people inside and outside your organization. Teams can simplify your work by integrating with the other apps and processes you use.

Teams provides a phone system with calling and phone system direct routing, making it possible for users to use Microsoft Teams to make, receive, and transfer phone calls. Before an organization can roll out a phone system solution, it needs to understand the benefits and restrictions for each option.

Microsoft 365 is the productivity cloud developed to support every need to achieve what matters in your work life with best-in-class Office apps, intelligent cloud services, and advanced security. Microsoft Teams is part of Microsoft 365, meaning your collaboration experience in Teams will be integrated with the files, information, and services your team needs to get things done. Teams provides various features, including instant messaging one-to-one and with groups, real-time presence, collaboration, audio-video meetings with app sharing, dial-in conferencing, apps and workflows, and phone calls. Microsoft Teams produces advanced security and compliance abilities that enable safe and trustworthy online collaboration. These features depend on different services and applications, making Teams a vast and complex product. Teams provides real-time communication, which is latency- and packet loss-sensitive, so when a Teams call quality degrades, it is very complex to troubleshoot.

Troubleshooting is the procedure of diagnosing and fixing a system that is acting abnormally. It involves conducting different diagnostic and restoration actions. Completing these actions may incur costs, and standard troubleshooting algorithms strive to minimize costs until the system is fixed. Prognosis deals with predicting future failures. The event-based troubleshooting approach provides more intelligent decision-making concerning the repair actions to minimize troubleshooting costs over time. Figure 1-1 shows how the administrator supports the different functionalities in Teams, which will give you an idea about the difficulty level.

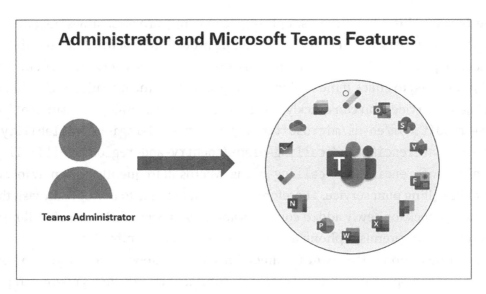

Figure 1-1. *Administrator and Teams functionality*

Introduction of Teams Phone System (Voice)

The Covid-19 pandemic increased the need for remote communication, and a phone call is one of the main communication instruments that allows us to stay connected. Fortunately, Microsoft Teams calling provides seamless connectivity and optimal call quality to communicate with coworkers and customers.

Teams brings together calling, meeting, chat collaboration, and content sharing, helping an organization easily stay connected right in their workflow. With capabilities like spam identification, users feel more confident answering their essential calls. It is easy to take calls from anywhere a user goes.

Microsoft Teams has a robust calling platform that provides call queue and auto-attendant for menu-driven call routing and for critical call scenarios like sales office or branch office scenarios. Teams have Survivable Branch Appliances (SBAs), keeping the user connected even with outages. At the Microsoft Ignite November 2021 event, Microsoft announced that Teams users made 650 million calls in October 2020, which indicates the popularity of the Microsoft Teams calling capabilities.

Microsoft Teams has simple, seamless, and global options for PSTN calling. Teams has a critical and innovative calling value for the board and sophisticated calling scenarios. Since every organization is different, Microsoft Teams calling offers three deployment options: Teams calling plans, Operator Connections, and Teams direct routing.

The **Teams calling plans** are a simple way to instantly procure, provision, and assign phone numbers to end users. In the calling procedure, Microsoft itself is the PSTN service provider. However, calling plans are not available everywhere; hence you, as an admin, need to check if the calling plan is available in the intended region before deploying the service. You can quickly check calling plan availability by visiting `https://docs.microsoft.com/en-us/microsoftteams/country-and-region-availability-for-audio-conferencing-and-calling-plans/country-and-region-availability-for-audio-conferencing-and-calling-plans`. Microsoft frequently adds new locations as part of its calling plan service. Therefore, it is a best practice to periodically visit the above site to check for newly added countries and switch over to a Microsoft calling plan by porting your on-premises phone numbers to Microsoft as a provider.

The second option is **Operator Connect.** This option allows organizations to stay with their existing operator service experience, contracts, and business relationships. It is a simplified and seamless experience to use an operator-manage service for Teams PSTN calling using a qualified operator. Figure 1-2 shows the high-level connectivity. Operator known as service provider manages PSTN (phone) connectivity to Microsoft 365 Teams cloud and the Session Broder Controller with user provisioning like phone number assignment, policy assignment, etc. The organization must procure the Teams licenses and maintain user profile configurations.

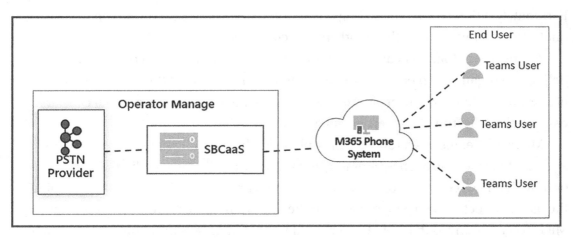

Figure 1-2. *Operator connect*

Operator connect offers multiple advantages:

- Organizations can bring their own telecom operator. This allows them to maintain operator contracts and relationships while providing users a modern calling experience in Teams.

- Using the Operator Connect setup, the Teams admin can set up quickly, including provisioning and management. As part of the setup, it establishes the connection to the operator, provisions users, and assigns phone numbers from the Teams admin center.

- You can save on infrastructure purchases and management. Since the session border controllers (SBCs) are in the operator cloud, they manage the call control in the cloud with the phone system, eliminating the need to purchase and maintain equipment.

- Another advantage is that the organization experiences confidence with enterprise-grade reliability and support. The operator provides the technical support and the service level agreement (SLA). It offers direct peering powered by Azure, which creates a one-to-one network connection to enhance resiliency.

Setting Up Operator Connect

In the Teams admin center, under Voice, click Operator Connect. This will show all the qualified operators. You, as an admin, can filter operators based on country name and service available. To add an operator, simply click the operator name and select. Once the operator is added, you can add the phone number under the Phone number tab in the Teams admin center. Figure 1-3 shows how to add Operator Connect.

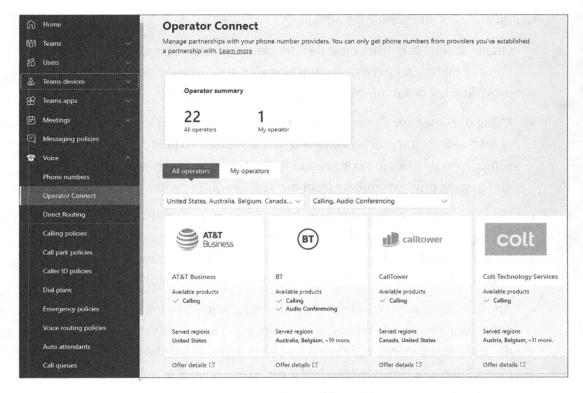

Figure 1-3. *Adding Operator Connect*

Finally, **Teams Direct Routing** allows organizations to keep their existing infrastructure (SBC appliance) service provider relationships and allows custom call routing options. Direct routing allows you to use an existing infrastructure and is supported in 180 countries. In Teams direct routing, you, as an admin, must use certified SBCs such as Ribbon, AudioCodes, Oracle, Cisco, Avaya, and many more. Additionally, you can add resiliency to most critical locations using an SBA, which enables PSTN calling in the event of a network outage that doesn't allow Teams clients to connect to Teams backend services. See Figure 1-4.

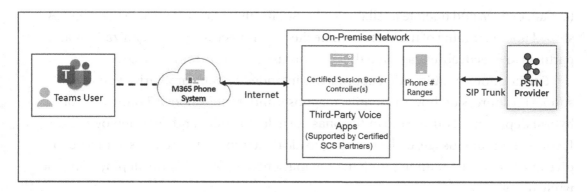

Figure 1-4. *Teams Direct Routing*

For detailed information on Teams Direct routing, calling plans, and Operator Connect configuration and troubleshooting, refer to Chapter 5.

Why Is the Troubleshooting Approach Critical?

The Microsoft Teams troubleshooting approach is intended to be used at the beginning of the Teams pilot and adopted into base operating procedures used throughout the lifetime of the deployment. This approach is designed to help familiarize you with support resources for diagnosing and troubleshooting Teams during the initial deployment phase. It covers tools and usage, collecting data from Teams' clients, and a deep dive into the most common problems support resources may encounter during and after deployment. This topic focuses explicitly on troubleshooting access to Teams' capabilities and features.

Understanding the appropriate tool to use and when to use it will help you make progress when diagnosing and troubleshooting any Teams problems users may encounter. The troubleshooting approach starts with identifying the issue and marking it to the appropriate category. Creating a plan of action and executing the outlined plan helps resolve issues systematically and adequately.

In this book, we are emphasizing a **multi-sided approach**, as Teams is a cloud-only service that requires rethinking how organizations plan, design, implement, and operate Microsoft Teams. Why is a multi-sided method suitable? This approach allows you to contemplate and check through different angles for effective deployment, maintenance, and troubleshooting of Microsoft Teams. This approach provides a step-by-step approach, practical guidance, and recommended practices plus tools and assets to enable you to plan, deliver, and operate a reliable and cost-effective Teams Service in the cloud. A shared understanding of the Teams online lifecycle is necessary for organizations and partners to effectively engage and drive Teams usage and customer success.

Furthermore, a multi-sided approach is intended to help familiarize you with support resources on how to identify, diagnose, and troubleshoot a Teams-only or hybrid deployment during the initial phase of a deployment and after deployment. It covers tools and usage, collecting diagnostic data from Teams' clients, and a deep dive into the most common problems you may encounter during the deployment and while using.

Microsoft Teams is a vast cloud-only service accessible via the Internet and thus it requires good networks, multiple hops, and multi-sites and routers from several independent administrative domains. As a result, users tend to see significantly higher failure probabilities in more extensive networks. Troubleshooting such problems is challenging because of increased network and protocol complexity. The many domains typically involved may have different administrative policies and provide varying access to information. Each domain may also use specialized or proprietary equipment and protocols, so troubleshooting from the outside may be complex.

The Teams client application runs on desktops (Windows, macOS, Linux), mobile apps (iOS and Android), and a web app client; client-installed components are generally quite reliable. Still, there are a variety of failures with software causes, operating systems, resource constraints, and devices, and they can be quite difficult to detect and correct. Detecting and fixing network problems have historically been regarded as the responsibility of network operations centers (NOCs). End users have played no role in the process beyond reporting problems to the admin and NOCs. However, this model does not scale well and becomes increasingly untenable as networks grow.

Work to date in network management has concentrated on effectively managing a single network. In this intra-domain context, it is assumed that the management software, the cloud service, and the managed devices are all owned by the same administration or that network management entities are mutually trusted. In contrast, little has been done to address the problem of coordinated network management across administrative domains. Since multiple components are involved, this makes Microsoft Teams troubleshooting quite complex. To troubleshoot, you must first understand the Microsoft Teams architecture, client architecture, call setup, signaling and media traffic flow, and authentication to develop the troubleshooting methodology.

Systematic Troubleshooting Approaches

Troubleshooting approaches are the standard procedures used to find the root cause of the symptoms discovered by any frequently used methods such as user reports, incident records, monitoring alerts, or other sources. The following methodologies are scoped to apply to many escalation paths yet contain enough details to help discover the root cause.

For example, say a user reports poor call quality when joining a meeting using a branch office's wired and wireless network. To troubleshoot this issue, isolating a network segment helps you troubleshoot network impairment (refer to the Microsoft Teams call quality impediment topic) issues in a specific network segment or network types (wired or wireless) rather than the entire network. If this methodology attempted to cover all network issues, there would be too many starting points, making the subject cumbersome. Suppose it only covered specific entities in the network. In that case, you, as an admin, need to know which entities or network subnets, types, or devices are relevant to your investigation in advance.

Figure 1-5 shows troubleshooting approach. The first step is to assess the issue from the initial report. If all you have in terms of a description of the problem is "Teams audio is poor at an office network," you can still use the process of elimination to isolate the issue. The Microsoft Teams call quality impediment topic describes the different types of audio quality issues and their causes, such as environmental, device, traffic type, and network-related reasons. Assuming that the audio quality problem is confined to an office network, you can probably eliminate all potential causes except network issues. There's always the slight possibility of a non-network issue (for instance, a software update or Teams service) but the possibility is low. The most efficient approach is starting your investigation with the highest probable cause. So, start with the highest possible cause and then review every cause until you reach the root cause.

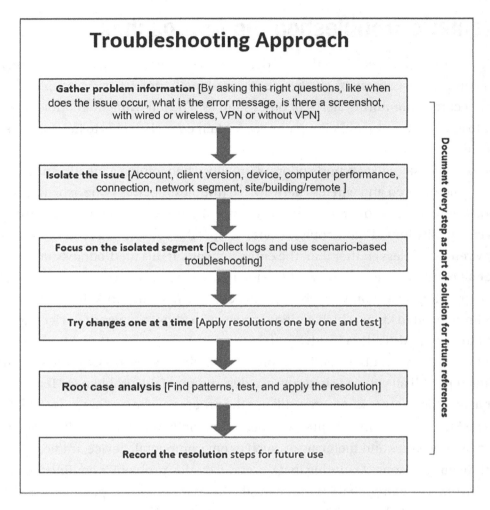

Figure 1-5. *Troubleshooting approach*

Troubleshooting Approach

Microsoft Teams service applications and clients can be complicated to troubleshoot. These applications are often composed of various cloud services and client-managed services. Teams faults are often unpredictable and can occur at multiple points, even in a simple Teams login, chat, or one-to-one call. Each additional function or service in a Teams composition introduces a new possible fault source and a new layer to obfuscate faults. Currently, Microsoft Teams service platforms offer limited service support through Microsoft service tickets. Still, client-side troubleshooting, some service-side troubleshooting, and the identifying defect are on the team administrator. You, as an administrator, must build service-side and client-side troubleshooting methodologies because the Teams main troubleshooting still relies on scattered Teams diagnostic logs and ambiguous error messages to pinpoint root causes. This topic presents and discusses the simple but effective troubleshooting methodology that helps solve day-to-day client-side and service-side issues.

Since Microsoft Teams provides multiple features (chat, audio/video calls, meetings, phone systems, applications, and content sharing) and third-party apps integration adds complexity to the product, diagnostics and troubleshooting methods are necessary to understand the root causes of process problems related to Teams functionality to fully solve them. Different traffic flows based on Teams signaling (chat) and media (audio/video/desktop sharing) traffic types make troubleshooting complex. Additionally, Teams integration with Microsoft apps and third-party apps adds more complexity. A rational, systematic approach is required, one that uses facts and evidence that are then combined with experience to drill down to find the true causes of the process issues encountered. The subsequent chapters cover detailed troubleshooting steps for each Teams capability and workload. This chapter covers the general method involved with troubleshooting and provides details related to specific processes and field experience.

Figure 1-5 describes the following troubleshooting steps.

1. **Gather problem information**: When an issue is reported, the first thing you need to do is to read and understand the issue. Interacting with the end user provides more details like when/what/how the issue occurs. Capture error messages and screenshots, and check if the issue is reproducible and if it is persistently happening or intermittent. This information helps you understand the problem. Once you have this information, move on to next step.

2. **Isolate or categorize the issue**: Try to isolate the issue starting from the highest possible cause. Isolate one thing at a time, like user account, Teams client, user's computer, wired or wireless network, office of remote network, and so on.

3. **Focus on the isolated part**: Once the issue has been isolated, focus on the isolated part and do deep dive. Checking one thing at a time is key.

4. **Core troubleshooting**: Change one thing at a time. Apply a resolution, propagate the change, and then test. If you were unable to fix it, check if there is a product bug or known issue and then open a support case with Microsoft.

5. **Root cause analysis**: Analyze and document the resolution of the problem.

6. **Record the solution for future use**: This is highly recommended.

Microsoft Teams Call Quality Impediments

VPN client network: Virtual private networks (VPNs) are generally utilized for securing external connections when end users are outside the corporate network. VPNs technically extend an organization's private network by transferring encrypted traffic with tunneling protocols. When an end user initiates a VPN connection, the traffic is sent through the VPN tunnel. This added tunneling layer affects Microsoft Teams traffic by increasing network latency and jittering. Encrypting and decrypting Teams traffic can potentially impair a VPN concentrator and affect the end user experience, which is why a VPN is not recommended for media traffic. The VPN client must utilize split tunneling and route Teams media traffic like any external non-VPN user (directly to the Internet, splitting from VPN tunnel).

Packet shapers (WAN optimizer): WAN optimizers (or packet shapers) are generally utilized for mitigating issues generated by high delays or low network bandwidth. *WAN optimization* is a term commonly used for devices that operate different techniques to enhance data transfer efficiency across WANs. Traditionally used optimization methods include caching, compression, protocol substitution, various forms of bandwidth throttling, and forward error correction (FEC). Packet snippers, packet inspections, and packet shaper devices are not recommended for Teams media traffic and may degrade quality significantly.

Packet loss: Packet loss directly affects the receiver attempting to recover from the loss utilizing advanced corrective or healing algorithms. Single (or some) packet losses can be healed with minimal distortion. Back-to-back packet losses may cause audio/video call disturbance. More significant packet bursts of loss result in speech cutout. Of course, the actual speech content plays an essential role in how the listener senses the healed audio. For instance, lost packets containing silence will not be missed; lost packets containing substantial financial numbers will be missed much more.

Jitter: Jitter is the change in delay from packet to packet. The expected delay is equal to the packetization time (or p-time). For instance, if 20ms of data is sent simultaneously, a packet of data is sent every 20ms. Any variation from the 20ms mark is considered jitter. A jitter value of 5ms means, on average, that the packet was early or late 5ms from the expected arrival time. Jitter can cause poor audio performance because the receiving endpoint tries to minimize the delay by playing the audio as soon as it is received. If a packet is delayed, the endpoint can either play a frame of zeros and glitch or stretch out the previous frame to buy more time. Microsoft Teams client use an adaptive jitter buffer. The first time a significant glitch is experienced, the buffer grows to accommodate any additional jitter. If no jitter is experienced for some time, the buffer slowly shrinks. This means that maintained high jitter is better than sporadic high jitter.

Packet delay: Delay is often measured using the round-trip delay calculation via the RTCP channel. Delay should be directly correlated to the distance between the Teams callers; therefore, absolute thresholds do not help determine whether an issue exists. Although delay figures in the end users' perception of overall quality, problems caused by loss and jitter generally substitute those caused by delay.

Firewall policies: Microsoft Teams uses a variety of workloads such as real-time presence, chat, audio, video, application sharing, phone (PSTN) calls, and content sharing. These workloads use multiple protocols (HTTPS-based REST, SDP, SRTP, SRTPC, SIP, ICE, and HTTPS). Modern corporate networks are extensively secured and segmented by using firewalls. Incorrect firewall policies may cause Teams communication issues. That is why it is a best practice to ensure that the firewall device's performance and the protocol support of the device's firmware and software are at the required levels.

Summary

This chapter presented and discussed the simple but effective troubleshooting methodology that helps solve day-to-day client-side and service-side issues. Additionally, you learned about Teams phone system (voice) basics. The Microsoft Teams troubleshooting approach is intended to be used at the beginning of the Teams pilot and adopted into base operating procedures used throughout the lifetime of the deployment. This asset is designed to help familiarize you with diagnosing and troubleshooting teams during the initial deployment phase. It covers tools and usage, collecting data from Teams clients, and a deep dive into the most common problems you may encounter during and after deployment. Knowing the right tool to use and when to use it will help you effectively make progress when diagnosing and troubleshooting any Teams problems users may encounter. The troubleshooting approach starts with identifying the issue and marking the appropriate categories. Then you create a plan of action. Executing the outlined plan helps resolve the problem systematically and adequately. Last but not least, documenting the entire process is key.

References

Hasidi, Netanel and Kalech, Meir. (2021). Anticipatory Troubleshooting. Applied Sciences. 11. 995. 10.3390/app11030995.

Microsoft Teams training videos, `https://support.microsoft.com/en-us/office/microsoft-teams-video-training-4f108e54-240b-4351-8084-b1089f0d21d7`

Teams client troubleshooting articles, `https://support.microsoft.com/en-us/office/troubleshoot-6fa7c08a-6fd4-47a0-b275-90a5f60f1df9`

Microsoft Teams admin Training videos, `https://docs.microsoft.com/en-us/microsoftteams/training-microsoft-teams-landing-page`

Microsoft Teams admin training, `https://docs.microsoft.com/en-us/microsoftteams/itadmin-readiness`

Microsoft Teams Ignite sessions, `https://docs.microsoft.com/en-us/microsoftteams/ignite-2020-landing-page`

"Microsoft Teams call flow and quality impairment information." `https://docs.microsoft.com/en-us/microsoftteams/microsoft-teams-online-call-flows`

"Reconnect with Microsoft Teams Calling" retrieved from the microsoft.com archives, `https://myignite.microsoft.com/archives/IGFY21Q3-OD378`

"Unified communication and how it transforms businesses." `www.techradar.com/news/unified-communication-and-how-it-can-transform-your-business`

CHAPTER 2

Microsoft Teams Overview

Communication and collaboration tools are essential factors of organizational success. One such tool is Microsoft Teams, widely used in various businesses and education sectors. With the help of Teams, users in the organization collaborate and communicate effectively by using Microsoft 365 and Microsoft Teams. Users and scholars rely on the collaboration and communication features in Microsoft Teams. It is now a critical service within organizations and educational institutes. As a Teams administrator, you need to administer and configure Microsoft Teams features and components.

This chapter provide the complete Teams overview, Teams service architecture, Teams capabilities, Teams licensing, Teams client architecture, Teams Phone System (calling plans, Operator Connect, and Direct Routing), Teams live events, and the Teams user and service administrator through the Microsoft Teams admin center. After completing this chapter, you will know Teams' service and client architecture and how to manage and administer Teams. Also, you'll be able to identify common Teams problems and explain how to troubleshooting Teams issues.

What Is Microsoft Teams?

Microsoft Teams is a cloud-based communications platform that incorporates various services for collaboration, such as chat, meetings, calling, and files. Teams are tightly integrated into Microsoft 365 and integrate multiple workloads in a unified communication and collaboration system. In addition, Teams offers integration capabilities for other tools and third-party products. Microsoft Teams is a purely cloud-based service; hence there is not much an admin can manage on-premises to make sure it's up and running. Microsoft Teams creates a hub for teamwork where people connect, communicate, and collaborate from within a single interface.

Teams is the central collaboration workspace in Microsoft 365. Teams provides the cost and agility benefits of cloud-based IM, presence, audio, video, and meetings,

© Balu N Ilag and Arun M Sabale 2022
B. N. Ilag and A. M. Sabale, *Troubleshooting Microsoft Teams*, https://doi.org/10.1007/978-1-4842-8622-7_2

without sacrificing the business-class capabilities of Skype for Business Server (the previous product). With Teams, Microsoft deploys and maintains the required server infrastructure in the cloud, and it handles ongoing maintenance, security updates, and upgrades. An admin can selectively enable users for a Teams subscription in a Microsoft 365 tenant.

Additionally, Teams adds significant collaborative capabilities, including a SharePoint site and an Exchange mailbox for each team. Admins have the Windows PowerShell command-line interface to manage settings specific to Teams.

Microsoft Teams License Requirements

Microsoft provides different licensing plans, and Teams is part of most Microsoft 365 licensing plans but is not accessible as a standalone plan. It unifies services from Exchange Online, SharePoint Online, and OneDrive. The Teams native license provides chat, presence, Teams to Teams VoIP calls, meetings, file sharing, and more. However, some features are dependent on the add-on license, which enhances functionalities like the Teams phone system, which allows users to make external phone calls and audio conferencing with a dial-in number in Teams meetings.

If you plan to deploy Teams in your organization or support Teams, you must know what subscriptions offer Teams. Table 2-1 shows the list of Microsoft 365 subscriptions with Teams.

Table 2-1. *Teams Licenses*

Small Business Microsoft 365 plans	Enterprise Office 365 plans	Education Microsoft 365 Plan	Developer Plans	Government plans
Business Basic	Enterprise E1	Education A1	Developer	Government G3
Business Standard	Enterprise E3	Education A3		Government G5
Business Premium	Enterprise E5	Education A5		

Even though the Enterprise E4 and Education E3 plans are no longer available for purchase, they do support Teams if you have an existing license for them. Additionally, Microsoft Teams has a few add-on licenses including SKUs for licensing meetings and calling on a per-device basis for meeting room devices (such as Microsoft Teams Rooms, Microsoft Surface Hub, and collaboration bars for Microsoft Teams).

1. Teams Room (standard and premium) license for room accounts

2. Teams common area phone license for common area phone accounts

3. The Teams Phone system license is an add-on license for enabling phone systems for Teams users. If you want to use a calling plan, you will need a calling plan license such as a domestic calling plan or an international calling plan.

Microsoft Teams Capabilities

Teams Chat: Chat is at the center of whatever end users do in Teams. Chat conversations span individual chats with just one person to group chats and conversations in channels. Once in a chat, you can send messages that include files, links, emojis, stickers, and GIF files. There are a few different ways to chat with people in Teams:

- **Private chat:** Private chats enable quick chats with a specific person or a group of people. It reduces email mess and allows for sharing pictures and documents. End users can start one-on-one or group chats by selecting the Chat icon in Teams. This includes one-on-one chats and group chats with a few people at once but outside a channel.

- **Channel messages:** Channels are where the work gets done. Channel conversations are public and visible to members of the channels. End users can start conversations and make announcements in one or multiple channels simultaneously by selecting new discussions in the Posts tab of channels. Channel messages are with everyone on the team who pays attention to that channel.

Teams Collaboration Using Teams and Channels

Microsoft Teams allows users to quickly pull together a team with people inside and outside your organization. End users can chat with others to drive fast and inclusive conversations, securely share and co-author documents, and iterate on projects. To achieve its efficiency goal through a flat hierarchy, Teams only provides two user roles: Owners and Members.

- **Team**: A team is a collection of people, content, and tools surrounding different projects and outcomes within an organization. There are three types of teams. *Org-wide teams* provide an intuitive way for everyone in a small to a medium-sized organization to be a part of a single team for collaboration and are limited to organizations with no more than 10,000 users. *Public teams* are open and anyone within the organization can join. *Private teams* consist only of invited users.

- **Channels**: A team is made up of channels. Channels are the collaboration spaces within a team where the real work is done. Channels are where users hold meetings, have conversations, and work on files together. *Standard channels* are visible to all team members and are available for conversations that everyone on a team can participate in. *Private channels* are similar to standard channels, but they restrict conversations, files, and apps to a limited subset of team members. This enables private collaboration within a project or department. *Shared channels* enable you to share channels with any user or group with Azure Active Directory to your organization (this feature is not generally available as of February 2022).

Teams can be dynamic for project-based work (such as running projects) and ongoing to reflect the internal structure of your organization (such as departments and office locations). All data within a team, such as conversations, files, and notes across team channels, are only visible to members of the team. Users will find tabs at the top of each channel, which are basically links to their favorite files, apps, and services. Figure 2-1 shows the structure of channels in Teams.

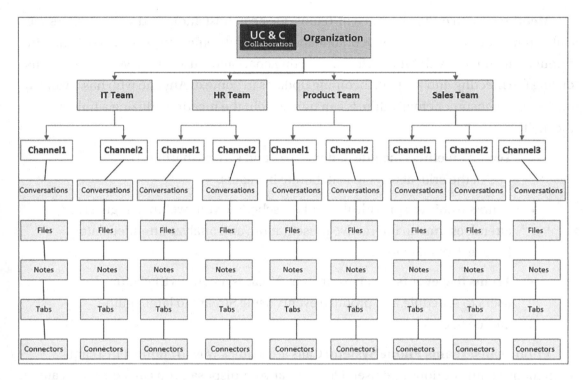

Figure 2-1. *Team and channels hierarchy*

Apps and workflows: Teams are designed to enable this new working method. Teams allow users to integrate simple work apps for a unified work experience in a single place. Users can add an app to a channel, chat, or meetings tab. Tabs serve like bookmarks so users no longer need to jump between different apps, clients, and services.

There are various apps that users can add to their teams, channels, and personal views to help them get things done. As a Teams administrator, you can manage apps, connectors, and bots across all team members.

- **App store**: Adding apps from the Teams App Store lets users do more in Microsoft Teams.

- **Low-code solutions**: Use Microsoft Power Platform to create low-code solutions to simplify work, all from within Teams.

- **Professional developer apps**: Create custom apps to fit your organization's needs.

Meetings: With online sessions in Teams, user can host audio and video conference calls from any device. Share your content and collaborate efficiently during your meeting through integration with Microsoft 365. Meeting chats allow users to have conversations during the meeting and keep forthcoming updates in context. Anyone who has a valid business or consumer email address can quickly join the meeting utilizing a link in the invite.

- **Teams meetings** include audio, video, and screen sharing. They're one of the critical ways to collaborate in Teams.

- **Teams webinars** provide the tools to schedule your webinar, register attendees, run an interactive presentation, and analyze attendee data for effective follow-up.

- **Teams live events** are an extension of Teams meetings that allow users to schedule and produce events using Stream to large online audiences.

Phone calls/Teams Phone System: Calls are a quick way to connect in Teams. With many calling options and useful features at your disposal, you can communicate with people or groups in familiar ways. Users can make and receive calls instantly in Microsoft Teams with advanced features like group calling, cloud voicemail, and call transfers. There are two kinds of calls in Teams.

Calls between Teams clients: Out of the box, Teams supports the ability for users to make voice over IP (VoIP) one-to-one or group calls from Teams clients to Teams clients.

Make and receive PSTN calls: Microsoft Teams Phone System allows users to make and receive PTSN phone calls with a traditional phone service. To enable users to make and receive PSTN calls, you need to connect the phone system to the PSTN. Users can then use the dial pad (shown in Figure 2-2) to call landlines or mobile phones on the PSTN and users can see their phone as a work number under the Calls tab. This figure also shows the Calls, Phone, and Contacts tabs that allow users to add or remove contacts.

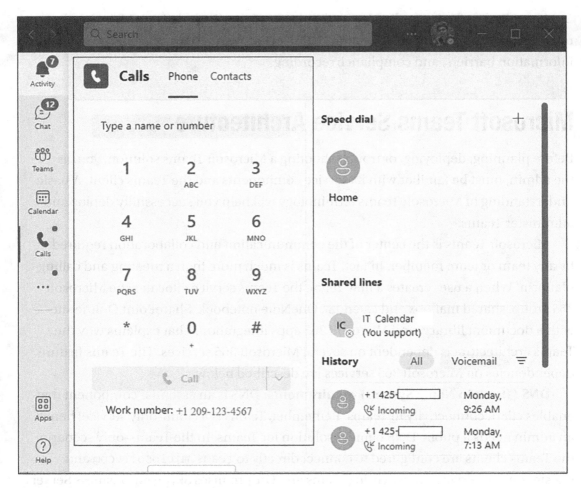

Figure 2-2. *Teams dial pad*

Security and compliance: Microsoft Teams provides enterprise-grade security, compliance, and manageability. With Microsoft Teams, organizations can adopt user collaboration and communication while protecting their business data and interests on an enterprise scale.

Security: Teams enforces two-factor authentication, single sign-on through Active Directory, and data encryption in transit and at rest. The security capabilities for Teams include Microsoft Defender for Office 365, safe links, safe attachments, conditional access policies, multi-geo support, end-to-end encryption, meeting safety controls, and cloud app security.

Compliance: The compliance capabilities for Teams includes sensitivity labels, retention policies, data loss prevention (DLP), eDiscovery, communication compliance, information barriers, and compliance recording.

Microsoft Teams Service Architecture

Before planning, deploying, or troubleshooting a Microsoft Teams solution, you, as the admin, must be familiar with its service components and the Teams client. A basic understanding of Microsoft Teams terminology will help you successfully deploy and administer Teams.

Microsoft Teams is the center of the communication and collaboration required by any team or team member. In fact, Teams is much more than a meeting and calling platform. When a user creates a new Team, the Teams service allocates the Microsoft 365 group, shared mailbox and calendar, OneNote notebook, SharePoint Online site with a document library, and Microsoft 365 apps integration. That explains why the Teams architecture is dependent on several Microsoft 365 services. The Teams feature dependencies on Microsoft 365 services are described below.

DNS (Domain Name System) requirements: DNS is an essential component that enables client connectivity to Teams. Remember, Teams is a cloud-only service; hence an admin needs a public DNS name resolution for Teams. In the Teams-only scenario, the Teams clients are configured to connect directly to `teams.microsoft.com` and register online services. In a hybrid (Teams and On-premises Skype for Business Server) scenario, you, as a Teams admin, must configure all DNS records for Skype for Business Server so that they point to on-premises. Additionally, if you want to configure a hybrid deployment, you must confirm that the following records exist:

- `_sipfederationtls._tcp.domain` name is a service resource record that must reference `sipfed.online.lync.com`.

Remember, the Teams infrastructure uses an Azure back end. Teams uses a REST-based protocol. Teams is designed, developed, and deployed on the Azure cloud. In Teams, microservices are used to scale elastically. Teams services are frequently updated globally. Teams has a client infrastructure across desktops (Windows, macOS, and Linux), mobile (iOS and Android), and web clients. Teams has native devices, including the Teams Room system and IP phones, which are run on Teams clients to support capabilities.

Users don't need a SharePoint license, but the tenant must be provisioned for SharePoint Online. OneDrive is required for sharing files between one-to-one chats and storing meeting recordings.

Microsoft Teams is all HTTPS traffic. The Teams client connects to a back-end Teams services infrastructure using HTTPS and connects to chat services using HTTP. Transport Relay (TR) is deployed in the cloud for media using RTP and RTCP. Teams clients make the connection to the Exchange server via Teams services. Microsoft Teams has auditing that tells who made a change that broke the team's functionality. Multiple Teams activities are audited, including Teams creation, deletion, channel addition/deletion, and changes in Teams settings.

Figure 2-3 demonstrates the Teams apps' dependencies on underlying communication and collaboration service technologies from Teams to the Office 365 services. Creating a team back-end service creates a new Microsoft 365 Group, a document library to store team files, a SharePoint Online site, an Exchange Online shared mailbox and calendar, and a OneNote notebook.

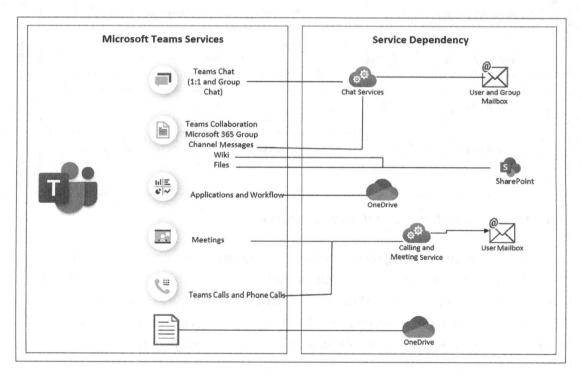

Figure 2-3. *Microsoft Teams feature and service dependency*

Microsoft Teams uses the most effective storage location for different Teams data. Figure 2-4 shows the key data entities and locations stored at rest. For example, Teams meeting recordings are saved to SharePoint and OneDrive.

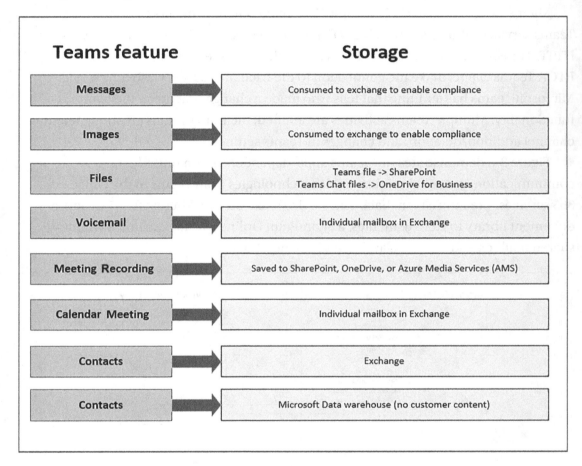

Figure 2-4. *Teams feature and storage location*

Suppose a Teams meeting recording fails to successfully upload to SharePoint or OneDrive. In that case, the recording will instead be temporarily kept in Azure Media Services (AMS). Once stored in AMS, no retry attempts are made to automatically upload the recording to SharePoint or OneDrive. Meeting recordings stored in AMS are available for 21 days before being automatically deleted. Users can download the video from AMS if they need to keep a copy.

Microsoft Teams Security and Compliance Capability

The Teams architecture enables data governance, security, and compliance capabilities. You can protect Teams data with various security and compliance features in Microsoft 365. This protects against leakage and loss of business data by supporting compliant business processes when discovering sensitive business data. Figure 2-5 illustrates the Microsoft security and compliance tools that help in information protection like eDiscovery, content search, hold, retention, and audit logs.

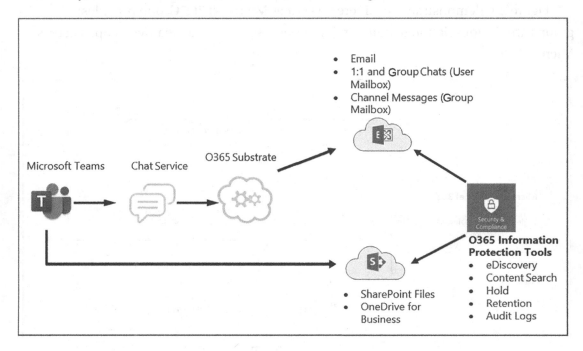

Figure 2-5. *Teams security and compliance*

These tools are very useful. For example, the eDiscovery tool can be used to search and export content in Microsoft 365. Additionally, you can use eDiscovery to place an eDiscovery hold on content locations, such as Exchange mailboxes, SharePoint sites, OneDrive accounts, and Microsoft Teams, as shown in Figure 2-5.

Microsoft Teams and Other Core Microsoft 365 Services

Microsoft Teams uses multiple services such as Microsoft 365 Group, SharePoint, OneDrive for Business, and Exchange (mailbox). Each of these services and their Teams connections are explained below.

Microsoft 365 Group and Teams

Microsoft 365 Groups is the cross-application membership service in Microsoft 365. It is an object in Azure Active Directory. A Microsoft 365 Group can be created directly from Microsoft 365 admin center or indirectly from creating associated workloads. When you create a team in Microsoft Teams, you're creating a Microsoft 365 Group and the related cloud applications on the back end. Teams share the same group privacy and membership roles with the associated Microsoft 365 group.

Figure 2-6 demonstrate the different services Microsoft 365 Group provides; groups are the foundational membership service that makes all teamwork apps across Microsoft 365.

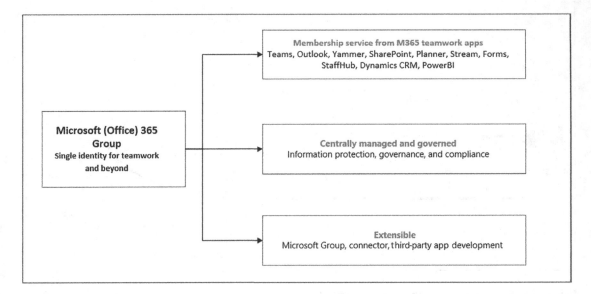

Figure 2-6. *Microsoft 365 Group and capability*

You, as an admin, can give a group of people access to a collection of shared resources, including a shared Outlook inbox, calendar, SharePoint document library, planner, OneNote for Notebook, PowerBI, Yammer (if the Group was created from Yammer), A-Team (if the Group was formed from Teams), and Stream.

SharePoint and OneDrive for Business Together with Microsoft Teams

SharePoint and OneDrive for Business are the primary content services in Microsoft 365. Microsoft Teams uses SharePoint and OneDrive in Microsoft 365 for content collaboration. Team files are stored in SharePoint sites, and chat files are stored in OneDrive. Additionally, all Teams meeting recordings are saved to OneDrive or SharePoint. If users aren't assigned SharePoint licenses, they don't have OneDrive storage in Microsoft 365. File sharing works in standard channels, but users won't share files in chats without OneDrive storage in Microsoft 365. By keeping the files in the SharePoint document library and OneDrive, all compliance rules configured at the tenant level will be followed.

Teams with SharePoint

Each team in Microsoft Teams has a SharePoint team site associated with it. Files shared within a conversation are automatically added to the document library. Permissions and file security options set in SharePoint are automatically reflected within Teams. Permissions for the SharePoint team site are best managed through the associated Microsoft 365 group or Teams team. Figure 2-7 illustrates this connection between Teams and SharePoint and OneDrive.

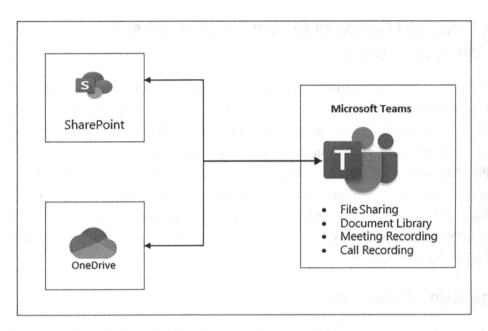

Figure 2-7. *Teams with SharePoint and OneDrive*

The SharePoint team site is provisioned with *Everyone except external users* access for public teams. The public team isn't displayed in Teams for people who aren't members of that team. However, they can access content on the SharePoint team site using the SharePoint team site URL. Each channel in a team gets a folder within the default Shared Documents library. The channel folder could be in the different SharePoint team sites depending on the channel type.

Standard channel: Each standard channel, including the general channel (the default channel for each team), gets a folder within the default SharePoint team site document library.

Private channel: Each private channel has a folder in the Shared Documents library of its own SharePoint team site that's separate from the parent team site. This ensures that access to private channel files is restricted to only members of the private channel. A private channel SharePoint site is created in the same geographic region as the SharePoint site of the parent team. Site membership is synced with the membership of the private channel within Teams.

Additionally, the recordings for channel meetings are stored in the channel folder in the document library for that team. The person who started the recording has edit permission. Permissions for all other channel members are inherited from the Teams channel permissions. If a user can access the channel in Teams, they can access the meeting recording just like any other file saved in the channel.

OneDrive for Business in Teams

For every user, the OneDrive folder `Microsoft Teams Chat Files` stores all files shared within private chats with other users (1:1 or 1:many), with permissions configured automatically to restrict access for the intended use only.

Additionally, the recordings for non-channel meetings are stored in a folder named `Recordings` in the OneDrive for the person who started the meeting recording. The meeting organizer and the person who started the recording will have edit permissions and share the record. People who were invited to the meeting will have view permissions. Guests will not have access by default, but they can request access, or the recording can be shared with external users proactively.

Microsoft Teams with Exchange (Mailbox)

Another core service of Microsoft Teams is Exchange Online. When you create a team, a corresponding Microsoft 365 Group and a mailbox for the group are automatically created behind the scenes. This group mailbox provides messaging capabilities and a mail-based storage location for data processed and produced in Teams. Figure 2-8 shows multiple features like email sent to the team, chat and channel messages, meeting information, and the profile picture depend on Exchange and Teams communication.

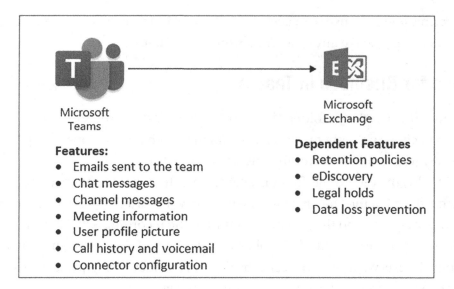

Figure 2-8. *Teams and Exchange*

Every Microsoft 365 Group associated with a team has a corresponding group mailbox in Exchange Online that provides resources to use messaging and a calendar for planning meetings. Data created in Teams is stored in different Exchange locations:

- **Emails sent to the team:** When an email is sent to the Microsoft 365 Group email address, the email is stored in the Microsoft 365 Group mailbox. A copy is distributed to the user mailboxes of all subscribers.

- **Chat messages:** Chat messages and users' chat history are stored in their user mailboxes.

- **Channel messages:** Messages posted into channel conversations are stored in a hidden folder in the Microsoft 365 Group mailbox.

- **Meeting information:** When planning meetings for a team, the meetings are stored as meeting elements in the Microsoft 365 Group mailbox.

- **User profile picture:** When a user changes their profile picture in Teams, it is also stored in the user's mailbox.

- **Call history and voicemail:** Call history and voicemail messages are delivered to the associated user's mailbox.

- **Connector configuration:** The configuration data for connectors are stored in the Microsoft 365 Group mailbox. An example is the connector data required to subscribe to RSS feeds.

These Exchange locations support the security and compliance tools provided by Microsoft 365, such as retention policies, eDiscovery, legal holds, and data loss prevention.

Teams can be deployed with Exchange hybrid, where either some or all mailboxes are hosted on an on-premises servers. In a hybrid deployment, Exchange must be deployed so that it's ready to use the supported Teams feature for storing and discovering data from on-premises Exchange locations.

Different Clients in Microsoft Teams

Microsoft Teams has clients available for desktops (Windows, Mac, and Linux), the Web, and mobile (Android and iOS). There are different ways to deploy Teams clients based on devices. The Microsoft Teams desktop clients provide real-time communications support (audio, video, and content sharing) for team meetings, group calling, and private one-on-one calls.

- The desktop client is available for the following operating systems:

    - **Windows:** Windows (8.1 or later) and Windows Server (2012 R2 or later), 32-bit and 64-bit versions

    - **macOS:** The three most recent versions of macOS

    - **Linux:** .deb and .rpm formats

- The Teams app is available for mobile phones (iOS and Android) and iPads.

- Teams also has web apps that eliminate installing apps on your devices.

As a Teams administrator, you can choose your preferred method to distribute the installation files to computers in your organization. For instance, the admin can use Microsoft Endpoint Configuration Manager for Windows operating systems or Jamf Pro for macOS. There are several methods to deploy Teams desktop clients:

- As a part of the Microsoft 365 Apps for Enterprise installer

- MSI files (both 32-bit and 64-bit) for IT bulk deployment, such as through Microsoft Endpoint Configuration Manager, Group Policy, or any third-party distribution mechanism for broad deployment

- A standalone (.exe) installer for user installation

The Teams desktop client on the Windows OS doesn't require elevated permissions. Every user can install the client to their profile path. On macOS systems, administrative permissions are required.

For the Windows Operating System

The Microsoft Teams installation for Windows provides downloadable installers in 32-bit and 64-bit architectures. The Windows client is deployed to the `AppData` folder located in the user's profile. Deploying the user's local profile allows the client to be installed without requiring elevated rights.

The Windows client uses the following locations:

- `%LocalAppData%\Microsoft\Teams`

- `%LocalAppData%\Microsoft\TeamsMeetingAddin`

- `%AppData%\Microsoft\Teams`

- `%LocalAppData%\SquirrelTemp`

Teams Phone System and Calling

Microsoft Teams is often perceived to be an internal messaging and communications platform, enabling users inside an organization to converse securely. However, Microsoft has now integrated it with their Phone System solution to provide traditional private branch exchange (PBX) capabilities through your existing Teams application framework. This integration enables users to make outbound calls and receive incoming calls to and from external sources. Phone System can work with your existing PBX or be used instead of a PBX to allow your users to make inbound and outbound calls.

The Microsoft Teams calling capability enables users to make and receive calls using their work number from any location. You can connect from Teams to landlines and mobile devices through the PSTN. Microsoft Teams works with Microsoft Teams Phone System, to enable call control and PBX capabilities through the Office 365 cloud.

Phone System supports three primary options to implement PSTN connectivity with Microsoft Teams:

- Using a Microsoft calling plan

- Using Teams Operator Connect

- Using Direct Routing

Microsoft Calling Plans

Using a calling plan, Microsoft acts as your PSTN career. The phone system operates with a PSTN calling plan and acts as part of Office 365 to enable external calls. You don't need to purchase or deploy any additional equipment or enter a contract with a third-party carrier. All you need is an uninterrupted connection to Office 365.

You can purchase a domestic calling plan or an international calling plan. A domestic calling plan allows users to connect to phone numbers located in the country/region where they are assigned in Office 365. An international calling plan extends the reach to international numbers. This option supports Teams and Skype for Business users. However, not all Office 365 regions support the calling plans. Figure 2-9 demonstrate the calling plan connectivity where a Teams client connects to Teams back-end service, which is directly connected to the PSTN component. In the calling plan, Microsoft acts as a provider; hence you don't need to configure or provide any PSTN connectivity. A calling plan is a license that combines a user's phone number with many minutes. Each phone number requires a calling plan. Two types of calling plans are available:

- **Domestic calling plan**: This calling plan enables a user to place calls outside of the organization to telephone numbers located in the same country/region in which they are assigned in Office 365 or Microsoft 365.

- **Domestic and international calling plan**: This plan allows users to make domestic calls to other numbers in their country/region and international phone numbers.

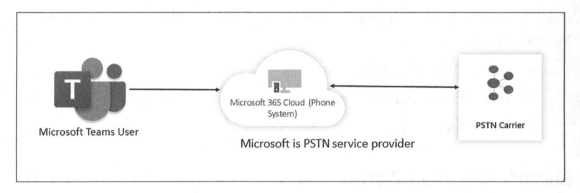

Figure 2-9. *Microsoft Teams calling plan service*

A calling plan includes several pre-paid minutes. Once the minutes in a calling plan have been exhausted, calls are charged on a per-minute basis. All users in the same country/region with the exact calling plan pool their minutes. For example, 100 users in the same country/region that each have a domestic calling plan with 120 minutes each have access to a shared pool of 12,000 minutes in total.

An administrator can purchase a calling plan using the Microsoft 365 admin center. Depending on the requirements, you can buy different calling plans and assign them to users as appropriate.

Microsoft Teams Calling with Operator Connect

Operator Connect provides an operator-managed voice solution. Using a connector operator, you can provide Teams calling in locations where a Microsoft calling plan isn't available. Furthermore, you can make sure the preferred operator is a participant in the Microsoft Operator Connect program. Additionally, you can find a new operator to enable calling in Teams. Figure 2-10 shows the Microsoft 365 cloud where Teams service and Phone System reside.

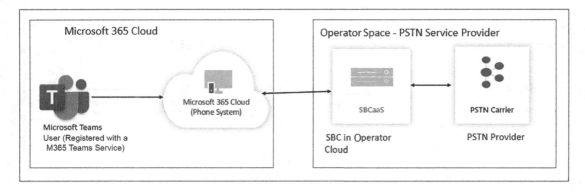

Figure 2-10. *Teams calling with Operator Connect*

Teams calling with Operator Connect is a managed service by the operator; it provisions and manages the SBC in the cloud infrastructure with a user configuration.

Operator Connect is another option for providing PSTN connectivity with Teams and a phone system. If you, as an admin, decide Operator Connect is the right solution for your organization, refer to Chapter 1 for Operator Connect setup and other information.

The last connectivity type is Teams Direct Routing (DR), which is available across the globe and allows you to bring your own carrier.

Microsoft Teams Phone System Using Direct Routing

Teams Direct Routing connects the Phone System through an on-premises PBX, using your on-premises telephony network and existing carrier to connect to the PSTN to place external calls. This option requires a supported session border controller (SBC) for interoperability with a third-party PBX and other telephone equipment, depending on the telephony configuration you have running on-premises.

Figure 2-11 shows Teams DR connectivity; the Teams client connects to the Teams back-end service (Microsoft 365 Phone System), which communicates to the on-premise (or cloud-hosted) SBC, which connects to the PSTN provider. You can use almost any telephony carrier with Phone System but you (or a partner) must configure interoperability between your on-premises telephony equipment and it.

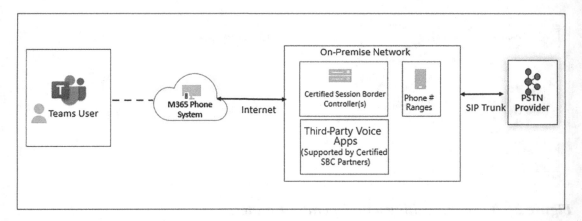

Figure 2-11. *Teams Direct Routing*

Unlike using a calling plan, this option is available worldwide. It still requires an uninterrupted connection to Office 365.

This solution is suitable for Teams users. If you also need to support Skype for Business users, connect Skype for Business Server to the PSTN through your on-premises PBX or telecommunications gateway. If you don't have an existing Skype for Business Server available, you can deploy Cloud Connector Edit. Phone System connects to your SBC through Skype for Business Server or Cloud Connector Edition.

Teams Meeting, Audio Conferencing, and Teams Live Events

Microsoft Teams offers different scenarios for meetings and live events within an organization, with both internal and external attendees. To choose the optimal solutions for your environment, you must familiarize yourself with the settings and policies that can be applied in Microsoft Teams meetings and live events.

In this section, you'll go over the step-by-step processes that will guide you as a Microsoft Teams administrator in the following tasks associated with meetings and virtual events, including planning, organizing, assigning roles, and configuring policies and settings.

Microsoft Teams supports all communication needs across the spectrum in the hybrid workplace, from one-to-one meetings to virtual events. Additionally, people can join meetings with different kinds of clients. For example, users can attend meetings from regular phones by dialing into the meeting using audio conferencing.

Figure 2-12 shows the Teams meeting types. There are three kinds of meetings that can be created in Microsoft Teams, depending on the nature of the conference:

- **Microsoft Teams meetings** include audio, video, and screen sharing. A Teams meeting is one of the critical ways to collaborate in Teams.

- **Microsoft Teams webinars** provide the tools to schedule a webinar, register attendees, run an interactive presentation, and analyze attendee data for effective follow-up.

- **Microsoft Teams live events** enable users to broadcast video and meeting content to a large online audience, such as a company town hall meeting.

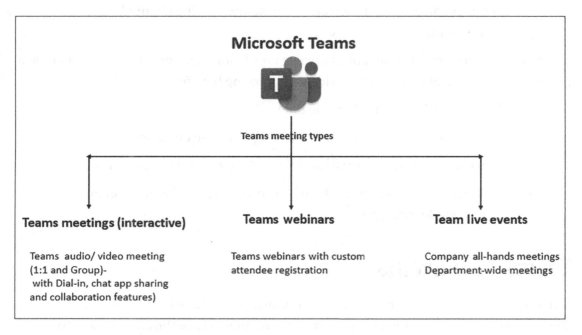

Figure 2-12. *Teams meeting types*

A Microsoft Teams admin controls meeting types through policies and settings. These configurations are based on administrative regulations, such as video or screen sharing. Each of these meeting types is examined in greater detail in the following sections.

Teams Meetings

Microsoft Teams offers two kinds of meetings: channel meetings and private meetings.

Channel meetings: If a team has a dedicated channel in Microsoft Teams, it can schedule a channel meeting. Channel meetings have multiple benefits:

- All members can see and join a meeting.

- Any meeting-related discussion held before, during, or after a meeting is part of the channel discussion.

- Non-private meetings and discussions are visible to any member of the team.

- Meetings can also be started ad-hoc from the existing channel conversation.

Private meetings: When meetings involve non-team members, users can schedule a private meeting. Private meetings provide the following benefits:

- They're visible to invited people only.

- They can be started ad-hoc from existing chat conversations.

- They can be scheduled from the Teams client or an Outlook add-in.

- Meeting-related discussions held before, during, or after the meeting are accessible through chat.

Teams Live Events

Live events are meant for one-to-many communications where the host of the event leads the interactions. Audience participation is mainly to view the content shared by the host. The attendees can watch the live or recorded event in Yammer, Teams, or Stream. They can also interact with the presenters using moderated Q&A or a Yammer conversation. Teams live events include the following features:

- **Event group roles**: Teams live events use the following roles to successfully broadcast and participate in an event. To learn more, see "Event group roles" at `https://support.office.com/article/get-started-with-microsoft-teams-live-events-d077fec2-a058-483e-9ab5-1494afda578a?ui=en-US&rs=en-US&ad=US#bkmk_roles?azure-portal=true`.

- **Organizer**: Schedules a live event and ensures the event is set up with the right permissions for both attendees and the event group, who will manage the event.

- **Producer**: As a host, ensures attendees have a great viewing experience by controlling the live event stream.

- **Presenter**: Presents audio, video, or a screen to the live event. The presenter often moderates a Q&A session at the end of the event.

- **Attendee**: A viewer who watches the event live or on-demand, either anonymously or authenticated using DVR controls. Attendees can participate in Q&A events.

- **Production options**: Teams live events can be produced either in Teams using a webcam or an external app or device.

  - **Teams**: Users can produce their live events in Teams using either their webcam or an A/V input from Teams room systems. This option enables users to easily use their webcams and share their screens as input in the event.

  - **External app or device**: External encoders enable users to produce live events directly from an external hardware device or a software-based encoder using Stream. An example of a software-based encoder includes studio-quality media mixers that support streaming to a real-time messaging protocol (RTMP) service.

- **Streaming platform**: The live event streaming platform consists of

  - **Azure Media Services**: Azure Media Services enhances accessibility, distribution, and scalability. It also makes it easy and cost-effective to stream content to your local or worldwide audiences while protecting your content.

  - **Azure Content Delivery Network (CDN)**: Once your Stream goes live, it's delivered through the Azure CDN, which provides integrated CDN for streaming endpoints. This feature enables Streams to be viewed worldwide with no buffering.

- **Enterprise Content Delivery Network (eCDN)** - The objective of eCDN is to take the video content from the Internet and broadcast the content throughout an organization without affecting network performance. Figure 2-13 identifies the certified, third-party eCDN partners that an organization can use to optimize its network for live events.

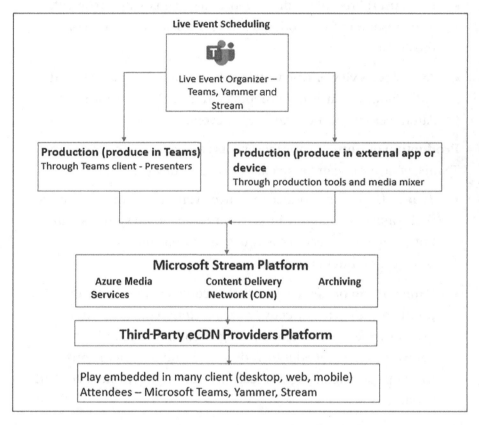

Figure 2-13. *Teams live event scheduling*

Flow Chart of Teams Live Events Scheduling

Figure 2-13 displays the high-level components involved in Teams live events and how they're connected, and it shows the live event scheduling flow.

Teams live events are very useful for hosting large events such as company or departmental all-hands meetings. Attendees join through invites or links, but what if you want to allow the user to register before the webinar-type event? This is where Teams webinars come in handy, and it is the next topic.

Teams Webinars

Webinars are formal meetings where presenters and participants have clear roles. They are frequently used for training or sales and marketing lead generation scenarios. After setting up Teams webinars in your organization, your users can schedule webinars and open registration to attendees. Unlike traditional meetings that include many discussions and task assignments, webinars are meant for interactive presentations and provide tools for attendee analysis. Teams webinars provide the following management features that enable the Teams admin to manage participation and follow up with webinar attendees:

- Custom registration pages and attendee emails

- Rich presentation options

- Host controls, such as the ability to disable attendee chat and video

- Post-event reporting

Team webinars include the following features:

- Polls, chat, and reactions for up to 1,000 attendees

- View-only broadcast of the webinar for up to 10,000 attendees

- Content layouts that can be customized for Presenter Mode

- Attendee registration page and email confirmations

- Downloadable attendee reporting for CRM and Marketing apps

- Video and audio can be turned off by default for all attendees

- Options for in-tenant and public attendees

- Attendee reporting for up to 1,000 attendees

Allowing Webinars in Teams Admin Center

First, you, as the admin, need to enable webinars in the Teams admin center under
Meetings ➤ Meeting policies. Setting up a webinar is quite simple.

1. You can do meeting registration, which is by default enabled. You
    may check the meeting policy and set the policy to On

2. Next, set who can register. All users can register for and attend
    webinars, including anonymous users, if you select *Everyone*.
    If you choose *Everyone in the organization*, only users in your
    organization can register for webinars

3. The last option to set up is the engagement report. When this is
    on, organizers can see reports of who registered and attended
    the webinars they set up. Figure 2-14 shows the webinar setup
    options.

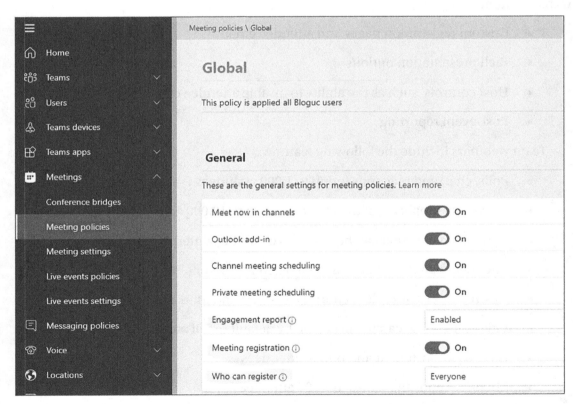

Figure 2-14. *Teams webinar setup options*

You, as an admin, can enable webinar options using the PowerShell command `Set-CsTeamsMeetingPolicy` with attributes `AllowMeetingRegistration`, `WhoCanRegister`, `AllowPrivateMeetingScheduling`.

It is crucial that `AllowPrivateMeetingScheduling` is set to `True` for `AllowMeetingRegistration` to work. Then you can run a command like `Set-CsTeamsMeetingPolicy -AllowMeetingRegistration $True` to enable registration.

Teams Audio Conferencing

Audio conferencing is the capability to join a Teams meeting from a regular phone and call out from a meeting to a phone number. This functionality enables users to call into meetings when they can't use a Teams client. Conference bridges let people dial into meetings using a phone. You can use the default settings for a conference bridge or change the phone numbers (toll and toll-free) and other settings such as the PIN or the languages used.

Calling into meetings is helpful for users on the road if they can't attend a meeting using the Microsoft Teams app on their laptops or mobile devices. There are different scenarios in which utilizing a phone to attend a Microsoft Teams meeting can be a more suitable option than using an app on a computer, such as

- When internet connectivity is limited

- When a meeting is audio-only

- When there's an inability to join from Teams

The advantages of calling into meetings include

- The call quality is better when calling in.

- People can join a meeting *hands-free* using Bluetooth devices.

- People discover it's more comfortable and more convenient for their situation.

Audio conferencing must be set up for people who plan to schedule or lead meetings. One audio conferencing license is required for each person who will organize/ host an audio meeting. Meeting attendees who call in don't need a license assigned to them or any other setup. After attendees have joined a Microsoft Teams meeting, they can call out and invite other callers into the meeting.

Verify that this feature is available in your country/region. A full list of country/region capabilities is available at `https://docs.microsoft.com/en-us/microsoftteams/country-and-region-availability-for-audio-conferencing-and-calling-plans/country-and-region-availability-for-audio-conferencing-and-calling-plans`. Determine which business users and sites require access to the audio conference. Consider rolling out audio conferencing on a site-by-site basis. Obtain service numbers or numbers for toll-free calling; you may be able to transfer existing toll-free numbers. Configure the default bridge number, set up languages for conference bridge phone numbers, and configure the meeting join experience (entry/exit announcements, PIN length, and so on). Customize meeting invitations to include additional legal or help information and add logos to ensure that invitations match the corporate look and feel.

Introduction to Microsoft Teams Admin Center

In day-to-day work as a Teams admin, you must keep Teams behavior optimized to your users and organization. Microsoft is on a mission to continually optimize the experience for admins. Microsoft is constantly evolving management capabilities to enable admins to manage Teams simply and effectively using granular control while keeping it secure and straightforward. The Teams admin center is the one place to do all the Teams management and operational work. If you are supporting Teams, you must learn the Teams administration tools that will help you manage Teams workload effectively. Microsoft Teams has multiple admin tools that you need to learn, such as Microsoft 365 admin center, Teams admin center, Teams PowerShell module, and Azure Active Directory.

Even though Microsoft Teams focuses considerable attention on self-service, some essential management and implementation tasks must be completed to maximize a deployment's effectiveness. For example, even when implementing self-service features, some policies that you create to guide users are essential and should be planned with the appropriate diligence. You should have insight into the different management tools available with Teams and the various clients that can work with Teams content. You will also learn how to interpret Microsoft 365 and Teams usage reports to understand user adoption.

There are different management tools available to manage Teams workloads, features, policies, client deployment, Phone System management, and such. One of the main tools that a Teams admin must know is the Microsoft Teams admin center, which is helpful for Teams client deployment, user provisioning, policy creation and assignment, call quality analysis, and analyzing usage patterns by monitoring Microsoft 365 and Teams usage reports.

Teams Admin Role for Management

Managing the various aspects of Microsoft Teams can be performed using multiple tools. Basic tasks, such as creating and editing Teams settings, adding or removing members, and adding, removing, and configuring apps, can be performed by users through one of the Teams clients. Administrative tasks must be performed with administrative roles and through the Teams admin center, the Teams PowerShell module, or Microsoft Graph API. Microsoft 365 provides various preconfigured administrative role groups so that selected users can receive elevated access to administrative tasks within the Office 365 services. The role groups are assigned through different portals, such as the Microsoft 365 admin center, the Azure portal, and PowerShell.

Several administrative roles have full access to all of the Teams' service settings, such as the Global Administrator and the Teams Admin. Other roles only provide access to specific parts of Microsoft Teams to perform recurring tasks, such as troubleshooting call quality problems and managing telephony settings. The specialized Teams admin roles include Teams Administrator, Teams Device Administrator, Teams Communications Administrator, Teams Communications Support Engineer, and Teams Communications Support Specialist. The Teams Administrator role in the Azure portal is the same role as the Teams Service Administrator in the Microsoft 365 admin center. If you assign this role to a member in the Azure portal, you can also see it in the Microsoft 365 admin center (and vice versa).

To configure and manage Teams, you must sign into your Microsoft 365 tenant with the appropriate privilege for the task you need to accomplish. There are multiple admin roles available in Azure AD, including the following:

- **Global Administrator**: It is not a Teams administrative role; however, users with this role can perform any administrative task in Teams, SharePoint, Exchange, and OneDrive.

- **Teams Administrator**: This role has full access to manage and administrator Teams capabilities, manage Microsoft 365 groups service requests, and monitor service health.

- **Teams Communication Administrator**: This role is used to assign phone numbers, create and manage voice and meeting policies, and view call analytics.

- **Teams Communication Support Engineer**: This role has access to call record details for all participants to troubleshoot communications difficulties.

- **Teams Communication Support Specialist**: This admin role provides access to read Teams call details only for a specific user to troubleshoot communication problems.

- **Teams Device Administrator**: This admin role configures and manages devices used for Microsoft Teams services, including Teams phones, Rooms, and Teams displays.

- **Skype for Business Administrator**: This admin role has full access to all Teams and Skype for Business capabilities and Skype user attributes, and it manages service requests and monitors service health.

Microsoft 365 Admin Center

Using Microsoft 365 admin center, you can manage user licenses, password resets, and group membership. You can use the Microsoft 365 admin center to manage admin roles. Also, you can assign the Teams admin role to one or more user accounts. Once you have signed in with the required permission, you can use both the Microsoft Teams admin center and Windows PowerShell to manage your Teams environment.

Microsoft Teams Admin Center

The Teams admin center portal is a centralized place to manage all Teams-related activities. This is an excellent resource for administration, analytics, reporting, and information. Most of the admin functions for managing Teams can be found in the admin center. This admin tool allows you to do all admin functions in a user-friendly way. Other administration methods like PowerShell and Graph API are still there to automate some admin work.

The Microsoft Teams admin center is available from the Microsoft 365 admin center or by navigating to https://admin.teams.microsoft.com/. The Microsoft Teams admin center provides a dashboard that shows the Teams usage and user activity in an organization and the entire administrative capabilities required to configure all aspects of Teams in a tenant. Once you log in, you will see multiple components that you can use to review and configure Teams settings:

- **Home:** This page shows the dashboard with user search and activity logs.

  - **Teams:** It enables you to perform team management, create and apply team policies, and define team templates.

  - **Manage teams:** Teams and channels are collections of people, content, and tools used for projects or outcomes within your organization. You can manage all the teams and channels, create new ones, and manage the existing ones. Go to Admin center > Groups to manage Microsoft 365 groups. This page shows the user's summary and team count.

  - **Teams settings:** Teams settings let you set up your teams for features such as email integration, cloud storage options, and device setup. When you make changes to the settings here, they will be applied to all the teams within your organization.

  - **Teams policies:** Teams and channel policies are used to control what settings or features are available to users when they are using teams and channels. You can use the Global (org-wide default) policy and customize it or create one or more custom policies for those people who are members of a team or a channel within your organization.

  - **Team templates:** Team templates are pre-built definitions of a team's structure designed around a business need or project. You can create a template using the Teams client and then upload and manage the templates stored in your organization. These templates can be assigned to a specific group using team policies.

  - **Templates policies:** Teams template policies let you create and set up policies for people in your organization so they can see only specific templates. You can use the Global (org-wide default) policy and customize it or create one or more custom policies for the people who will be using templates.

- **Teams update policies:** Update policies are used to let Teams and Office preview users see prerelease or preview features in the Teams app. You can use the Global (org-wide default) policy and customize it or create one or more custom policies for your users.

- **Teams upgrade settings:** Teams upgrade lets you set up your upgrade experience from Skype for Business to Teams for your users. You can use the default settings or make changes to the coexistence mode and app preferences to fit your organizational needs.

- **Users:** This provides access to your Microsoft 365 users and enables you to manage Teams-related settings for them.

  - **Manage users:** You can manage audio conferencing settings, policies, phone numbers, and other features for people in your organization. Go to Admin center > Users to manage different user settings such as adding or deleting users, changing passwords, and assigning licenses.

  - **Guest access:** Guest access in Teams allows people outside of your organization access to teams and channels. When you, as an admin, turn on Guest Access, you can turn on or off features for guest users so they can or can't see them. Make sure to follow the steps in this checklist to set up the prerequisites, so team owners can add guest users to their teams.

  - **External access:** External access lets your Teams and Skype for Business users communicate with other users outside of your organization. Your users can add apps when they host meetings or chats with external users. They can also use apps shared by external users when they join meetings or chats hosted externally. The data policies of the hosting user's organization, as well as the data-sharing practices of any third-party apps shared by that user's organization, are applied.

- **Teams devices:** This enables you to control and manage IP phones, team rooms, and collaboration bars.

  - **Teams Rooms on Windows:** Here you control and manage Teams Rooms on Windows devices such as consoles, microphones, cameras, and displays. You can configure settings, view activity information, manage updates, set up alert rules, and perform diagnostics to help with troubleshooting.

  - **Teams Rooms on Android:** Here you control and manage your Teams-certified Teams Rooms on Android devices across your organization, create and upload configuration profiles to make changes, set up alert rules, and apply updates for each device.

  - **Surface Hubs (Preview):** Surface Hubs offer an all-in-one digital whiteboard, meetings platform, and collaborative computing experience.

  - **Panels:** Panels are devices mounted outside conference rooms, typically next to the room entrance. They show room availability, room names, and reservations.

  - **Phones:** Here you control and manage Teams-certified phones across your organization, create and upload configuration profiles for each type of phone you have, make changes to their settings, set up alert rules, and apply software updates.

  - **Displays:** Here you manage displays in your organization, create and upload configuration profiles so you can make setting changes, set up alert rules, and apply updates for each type of device.

  - **SIP devices:** Here you control and manage Teams-certified SIP devices across your organization.

- **Teams apps:** This provides access to manage apps for your users, configure app permissions policies, and create and configure app setup policies.

  - **Manage apps:** When you manage apps for your organization, you control what apps are available to users in your organization's app store. You can then use app permission and app setup policies to configure what apps will be available for specific users.

- **App permission policies:** App permission policies control what apps you want to make available to Teams users in your organization. You can use the Global (org-wide) default policy and customize it, or you can create one or more policies to meet the needs of your organization.

- **App setup policies:** App setup policies control how apps are made available to a user with the Teams app. You can use the Global (org-wide default) policy and customize it, or you can create custom policies and assign them to a set of users.

- **Customize app store:** You can customize the Teams app store with your organization's logo, logomark, and custom background or color.

- **Meetings:** This feature provides access to conference bridges, meeting policies, meeting settings, live event policies, and live event settings.

  - **Conference bridges:** Conference bridges let people dial into meetings using a phone. You can use the default settings for a conference bridge or change the phone numbers (toll and toll-free) and other settings such as the PIN or the languages that are used.

  - **Meeting policies:** Meeting policies are used to control what features are available to users when they join Microsoft Teams meetings. You can use the Global (org-wide default) policy and customize it or create one or more custom meeting policies for people that host meetings in your organization.

  - **Meeting settings:** Meeting settings are utilized to control whether anonymous people can join Teams meetings, what is incorporated in the meeting invitations, and if you want, you can enable Quality of Service (QoS) and set the ports for real-time traffic. These settings are used for all Teams meetings that people schedule in your organization.

- **Live events policies:** Teams live events policies cover who can join a live event, if the transcription is provided for attendees, or if live recording events are available for people who schedule and hold live events. You can use the Global (org-wide default) policy and customize it or create additional policies with different settings and assign them to people who hold live events in your organization.

- **Live events settings:** Teams live events settings lets you control org-wide settings for all live events that are scheduled. You can choose to include a support URL when live events are held and set up a third-party video distribution provider for all live events organized and planned by people in your organization.

- **Messaging policies:** Messaging policies are used to control what chat and channel messaging features are available to users in Teams. You can use the Global (org-wide default) policy or create one or more custom messaging policies for people in your organization. This enables you to update messaging policies and control available chat and channel messaging features for your Teams users.

- **Voice:** Here you configure the voice settings for your organization.

    - **Phone numbers:** To set up calling features for users and services in your organization, you can get new numbers or port existing ones from a service provider. You can assign, unassign, and release phone numbers for people or services, like audio conferencing, auto attendants, or call queues.

    - **Operator Connect:** Manage partnerships with your phone number providers. You can only get phone numbers from providers you've established a partnership with.

    - **Direct Routing:** Direct Routing lets you connect a supported SBC to the Microsoft Phone System to enable voice calling features. You can add, edit, and view information about your SBCs, voice routes, and PSTN usage records.

    - **Calling policies:** Calling policies are used to control what calling features are available to people in Teams. You can use the Global (org-wide default) policy and customize it or create one or more custom calling policies for people who have phone numbers in your organization.

- **Call park policies:** Call park lets people put a call on hold and transfer it to other people within your organization. Call park policies to let you control which users are call park enabled and make other call park setting changes for them. You can use the Global (org-wide default) policy and customize it or create one or more custom policies and assign them to users.

- **Caller ID policies:** Caller ID policies are used to change or block the Caller ID (also called a Calling Line ID) for users. By default, the user's phone number is displayed when a call is made to a PSTN phone number such as a landline or mobile phone. You can use the Global (org-wide default) policy and customize it or create a custom policy that provides an alternate number to display or to block any number from being displayed.

- **Dial plans:** A dial plan is a set of rules that translates a phone number that a user dials into a standard E.164 number for call authorization and routing. You can use the Global (org-wide default) policy or create one or more custom dial plans for people in your organization.

- **Emergency policies:** There are two policies under the emergency policy option.

  - **Calling policies:** Emergency calling policies are used to control how users in your organization can use dynamic emergency calling features. You can use the Global (org-wide default) policy and customize it or create one or more custom policies for those people within your organization.

  - **Call routing policies:** Emergency call routing policies are utilized to set up emergency numbers for Direct Routing and then specify how those emergency calls are routed. You can use the Global (org-wide default) policy and customize it or create one or more custom policies for people within your organization.

- **Voice routing policies:** A voice routing policy is linked to a voice route using a PSTN usage record. You can add existing PSTN usage records, change the order in which the usages will be processed, and assign the voice routing policy to users.

- **Auto attendants:** Auto attendants let people who call in navigate a menu system so they can be connected with the correct department, person, or the operator in your organization. When you create an auto-attendant, you choose your greetings, set up your menus, and then decide how to redirect calls.

- **Call queues:** Call queues deliver a method of routing callers to people in your organization who can assist with a particular issue or question. Calls are distributed one at a time to the people in the queue (who are known as agents). While waiting for an agent, a greeting message and music may be played to callers.

- **Holidays:** This is used to set specific dates and times that your organization will take time off from work and won't be available during business times. The holidays you create here can then be linked to auto attendants that you make within your organization.

- **Resource accounts:** Resource accounts are non-enabled user accounts that are used to represent system resources. In Teams, you can create resource accounts and assign them to voice features such as call queues and auto attendants.

- **Locations:** This enables you to define reporting labels for IP subnets. You can also define a network topology and networks and sites.

  - **Emergency addresses:** An emergency address is a civic address, which is a physical street address of a place of business for your organization. An emergency location is a civic address with an optional place. If your company has more than one physical location, you'll likely need more than one emergency location.

  - **Network topology:** You can use a network topology to define the network regions, sites, and subnets that are used to determine the emergency call routing and calling policies that are to be used for a given location.

- **Network and Locations:** There are four different network access support options.

  - **Subnet:** Every subnet must be associated with a specific network site. A client's location is determined based on the network subnet and the associated network site. You can associate multiple subnets with the same network site, but you can't associate various locations with the same subnet.

  - **Wi-Fi access points:** A wireless access point (WAP), or generally just an access point (AP), is a networking device that lets other Wi-Fi devices such as PCs, laptops, and mobile phones connect to a wired network. Each Wi-Fi access point is assigned a BSSID (Basic Service Set Identifier) to group wireless network devices that operate with the same network parameters.

  - **Switches:** A network switch is a device that connects multiple LAN (local area network) devices using Ethernet connections, like desktops running the Teams app, to receive and forward data to other devices plugged into the switch. Each network switch is stamped with the chassis ID used to identify a specific switch on a network.

  - **Ports:** A network port is a physical Ethernet connection that connects multiple LAN devices like a desktop computer that is running the Teams app. Each port will require you to put in the switch's chassis ID, which connects the port to a switch in Teams.

- **Policy packages:** This provides access to defined policy packages. A policy package is a customizable collection of settings and policies that you can apply to a group of users with similar roles in your organization. The definitions in these policy packages aren't designed for regulatory compliance, but they can be customized based on your own regulatory requirements. You can manage packages and use Group package assignments to assign the package.

- **Planning:** This enables access to the Teams advisor and the Network planner tool.

  - Teams Advisor provides guidance and help in Microsoft Teams deployment. It evaluates your Microsoft 365 tenant setting and recognizes the most typical configurations you may require to correct or change before you can deploy Teams.

  - **Network planner:** A network planner helps you determine and organize network requirements for connecting people who use Teams across your organization in a few steps. By providing your networking details and Teams usage, you get calculations and the network requirements you need when deploying Teams and cloud voice across organizational physical locations.

- **Analytics & reports**: This provides access to usage reports. Available reports include apps usage, Teams device usage, and Teams user activity.

  - **Usage reports:** This helps you create different types of reports to gain insights and information about Teams usage. These reports support you in better understanding usage patterns, so you create better business decisions.

  - **Reporting labels:** Reporting labels are used to give an IP subnet a name that links it to a physical location such as offices, buildings, or organizational sites within your organization. They are used by Call Analytics to make it easier to see a name of a place instead of just an IP subnet in reports. You can upload a CSV that has a list of physical locations and their associated network subnets.

  - **Call quality dashboard:** This provides a link to the Microsoft Call Quality Dashboard.

- **Notifications & alerts:** This page allows you to create notification rules for app submission and device state rules.

  - **Rules:** Edit and configure alert rules to monitor critical metrics and get notified if they meet a threshold that you set. See Figure 2-15.

Figure 2-15. *Teams admin center dashboard*

The Teams admin center enables administrators to manage and create Teams policies; manage phone devices and telephony numbers, locations, and emergency addresses; and manage meeting settings and policies, such as live event settings and policies, messaging policies, the Teams apps settings and policies, organization-wide settings for sharing, guest access, resource accounts, and all calling settings. The portal also provides links to the legacy portal, the call quality dashboard for troubleshooting, and to StaffHub. For access the Teams admin center, a user must be assigned to one of the admin roles (Global Administrator, Teams Administrator, Teams Communication Administrator, and Skype for Business Administrator (might be deprecated in the future)). Figure 2-15 shows the Teams admin center Dashboard landing page.

- **Dashboard**: It shows relevant information about your Teams deployment status.

- **User Search**: You can quickly search for your users and view their information.

- **Navigation (Home/Teams/User/Teams devices/ Teams apps)**: Find all the areas supported by your Teams deployment.

- **Navigation**: Select a place within the navigation bar to show and hide the navigation.

New Capabilities Added to Teams Admin Center

Microsoft has made multiple enhancements in the Teams admin center to manage Teams capabilities effectively. Also, the Teams admin center has been simplified for a better experience.

Teams admin center interface improvements: It has a new look with improved left navigation to find appropriate options. Drag-and-drop customization is on the Home page, which allows admins to add/remove effective options. Additionally, login improvements to the Teams admin center without using third-party cookies and login pop-ups helps you to log into the Teams admin center in all modern browsers in private browsing and have strict tracking prevention on Edge or incognito mode in Chrome and Safari. In addition, Microsoft has increased the time of the inactive session to 24 hours, allowing the admin to use the existing browser. Furthermore, simplified external access management enables you to select one of the four access control configurations that best fits your organization's needs, allowing all domains or specific domains or blocking particular domains while letting everything else or blocking all domains. This is an improvement, so it doesn't impact any existing settings. Figure 2-16 shows all options available in the Teams admin center.

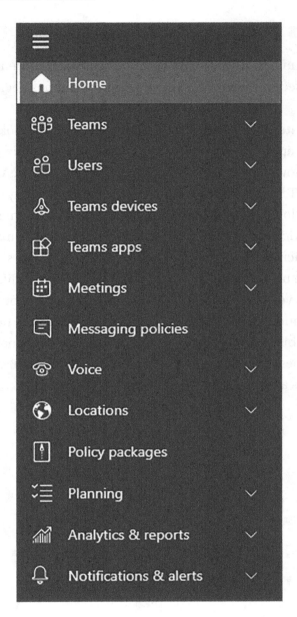

Figure 2-16. *Teams admin center options*

Home page customization: You, as an admin, can customize the options shown on the dashboard.

Export data: This is a significant improvement that makes a Teams admin's life easier by providing the ability to export data from Teams, users, and devices. Exported data will show in the downloads section in the header supported download types. Figure 2-17 shows Teams device report options.

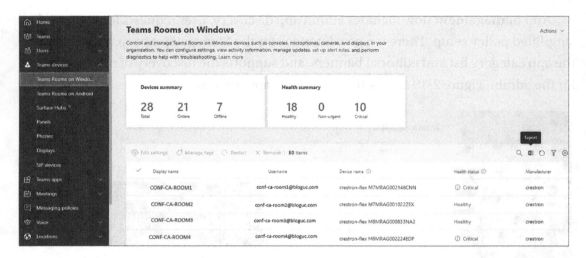

Figure 2-17. *Exporting a Teams device report*

Teams admin center search: Microsoft has improved the search capability for the admin enter, which makes everything easy to find, including users, teams, and apps. Search results are updated based on the query entered. Figure 2-18 shows user search options.

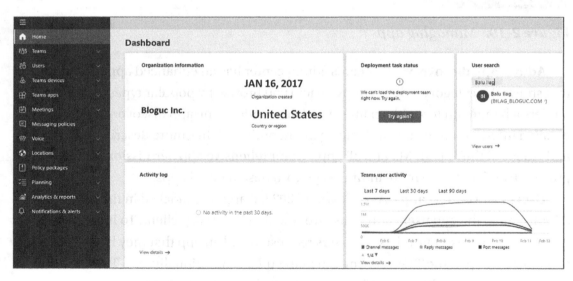

Figure 2-18. *User search*

App management now includes admin app discovery, user requests for apps, and a simplified policy setup. There is a new interface for the Manage App page, which shows the app category list and editorial banners, and supports the discovery of relevant apps for the admin. Figure 2-19 shows Teams manage app options.

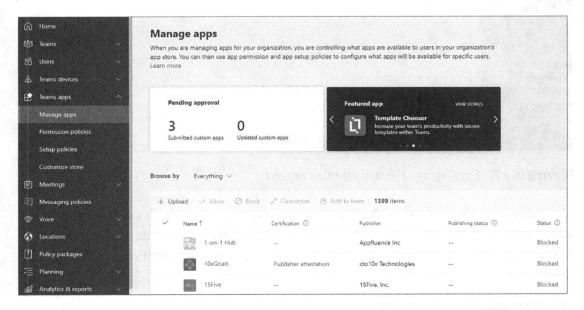

Figure 2-19. *Managing apps*

Admin app discovery: The Teams admin center has an enhanced app details page that shows the category of listed apps to help you browse by popular types. Furthermore, it offers a banner on top with an image and description. The app discovery page provides detailed information on app and management options. It has more descriptive images and videos of the app for MS and 3P apps. Comprehensive app permission info is provided, and it offers a more intuitive app card design for all apps.

Users can request apps: As of February 2022, if apps are blocked in the Teams admin center, the end user cannot discover them in the Teams client. To improve this experience, Microsoft now lets end users request to add an app that they have discovered as a blocked app in the Teams client app marketplace. Additionally, as a Teams admin, you will get insights about apps desired by the end users on the Manage apps page.

App setup policy enhancement: App setup policy is helpful for the admin to manage the App setup policy. In-app setup policies have additional improvements such as messaging extensions, apps pinned in-app setup policy for admin, and admin control with policy order change and appearance. End-user can pinned the app once the admin renders the pinned apps. Figure 2-20 shows the app setup policies with *Upload custom apps* and *User pinning* options.

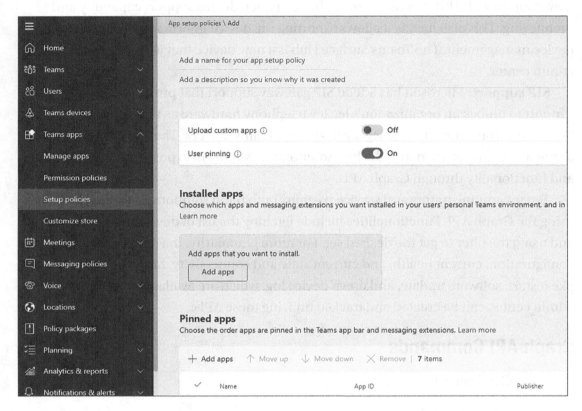

Figure 2-20. *App setup policies*

Additionally, it allows group assignment such as a setup policy to be assigned to a group or a distribution list. Also, existing precedence rules and rankings are applied.

From a security and compliance angle, these app discovery capabilities are vast components of security sanitation. Across the security landscape, we talk a lot about risks and shadow IT because unknown apps or services within your environment are approved and regulated by information security.

Device Management

Teams device management in the Teams admin center shows device types that are newly supported. This means Microsoft has extended device support capability and monitoring. This also means it allows exporting the device information to automate device management. The Teams Surface Hub is a new device that is managed under the admin center.

SIP support: Microsoft has added SIP gateway support that provides basic telephony support to unlock an organization's legacy telephony hardware as they move to Teams. This allows you connect these legacy devices as Teams devices. These devices will have a similar UI as a Teams-native device. Additionally, Microsoft exposes the manageability and functionality through Graph APIs.

Tenant administrators and service partners both build solutions and enhancements using the Graph API. Functionalities include fetching the list of devices and enrollment and using the filter to get the desired set. For more granularity, the API provides device configuration, current health, and current state and connectivity. Moreover, operations like restart, software update, and down device log, which are available from the Teams admin center, can be created and tracked utilizing these APIs.

Graph API Commands

- Get device list

- GET device details

- GET Device configuration

- GET device health details

- GET device activity details

- GET device operation history

- POST initiate device

The Teams admin center adds device support for these activities:

- Monitor and manage device health

- Workspace management

- Scoped Teams device administration role

- Device managed services

- Device analytics – Dashboard

- Device management alerts

Device Management Workflow

The Teams device management workflow is straightforward; it starts with a simple setup of devices and then goes to a seamless auto-enrollment for a new device, remote provisioning of devices, and remote sign-in or sign-out for Android devices.

It also supports continued granular inventory management capabilities including tracking and managing the device inventory, creating and assigning configuration profiles, organizing views and tag devices, and easy lookup through flexible search and filters; you can also perform scheduled tasks such as software updates and bulk actions such as device settings application.

There is a view of workspaces that is location-based with all the connected devices and inventory management insights. The Teams admin center also provides various options to delegate admin access to manage devices securely. The possibilities include *Teams device administrator role, Securely managed by a Microsoft partner*, and *Scoped administrator role for admins.*

Specific to monitoring and diagnosis, the Teams admin center can monitor the active device health with an alerting capability that supports immediate troubleshooting and the ability to analyze call quality details. As an admin, you can also inspect the health status, including connected peripherals, and configure the health impact of peripherals.

Device Health Monitoring and Control

Multiple factors can affect the device health service status, varying from healthy to problematic and critical to non-urgent.

For instance, in a scenario where the display device is disconnected, the device's health will show as critical status; however, the admin might have routinely turned off the device display power, so it shouldn't be considered critical. Now you can control and configure the status from critical to non-urgent. Figure 2-21 shows the health status of peripherals and management options with impacts of critical, non-urgent, or no impact.

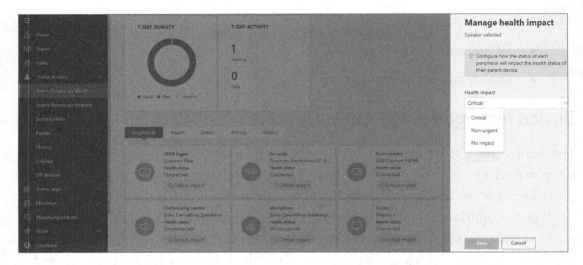

Figure 2-21. *Teams room peripherals status and health impact management*

Also, the critical status generates alerts; hence changing the status to non-urgent helps to reduce alerts.

Specific Device Management Alerts

For a device's health change status, a notification to the IT admin can be turned into an immediate corrective action. They have been enriched with a set of rules to flexibly manage the alerts according to prioritized devices. Also, you can integrate alerts with ITSM providers through webhooks to facilitate auto ticket generation.

To generate alerts, first define the role. Log into the Teams admin center and choose Rules on the left navigation bar. Then create a rule for device alerts. Figure 2-22 shows the device alerts creation option.

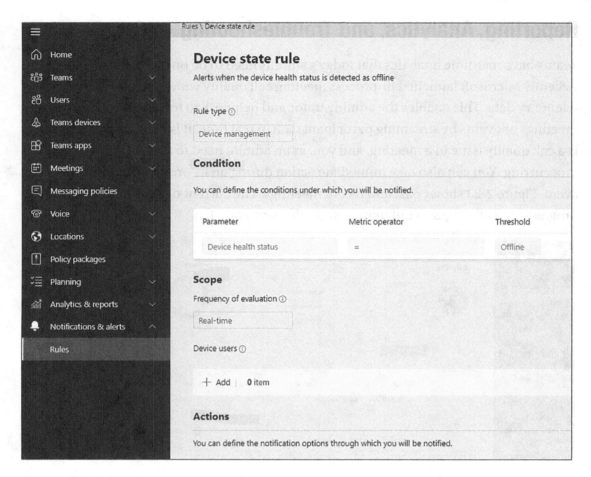

Figure 2-22. *Device alerts setup*

Device alert rules are beneficial for admins to proactively support Teams rooms, so it is essential to set up rules that will monitor the rooms. The next topic is reporting and call analytics, which help with troubleshooting.

Workspace Management Preview

By corresponding physical locations of workspaces to all related devices and peripherals, a Teams admin can segregate devices based on their physical location. For example, say your org has 10 devices in a Tracy, California location with the health status and utilization. You can monitor workspace health, utilization, and performance to standards at any location of your organization. Also, you can manage and perform everyday administrative actions on workspaces.

Reporting, Analytics, and Troubleshooting

Teams have real-time analytics that today's admins need to be on top of during meetings. Recently Microsoft launched in-process meeting call quality with real-time network telemetry data. This enables the administrator and helpdesk to troubleshoot during meetings or events by streaming participant data in real time. It is beneficial when there is a call quality issue in a meeting, and you, as an admin, need to explain why this issue is occurring. You can also take immediate action during an in-progress meeting or event. Figure 2-23 shows past and recent meetings. The current meeting status shows In progress, and all the past conferences and calls have ended.

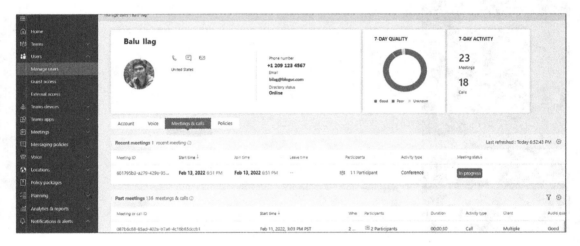

Figure 2-23. *An in-progress meeting*

This real-time data provides detailed network parameter information like jitter, packet loss latency, frames per second during the audio and video, and screen sharing per user. Additionally, it offers real-time information about users' locations, device details, and operating systems.

Teams call quality real-time analytics features are highly useful for executive or management people as they provide practical information about their participants' network conditions, which may cause meeting call quality issues. And it will ensure that you can troubleshoot call quality problems on the spot.

For instance, say you're looking for a specific user's call quality status. Log into the Teams admin center, click Managing users, and search for that particular user. Open the user's profile, and you will see a list of meetings joined, including the meeting that is in process. Clicking the in-process meeting will show all the participants' names and details and the audio health of each participant in the conference. Figure 2-24 shows one of the participant's audio stream details (inbound).

Figure 2-24. *Real-time quality information*

When you click the username, it will show more details about the audio and video streams, and some troubleshooting options for why the inbound audio stream has higher packet loss than average conditions.

Teams Admin Center Notification Framework

This rule-based alert and notification platform is helpful for various critical scenarios based on a specific matrix and its threshold. It also keeps the admin informed when monitoring thresholds are breached so they can take the necessary steps to remediate the issue.

You can define rules, set up a monitor matrix, set the threshold to get alerts, trigger alerts or notifications, and perform actions.

You can also set Teams devices monitoring, call quality monitoring and user feedback rating monitoring, and apps "submit for approval" notifications.

Priority account monitoring can be utilized in the Microsoft 365 admin center and can be monitored for their collaboration experiences.

Microsoft Teams Management Using PowerShell (Teams PowerShell Module)

The Microsoft Teams Management Shell is another tool for administrating a Teams unified communications system. The decision to use the Teams admin center or Teams Management Shell is yours. You can perform almost all the Teams admin center management tasks by using either tool. One advantage of the Teams Management Shell is that you can use it to run scripts to automate everyday administrative tasks.

You can create a Teams module Windows PowerShell script by saving the commands you would type in the shell to a file with a .ps1 extension. You can create a script in any text editor. It is easier to use the Windows PowerShell Integrated Scripting Environment (Windows PowerShell ISE), which is installed on all servers running the Windows Server operating system. However, you must consider a few limitations. Windows PowerShell ISE does not automatically load the Teams PowerShell module. To load the module, you must include the `Import-Module MicrosoftTeams` command as the first line in your script.

You also must remember that Windows PowerShell does not permit you to run scripts in their default state. You should set the execution policy as `RemoteSigned` and digitally sign the script. You must select the execution policy as `UnRestricted` if you cannot digitally sign it. To sign a script, you must install a script-signing certificate in the local user certificate store and then apply the Set-Authenticode cmdlet to the script.

Another way to administer and control Teams features is by using PowerShell. You can use Windows PowerShell to perform the same management tasks that you can perform in the admin canter. However, using PowerShell, you can do configuration tasks more quickly, perform repetitive tasks, and automate complex tasks using scripts. Connecting to the Teams PowerShell module is relatively easy; however, you must have the Microsoft Teams Windows PowerShell module installed before connecting to your Teams tenant.

Installing and Connecting Teams PowerShell

The Teams PowerShell module installation and connection is quite simple. Follow these steps:

a. First, open the Windows PowerShell command prompt as an admin. Once it opens, run this command: `Install-Module MicrosoftTeams`

b. After the above command runs, it will prompt you to enter *Y*.

c. It will take a couple of minutes to install the Teams module. Then you connect to Teams in your Office 365 tenant by employing the below commands.

d. On the PowerShell command prompt, run these commands:

```
Import-Module MicrosoftTeams
$credential = Get-Credential
Connect-MicrosoftTeams -Credential $credential
```

It will prompt you to sign in as a global admin or Teams admin into your tenant. Refer to Figure 2-25. Once it connects to the Teams tenant, you can run different commands to complete your administrative tasks.

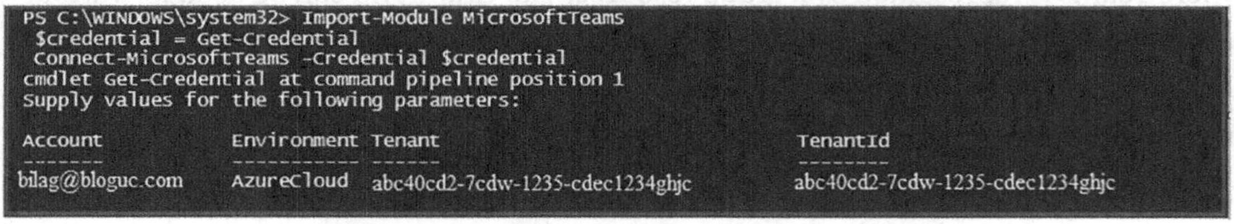

Figure 2-25. Importing and connecting to PowerShell

Teams PowerShell Commands for Managing Different Workloads

If you are unsure of the command or need any help, simply use the command `Get-Help`. For example, suppose you want to create new Teams using PowerShell but are unsure about the command syntax and parameters. In that case, run the command `Get-Help New-Team`. It will return with the command syntax and different parameters, for example. See Figure 2-26.

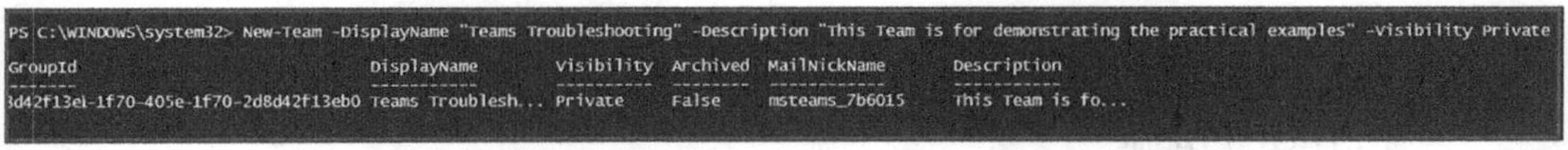

```
PS C:\WINDOWS\system32> New-Team -DisplayName "Teams Troubleshooting" -Description "This Team is for demonstrating the practical examples" -Visibility Private

GroupId                              DisplayName        Visibility  Archived  MailNickName       Description
-------                              -----------        ----------  --------  -----------        -----------
3d42f13ei-1f70-405e-1f70-2d8d42f13eb0 Teams Troublesh... Private    False     msteams_7b6015     This Team is fo...
```

Figure 2-26. *New team PowerShell command*

Managing Teams and Channels with PowerShell

PowerShell provides various commands that you can use to manage teams such as New-Team, Get-Team, Set-Team, and Remove-Team. You can use add or remove to manage Teams users: Add-TeamUser and Remove-TeamUser. Additionally, you can use new or remove commands to manage Teams channels (New-TeamChannel and Remove-TeamChannel).

Teams Graph API

Microsoft Teams also provides management capabilities through Microsoft Graph, where Teams is represented by a group resource. The Graph API can be used for various tasks regarding managing team settings, members, and resources. The primary use of the Graph API is its automation capabilities because Graph API calls can be embedded into tab pages and easily called from other sources.

Summary

Teams is the center of teamwork and it provide better collaboration mechanisms. This Microsoft Teams overview chapter outlines Microsoft Teams capabilities, service architecture, license requirements, clients and different meeting types, Phone System (calling plans, Operator Connect, and Direct Routing), and admin tools. Now you can explain what Teams is and features including the Teams admin center and the Teams PowerShell module and their management capabilities.

References

"GitHub MicrosoftDocs/msteams-docs: Source for Microsoft Teams." https://github.com/MicrosoftDocs/msteams-docs

Computer Services Tech, http://computerservicestech.com/

"How to collaborate with Microsoft Teams." https://help.delcocitizencorps.
org/microsoft-teams/teams-how-to/collaborating-with-microsoft-teams/
1-introduction-to-collaborating-with-microsoft-teams/3-how-to-collaborate-
with-microsoft-teams

"Get started with Microsoft Teams live events." https://support.microsoft.com/
en-us/office/get-started-with-microsoft-teams-live-events-d077fec2-a058-
483e-9ab5-1494afda578a

GitHub frbori/TeamsMeetingRecordingsNoDownloadAzureFunctions. https://
github.com/frbori/TeamsMeetingRecordingsNoDownloadAzureFunctions

SOLUTION: Missing Teams Video Recordings!! Microsoft Tech Community,
https://techcommunity.microsoft.com/t5/microsoft-stream-classic/solution-
missing-teams-video-recordings/td-p/2129450

"Office 365: How Microsoft Teams and SharePoint Work Together." https://
services.stthomas.edu/TDClient/1898/ClientPortal/KB/ArticleDet?ID=119046

"MS TEAM – Part II - SharePoint Pals." www.sharepointpals.com/post/ms-
team-part-ii/

Ilag, B.N. "Microsoft Teams Overview" in *Understanding Microsoft Teams
Administration* (Apress, 2020). https://doi.org/10.1007/978-1-4842-5875-0_1.

"Microsoft Teams Operator Connect – Digital Transformations." https://
agarwalronak.com/microsoft-teams-operator-connect/

"Live events." Microsoft Q&A, https://docs.microsoft.com/en-us/answers/
questions/102797/live-events.html

"What are Microsoft Teams live events?" Microsoft Teams, https://docs.
microsoft.com/en-us/microsoftteams/teams-live-events/what-are-teams-
live-events

"A Creative Event Studio Perfect for Networking Events Designed for Social Media."
www.peerspace.com/pages/listings/624e4f13f4033e000e3c8b27

"Configure Audio Conferencing settings." Microsoft Teams, https://docs.
microsoft.com/en-us/microsoftteams/deploy-audio-conferencing-teams-
landing-page

"Microsoft Teams Audio Conferencing with dial-out to select geographies." www.
schneider.im/microsoft-teams-audio-conferencing-with-dial-out-to-select-
geographies/

"Chat, teams, channels, & apps in Microsoft Teams." Microsoft Teams, https://
docs.microsoft.com/en-us/microsoftteams/deploy-chat-teams-channels-
microsoft-teams-landing-page

"Voice Calling with Microsoft Teams Schedule to the General Terms." BT, https://
business.bt.com/content/dam/terms/Voice-Calling-with-Microsoft-Teams/BTL_
BTE_VoiceCallingwithMicrosoftTeams.pdf

"Exam MS-740 topic 1 question 6 discussion." ExamTopics, www.examtopics.com/
discussions/microsoft/view/69867-exam-ms-740-topic-1-question-6-discussion/

"Microsoft Teams third-party apps now available in Government Community Cloud
(GCC)." https://techcommunity.microsoft.com/t5/public-sector-blog/microsoft-
teams-third-party-apps-now-available-in-government/ba-p/1132197

"Office 365: Manage meeting settings in Microsoft Teams." https://global-
sharepoint.com/sharepoint-2/office-365-manage-meeting-settings-in-
microsoft-teams/

"Manage Live Events Policies and Live Events Settings in Microsoft Teams." https://
global-sharepoint.com/sharepoint-2/manage-live-events-policies-and-live-
events-settings-in-microsoft-teams/

"Network settings for cloud voice features." Microsoft Teams, https://docs.
microsoft.com/en-us/MicrosoftTeams/cloud-voice-network-settings

"Microsoft Ignite Fall 2021: Innovations coming to Microsoft Teams." https://
techcommunity.microsoft.com/t5/microsoft-teams-blog/microsoft-ignite-
fall-2021-innovations-coming-to-microsoft-teams/ba-p/2824127

CHAPTER 3

Microsoft Teams Phone (Voice) Configuration and Management

Teams brings together calling, meeting, chat collaboration, and apps, thereby helping users easily stay connected right in their workflow. Microsoft Teams provides calls (1:1 and group) and multiparty meetings with optimal audio/video quality. Apart from VoIP communication, Teams provides external calling (PSTN calling) through calling plans, Operator Connects, and Direct Routing. Teams (Microsoft 365) Phone System is Microsoft's technology for enabling call control and PBX capabilities in the Microsoft 365 cloud.

In this chapter, you will learn how to plan and configure Microsoft Teams Phone System (calling plans, Operator Connect, and Direct Routing) with voice and emergency call routing policies and phone number management. Additionally, you will learn how to configure Teams calling features such as group call, auto attendant, and call queue. This chapter describes configuring Teams phone devices (Teams IP phone, CAP, Teams Room, and Teams Display).

Planning and Configuring Microsoft Teams Phone System

Microsoft Teams VoIP calls between two users in an organization are handled within Teams Phone System and never go to the PSTN. This also applies to multiparty calls between organization users, regardless of if they are in the same or different physical locations, removing long-distance costs on these internal calls. Specific to Teams, PSTN

© Balu N Ilag and Arun M Sabale 2022

B. N. Ilag and A. M. Sabale, *Troubleshooting Microsoft Teams*, https://doi.org/10.1007/978-1-4842-8622-7_3

call referring as an external phone call routed through the phone service provider is not available by default. As a Teams admin, you need to connect the Teams Phone System to the PSTN. There are three different options available:

1. **Teams Phone System with calling plans**: This is provided by Microsoft as a PSTN provider in a cloud-only solution. Calling plans are a simple way to quickly procure, provision, and assign phone numbers to organization users. In the calling plan, Microsoft is the PSTN service provider.

2. **Teams Phone System with Operator Connects**: This option allows you to stay with your existing operator service experience and contacts and relationships. It is a simplified and seamless operator management service for adding PSTN calling for Teams using the qualified operator.

3. **Teams Phone System with Customer's Own PSTN Carrier by Using Direct Routing to Connect Your On-Premises Environment to Teams**: This allows the customer to keep its existing infrastructure and service provider relationships and provide customer call routing. Direct routing allows you to keep your existing infrastructure and is supported in 180 countries. In Teams Direct Routing, you must use certified SBCs such as Ribbon, AudioCodes, Oracle, Cisco, and Avaya. Additionally, to add resiliency to most critical locations, a Survivable Branch Appliance (SBA) is generally available, enabling PSTN calling in a network outage that doesn't allow Teams clients to connect to a Teams back-end service.

Configuring Teams Calling Plans

Teams Phone System with calling plans is a simplified solution provided by Microsoft where everything is in the cloud, which means no infrastructure required for this solution and Microsoft acts as the carrier. Microsoft provides the PBX functionality and calls to the PSTN, as demonstrated in Figure 3-1.

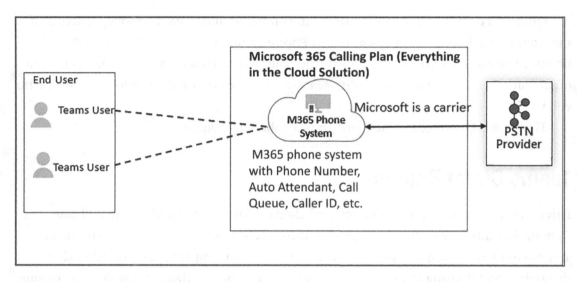

Figure 3-1. *Teams calling plan*

You, as the admin, need to be aware that the Teams calling plans are not available worldwide. Check the Teams website to see if your intended region has a calling plan available. Also, you need to check if the current PSTN carrier has any contractual terms and if there is a contact center and call recording requirements as calling doesn't provide those.

Note   Teams in general, and Phone System calling plans in particular, require an uninterrupted connection to Microsoft 365.

Using a Phone System calling plan, you get the following features:

- You get Microsoft Teams Phone with added domestic or international calling plans that enable calling to phones worldwide (depending on the level of service being licensed).

- Customers do not require deployment or maintenance of an on-premises deployment because the calling plans operate out of Microsoft 365 or Office 365.

- If required, you can use a combination of a calling plan and Teams Direct Routing, which means some users will have a calling plan license assigned with Microsoft's provided phone number. The rest of the users will have on-premises phone numbers, although Teams Direct Routing is not available everywhere.

Once you decide to use the Teams calling plan, purchase Teams Phone System and the calling plan licenses. Microsoft Teams Phone system is configured as an add-on license. The add-ons provide admins the flexibility to add features only for users in your organization who need them. To add a feature, buy one add-on license for each user who will use it.

The Teams Operator Connect option is detailed in Chapter 1.

Teams Direct Routing

Direct Routing allows you to connect a certified customer-provided SBC to a Phone System. The admin can configure on-premises PSTN connectivity with the Microsoft Teams client, as shown in Figure 3-2. You can choose to connect a supported SBC through Direct Routing for interoperability with third-party PBXs, analog devices, paging systems, and other third-party telephony equipment supported by the SBC.

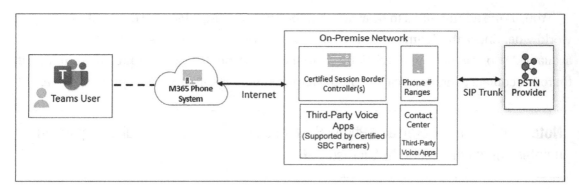

Figure 3-2. *Teams Direct Routing connectivity*

Direct Routing requirements:

- Your SBC must be supported. Here is the supported SBC list: https://docs.microsoft.com/en-us/microsoftteams/direct-routing-plan#supported-session-border-controllers-sbcs/.

- The PSTN must be connected to an SBC. One or more telephony trunks (SIP or PRI) must be connected to the SBC. On one end, the SBC connects to Teams Microsoft 365 Phone System through Direct Routing. The SBC can also connect to third-party telephony entities, like PBXs, analog telephony adapters, etc.

- A Microsoft 365 tenant (Teams) is used to host Teams users and the voice configuration. Users must be on Teams Only mode.

- The domain name is added to your Microsoft 365 organizations. Note that you cannot use the default domain, `*.onmicrosoft.com`, which is automatically created for your tenant (for `example, bloguc.onmicrosoft.com`). You can use the domain added to your domain (`Bloguc.com`).

- You need a public IP address to connect to Microsoft Teams in the cloud, one that can be used to connect to the SBC. Based on the type of SBC, the SBC can use NAT, but it must be 1:1.

- You need a FQDN for the SBC, where the domain portion of the FQDN is one of the registered domains in your Microsoft 365 (for example, `SBC1.bloguc.com`). This is used for mapping the SBC FQDN to the public IP address.

- You need a public trusted certificate for the SBC to be used for all communication with Direct Routing. The certificate provider list is at `https://docs.microsoft.com/en-us/microsoftteams/direct-routing-plan#public-trusted-certificate-for-the-sbc`.

- Firewall IP addresses and ports for Direct Routing media must be allowed for SBC communication, specifically for a SIP proxy, which handles the signaling, and Media Processor, which handles media, except when Media Bypass is on. For IP addresses and URL links, go to `https://docs.microsoft.com/en-us/office365/enterprise/urls-and-ip-address-ranges`.

- The SBC media transport profile should be TCP/RTP/SAVP and UDP/RTP/SAV.

- Direct routing requires licenses assigned to the user account in Microsoft 365: Microsoft Phone System, Microsoft Teams + Skype for Business Plan 2, and Microsoft Audio Conferencing (required only if you are migrating users from Skype for Business on-premises with enterprise voice to Microsoft Teams).

- Teams Direct routing supported clients:

  - Any Teams client

  - Common area phones

  - Skype for Business 3PIP phones

- Teams Direct routing connection points to three FQDNs:

  - `sip.pstnhub.microsoft.com`: The global FQDN must be tried first. When the SBC sends a request to resolve this name, the Microsoft Azure DNS servers return an IP address pointing to the primary Azure datacenter assigned to the SBC.

  - `sip2.pstnhub.microsoft.com`: The secondary FQDN geographically maps to the second priority region.

  - `sip3.pstnhub.microsoft.com`: The tertiary FQDN geographically maps to the third priority region.

- The FQDNs (`sip.pstnhub.microsoft.com`, `sip2.pstnhub.microsoft.com`, and `sip3.pstnhub.microsoft.com`) will be resolved to IP addresses from the subnets: 52.112.0.0/14 and 52.120.0.0/14

Note   As a requirement, you need to open ports for all these IP address ranges in your firewall to allow incoming and outgoing traffic to and from the addresses for signaling.

- **SIP signaling ports for Direct Routing**: Software that must use the following ports for Microsoft 365 environments where Direct Routing is offered are Microsoft 365, Office 365 GCC, Office 365 GCC High, and Office 365 DoD. See Table 3-1.

Table 3-1. *Signaling and Media Ports*

Traffic	From	To	Source port	Destination port
SIP/TLS	SIP proxy (Teams service)	SBC (your SBC public IP address)	1024 – 65535	Defined on the SBC (for Office 365 GCC High/DoD, only port 5061 must be used)
SIP/TLS	SBC (your SBC public IP address)	SIP proxy (Teams service)	Defined on the SBC	5061

Media ports for Direct Routing:

Traffic	From	To	Source port	Destination port
UDP/SRTP	Media Processor (Teams service)	SBC (your SBC public IP address)	3478-3481 and 49152 – 53247	Defined on the SBC
UDP/SRTP	SBC (your SBC public IP address)	Media processor (Teams service)	Defined on the SBC	3478-3481 and 49152 – 53247

Configuring Teams Direct Routing

First, you need to read the Teams Direct routing requirements to connect your SBC to Microsoft Phone System using the following steps.

1. Log into the Teams admin center at `https://admin.teams.microsoft.com`, select Voice in the left pane, and select Direct Routing.

2. Then select the SBCs tab, select Add to create a new entry, and enter a valid FQDN for the SBC. Ensure that the domain name portion of the FQDN matches a domain registered in your tenant, and keep in mind that the `*.onmicrosoft.com` domain name isn't supported for the SBC.

3. For FQDN, domain names added in Microsoft 365 are multiples; for instance, if you have two domain names, `bloguc.com` and `bloguc.onmicrosoft.com`, use `sbc.bloguc.com` as the SBC FQDN

name. If you're using a subdomain, make sure this subdomain is also registered in your tenant. For instance, if you want to use `sbc.test.bloguc.com`, then `test.bloguc.com` must be registered.

4. The next thing is to configure the below settings for the SBC based on your organization's needs (Figures 3-3 and 3-4):

   a. **Enabled (On/Off)**: Used to allow the SBC for outbound calls. You can temporarily remove the SBC from service while it's being updated or during maintenance.

   b. **SIP signaling port (5067 (can be changed during setup))**: This is the listening port that's used to communicate with Direct Routing by using the TLS protocol.

   c. **Send SIP options (On/Off)**: This setting defines if an SBC will or won't send SIP options messages. If this isn't turned on, the SBC will be excluded from the monitoring and alerting system. We recommend that you enable SIP options.

   d. **Forward call history (On/Off)**: Indicates whether call history information is forwarded

      through the trunk. When you turn this on, the Microsoft 365 or Office 365 proxy sends a history-info and Referred-by header.

   e. **Forward P-Asserted-Identity (PAI) Header (On/Off)**: Indicates whether the PAI header will be forwarded along with the call. The PAI header provides a way to verify the identity of the caller.

   f. **Concurrent call capacity (number, such as 50)**: When you set a value, the alerting system will notify you when the number of simultaneous sessions is 90 percent or higher than this value. If you don't put a value, alerts won't be generated. However, the monitoring system will report the number of concurrent sessions every 24 hours.

   g. **Failover response code (408, 503,504)**: If Direct Routing receives any 4xx or 6xx SIP error code in response to an outgoing Invite, the call is considered completed by default. Outgoing means a call from a Teams client to the PSTN with a traffic flow of Team's client ➤ Direct Routing ➤ SBC ➤ telephony network. When you specify a failover response code, this forces Direct Routing to try another SBC (if another SBC exists in the voice routing policy of the user) when it receives the specified codes if the SBC can't make a call because of the network or other issues.

h. **Failover time (seconds) (10)**: When set to 10 (default value), outbound calls that aren't answered by the gateway within 10 seconds are routed to the next available trunk. If there are no additional trunks, then the call is automatically dropped. Calls may be unintentionally dropped in an organization with slow networks and slow gateway responses.

i. **SBC supports PIDF/LO for emergency calls (On/Off)**: Specifies whether the SBC supports Presence Information Data Format Location Object (PIDF/LO) for emergency calls.

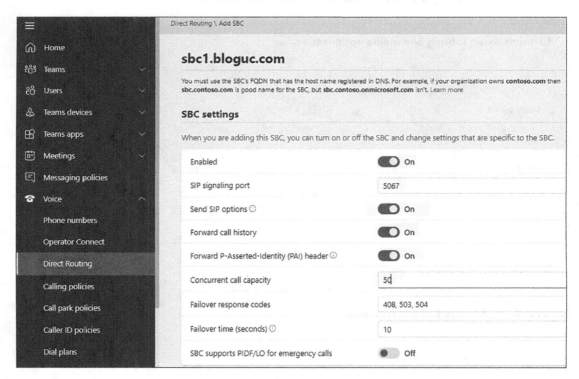

Figure 3-3. *Teams Direct routing*

j. **Bypass mode (None)**: Media bypass enables you to shorten the path of media traffic and reduce the number of hops in transit for better performance.

k. **Preferred country/region for media traffic (None)**: Manually set your preferred country or region for media traffic. We recommend that you set this only if the call logs indicate that the default assignment of the datacenter for the media path doesn't use the approach closest to the SBC datacenter. By default, Direct Routing assigns a datacenter based on the public IP address of the SBC. It always selects the path closest to the SBC data center. However, in some cases, the default path might not be optimal. This parameter allows you to manually set the preferred region for media traffic.

l. **Location-based routing (On/Off)**: Allows for network-based routing to the nearest SBC.

m. **Gateway site ID (None)**: Select the site name.

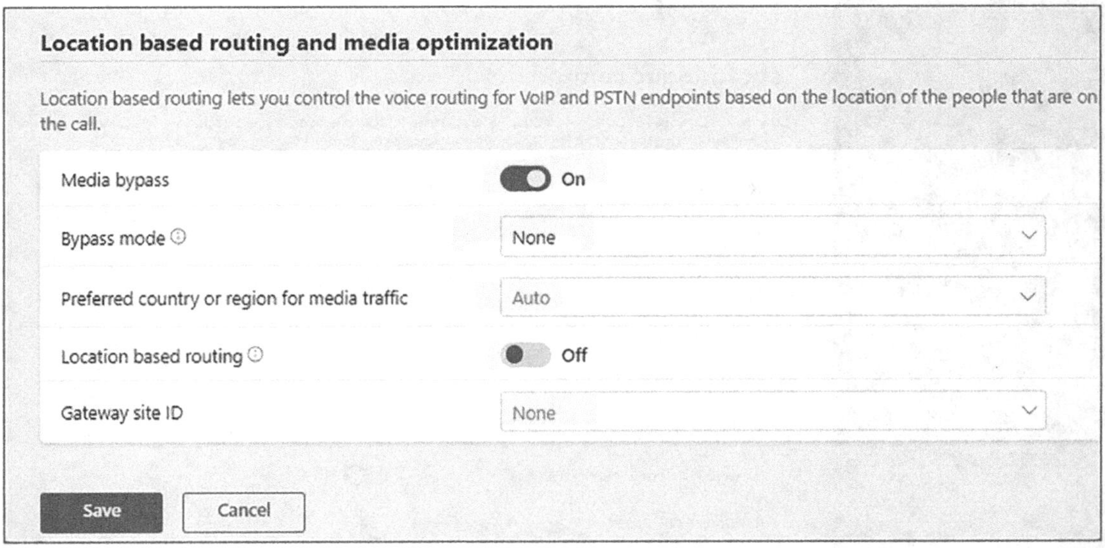

Figure 3-4. *Teams Direct routing*

5. Finally, select the Save button to save the SBC Teams Direct Routing configuration. After successfully configuring Direct Routing to an SBC from Microsoft Teams, the configuration of the SBC can be done through the GUI or through PowerShell. The Resources section contains how you can configure Direct Routes through PowerShell if required.

6. For an SBC configuration, you can contact the SBC vendor and refer to their documentation for Teams DR call routing to PSTN.

Reference link: https://docs.microsoft.com/en-us/microsoftteams/direct-routing-plan#supported-session-border-controllers-sbcs

Media Bypass and Non-Media Bypass Scenarios Specific to Direct Routing

In Direct Routing scenarios, the Direct Routing interface on the leg between the SBC and the cloud media processor (without media bypass) or between the Teams client and the SBC (if media bypass is enabled) can use the codecs *Non-Media bypass (SBC to Cloud Media Processor): SILK, G.711, G.722, G.729* and *Media Bypass (SBC to Teams client): SILK, G.711, G.722, G.729*. Admin can force the use of specific codec on the SBC by excluding undesirable codecs from the offer. On the leg between the cloud media processor and the Microsoft Teams client, either SILK or G.722 is used. The codec choice on this leg is based on Microsoft algorithms, which consider multiple parameters.

Managing Phone Numbers

In Teams, the admin mainly manages two phone types: phone numbers acquired from Microsoft for calling plans and phone numbers (on-premises) for Direct Routing.

Phone Numbers Acquired from Microsoft (Calling Plan)

Phone numbers are obtained from Microsoft using the Teams admin portal. These numbers are of different types: user (subscriber) number, call queue, auto attendant, and conference bridge number.

- **User (subscriber):** These are numbers for users in your organization that need a phone number.

- **Call queue (toll/toll-free):** These are service numbers used when you create a call queue, and they will be used on resource accounts.

- **Auto attendant (toll/toll-free):** These are the service numbers that are used when you create an auto attendant, and they will be assigned to a resource account.

- **Dedicated conference bridge (toll/toll-free):** These are service numbers used on conference bridges so users can dial into meetings.

To acquire the new phone number, log into the Teams admin center (`https://admin.teams.microsoft.com/`), click Voice and then Phone numbers, and click Add. Then type the name and description, select the country or region and number type, and click Next get the phone numbers, as shown in Figure 3-5.

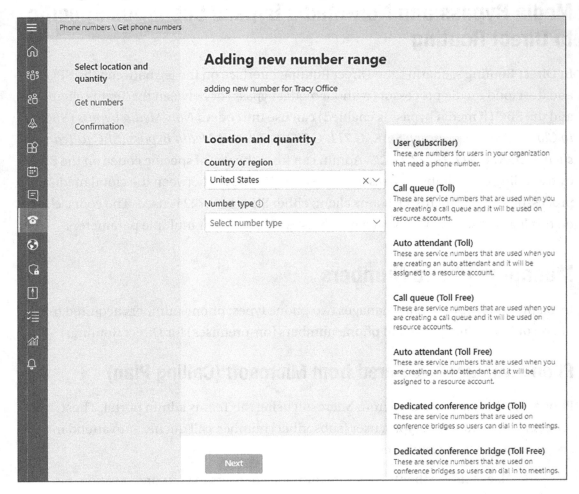

Figure 3-5. *Acquiring a number from Microsoft*

86

Once you get the numbers, you can assign them to the users or resource account; the remaining phone number you can keep and manage.

Phone Numbers (On-Premises) for Direct Routing

Teams Direct Routing allows the admin to configure existing on-premises PSTN connectivity to Teams through the SBC external interface. You cannot see the on-premises phone number listed in the Teams admin center; however, you can manage it locally using an Excel file and assign the number using a PowerShell command.

Configuring Unassigned Numbers for Better Management

When you use a bulk phone number range, not all numbers are assigned to the user. Those free phone numbers are the unassigned numbers applicable to your organization. Still, they are not assigned to a user or a phone or room account. The unassigned number table identifies how you want calls to unassigned numbers to be treated. As an administrator, you can route calls to unassigned numbers in your organization. For example, you might want to route all calls to a given unassigned number to a custom announcement or route all calls to a given unassigned number to the main switchboard.

You can configure unassignment number announcements through PowerShell only. You cannot do so using the Teams admin center because on-premises phone number ranges do not show in the Teams admin center.

You can route calls to unassigned numbers to a user, or a resource account associated with an auto attendant, or a call queue, or an announcement service that will play a custom audio file to the caller.

To configure route calls to an unassigned number, you can use the New/Get/Set/ Remove-CsTeamsUnassignedNumberTreatment command available in Teams PowerShell module 2.5.1 or later.

Example 1 with One Unassigned Number

As an admin, you need to require the called number or range of numbers and the associated routing for calls to these numbers. For instance, the following command specifies that all calls to the number +1 (408) 123-4567 will be routed to the resource account testAA@bloguc.com:

```
$RAObjectId = (Get-CsOnlineApplicationInstance -Identity
testAA@bloguc.com).ObjectId
New-CsTeamsUnassignedNumberTreatment -Identity MainAA -Pattern
"^\+14081234567$" -TargetType ResourceAccount -Target $RAObjectId -Treatment
Priority 1
```

Example 2 with an Unassigned Phone Number Range

in this example, you route calls coming to an unassigned phone number range to an announcement service:

```
$Content = Get-Content "C:\test\MainAnnoucement.wav" -Encoding
byte -ReadCount 0
$AudioFile = Import-CsOnlineAudioFile -FileName "MainAnnouncement.wav"
-Content $Content
$fid = [System.Guid]::Parse($AudioFile.Id)
New-CsTeamsUnassignedNumberTreatment -Identity TR1 -Pattern
"^\+1408123\d{4}$" -TargetType Announcement -Target $fid.Guid -Treatment
Priority 2
```

You can add or remove the unassigned number ranges using the PowerShell commands New/Get/Set/Remove-CsTeamsUnassignedNumberTreatment.

Note   You need to connect to the Teams PowerShell module before running the above commands.

Phone Number Translation

Phone number translation is critical because sometimes you, as the admin, may want to change the number for outbound and/or inbound calls based on the patterns they created to ensure interoperability with SBCs. The number translation rules policy is mainly used to translate numbers to an alternate format. You can use the number translation rules policy to translate numbers for the following:

- **Inbound calls**: The calls from a PSTN endpoint (caller) to a Teams client (callee)

- **Outbound calls**: The calls from a Teams client (caller) to a PSTN endpoint (callee)

The number translation policy is applied at the SBC level. You can assign multiple translation rules to an SBC, which are involved in the order that they are seen when you list them in PowerShell. You can also change the order of the rules in the policy.

To create, modify, view, and delete number manipulation rules, use the `New-CsTeams TranslationRule`, `Set-CsTeamsTranslationRule`, `Get-CsTeamsTranslationRule`, and `Remove-CsTeamsTranslationRule` commands.

To assign, configure, and list number manipulation rules on SBCs, use the `New-CS OnlinePSTNGateway` and `Set-CSOnlinePSTNGateway` commands together with the `InboundTeamsNumberTranslationRules`, `InboundPSTNNumberTranslationRules`, `OutboundTeamsNumberTranslationRules`, `OutboundPSTNNumberTranslationRules`, `InboundTeamsNumberTranslationRules`, `InboundPSTNNumberTranslationRules`, `OutboundTeamsNumberTranslationRules`, and `OutboundPSTNNumberTranslationRules` parameters.

Configuring Phone Policies
Teams Voice Routing Policy

The Teams Voice routing policy (also called an online voice routing policy) is assigned to the end user. The Voice routing policy contains PSTN usage; in other words, a call routing policy is a container for PSTN usage records. PSTN usages have voice routes added, and voice routes have calling patterns with the SBC FQDN to route calls. You cannot assign PSTN usage or a voice route to an end user configuration. The process is to create PSTN usage as a container, add a voice route to it, and the associate PSTN usage to the Teams Voice routing policy to get them assigned to the end user.

Note   Teams Voice route policy, PSTN usage, and Voice route all have the Online word added in front, so do not get confused by the name.

You can create Teams Voice routing policies, PSTN usages, and voice routes using the Teams admin center and PowerShell.

Teams Voice route and PSTN usage: The voice route points to the SBC. So, creating multiple voice routes and associating them with all local, national, and international PSTN usages for call authorization is a best practice because you can then add appropriate voice routes to the PSTN usage in priority. For instance, if you create a voice route for making calls to the US offices, use `sbc1.bloguc.com` for the SBC and set the route to priority one. If you have more than one SBC on the same site, you can add more than one SBC you want calls to route to. However, all of the SBCs that you added will be tried in a random order; it does not give high availability. For high availability, you can create a separate voice route for each SBC with priority and then add them to PSTN usage to get them checked.

Creating a Voice Routing Policy with PSTN Usage and Voice Routes

First, you need to create PSTN usage, and then you can associate it with a voice route. As mentioned, you can create a voice routing policy, PSTN usage, and voice using the Teams admin center and PowerShell. To use the Teams admin center for creating PSTN usage and voice routes, follow these steps:

1. Login into the Teams admin center, then on left navigation of the Teams admin center, go to Voice ➤ Voice routing policies, and click Add. Enter a name and description for the policy. Figure 3-6 shows a voice routing policy named NA-CA-Tracy-National.

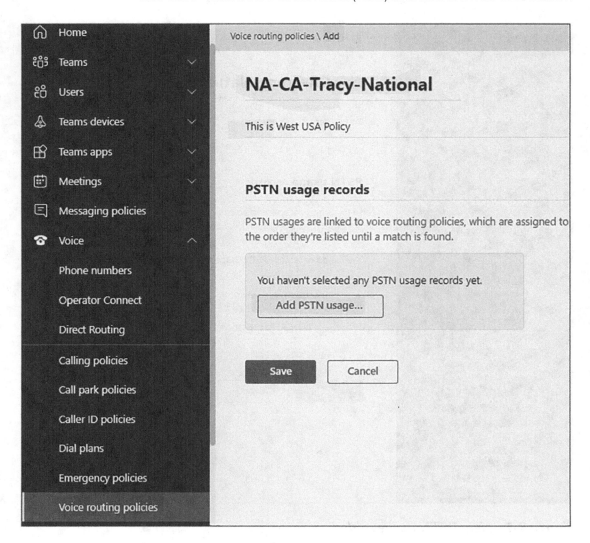

Figure 3-6. *Creating a voice route policy*

2. Under PSTN usage records, click Add PSTN usage and select the
    records you want to add. If you need to create a new PSTN usage
    record, click Add and give it a meaningful name. The best practice
    is to use a similar name as the voice routing policy to correctly
    identify the PSTN usage and route. Figure 3-7 shows a new PSTN
    usage added as NA-CA-Tracy-National.

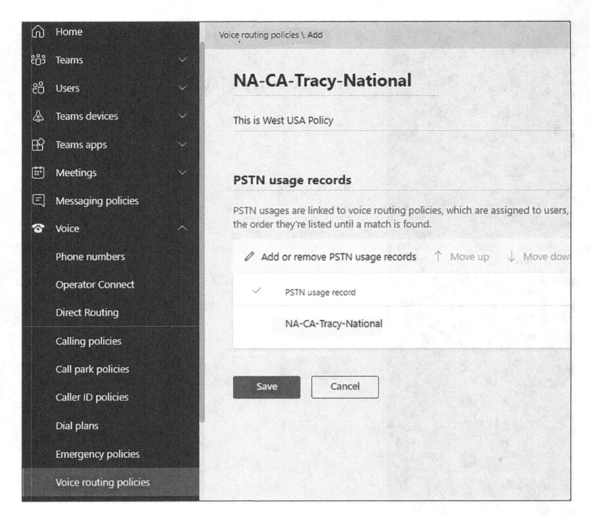

Figure 3-7. *New PSTN usage added*

3. If you added multiple PSTN usage records, arrange them in the
    order you want. Once you are done adding PSTN usages, click
    Apply. Finally, click Save to create the policy.

4. The next step is to add voice routes to the PSTN usage. In Teams,
    go to the admin center ➤ Voice ➤ Direct Routing ➤ Add to add
    new voice route associate to a PSTN usage. Figure 3-8 shows the
    voice route, PSTN gateway, and PSTN usage association.

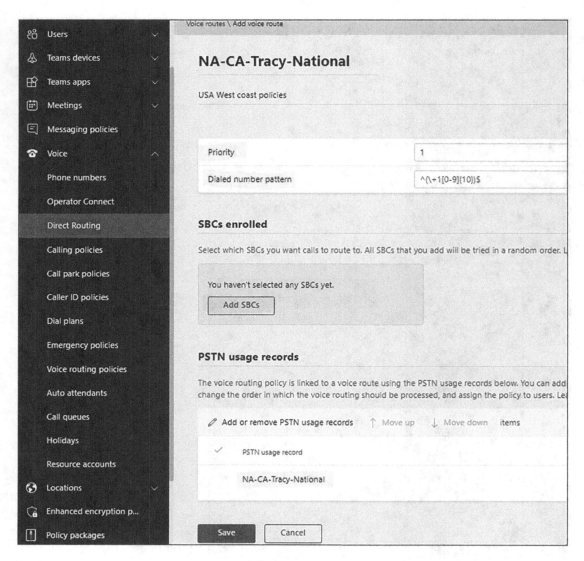

Figure 3-8. *Voice route creation*

5. Finally, assign the custom voice routing policy to a user account, either individually or at scale, through a batch assignment (if supported for the policy type) or to a group that the users are members of (if supported for the policy type). Figure 3-9 shows the individual user policy assignment.

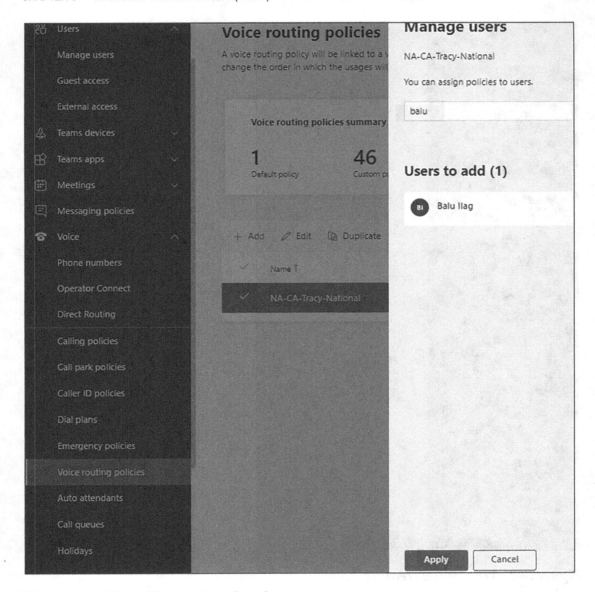

Figure 3-9. *The policy assigned to the user account*

Creating a Voice Routing Policy with PSTN Usages and Voice Routes Using PowerShell

You can create a voice routing policy with PSTN usage and voice routes using the following PowerShell commands from the Microsoft Teams PowerShell module.

First, create a voice route and PSTN usage using the `New-CsOnlineVoiceRoute` command, which has multiple parameters:

- `Identity`: The name of the route. This can be the same name as the usage.

- `NumberPattern`: Number patterns to match. You can use .* to match all number patterns.

- `OnlinePstnGatewayList`: The name of your SBC

- `Priority`: The priority position of this route.

- `OnlinePstnUsages`: The usage you want to associate with this voice route

```
New-CsOnlineVoiceRoute -Identity "NA-CA-Tracy-National" -NumberPattern
".*" -OnlinePstnGatewayList sbc1.bloguc.com -OnlinePstnUsages "NA-CA-Tracy-
National"
```

Create a custom voice routing policy using PowerShell: Create a voice routing policy and link it with your PSTN usage:

```
New-CsOnlineVoiceRoutingPolicy "NA-CA-Tracy-National" -OnlinePstnUsages
"NA-CA-Tracy-National"
```

Finally, assign the voice routing policy to the user account, which is the final step:

```
Grant-CsOnlineVoiceRoutingPolicy -Identity Balu Ilag -PolicyName
"NA-CA-Tracy-National"
```

Creating Dial Plans (Normalization Rule)

A dial plan is a called set of normalization rules that interpret dialed phone numbers by an individual user into an alternate format (typically E.164) for call authorization and voice routing purposes. Every dial plan consists of one or more normalization rules that describe how phone numbers stated in different formats are translated to alternate formats. The same dial string may be interpreted and translated differently in other dial plans. Depending on which dial plan is assigned to a given user, the same dialed number may be translated and routed differently. You, as an admin, can create up to 1,000 custom tenant dial plans. Dial plans can be made using the Teams admin center and PowerShell.

Creating a Dial Plan

A dial plan is a set of rules that translates a phone number that a user dials into a standard E.164 number for call authorization and routing. You can use the Global (org-wide default) or create one or more custom dial plans for people in your organization. You, as an admin, can check end user dialing requirements and then think out all the normalization rules that need to be created for voice routing. Once you have gathered information about your users' dialing habits and extension dialing requirements, you can make the dial plans. You can create a dial plan using the Teams admin center or Windows PowerShell.

Using Teams Admin Center

1. Log into the Teams admin center, then go to Voice ➤ Dial plan and click Add, and then enter a name and description for the dial plan. Figure 3-10 shows the Add page for creating a dial plan.

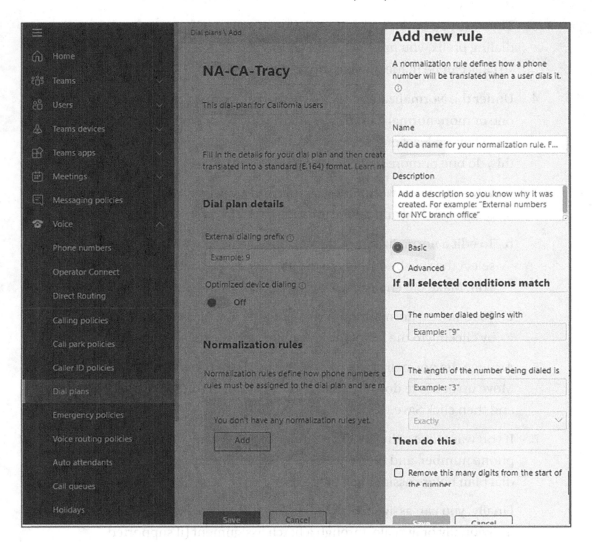

Figure 3-10. *Dial plan with basic options*

2. Next, under Dial plan details, specify an external dialing prefix
   if users need to dial one or more additional leading digits (for
   example, 9) to get an external line. To do this, in the External
   dialing prefix box, enter an external dialing prefix. The prefix can
   be up to four characters (#,*, and 0-9). Figure 3-10 shows adding
   a normalization rule option, and it shows basic and advanced
   normalization types. So, choose one based on your need.

3. Then turn on optimized device dialing. If you specify an external dialing prefix, you must also turn on this setting to apply the prefix so calls can be made outside your organization.

4. Under the Normalization rules section, configure and associate one or more normalization rules for the dial plan. Each dial plan must have at least one normalization rule associated with it. To do this, do one or more of the following:

    a. To create a new normalization rule and associate it with the dial plan, click Add and define the rule.

    b. To edit a normalization rule already associated with the dial plan, select the rule by clicking to the left of the rule name and then click Edit. Make the changes you want, and then click Save.

    c. To remove a normalization rule from the dial plan, select the rule by clicking to the left of the rule name and then click Remove.

5. Arrange the normalization rules in the order that you want. Click Move up or Move down to change the position of rules in the list, and then click Save.

6. If you want to test the dial plan, under Test dial plan, enter a phone number, and then click Test. It is a best practice to test the dial plan before assigning it to the user.

7. Finally, you can assign a dial plan policy directly to users, either individually or at scale, through a batch assignment (if supported for the policy type) or to a group that the users are members of (if supported for the policy type).

Creating a Dial Plan Using PowerShell

1. First, you need to connect the Microsoft Teams PowerShell module:

```
Import-Module MicrosoftTeams
$credential = Get-Credential
Connect-MicrosoftTeams -Credential $credential
```

2. Once connected to the Teams PowerShell module, run the following command to create a dial plan. This command is an example command; modify the parameters as per your need.

```
New-CsTenantDialPlan -Identity NA-CA-Tracy -Description "Dial Plan
for California Tracy" -NormalizationRules <pslistmodifier>
-ExternalAccessPrefix 9 -SimpleName "Dial-Plan-for-California"
```

3. Finally, assign the dial plan policy to the user account using this command:

```
Grant-CsTenantDialPlan -Identity bilag@bloguc.com -PolicyName
NA-CA-Tracy
```

The following are additional PowerShell commands for management purposes to view, remove, and check effective dial-plan:

- To view a dial plan: `Get-CsTenantDialPlan -Identity NA-CA-Tracy`

- To remove a dial plan: `Remove-CsTenantDialPlan -Identity NA-CA-Tracy -Force`

- To check an effective dial plan: `Get-CsEffectiveTenantDialPlan -Identity bilag@bloguc.com`

Configuring Teams Calling Features (Auto Attendant and Call Queue)

Auto attendant (AA) is the component of a Teams cloud phone system that provides a caller a series of voice prompts or audio files they hear instead of a human operator. When you create an auto attendant, you choose your greetings, set up your menus, and then decide how to redirect calls. When people call a number associated with an auto attendant, their choices can send the call to a user or locate someone in your organization and then connect to that user. They can express their preferences and interact with the menu system using a phone keypad or speech recognition. Their choices can also redirect the call to another auto attendant or a call queue.

There are multiple functionalities that AA provides, such as formal or informal greetings, custom menu choices, searching a directory name, allowing the caller to leave a voicemail, supporting multiple languages for prompts, text-to-speech and speech recognition, specifying holidays and business hours, call transfers, and call queue.

Configuring the Auto Attendant

You need to gather some required data before configuring the auto attendant:

- A resource account for each auto attendant and each call queue

- A free Phone System - Virtual User license for each resource account

- At least one Microsoft service number, direct routing number, or a hybrid number for each resource account that you want to be directly dialable

- The service number may be a toll or toll-free number.

- Agents who receive calls from the call queues must be Enterprise Voice enabled online or on-premises users.

- In addition, if the call queues are using Direct Routing numbers, agents who need to conference or transfer calls also require the following:

  - If a call queue uses transfer mode, an online voice routing policy must be assigned.

  - A voice routing policy or audio conferencing license must be applied if the conferencing mode is enabled.

  - If your agents use the Microsoft Teams app for call queue calls, they need to be in TeamsOnly mode.

When transferring calls to an external phone number, the resource account performing the transfer (that is, the one associated with the auto attendant or call queue) must have a Microsoft 365 Phone System Virtual User license and have a Calling Plan license and a phone number assigned or an online voice routing policy (the phone number assignment is optional when using Direct Routing).

Note   Direct Routing service numbers for auto attendant and call queues are supported for Microsoft Teams users and call agents only. Transfers between calling plan trunks and Direct Routing trunks aren't supported. In a hybrid scenario, the resource account must be created on-premises.

You can configure an auto attendant using the Microsoft Teams admin center and PowerShell. The following steps are via the Teams admin center.

1. Log into the Teams Admin center, go to Voice ➤ Auto Attendant ➤ Add, and give a meaningful the name to the auto attendant (like Bloguc – Helpdesk).

2. From the operator list, select a person in your organization (for example, Balu Ilag).

Note   The account you are using must be enabled for enterprise voice.

---

1. Select the time zone for this auto attendant (for example, (UTC-08:00) Pacific Time (US & Canada)).

2. Choose the language you want to use for prompts, greetings, and such (for example, English (United States)).

3. Selecting Enable voice inputs will enable voice commands in menus. It will also allow callers to say "Operator" and get transferred directly to the operator. Figure 3-11 shows the AA options.

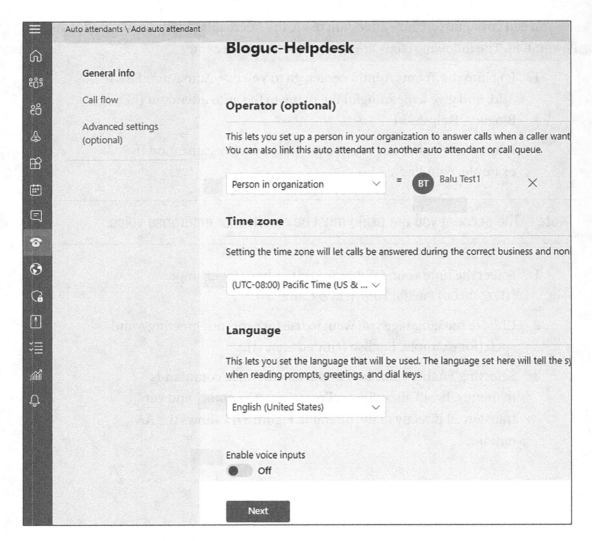

Figure 3-11. *Auto attendant setup*

1. Next, you can set up call flow for the main menu. For a greeting message, type the message that you want to be read to the caller (for example, "Welcome to Bloguc IT Helpdesk support").

2. In the route the call section, type the message that the caller will hear before hearing the options (for example, "Press 1 for Laptop support, Press 2 for mobile support, Press 3 for telecom support").

3. From the Set menu options, add in each of the options that you want. Here are some examples:

- Menu option 1 for the laptop support call queue.

- Menu option 2 for the mobile phone support call queue.

- Menu option 3 for the telecom support call queue. Refer to Figure 3-12 for the call flow menu.

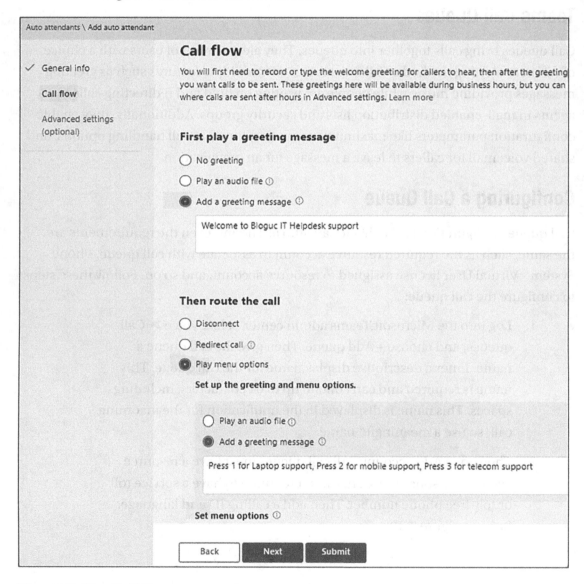

Figure 3-12. Call flow route and menu options

4. Finally, select the Directory Search, select Dial by name, and
    Submit because advance settings are optional.

Generally, a welcome greeting is only set on the main menu. A nested auto attendant
usually flows straight through to the custom prompt. From here, you can typically leave
the defaults set for call flows outside business hours, custom call flows during holidays,
and dial scope.

Teams Call Queues

Call queues bring calls together into queues. They alert a group of users with a choice
of different alerting methods. Call queues can offer multiple features such as greeting
messages providing music while people are waiting on hold and redirecting calls to
agents in mail-enabled distribution lists and security groups. Additionally, they enable
configuration parameters like maximum queue size, timeout, call handling options, and
shared voicemail for callers to leave a message for an organization.

Configuring a Call Queue

Call queue configuration is like that for an auto attendant. Even the requirements are
the same, such as the required resource account to associate with call queue, Phone
System - Virtual User license assigned to resource account, and so on. Follow these steps
to configure the call queue:

1. Log into the Microsoft Teams admin center, select Voice ➤ Call
    queues, and choose + Add queue. Then give the call queue a
    name. Enter a descriptive display name for the call queue. This
    name is required and can contain up to 64 characters, including
    spaces. This name is displayed in the notification for the incoming
    call, so use a meaningful name.

2. Then go to Add accounts. All call queues must have a resource
    account. Resource accounts aren't required to have a service toll
    or toll-free phone number. Then add a calling ID and language.
    Refer to Figure 3-13.

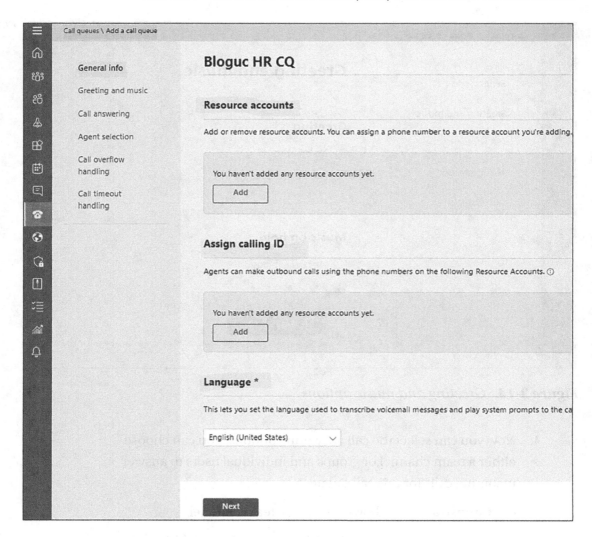

Figure 3-13. *Setting up a call queue*

3. The following steps are to set the greeting:

    - **Greeting**: The optional greeting played for people who call the call queue number. You can upload an audio file (.wav, .mp3, or .wma formats).

    - **Music on hold**: You can use the default music on hold provided with the call queue. You can also upload an audio file in .wav, mp3, or .wma formats as your custom music on hold. Refer to Figure 3-14.

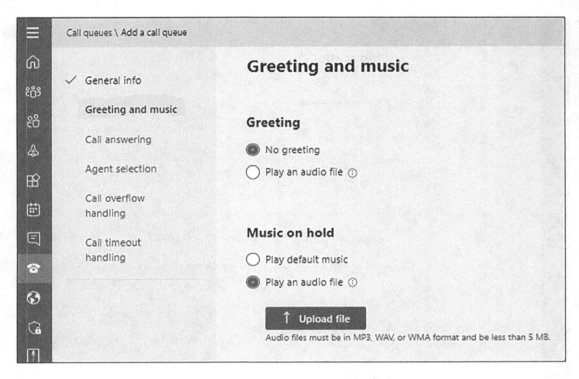

Figure 3-14. *Greeting and music options*

4. Now you can select the call answering options. You can choose
    either a team channel or groups and individual users to answer
    incoming calls for this call queue.

    • **Choose a team**: Allows selecting a team channel

    • **Choose users and groups**: Gives two options: *Add user* allows
       you to add individual agents directly, without adding them
       to a group, up to 20 individuals, or *Add group* for a group of
       users up 200.

    • **Conference mode**: Conference mode significantly reduces the
       time it takes for a caller to be connected to an agent after the
       agent accepts the call. If you have more than one call queue, you
       can enable conference mode on some or all your call queues;
       enabling or disabling conference mode on one call queue doesn't
       impact any other call queues. Refer to Figure 3-15.

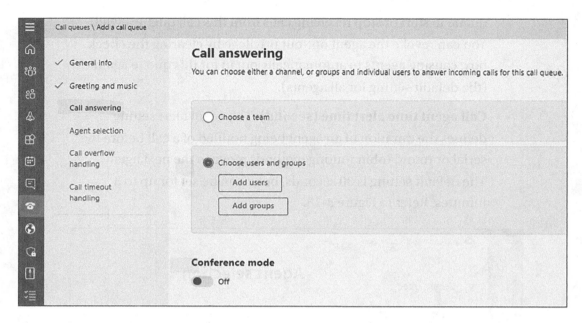

Figure 3-15. *Call answering options*

5. The next option is the agent selection:

    • **Routing method**: You can choose either attendant, serial, longest
       idle, or round robin as the distribution method. All new and
       existing call queues have attendant routing selected by default.
       When attendant routing is used, the first call in the queue rings
       all call agents simultaneously. The first call agent to pick up the
       call gets the call.

    • **Presence-based routing**: Presence-based routing uses the
       availability status of call agents to determine whether an agent
       should be included in the call routing list for the selected routing
       method. Call agents whose availability status is Available are
       included in the call routing list and can receive calls. Agents
       whose availability status is set to any other status are excluded
       from the call routing list and won't receive calls until their
       availability status changes back to Available.

    • **Agent can opt out of getting calls**: You can allow call queue
       agents to opt out of taking calls from a particular queue by
       enabling this option. Enabling this option allows all agents in this

queue to start or stop receiving calls from this call queue at will.
You can revoke the agent opt-out privilege by clearing the check
box, causing agents to automatically opt in for this queue again
(the default setting for all agents).

- **Call agent time alert time (second)**: The agent alert setting
  defines the duration of an agent being notified of a call before the
  serial or round robin routing methods move to the next agent.
  The default setting is 30 seconds, but it can be set for up to 3
  minutes. Refer to Figure 3-16.

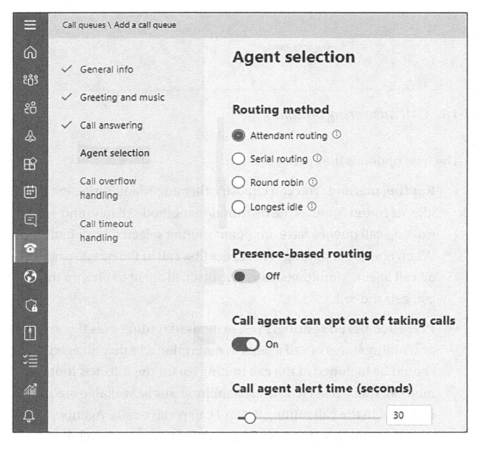

Figure 3-16. *Agent selection*

6. The next option is to select call overflow handling. After the maximum number of calls in the queue is reached, any additional calls will be disconnected or redirected, depending on your selection.

    •   **Maximum calls in the queue**: Use this to set the maximum calls that can wait in the queue simultaneously. The default is 50, but it can range from 0 to 200. When this limit is reached, the call is handled in the way you set when the maximum number of calls is reached.

    •   **When the maximum number of calls is reached**: When the call queue comes to its maximum size (set using the *Maximum calls in the queue* setting), you can choose what happens to new incoming calls. Refer to Figure 3-17.

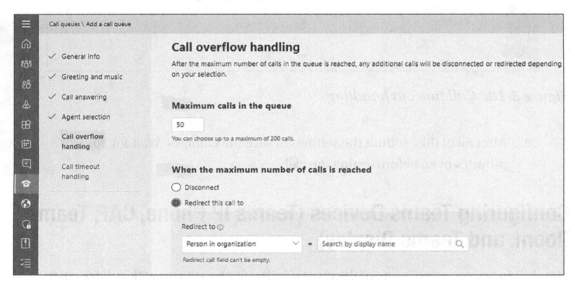

Figure 3-17. *Call overflow handling*

7. Finally, select the call timeout handling options:

    •   **Maximum wait time**: You can also decide how much time a call can be on hold in the queue before it times out and needs to be redirected or disconnected. Where it's redirected is based on how you set the *When a call times out* setting. You can set a time from 0 to 45 minutes.

- **When call times out**: When the call reaches the limit you set on the *How long a call can wait in the queue* setting, you can choose what happens to the ring. See Figure 3-18.

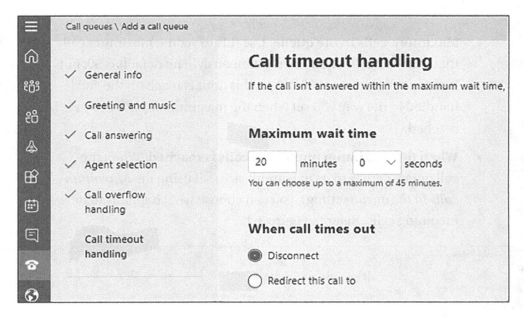

Figure 3-18. *Call timeout handling*

8. After all of this, submit the settings to save the changes. Wait for 30 minutes or so before testing the call.

Configuring Teams Devices (Teams IP Phone, CAP, Teams Room, and Teams Display)

The shift to remote work is one of the most significant changes in work culture since the Industrial Revolution. In the complex world of hybrid work, it will be challenging to ensure people can meet from anywhere without compromises and continue to feel included. In this section, we will share some of the latest features coming to Microsoft Teams, Teams devices (including Surface Hub), and Microsoft 365 that are designed to support the diverse needs and work styles of today's employees.

Teams Room on Surface Hub

Microsoft whiteboard works effectively on Microsoft Surface Hub. Surface Hub is part of the Microsoft Teams Room system, which means Surface Hub is your Teams Room. Surface Hub has similar features like a Teams desktop client, including meeting control, together mode, chat and live reactions. Additionally, you can log into Microsoft Surface Hub with Microsoft 365 apps.

Microsoft Teams Display

Hotdesking on Teams Display makes it easy to quickly locate and reserve flexible workspaces that even touchdown, take calls, or sing to personalize the Teams experience. You can reserve space right from the device. This experience is available on Lenovo Think smart view.

Deploying Microsoft Teams Rooms System

As a Teams admin, you can manage Teams Room in the Teams admin center with several improvements, including the ability to customize dashboard views, improve search functionality for faster discovery, and make bulk updates even more accessible. Surface Hub can be managed from the Teams admin center and all other Teams devices.

Teams Room standard deployment: The goal of a typical deployment is to make sure that you can have a simple and repeatable rollout, not only at one office or in one office space but in many locations across your geography, be that within a city, country or globally.

You will want to standardize on procurement and have the same options in as many rooms as possible. You will have to decide on shipping. Will you ship all the devices to a central location, configure them there, and then ship them out to the remote locations for installation, or will you drop-ship everything directly to the final location and do all the configuration on site? The more consistent you can be with these practices, the better you will be in supporting, implementing, and operating Teams Rooms in the future. You will be able to scale up from setting up Teams Rooms in just one building to setting up globally.

Here are the overall details of a Teams deployment project plan with a critical milestone in Teams Room deployment:

- Start with envisioning the room inventory and plan capabilities, then device selection, and then procurement.

- Onboard site readiness, then service readiness, then configuration and deployment.

- Drive values of adoption and maintenance and operation.

Make sure you standardize your deployment. Try to create all resource accounts in as standardized a way as possible. Have step-by-step instructions designed for how you intend all rooms to be configured and installed. Make sure you have standards for how you will run and organize the cables and where you are going to mount devices. If you are going to mount compute devices behind displays, make that a standard. Be sure you have a good understanding of the device setup instructions and any necessary configuration files. Know basic troubleshooting instructions you can take before escalating. Teams themselves are a better place to store all the information for each of your Teams Rooms.

Teams configuration steps:

1. The first step is to plan, purchase, and do physical connectivity of the Teams Room components.

2. The next step is to provision a resource account with a proper license.

3. The last step is to prepare login and how-to instructions for end users.

How are Microsoft Teams Room Components Connected?

So, how does a Teams Room connect? Here is a small example of a Teams Room connection configuration. You start with the computer module, the heart of Teams Rooms. Everything is eventually connected to the compute. The middle of the table console connects to the compute via USB, and this console is what people will be interacting with. Microphone, audio, and camera are all contained in one unit. In this example, they connect via USB to the compute module. A monitor or display already in-room or just recently added is connected via HDMI to the compute module. You may also enable a USB touch screen for the monitor. This all-components connection is pretty straightforward connectivity to bring a Teams Rooms up and have complete audio, video, and even touchscreen displays for inking. Figure 3-19 shows the small room connectivity.

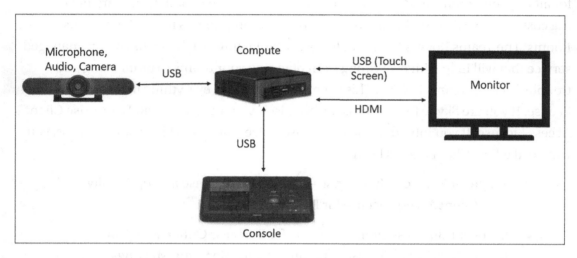

Figure 3-19. *Teams room connectivity*

For a large room, the configuration is a bit more complex. The same as the small room configuration, it starts with the compute module. A console on the center of the table connects to compute via USB. Display extensions extend cabling beyond the standard. A separate camera can connect to the display extension and directly to the compute module. Multiple speakers can be added to the room and extend to the display extension. It could use an analog cable, so the first cable would be different from USB or HDMI. A cable extension could connect devices such as microphones. The microphones could connect to the table extension via USB. The table extension could connect to the display extension via category 6 cabling. In this larger room, you may have dual monitors and both monitors could connect to compute with HDMI. So, there would be two HDMI cables, and then one of those monitors would be enabled for USB touchscreen.

Microsoft Teams Rooms Resource Account

What is the resource account? Well, it's technically a Microsoft exchange mailbox. Specifically, it's a Microsoft Exchange resource account. When people schedule a room, it is a mailbox or resource that they invite to their meeting. This resource mailbox will be used on behalf of the room to accept or decline the meeting invite. This resource account is also the account that signs into the Microsoft Teams Rooms app.

Resource Account Licensing

Microsoft strongly recommends using the Teams Rooms Standard or Premium license for all meeting rooms used for Microsoft Teams. The Teams Rooms Standard license is a cost-effective license that includes all the core components needed for Teams Rooms. The Teams Rooms Premium license adds features such as a Microsoft-managed service that will help with everything from planning your rooms to monitoring and troubleshooting Teams Rooms. This license also includes everything in the Standard license. If you are Skype for Business on-premises, you must assign an Enterprise Client Access License. If you intend to use Enterprise Voice features of Skype for Business, you will need a Plus Client Access license.

- Skype for Business: Enterprise Client Access License and optionally, Plus Client Access License for PSTN calling

- Skype for Business Online: A Skype for Business Online Plan 2 or Office 365 E1 or E3 license is required to enable Skype Meetings.

- Microsoft Teams: Acquire and assign the Teams Rooms Standard or Teams Rooms Premium license.

- Dial-in to a Microsoft Teams meeting and "call me at" features are included in the Audio-Conferencing license.

- Non-meeting PSTN calling requires a Calling Plan license or Direct Routing configuration.

Dial-in to Microsoft Teams meeting and "call me at" features are included in the Audio-Conferencing license. *Dial-in to Microsoft Teams meeting* is if someone is remote or driving and they want to join with a mobile phone, they would then dial the phone number and be able to join the meeting.

For Teams Rooms connected to Microsoft Teams, if you would like to make and receive any phone call outside of an audio conference, you will need to assign a calling plan license or configure Direct Routing. If you are configuring Direct Routing, no additional licenses are required. The Phone System license is already included with a Teams Rooms Standard or Premium license. Every Teams Rooms device requires its own unique account. You cannot share a resource account across multiple rooms. If you do, only one of those devices will be able to join a meeting, and other rooms' devices with the same account will not be able to join any meetings simultaneously.

Creating a Resource Account for a Teams Room

It is a best practice to create the account well in advance of the hardware installation. You may need to open up tickets within your internal IT infrastructure team to have these accounts created. Then you need to test and review to make sure the account was set up correctly as per the requirements. You can create resource accounts via different ways, including Microsoft 365 admin center, PowerShell, or on-premises case Active Directory Users and Computers (ADUC). Again, considering the naming standard for this account will simplify future management.

Steps to create a resource account: Here are the steps to create a resource account:

1. Log into `https://admin.Microsoft.com` and then navigate to Resources ➤ Rooms & equipment.

2. Edit the current room inventory or click the +Add button on the left-hand side to create a new room.

3. Later, fill in the values; select the resource account type as room; give a friendly display name, capacity, and location; and then assign a license. Refer to Figure 3-20 for additional resources.

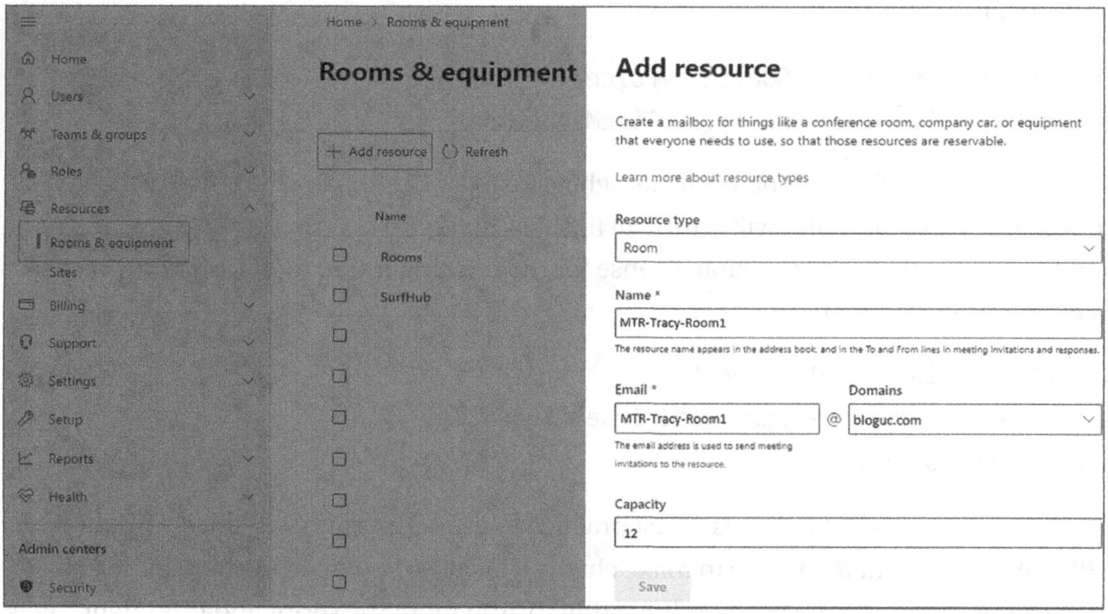

Figure 3-20. *Adding a room account*

4. After clicking Add, it will take 1-2 minutes. You will get the acknowledgment that the room has been created. This gives confirmation that a room mailbox is created.

5. The next step is to set scheduling options, including allowing scheduling and auto declining a meeting outside 180 days and 24 hours. By default, auto-accepting meeting requests is enabled.

6. The next step is to navigate to Users ➤ Active Users and then click the key icon and reset the password. Type in a new password. Do not tick the box to require a password change.

Note   Teams Room does not support changing the password interactively within the Teams Rooms app after first sign-in.

You can also use PowerShell to configure resource accounts. PowerShell can expedite resource account provisioning and add users in bulk through scripts.

There are two mandatory PowerShell modules as prerequisites: the MS Online PowerShell module for Microsoft Azure Active Directory and the Exchange Online PowerShell Module.

```
Install-Module -Name MSOnline -Force
Install-Module -Name ExchangeOnlineManagement
```

First, you can check if you have enough licenses by running the Get-MsolAccountSku command. This command will return all licenses that have been acquired for your tenant. Once you see the available license for the meeting room, then assign the license to the resource account.

```
$UserCredential = Get-Credential
Connect-MsolService -Credential $UserCredential
Get-MsolAccountSku
```

When using PowerShell, it is a best practice to use scripts and variables. Variables will make it easier in the future to make changes because you need to change the values in one place. This value is used multiple times throughout the script and this change gets reflected automatically.

In this case, you create a few variables like account UPN, the mailbox name, mailbox alias, and your password. Note that the password is in clear text, so you may not want to set the password via PowerShell, or after you set it to this plain text password, you may want to go into the Microsoft 365 admin center and change it there so that this clear text password can't be used by anyone else.

Creating a Single Resource Account Using PowerShell

To connect to Office 365, get your user credentials and connect-MsolService and connect-ExchangeOnline, passing in your credentials:

```
$UserCredential= Get-Credential
Connect-MsolService -Credential $UserCredential
Connect-ExchangeOnline -Credential $UserCredentia -ShowProgress $true
```

Now create a mailbox. The resource account is really an Exchange mailbox. Here is the command. You can see the variable used throughout this command, plus DisplayName, mailbox alias, and account UPN. And here is the password in plain text. So be careful when using scripts and change the password right away.

```
New-Mailbox -MicrosoftOnlineServicesID $acctUpn -Name $DisplayName -Alias
$MailBoxAlias -Room -EnableRoomMailboxAccount $true -RoomMailboxPassword
(ConvertTo-SecureString-String $Password -AsPlainText -Force)
```

Setting to Auto-Accept

The next thing to do is enable calendar processing. Set Outlook to auto-accept meeting invites and add a response. The following command says automatic processing is auto-accepted, so it will accept any conference invites automatically:

```
Set-CalendarProcessing-Identity $MailBoxAlias -AutomateProcessing
AutoAccept -AddOrganizerToSubject $false -DeleteComments $false -DeleteSubject
$false -RemovePrivateProperty $false
```

Next, set the password to never expire:

```
Set-MsolUser -UserPrincipalName $acctUpn -PasswordNeverExpires
$true -UsageLocation $UsageLocation
```

Then assign the license:

```
Set-MsolUserLicense -UserPrincipalName $acctupn -AddLicenses $ADLicense
```

Assigning a Phone Number to the Resource Account

If you are setting a phone number using a calling plan, then use the Teams admin center or PowerShell. A calling plan phone number permits the Teams Room to call users and conference bridges. It provides a calling service for USA and Canada; however, you must create an emergency location first and assign a phone number.

PowerShell command:

```
$acctUpn=MTR-Tracy-Room1@bloguc.com
$PhoneNumber="+12091234567"
#Get Location ID via Get-CsOnlineLisLocation $LocationID="c94000cy-6bbc-4c
c8-510c - f7924578f792"
Set-CsOnlineVoiceUser-Identity $AcctUPN -TelephoneNumber
$PhoneNumber -LocationID $LocationID

Set-CsPhoneNumberAssignment -Identity abcRoom@bloguc.com -PhoneNumber
"+14081234567" -PhoneNumberType CallingPlan
```

Assigning a Phone Number Using Direct Routing

```
Set-CsUser -Identity MTR-Tracy-Room1@bloguc.com -EnterpriseVoiceEnabled
$true -OnPremLineURI tel:+12091234567
```

Planning and Configuring Teams IP Phone and Common Area Phone

Teams supports a range of desk phones for users who need a traditional phone experience. As a Teams admin, you must plan, deliver, and manage Microsoft Teams phones as part of your Microsoft Phone System solution. To provide a high-quality and reliable Microsoft Teams experience on phones, Microsoft has partnered with and is actively working with Yealink, Crestron, Lenovo, Polycom, and AudioCodes to develop and certify a broad portfolio of desk phones and conference room audio devices.

The admin needs to be a Global admin, Teams Service admin, or Teams Device admin to manage Teams phones.

Teams Phones Supported Features

Teams-certified phones provide multiple features:

- **Authentication**: Phones use Modern Authentication to simplify signing in and improve security. Users can sign in by entering their username and password on the phone or by signing in from another device like a PC/smartphone.

- **Speed dial and call history**: Users have quick access to their contacts, call history, and voicemail. They can easily manage their contacts and speed dial entries directly from their phone.

- **Meetings and calls**: Users can view their schedules and quickly join meetings using Teams' one-touch join.

- **Call groups**: Phone agents who participate in call groups can easily manage their availability and accept or decline incoming calls from the call queue.

- **User delegation**: Executive assistants and admins can manage their executives' phones, intercept incoming calls, make calls on behalf of the executive, take over calls that the executive has placed on hold, and monitor whether the executive is on a call, on hold, and such.

- **Hot-desking**: Users can get their contacts, meetings, and other preferences just by signing into a phone. They can sign out and leave the phone ready for subsequent use when they're done.

- **Video phones**: With video support, users can join calls and video conferences just like they were at their computers. Users can keep their privacy by using a phone's camera shutter and mute microphone switch.

- **Better together**: Phones can lock and unlock in an integrated fashion when connected to their Windows PC running a 64-bit Teams desktop client.

- **Accessibility**: Phones have several accessibility features, such as high contrast text, to make it easier for anyone to use them.

- **Dynamic and enhanced E911 support**: Signed-in users who call 911 will see their location on the phone.

Note   Since Teams Phone requires internet access to connect to the Teams back-end service, users cannot make or receive calls, including emergency calls (e.g., 911), if there is no internet or the user is not logged into the phone.

Managing Teams Phone

Microsoft Teams Phones, collaboration bars, Teams Displays, and Teams panels are automatically enrolled in Microsoft Intune if it is part of your Microsoft 365 subscription, as part of the user sign-in process. After a device is enrolled, device compliance is confirmed, and conditional access policies are applied to the device. Conditional access is an Azure Active Directory (Azure AD) feature that helps you ensure that devices accessing your Microsoft 365 resources are appropriately managed and secure.

If you apply conditional access policies to the Teams service, Teams Phones and Teams Displays that access Teams must be enrolled in Intune. Their settings need to comply with Intune policies. Suppose the device is registered with Intune or enrolled, but its settings don't comply with your policies. In that case, conditional access will prevent a user from signing in to or using the Teams app on the device.

Teams Android-based devices, including all Teams-certified phones, are managed by Intune via Android Device Administrator (DA) management. Before devices can be enrolled in Intune, there are a few basic steps to perform:

1. Set Intune as the mobile device management authority.

2. Enable Android device administrator enrollment.

3. Assign licenses to users.

4. Assign Device Administrator compliance policies.

Suppose users are already able to enroll Android devices via Device Administrator management into Intune. In this case, these steps should already have been performed, and users should already be licensed for Intune.

Managing Teams Phones Using Configuration Profiles

You can use configuration profiles to centrally manage settings and features for different Teams devices in your organization, including collaboration bars, Teams Displays, Teams Phone, and Teams Panels. You can create or upload configuration profiles to include settings and features you want to enable or disable and then assign a profile to a device or set of devices. Follow these step to create a configuration profile:

1. Log into the Teams admin center at `https://admin.teams.microsoft.com` and then select Devices and the Teams device type. For example, choose Devices ➤ Teams Phones to continue to create a new configuration profile for Teams Phones.

2. Select the Configuration profiles tab and select Add and then enter a name for the configuration profile and optionally add a friendly description.

3. Then specify the settings you want for the profile and select Save. The newly created configuration profile is displayed in the list of profiles.

After creating a configuration profile for a Teams device type, assign it to one or more devices by following these steps:

1. Log into the Teams admin center, select Devices, and select the Teams device type. For example, to assign a configuration profile to a Teams panels device, choose Devices and Teams panels and then choose one or more devices, and then select Assign configuration.

2. In assigning a configuration pane, search for a configuration profile to assign to the selected devices and select Apply. For the devices to which you applied the configuration policy, the Action column displays Config Update. The Configuration profile column indicates the configuration profile name. The devices in the scope of a configuration profile will be automatically configured with the setting defined.

3. This may take several hours to take effect. To validate that the
    configuration has been applied, select the device within the
    Teams admin center, then choose Device Configuration to
    examine the state.

Teams Common Area Phone

There is a separate license called a Teams Common Area Phone (CAP) license that
Microsoft has built; this license includes Microsoft Teams, SfB, and Phone System.

Step to provision Common Area Phone:

1. First, buy the Common Area Phone, get shifted, and acquire the
    CAP license.

2. The next step is to create a new CAP account:

    a. Log into Microsoft 365 admin center and go to Users ➤ Active
        Users ➤ Add a user.

    b. Enter a username like "Mainlobby" for the first name and "Phone"
        for the second name.

    c. Enter a display name if it doesn't autogenerate one like
        "Mainlobby Phone."

    d. Enter a username like "Mainlobby" (for example, mainlobby@
        bloguc.com).

    e. Set the password for your common area phone manually. To do
        this, uncheck *Automatically create a password* and require this
        user to change their password when they first sign in.

    f. Select the usage location of the device and assign the Common
        Area Phone license to the account. If any other licenses are
        needed, like calling plans, assign them.

    g. The last thing to do is assign the phone to the common area phone.

3. Assign policies. This is dependent on what Phone System
    deployment method you choose, such as Teams calling plan,
    Teams Direct routing, etc. If you have Teams Direct Routing
    configured, you need to assign a few policies such as call routing

policy, dial plans, and an emergency call routing policy and assign the IP phone policies. For example, if a common area phone is used in a public area, set an IP phone policy to restrict searching your organization's global address book and block hot-desking. If you want to override a phone's default interface, consider creating an IP phone policy.

Note   For Teams calling plan deployment, you don't need call routing policies but need a calling plan license and dial plan policy.

---

4. The next thing to do is assign the phone number to the common area phone. You can set the phone number acquired from Microsoft (calling plan) or from Teams Direct Routing on-premises PSTN connectivity.

5. After assigning a phone number, log into the phone device through a local login or sign in from a different device or through the Teams admin center. Refer to each option using the following links.

    a. Local sign-in: `https://docs.microsoft.com/en-us/microsoftteams/set-up-common-area-phones#local-sign-in`

    b. Sign in from another device: `https://docs.microsoft.com/en-us/microsoftteams/set-up-common-area-phones#sign-in-from-another-device`

    c. Sign in using the Teams admin center: `https://docs.microsoft.com/en-us/microsoftteams/set-up-common-area-phones#sign-in-using-the-teams-admin-center`

Updating Teams Device Software

As a Teams admin, particularly a Teams device admin, you need to update your Teams devices, which is an operational task. There are different ways to update the devices, such as updating Microsoft Teams devices remotely. Using the Microsoft Teams admin center, you can remotely update your Teams devices, such as Teams Phones, Teams Panels, and collaboration bars. You can choose device firmware automatic update behavior. You can update the following on your devices using the Teams admin center:

- Teams app and teams admin agent

- Company portal app

- OEM agent app

- Device firmware

Device firmware updates can be applied automatically or scheduled for a future date and time. Other available device updates aren't applied automatically but can be applied manually or scheduled for a future date and time. This can be useful when you need to test new device updates and document features before deploying them to users or scheduling updates to devices outside of business hours.

Automatic Update Options

Device firmware updates are installed automatically. You can decide whether to apply updates as soon as one is released (if you choose this option, updates are used on the first weekend after an update is released) or 30 or 90 days after an update is released. By default, device firmware updates are applied 30 days one release.

To choose the automatic update behavior for your devices, do the following:

1. Log into the Teams admin center at `https://admin.teams.microsoft.com`. Select Devices and then select IP phones ➤ Collaboration bars ➤ Teams panels.

2. Select one or more devices and choose Update. Under Firmware auto-update, select one of the following options:

   a. **As soon as available**: The second-newest device firmware update is applied on the first weekend after the latest update is released.

   b. **Defer 30 days**: The second-newest device firmware update is used 30 days after the newest update is released.

   c. **Defer 90 days**: The second-newest device firmware update is applied 90 days after the latest update is released.

3. After choosing the device update option, select Update to commit the changes.

It is recommended to use automatic updates were possible because automatic updates are not applied immediately upon release and allow for deferral; you have time to examine release notes and check for changes and share with your end user using the device for their support.

Additionally, suppose the user/admin needs to revert a device firmware update, such as in the event of unexpected issues. In that case, you need to reset your device to its factory settings. Reset your device using the instructions from its manufacturer. For instance, to reset the Yealink phone device, refer to Yealink support documents.

Manual Update Options

You, as an admin, can decide how to update your devices. Using the Teams admin center, you can update the devices immediately or schedule an update for a future date and time. But what if you want to use the latest version or pick and choose to update devices? Then the manual update process is helpful. Manual updates can be beneficial if you want to update a device immediately to the latest release, such as updating a test device and validating compatibility or seeing new software changes ahead of your users. Follow these steps to update remote devices:

1. Log into the Teams admin center by visiting `https://admin.teams.microsoft.com`. Then, select Devices and select one of the device categories, such as IP phones or Collaboration bars.

2. Select one or more devices and choose Update, and then under Manual updates, select Schedule if you want to schedule the update for a future date and time. The updates are applied at the date and time in the time zone selected in Timezone.

If you select multiple devices, you can choose which update types to apply to each selected device. Then select the update types you want to use and select Update.

If you select a single device, updates for the device are shown. Select each update type to apply if multiple update types are available for the device. You can view the current version used on the device and the new version applied. Select the update(s) you want to apply and select Update. After you choose to update, updates are applied to your devices at the date and time you decided if you scheduled an update. If you didn't select a future date and time, updates are applied to your devices within a few minutes.

Post-Update Verification

Post (automatic or manual) update, the update can be verified within the Microsoft Teams admin center by selecting a device to verify the update level and if additional updates are available. This is useful if you don't have physical access to the device. You've performed the update and want to verify the update is applied. When a device has been updated to the current update, the option to complete a manual update will no longer be available. The used version will be shown.

Managing Microsoft Teams Displays

Microsoft Teams Displays are a category of all-in-one dedicated Teams devices that feature an ambient touchscreen and a hands-free experience powered by Cortana. Users can use a microphone, camera, and speakers (or Bluetooth headset) for a reliable calling and meeting experience with Teams displays. Teams Displays integrate with users' Windows PCs to bring a companion experience that allows for seamless cross-device interaction.

Specific to the features supported by Teams Displays:

- **Dedicated displays for Teams**: Users can access all of the core Teams features, including chat, meetings, calls, teams and channels, files, and more.

- **Ambient experience**: Users can easily stay on top of their work with always-on and glanceable displays to see important activities and notifications without context-switching on their primary work device. Users can also personalize Teams displays by customizing the background through settings.

- **Hands-free with Cortana**: Users can interact with Teams Displays using their voice to effortlessly join and present in meetings, dictate replies to a Teams chat, check what's on the calendar, and more.

- **Leave a note on the lock screen**: Guests can choose to leave audio, video, and text notes, and users can check the notes left by guests and see who's stopped by.

Teams Display devices are typically used as companion devices alongside laptops or desktop PCs. The typical user for a Teams Display won't necessarily be a user that would otherwise use a Teams Phone and will not always require Teams Phone System capabilities. For example, some users of Teams Displays use their devices primarily to join meetings. From an administrator's perspective, a Teams Display provides the same management capabilities as a Teams Phone. It can be subject to identical policies or rules.

Configuring Teams Audio Conferencing

Audio conferencing is the capability to join a Teams meeting from a landline or mobile phone and call out from a meeting to a phone number, allowing users to call into meetings when they can't use a Teams client. Calling or dialing into meetings is very useful for users on the road who cannot attend a meeting using the Microsoft Teams client on their desktop or mobile devices or Teams web client. There are other scenarios in which utilizing a phone to attend a Microsoft Teams meeting can be a better option than using a Teams client on a computer, such as when internet connectivity is limited, when a meeting is audio-only, and when there's a failure to join from Teams.

You only need to set up audio conferencing for people who plan to schedule or lead meetings. Individual Audio-Conferencing licenses are necessary for each person who will organize/host an audio conference. Meeting attendees who call in don't need any licenses assigned to them or any other setup. After attendees have joined the meeting, they can also call out and invite other callers into a Microsoft Teams meeting.

Microsoft Teams Add-On Licenses

Above and beyond basic Teams features, there are add-on licenses for more features such as audio conferencing, Phone System, calling plans, and Microsoft Teams Rooms. Organizations will need to buy and assign an audio-conferencing license to each user to set up a dial-in meeting for audio conferencing.

Sometimes people in your organization need to make use of a phone to call into a Teams meeting instead of their computer. Set up audio conferencing for users who schedule or lead meetings. To find out whether audio conferencing is available in your country or region, see "Country and region availability for Audio Conferencing and Calling Plans." Figure 3-21 shows the sample dial-in information.

Microsoft Teams meeting

Join on your computer or mobile app
Click here to join the meeting

Or call in (audio only)
+1 209-123-4567,,619525359#   United States, San Jose
Phone Conference ID: 619 525 359#
Find a local number | Reset PIN

Teams meeting.

Learn More | Help | Meeting options

Figure 3-21. *Teams dial-in information*

Additional Information

Specific to the user migration, if the user is enabled for dial-in conferencing on-premises, the user must also have an Audio-Conferencing license assigned in Teams before you move the user online. Once migrated to the cloud, the user will be provisioned for audio conferencing in the cloud.

Suppose you want to move a user to the cloud for some reason but not use the audio conferencing functionality. In that case, you can override this check by specifying the BypassAudioConferencingCheck parameter in Move-CsUser.

Configuring Audio Conferencing

Audio conferencing helps users dial into or out from a Teams meeting via PSTN phone numbers. These numbers are sometimes described as *conference bridges*. They need a per-user Audio-Conferencing license. Even though this is a "meetings" feature because it involves the PSTN, it is often given to the Teams voice administrators to configure.

It is essential to set a default audio conferencing bridge in the meeting invite (Figure 3-21 shows the example). The default phone number of your conference bridge defines the caller ID that will be used when an outbound call is placed by a participant or the organizer from within a meeting. The phone number assigned as the default number of the bridge will be one from the country/region of the organization.

To set up or change the default audio conferencing bridge number for your organization, log into the Teams admin center, select Meetings, select Conference bridges, select a bridge number, and then select Set as Default. Figure 3-22 shows the conference bridge sets as the default option.

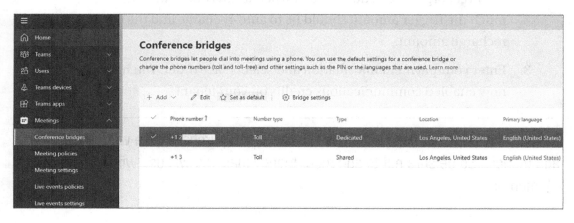

Figure 3-22. *The conference bridge default number*

Some audio-conferencing scenarios are charged on a per-minute basis. For instance, toll-free numbers are used with audio conferencing meetings, auto attendants, or call queues. Toll-free calls are billed per minute and require a positive communications credits balance. Any scenarios charged per minute are managed through communications credits. Communication credits are a prepaid bucket of credit. They can be a one-time funded bucket or an auto-recharge amount with a minimum balance that will trigger a purchase for that recharge amount.

Setting Up Communication Credits

Follow these steps to set up communication credits in Microsoft 365 admin center.

1. Log into the Microsoft 365 admin center at `https://admin.microsoft.com` and select Billing and Purchase Services.

2. Then select Add-ons and Communications Credits. On the Communications Credits subscription page, fill in your information. Here you add funds via a credit card and if it will auto-recharge (keep adding credit when it runs out) and how much the trigger amount should be to auto-recharge and the recharge amount.

3. Enter your payment information and select Place order. You have now enabled communications credits on your tenant.

Note   Any funds not used within 12 months of the purchase date will expire and be paid. So be sure not to add more money than you will use within the next 12 months.

If you are a volume licensing customer, you may choose your enterprise agreement number for payment rather than a credit card.

Assigning Communications Credit Licenses to Users

After enabling communication credit, you can assign the communication credits to the user account. This helps in managing acquire communication credits costs. To assign the communication credit license, follow these steps:

1. Log into the Microsoft 365 admin center at `https://admin.microsoft.com` and then select Users and then Active Users and then select a user from the list.

2. On the user account, select Licenses and Apps and then enable communications credits to assign this license and select Save to commit the changes.

3. After performing the defined steps, you have assigned the communications credits license to a user.

Configuring New Toll or Toll-Free Conference Bridge Numbers

Microsoft Teams provides audio conferencing that allows users to dial into meetings. Audio conferencing comes with various conference bridge/meeting PSTN numbers (shared) by default. You can acquire the dedicated toll or toll-free numbers used for your tenant only. These shared and dedicated numbers let users dial into meetings via landlines or mobile phone numbers rather than the VoIP data network. Many numbers are given by default to provide users worldwide with a local number to dial while minimizing their call costs.

Specific to the dedicated conference bridge number (Toll or toll-free) that is dedicated to the customer and allows to configure to a particular city or site users as a primary number to show in their meeting invite as a dial-in number with an area code.

You can acquire Microsoft's new toll or toll-free service number as an admin. Then you can assign it to the conference bridge service by following these steps:

1. Log into the Teams admin center at `https://admin.teams.microsoft.com/`, select Meetings and Conference bridges, and click Add to create a new entry.

2. Then select either toll or toll-free number and select the number and Apply.

You can define the default language for a conference bridge number. Since this is a dedicated number for your tenant, you can optionally choose the default and alternate languages used for the audio prompts when dialing into it. This can be useful to present a number to customers and have the default prompts be in their local language.

Designing and Configuring an Emergency Calling Policy

An emergency calling service provides treatment to the caller by providing help and medical assistance. In Microsoft Teams, you can deploy emergency calling through Teams Direct Routing and the calling plans. Each country has specific regulations and policies that require phone numbers associated with the user's physical address so that emergency calls are routed to the correct Public Safety Answering Point (PSAP). They are aware of the users' address to dispatch any emergency services. That is how users get expedited assistance.

How Do Emergency Calls Get Touted to PSAP?

When an end user makes an emergency call, it routes through a Teams calling plan or Teams Direct Routing quickly, reaching a PSAP; this call routing process involves multiple elements. Basically, a PSAP is a call center where emergency calls are routed. Once the call reaches a PSAP, someone will talk to the caller and dispatch the appropriate emergency responder services, like police, fire brigade, or ambulance. Microsoft Teams provide for emergency calling, which binds a specific static address to a phone number, and dynamic emergency calling, which provides the capability to provide the user's current location based on the network they are currently connected to.

It is essential to configure emergency calling addresses as a phone number must be aligned to an emergency calling address. How this is configured varies by country/region. In the United States, you need to associate an emergency location when assigning the user's phone number. In Europe, you need to associate an emergency location to the phone when you acquire the phone numbers from Microsoft or your Operator Connect provider. See Figure 3-23.

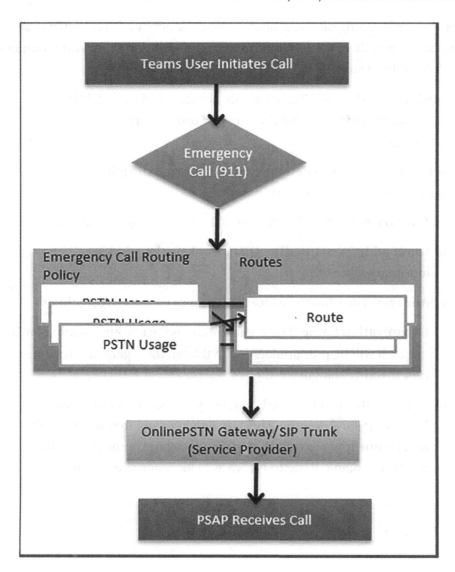

Figure 3-23. *Teams emergency call routing*

Describing the Emergency Calling Address

Before adding a phone number to the user account for Teams, you must first configure emergency addresses. This is mainly applicable to the calling plan, where you will acquire the phone numbers from Microsoft. To assign calling plan numbers successfully in countries where a calling plan is available, the emergency address must match the phone number area code of the number ordered from Microsoft. To add emergency addresses, follow these steps:

1. Log into the Microsoft Teams admin center at `https://admin.teams.microsoft.com` and then select *Locations and Emergency addresses*.

2. Select Add to create a new entry and then enter the following information for the new address:

    a. **Country or region**: The region of the new emergency address

    b. **Input address manually – Off**: To look up the address automatically

    c. **Address**: The office/site location address is like a street address

    d. **Organization name**: The organization name is your organization's name. It will be prepopulated with the tenant organization name. (For instance, bloguc.com.)

    e. **ELIN 1**: SBCs can include Emergency Location Identification Number (ELIN) records. They are only relevant for Direct Routing and do not apply to calling plans or Operator Connect. This field can be left blank. Refer to Figure 3-24 for emergency addresses.

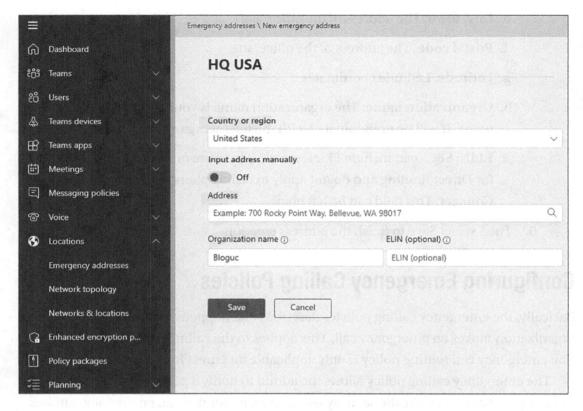

Figure 3-24. Location and emergency addresses

3. Select Save to commit the changes.

If you can't find the address, toggle to input addresses manually by following these steps:

4. Log into the Microsoft Teams admin center at `https://admin.teams.microsoft.com`. Then, select *Locations and Emergency addresses* and select Add to create a new entry.

5. Enter the following information for the new address:

   a. **Country or region**: The region of the new emergency address

   b. **Input address manually – On**: To look up, insert the address manually

   c. **House number/name**: The address of office/site

   d. **Street name**: The address of office/site

    e. **City/town**: The address of the office/site

    f. **Postal code**: The address of the office/site

    g. **Latitude**: Latitude coordinates

    h. **Organization name**: The organization name is your organization's name. It will be prepopulated with the tenant organization name.

    i. **ELIN**: SBCs can include ELIN records. These are only relevant for Direct Routing and do not apply to calling plans or Operator Connect. This field can be left blank.

6. Then select Save to finish the address creation.

Configuring Emergency Calling Policies

Basically, the emergency calling policies describe what happens when a user in your organization makes an emergency call. This applies to the calling plans approach only. The emergency call routing policy is only applicable for Direct Routing.

The emergency calling policy allows the admin to notify a person/group of people in their organization, typically the security team, when a user dials an emergency number. You can allocate emergency calling policies directly to users or network sites to be inherited by the users dynamically when located on those sites. Users will automatically get the global policy unless you create and assign a custom policy, or a network site policy applies. For example, an emergency calling policy might be assigned to the "California site" so that any user that roams from home or another location is configured. Therefore, the California security team is notified when they dial an emergency number when they are at the California site. Follow these steps to configure the emergency calling policy:

1. Log into the Teams admin center at `https://admin.teams.microsoft.com`, select *Voice and Emergency policies*, and add to add an emergency policy.

2. Enter a meaningful name and description and then select notification mode. The options are

    a. **Send notification only**: A Team chat message is sent to the users and groups you specify.

b. **Conferenced in muted and unable to unmute**: A Teams chat message is sent to the users and groups you specify. They can listen (but not participate) in the conversation between the caller and the PSAP operator.

c. **Conferencing is muted but can unmute**: A Teams chat message is sent to the users and groups you specify. They can unmute to listen and participate in the conversation between the caller and the PSAP operator.

3. Define the numbers to dial for emergency call notifications. If you select one of the conferences modes, you can put in an E.164 PSTN phone number or a security group, or you can put in both.

4. In *Users and groups for emergency calls notifications*, you can define one or more users and groups that will be notified for emergency calls via email. You can send information to the email addresses for users, distribution, and security groups. Figure 3-25 shows the calling policy.

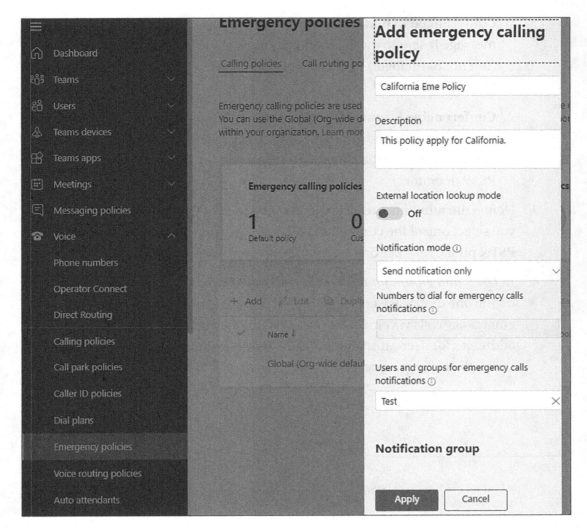

Figure 3-25. *Emergency calling policy*

    5.   Select Apply.

After applying the emergency calling policy, you, as the admin, need to understand the network locations that can map with a network site, physical address, and trusted IP addresses. The next topic describes the network topology configuration.

Configuring Network Locations for Dynamic Emergency Calling

First, you need to understand what dynamic emergency calling offers and how to configure it. Dynamic emergency calling offers the ability to configure and route emergency calls, provide the correct emergency calling address, and optionally notify security personnel (via emergency calling policies) based on the current network location of the Teams client. For Microsoft calling plan users, dynamic location for routing emergency calls is only supported in the United States. This works by the Teams admin populating a database that maps specific network addresses to physical locations/addresses. Location Information Service (LIS) is the service that provides the correct details to the Teams client.

During startup and periodically afterward, the Teams client sends a location request that contains its network connectivity information to LIS. If there is a match, LIS will provide the correct details.

To configure dynamic emergency calling, first you must map the relevant network regions, network sites, network subnets, and trusted IP addresses. This is accomplished in the Teams admin center under Locations ➤ Network topology. So, it is a best practice to gather and add the network sites that align with the emergency calling policy and trusted IP addresses.

Adding a Network Site to Network Topology

In the Teams admin center, select Add to add a network site. The network site is the level where you can align an emergency calling policy (as well as location-based routing and an emergency call routing policy for Direct Routing). Multiple network subnets can be associated with a single network site. A network region is a collection of network sites; you can configure your network region by selecting or adding one when adding a network site. Figure 3-26 shows the network topology configuration.

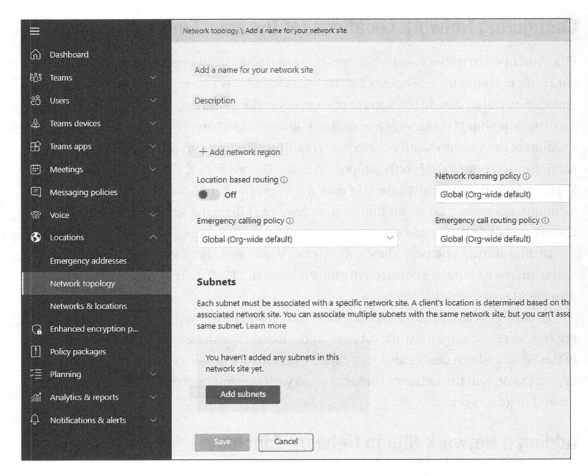

Figure 3-26. *Network topology configurations*

Adding a Trusted IP to Network Topology

Trusted IP addresses are the enterprise's public external IP addresses that a Teams user will show as routing from on the public internet. They are important as they validate that the user is on an enterprise network, and the system should check if they are on a mapped subnet. If the public IP of the user does not match a trusted IP address, the location map will not be checked. This prevents subnets on different networks, but with the same internal subnet numbering, being accidentally mapped to the wrong emergency address. You do not need to map trusted IPs to specific networks.

Mapping a Network to a Physical Location (Emergency Address)

After the network topology of the region, site, and subnet is complete, you can map specific network locations to physical emergency addresses. This populates the LIS database. Note that emergency locations and emergency addresses are the same.

You can map emergency location/addresses to the WAP, network switch, Ethernet port, and network subnets. Here are short descriptions:

- **WAP by BSSID (Basic Service Set Identifier)**: Each AP has a BSSID.

- **Ethernet switch by chassis ID**: Each network switch is stamped with a chassis ID used to identify a specific switch on a network.

- The Ethernet switch port maps both the chassis ID and the port ID. This allows a switch that spans multiple locations to be more accurately mapped down to the port.

- **Subnet**: Not tied to any physical equipment address; this is the user's network address. Unlike mapped subnets in the Teams network topology, the LIS doesn't maintain a list of networks and subnet masks; it relies on the NetworkID of the subnet.

To configure an emergency address, follow these steps:

1. Log into the Teams admin center at `https://admin.teams.microsoft.com`. Select Locations ➤ Networks & locations and then select the tab that represents the network identifier you want to add: subnets, Wi-Fi access points, switches, or ports. For instance, select subnets.

2. Then select Add to add a subnet and emergency location, and then select an IP version (IPv4 or IPv6, as appropriate for the network you wish to map).

3. For subnet, enter the network ID of the subnet to add and then enter a meaningful description.

4. Search for and select an emergency location from one of the emergency addresses you have already defined. Or, if you have not yet determined the emergency location you need, select Add to add an emergency location.

After performing the described steps, you have mapped a network to an emergency address location.

For Direct Routing scenarios: You can utilize emergency voice routing policies in Microsoft Teams to set up emergency numbers and specify how emergency calls are routed. An emergency voice routing policy determines whether enhanced emergency services are enabled for users assigned the policy, the numbers used to call emergency services (for example, 911 in the United States or 112/100 for India), and how calls to emergency services are routed.

You can manage emergency voice routing policies by going to Voice ➤ Emergency policies in the Microsoft Teams admin center or using Windows PowerShell. The policies can be assigned to users and network sites. You can use the Global (org-wide default) policy or create and assign custom policies for users. Users will automatically get the global policy unless you create and assign a custom policy. It is a best practice to create a separate policy for each country and assign it to users belonging to that country.

You can edit the settings in the global policy, but you can't rename or delete them. For network sites, you can create and assign custom policies. If you assign an emergency voice routing policy to a network site and a user, and if that user is at that network site, the policy assigned to the network site overrides the policy assigned to the user.

Creating a Custom Emergency Voice Routing Policy

A custom emergency voice routing policy can be created through the Teams admin center or Teams PowerShell module. Emergency call routing policies are applicable for Teams Direct Routing scenarios only. For a calling plan, there's no need to develop a call routing policy. Follow these steps to make a custom emergency voice call routing policy:

1. Log into the Microsoft Teams admin center at `https://admin.teams.microsoft.com`, click Voice, and select Emergency policies.

2. Then select the *Call routing policies* tab and select Add.

3. Give a meaningful name and description.

4. To enable dynamic emergency calling, turn it on. When dynamic emergency calling is enabled, Teams retrieves the policy and location information from the service. It includes that information as part of the emergency call.

5. Then define one or more emergency numbers. To do this, under Emergency numbers, select Add, and then do the following:

    a. **Emergency dial string:** Enter the emergency dial string. This dial string indicates that a call is an emergency call.

    b. **Emergency dial mask:** You can specify zero or more emergency dial masks for each emergency number. A dial mask is a number you want to translate into the value of the emergency dial string. This allows for alternate emergency numbers to be dialed and still have the call reach emergency services. For example, you can add 112 as the emergency dial mask, the emergency service number for most of Europe, and 911 as the emergency dial string. A Teams user from Europe visiting may not know that 911 is the emergency number in the United States, and when they dial 112, the call is made to 911. To define multiple dial masks, separate each value by a semicolon. For example, 112;911.

    c. **PSTN usage record:** Select the PSTN usage record. The PSTN usage record is used to determine which route is used to route emergency calls from users who are authorized to use them. The route associated with this usage should point to a SIP trunk dedicated to emergency calls or to an ELIN gateway that routes emergency calls to the nearest PSAP.

Note   Earlier, Microsoft added + in front of the emergency dial string from the Teams client, which was corrected. However, using + or without + in Voice, a route pattern is recommended to match an emergency dial string, like 911 and +911. For example, ^+?911.

Dial strings and dial masks must be unique within a policy. This means that for a policy, you can define multiple emergency numbers. You can set various dial masks for a dial string, but each dial string and dial mask must only be used one time.

---

6. After setting up all policy options, select Save to commit the changes.

After creating a location and routing information to allow emergency services to correctly find the location, should you require it? This is only suitable for static sites and will need to be amended should people start to work from other locations, homes, or hybrid working.

It is a best practice to test and validate the new rule you created. If you don't see the intended result, revert to the previous state.

Summary

Any deployment success is dependent on how you plan things, and your implementation is based on the plan you made. This chapter primarily focusing on the Teams voice aspect. You learned about the Microsoft Teams phone system (calling plan, Operator Connect, and Direct Routing) configuration, managing phone numbers, configuring phone policies (voice routing policy and dial plan), and configuring the Teams calling features (auto attendant and call queue). Additionally, you learned how to update plans to configure Teams devices such as Teams Room and Teams audio conferencing. You also learned how to configure emergency calls.

References

"Method: Interview. In this chapter you will learn how to…" https://medium.com/ocean-industries-concept-lab/method-interview-8bd0051c2b86

"Setting Up a New Year Title of document," Amazon S3, https://s3-eu-west-1.amazonaws.com/cjp-rbi-farmplan/sites/1/2021/03/Setting-Up-A-New-Cropping-Year-QSG-version-3.5.pdf

"Patton and Microsoft Teams Direct Routing: Together Better Stronger!" www.voipsupply.com/blog/voip-insider/patton-and-microsoft-teams-direct-routing-together-better-stronger/

"Plan Direct Routing." https://docs.microsoft.com/en-us/MicrosoftTeams/direct-routing-plan

"Azure direct routing infrastructure requirements." Azure Communication, https://docs.microsoft.com/en-us/azure/communication-services/concepts/telephony/direct-routing-infrastructure

"Plan for media bypass with Direct Routing." https://docs.microsoft.com/en-us/microsoftteams/direct-routing-plan-media-bypass

"Connect your Session Border Controller (SBC) to Direct Routing." https://docs.microsoft.com/en-us/microsoftteams/direct-routing-connect-the-sbc

"Create a new collection of trunk configuration settings in Skype." https://docs.microsoft.com/en-us/skypeforbusiness/deploy/deploy-enterprise-voice/trunk-configuration-settings

"Routing calls to unassigned numbers." https://docs.microsoft.com/en-us/microsoftteams/routing-calls-to-unassigned-numbers

"Translate phone numbers for Direct Routing." https://docs.microsoft.com/en-us/microsoftteams/direct-routing-translate-numbers

"Create and manage dial plans." https://docs.microsoft.com/en-us/microsoftteams/create-and-manage-dial-plans

"Manage call routing policies for Direct Routing." https://docs.microsoft.com/en-us/microsoftteams/manage-voice-routing-policies

"Understanding Microsoft Teams Administration: Configure, Customize, and ...." https://ebin.pub/understanding-microsoft-teams-administration-configure-customize-and-manage-the-teams-experience-1st-ed-9781484258743-9781484258750.html

"Plan for Teams auto attendants and call queues." https://docs.microsoft.com/en-us/microsoftteams/plan-auto-attendant-call-queue

"Create a call queue in Microsoft Teams." https://docs.microsoft.com/en-us/microsoftteams/create-a-phone-system-call-queue

"Shared voicemail for callers to leave a message for an organization." https://github.com/MicrosoftDocs/OfficeDocs-SkypeForBusiness/issues/4278

"Microsoft Teams Call Queues." Microsoft Tech Community, https://techcommunity.microsoft.com/t5/microsoft-teams/microsoft-teams-call-queues/td-p/1464285

"Call queue time out when no one is in queue." Microsoft Tech Community, https://techcommunity.microsoft.com/t5/microsoft-teams/call-queue-time-out-when-no-one-is-in-queue/td-p/1641146

"Call Queue Overflow." https://social.technet.microsoft.com/Forums/lync/en-US/70bc1f34-3d2b-4b09-a124-c43ef0f7f4f0/call-queue-overflow

"Microsoft 365 & Teams: Breakouts (Microsoft 365 & Teams)." https://docs.microsoft.com/en-us/events/ignite-nov-2021/microsoft-365-teams/breakouts/

"Phones for Microsoft Teams." https://docs.microsoft.com/en-us/microsoftteams/devices/phones-for-teams

"OfficeDocs-SkypeForBusiness/device-management.md at live ..." https://github.com/MicrosoftDocs/OfficeDocs-SkypeForBusiness/blob/live/Teams/devices/device-management.md

"Deploy Teams phones, Teams displays, Teams panels, and Microsoft Teams ...." https://docs.microsoft.com/en-us/microsoftteams/devices/phones-displays-deploy

"Set up the Common Area Phone license." https://docs.microsoft.com/en-us/microsoftteams/set-up-common-area-phones

"Microsoft Teams displays." https://docs.microsoft.com/en-us/microsoftteams/devices/teams-displays

"Set up Audio Conferencing for Microsoft Teams." https://docs.microsoft.com/en-us/microsoftteams/set-up-audio-conferencing-in-teams

"Lab 02: Configure your environment for Teams Phone." https://github.com/MicrosoftLearning/MS-720-Microsoft-Teams-Voice-Engineer/blob/master/Instructions/Labs/LAB_AK_02_configure_environment_teams_voice.md

"Understanding PSTN Dial-In Audio Conferencing with ...." Tom Talks, https://tomtalks.blog/understanding-pstn-dial-in-audio-conferencing-to-microsoft-teams/

"Manage emergency call routing policies for Direct Routing." https://github.com/MicrosoftDocs/OfficeDocs-SkypeForBusiness/blob/live/Teams/manage-emergency-call-routing-policies.md

"Manage emergency calling policies in Microsoft Teams." https://docs.microsoft.com/en-us/MicrosoftTeams/manage-emergency-calling-policies

CHAPTER 4

Microsoft Teams Client-Side Troubleshooting

Developing a systematic troubleshooting approach is an essential step in solving Teams problem. This chapter provides information about Microsoft Teams network configuration; collecting Teams diagnostic logs and analysis processes; diagnosing common Teams problems; troubleshooting problems with public and private channels; deploying and updating Teams client software; troubleshooting Teams client startup and configuration; troubleshooting audio and video devices; troubleshooting Teams desktop client performance issues; understanding and troubleshooting external (federation) access issues; enabling and troubleshooting Teams guest access issues; and troubleshooting issues with interoperability with Skype for Business. This chapter is primarily focused on Teams client issues and troubleshooting them.

Understanding, Reviewing, and Optimizing Network Connectivity for Teams

The network is the backbone of any cloud service so it is essential to understand network connectivity and how you can optimize it through best practices. This section discusses network connectivity, traffic flow, and how you can optimize it.

© Balu N Ilag and Arun M Sabale 2022
B. N. Ilag and A. M. Sabale, *Troubleshooting Microsoft Teams*, https://doi.org/10.1007/978-1-4842-8622-7_4

Connecting to Microsoft 365 Services Over the Internet?

You need internet connectivity to connect to any cloud hosting service like Microsoft 365. Even browsing a website requires internet connectivity. So here is how you generally connect to a website on the Internet. For instance, say you are trying to communicate to google.com. You are sitting in your corporate network, which is a managed and secure network, and you are trying to browse google.com. The process starts with connecting to the Internet, initializing a DNS lookup that resolves the name to the IP address, receiving the IP address, and establishing a TLS connection based on the IP address. Once DNS resolution happens, you get routed to the Internet. For the Internet, there is minimal control; you can only choose your ISP and maybe a DNS provider. After that, you are out of control of what you can do. The Internet is an unmanaged network, but it works very well, and users can access the intended website, like you can access google.com.

Specific to accessing Microsoft services (Office apps and Teams), the internet path is reduced, and the Microsoft network picks up most of the connection path. So, when you start on a corporate network, you are still looking to get to Microsoft 365, you are still looking to go to office.com, and you still have the strengths and weaknesses of a corporate network. But because of how the Microsoft network is designed, the time spent on the Internet is significantly reduced; refer to Figure 4-1. This reduces jitter, packet loss, and latency. It reduces latency which is critical when connecting Teams audio and real-time video traffic.

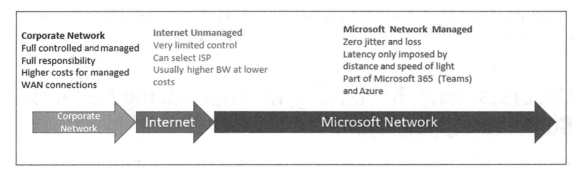

Figure 4-1. *Corporate network, internet, and Microsoft network*

Specific to optimizing network connectivity, the first thing that can be done is a local internet breakout. When we talk about a local internet breakout, don't forget local DNS resolution. It means that if you have a branch office with local internet, that branch office has to be able to go out to the Internet for DNS. Suppose you have DNS set up so that all DNS requests get forwarded to the corporate DNS server installed in a data center in a different country/region. The Microsoft DNS servers will see the DNS requests come from the corporate headquarters and not the local branch and assume that the user is at the corporate headquarters, not the local branch. Thus, it will return an accurate DNS entry for the corporate offices but not the local branch office. The local branch needs a local DNS so the Microsoft DNS servers can realize where they are located and give them the optimal (faster) DNS response, an IP address to an AFD (Azure Font Door) close to them.

Additionally, you want to remove as much internet as possible (by internet, we mean the unmanaged internet). The internet doesn't support QoS (Quality of Service). You cannot necessarily control the routing or network traffic or bandwidth controls. The less time you spend on the internet, the better the quality of service. The more time you spend on the Microsoft network, the faster your performance will be, which helps you get better audio and video in your Teams meeting.

Azure Active Directory and Conditional Access Policies

Azure Active Directory (AAD) is Microsoft's multi-tenant cloud-based directory and identity management service. It offers sign-in authorization and authentication for Microsoft Teams.

Azure Active Directory (Azure AD) business-to-business (B2B) collaboration permits organizations and users to invite guest users to collaborate with them using Microsoft Teams. With Azure AD B2B collaboration, organizations can enforce conditional access and multifactor authentication (MFA) policies for B2B users.

Azure Active Directory is also the registration and access control point for applications and bots when configuring features like policy-based compliance recording or contact center integration when using Azure Active Directory. Connecting other services tied to Azure AD identities allows a unified user experience across the many different tools business users consumes during their workday.

Specific to Microsoft Teams, you should first understand how to control external user access and then execute security by configuring conditional access, multifactor authentication, or threat management for Microsoft Teams. Ultimately, you will implement compliance for Teams by using data loss prevention (DLP) policies, eDiscovery cases, or supervision policies.

149

Multifactor Authentication Process

Multifactor authentication (MFA) is the process of prompting a user for a different form of identification during sign-in. They might be asked to enter a code on their cell phone or provide a fingerprint scan. MFA significantly reduces the chances of user accounts being compromised. Requiring MFA for all users considerably enhances identity security for the organization.

Conditional Access Policy

Conditional Access (CA) is an Azure AD capability that supports you in ensuring that computer and mobile devices accessing Microsoft 365 resources are appropriately managed and protected. This primarily helps protect access by adding multiple conditions.

CA utilizes multiple signals to verify whether a user or device is reliable. CA policies are if-then statements that permit security experts to offer defense-in-depth and are implemented after the first-factor authentication has been completed. Microsoft Teams is supported independently as a cloud app in Azure Active Directory Conditional Access policies.

A CC policy is made of if-then statements of assignments and access controls. The assignment part of the policy controls the who, what, and where of the CA policy. The access part of the policy contains how it's enforced. Based on the assignments, it may grant access, block access, or grant access provided one or more additional conditions are met.

Configuring a Conditional Access Policy

CA policies can be configured for Microsoft Teams. Teams are integrated with other Microsoft apps to execute features such as meetings, calendars, interop chats, and file sharing. CA policies can additionally be set for these apps. When a user signs into Microsoft Teams on any client, the CA policies set for Teams and any integrated cloud apps are applied. It's crucial to see that even though CA policies may be set up for Teams, without the correct policies on other apps like Exchange Online and SharePoint, users might still be able to access resources directly because Teams leverages other application services. If you have a service dependency configured, the policy might be applied to utilize early-bound or late-bound implementation; early-bound policy enforcement means a user must satisfy the dependent service policy before accessing the calling app. For example, a user must fulfill the SharePoint policy before signing into Teams. Late-bound policy enforcement occurs after the user signs into the calling app. Enforcement is deferred when the calling app requests a token for the downstream service, such as Teams accessing Planner. Conditional access policies make Teams authentication secure, which is why it is important to utilize them.

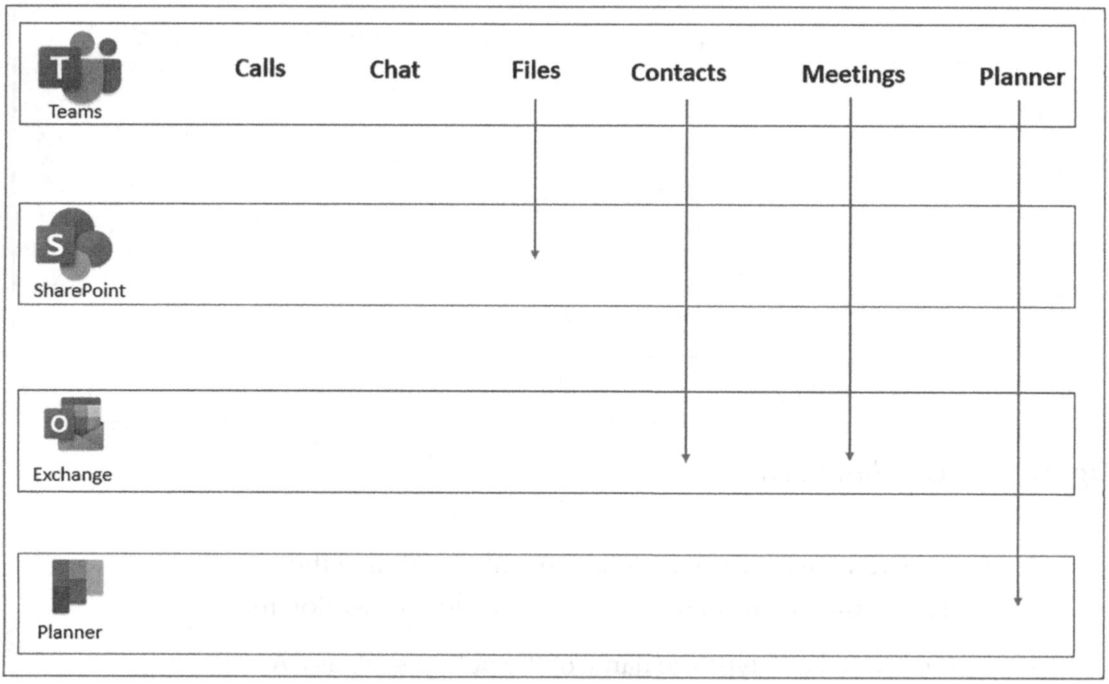

Figure 4-2. *Teams service needs*

Figure 4-2 demonstrates Teams service needs. Blue arrows indicate early-bound enforcement; the blue arrow for Planner indicates late-bound enforcement. Follow these steps to configure a CA policy, such as a CA policy for the Engineering department:

1. Sign into the Azure Active Directory admin center as a Global Administrator. Select All services, search for Conditional access on the left pane, and choose Azure AD Conditional Access.

2. On the Conditional Access - Policies page, select New Policy. Refer to Figure 4-3 for creating new CA policy.

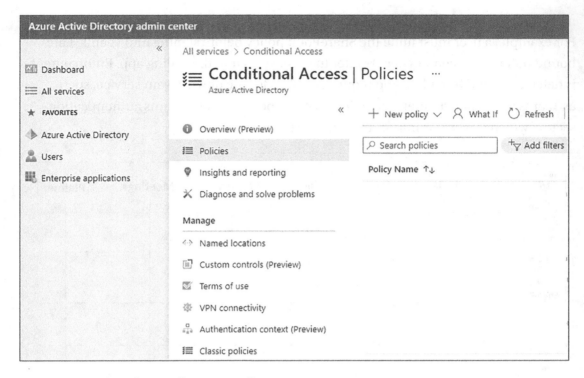

Figure 4-3. *Conditional access policy*

3. On the new page, insert the following information in the corresponding fields in the sections of the left navigation menu:

-   In the Name field, type the name of the policy, such as CA-Engineering-Policy. In the section Assignment, configure the following settings:

    a. Select the users or workloads that you would like to apply this policy to, for example, the Eng group.

    b. Select the cloud apps or actions that you would like to apply the policy to, and from the list of the apps, choose Microsoft Teams. Refer to Figure 4-4.

    c. Select the conditions that you would like to include in the policy, such as the level of sign-in risk, device platform, physical locations, client apps, and device state.

- Choose what type of access control you would like to deploy for the settings you configured in the Assignments section.

    a. Select Grant to choose which controls will be enforced, such as multifactor authentication.

    b. Select Session if you need to configure a limited experience within a cloud app, such as an app enforced restriction.

4. Enable the policy by selecting On in the Enable policy section and then click Create. Refer to Figure 4-4.

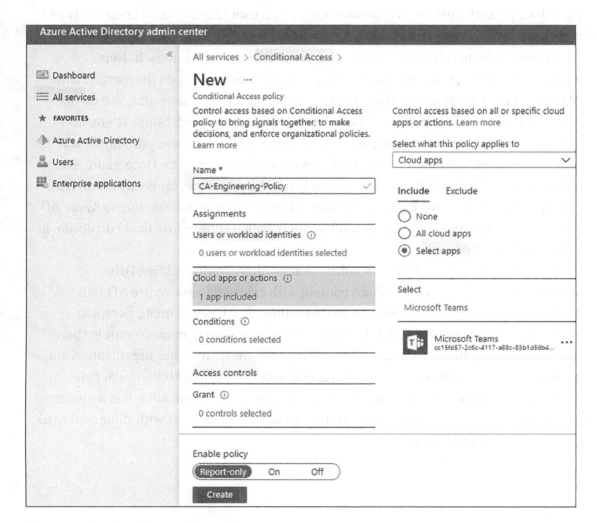

Figure 4-4. *Creating a CA policy*

Understanding Teams Identity and Troubleshooting Teams Account Issues

Azure AD is the cloud-based identity and access management service for Microsoft 365 application. You can utilize Azure AD to control access to your applications and resources based on your company's needs. For instance, you can utilize Azure AD for multifactor authentication when accessing valuable organizational resources. Furthermore, you can use Azure AD to systematize user provisioning among your Windows Server AD and your cloud apps with Microsoft 365. Ultimately, Azure AD provides a powerful means to automatically protect user identities and credentials and meet your access governance needs.

Microsoft Teams services need correct Active Directory attributes. If users' identities exist across multiple forests, Azure AD Connect should do the merge. Azure AD Connect automatically synchronizes the correct attributes, given that you do not modify either the Connectors or Sync Rules in Azure AD Connect. Suppose you don't synchronize from all forests that contain user identities. In that case, you should still make sure the appropriate identity attributes are correctly populated into Azure AD for any user using Teams online, which will likely require additional on-premises directory synchronization. Utilizing a non-standard configuration for synchronizing to Azure AD is risky because it could lead to misconfiguration, which could cause data corruption in your online directory.

Microsoft 365 applications, including Teams, SharePoint, and OneDrive, are utilized to collaborate and share content with external users. Azure AD B2B collaboration is a feature within External Identities that lets you invite guests to collaborate with your organization. With B2B collaboration, you can securely share Microsoft 365 applications and services with guests from any other organization while providing control over your own corporate data. With Azure AD B2B, the partner utilizes their own identity management solution, so your organization has no external administrative overhead. Guests sign into your apps and services with their own work, school, or social identities.

Azure AD Features

- **Application management**: Manage your cloud and on-premises apps using application proxy, single sign-on, the My Apps portal (also known as the Access panel), and Software-as-a-Service (SaaS) apps.

- **Authentication**: Manage Azure Active Directory self-service password reset, multifactor authentication, custom banned password list, and intelligent lockout.

- **Azure Active Directory for developers**: Build apps that sign in all Microsoft identities and get tokens to call Microsoft Graph, other Microsoft APIs, or custom APIs.

- **Business-to-business (B2B)**: Manage your guests and external partners while maintaining control over your own corporate data.

- **Business-to-customer (B2C)**: Customize and control how users sign up, sign in, and manage their profiles when using your apps.

- **Conditional Access**: Manage access to your cloud apps.

- **Device management**: Manage how your cloud or on-premises devices access your corporate data.

- **Domain services**: Join Azure virtual machines in a domain without domain controllers.

- **Enterprise users**: Manage license assignment, access to apps, and set up delegates using groups and administrator roles.

- **Hybrid identity**: Use Azure Active Directory Connect and Connect Health to provide a single user identity for authentication and authorization to all resources, regardless of location (cloud or on-premises).

- **Identity governance**: Manage your organization's identity through employee, business partner, vendor, service, and app access controls. You can also perform access reviews.

155

- **Identity protection**: Detect potential vulnerabilities affecting your organization's identities, configure policies to respond to suspicious actions, and then take appropriate action to resolve them.

- **Managed identities for Azure resources**: Provide your Azure services with an automatically managed identity in Azure AD that can authenticate any Azure AD-supported authentication service, including Key Vault.

- **Privileged identity management (PIM)**: Manage, control, and monitor access within your organization. This feature includes access to Azure AD and Azure resources and other Microsoft Online Services, like Microsoft 365 and Intune.

- **Reports and monitoring**: Gain insights into your environment's security and usage patterns.

Capturing and Analyzing Teams Sign-In Logs

In the previous section, you learned about identity access, Teams authentication, and how you can securely access Teams log-on. This section discusses how you collect Teams client diagnostic logs for troubleshooting.

Teams Diagnostic Logs and the Collecting Process

In any problem-solving process, diagnostic or system logs play a critical role, and Teams is no exception. Other than ensuring that end users are using the most current version of a Teams client, an essential element of troubleshooting is capturing the suitable logs from the Teams clients. The clients have rich logging capabilities that will assist in troubleshooting many end user problems. Teams diagnostic logs track valuable information that you, as an admin, need for troubleshooting problems. In Teams, log files are created automatically by the system. Log files have a primary source of information that you can turn to when troubleshooting particular issues. There are three kinds of log files: debug, media, and desktop. Out of the three logs, the debug log is used frequently. Microsoft support personnel utilize media and desktop logs when you open a specific support case. The support engineer will need the debug log if you generate a Microsoft support request.

Teams has multiple clients but not all clients generate all three types of logs. Log files are stored in locations specific to the client and the operating system. Table 4-1 lists Teams clients and the logs they generate. This section explains how to enable logging and collect the log files for the following Teams clients.

Table 4-1. *Teams Clients and Logs*

Teams client	Debug log	Media log	Desktop log
Teams Web	Yes	No	No
Teams Windows	Yes	Yes	Yes
Teams Mac OSX	Yes	Yes	Yes
Teams Linux	Yes	Yes	Yes
Teams mobile (iOS)	No	No	No
Teams mobile (Android)	No	No	No

Below is detailed information about each log type.

Microsoft Teams Debug Log

The Teams debug log data is produced by desktop (Windows and Mac) clients and web (browser-based) clients. These logs are text files, and they can be easily read using any text-based editor such as Notepad and Notepad++. Debug logs show the data flow: sign-in, connection requests to middle-tier services, and the call/conversation.

Note   Always read the debug logs from the bottom up. New log records are created when logging into the client.

Generating the Teams Debug Log

Teams debug logs are generated and downloaded differently for each operating system.

- **The Teams Windows client debug log** can be generated using the shortcut Ctrl + Alt + Shift + 1. This log is automatically stored in the Download folder at path %userprofile%\Downloads.

- **The Teams Mac OSx client debug log** can be generated using the shortcut Option + Command + Shift + 1. This log is automatically stored in the Downloads folder at path Downloads.

- **The Teams Linux client debug log** can be generated using the shortcut Ctrl + Alt + Shift + 1, and the file is stored in the Downloads folder at path ~/Downloads.

- The Teams web (browser) client log can be generated using the keys Ctrl + Alt + Shift + 1. Once the log is generated, you will be prompted to save it in the default save location.

Capturing the Teams Media Log

Teams Media logs are required when you are troubleshooting Teams call/meeting quality or media failure issues. Media logs include diagnostic data about audio, video, and screen sharing. These logs are necessary for support cases only when requested by Microsoft. They can only be inspected by Microsoft.

By default, the media log is turned off. To enable the media log as diagnostic data for Teams meetings, you must turn on the option in the Teams client. From the Teams client top status bar (**...**), select Settings, click *Settings* and then *General*, select the *Enable logging for meeting diagnostics (requires restarting Teams)* check box, and then restart the Teams client and reproduce the issue. Refer to Figure 4-5 to enable logging for meeting diagnostics.

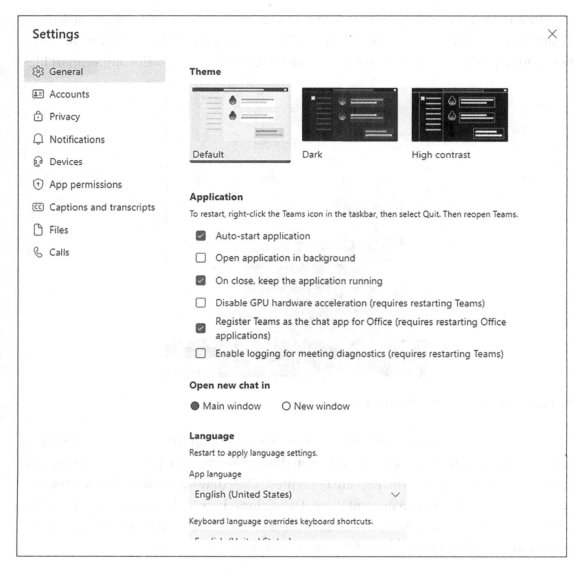

Figure 4-5. *Enabling meeting diagnostics*

Note   Sign out and log back into the Teams client after selecting *Enable logging for meeting diagnostics* (this requires restarting Teams). Just closing Teams and opening it again is not sufficient. Although the setting appears to have been saved, the changes won't take effect without signing out and logging back in again.

Once the log is enabled, collect the logs as soon as the issue occurs. Right-click the Teams icon in the systems tray and select *Collect support files*. All log file types are stored in one folder called `MSTeams Diagnostics Log`. Figure 4-6 shows collecting support files.

Figure 4-6. *Collecting support logs*

Most logs are text-based and are read from the bottom up. They can be read using any text-based editor, and new logs are created when logging into the client. Remember, Teams Media-stack and skylib logs are encrypted. They may be requested by Microsoft support engineers, who can decrypt them. Debug logs show login, connection requests, and call/conversion data flows. Media files contain information related to the media stack. Individual log files contain different information.

Teams Desktop log

Teams desktop logs, called bootstrapper logs, contain log data that occurs between the desktop client and the browser. Like media logs, these logs are only needed if requested by Microsoft. The logs are text-based and can be read using any text-based editor in a top-down format.

- **To collect the Linux OS client logs**: First, click on the Microsoft Teams icon in your system tray and select Get Log. These log files will be available in `~/.config/Microsoft/Microsoft Teams/logs.txt`.

- **To collect logs for Windows**: First, click the Microsoft Teams icon in your system tray and select *Collect support files*. These log files are located at `%appdata%\Microsoft\Teams` in Windows. When investigating problems signing into Teams, you may need to manually collect the desktop logs. You can open these log files in Notepad.

Teams Mobile Phone Log

1. To capture the log on a Teams mobile client, Open the Microsoft Teams mobile app, click your avatar, and click Settings.

2. Click on *Help and feedback* and toggle the Enable Diagnostic log button on the setting screen. Refer to Figure 4-7. You will be prompted to restart the app (to enable diagnostic log collection, the app needs to be closed. Please open the app after closing). Restart the app and check.

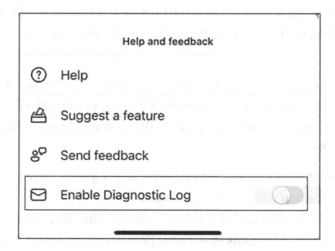

Figure 4-7. *Enabling diagnostic logs for a mobile device*

Teams Web Client Trace and WebRTC Logs

As described in Chapter 1, Teams has various clients, and the Teams Web client is one of them. Some scenarios require you to collect a browser trace. This information can present important details about the state of the Teams client when the error occurred. It is required to sign into Teams before you start the browser trace. It's crucial to do this before starting the trace so that it doesn't contain sensitive sign-in information. After you've signed in, start Teams on one of the browsers such as Chrome, Edge, Safari, and Firefox.

1. Log into the Teams web client (`https://teams.microsoft.com`). It's crucial to sign in before you start the trace so that it doesn't contain sensitive information related to your sign-in.

2. Press F12 or select settings or the more (**...**) browser settings icon. Then click on More tools and then select Developer tools.

3. The browser keeps trace information only for the currently loaded page by default. Select the Network tab and then select the Preserve log options so that the browser will support all trace information, even if your repro requires going to more than one page.

4. Select Record network log and then reproduce the issue in the Teams web client. After reproducing the unexpected web client behavior, select Stop recording network log, select Export HAR, and save the file.

You may need to share the HAR file with Microsoft support, so use a compressed format like .zip and share it with Microsoft support.

Apart from the web traces, you may have to generate the WebRTC log for Teams web client audio/video issues. Th Teams Web client (WebRTC) generates logs that provide connection details for audio and video calls and support an engineer when they are diagnosing and identifying the problem. Follow these steps to access the WebRTC logs in Edge (Chromium) or Google Chrome:

1. Open a new tab and visit the Edge (Chromium) browser by visiting Edge (`edge://webrtc-internals/`) or Chrome (`chrome://webrtc-internals/`). Refer to Figure 4-8 to create a data dump.

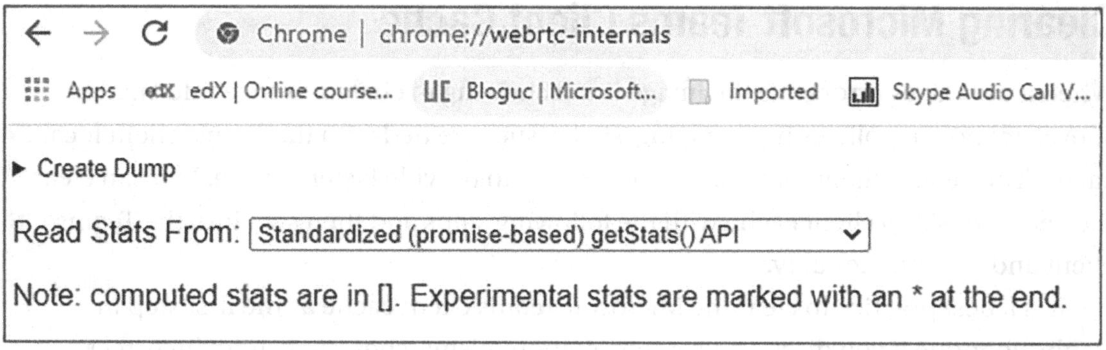

Figure 4-8. *Webrtc dump*

2. Open the Teams Web application and reproduce the problem.

3. Go back to the tab that was accessed in step 1, and you will see at least two charges, including GetUserMedia Requests and `https://teams.microsoft.com/url`.

4. Lastly, select the tab with the name of the Teams application and save the page content.

Now you have the Teams web (WebRTC) log, which you can share with the Microsoft support engineer.

Identifying and Resolving Common Teams Problems

In the previous section, you learned how to collect diagnostic logs. This section focuses explicitly on troubleshooting access to the Teams cloud service, Teams capabilities, and additional scenarios such as chat, Teams phone system, audio conferencing, and updated coverage.

Teams provides chat, calling, meeting, content sharing, app integration, and much more functionality that increase the possibility of standard errors. This topic section provides the information that you need to resolve standard or day-to-day Teams issues, including sign-in, presence information, chat and call issues, calendar sync issues, and known issues. We cover the most common and general problems with workarounds or resolutions.

Clearing Microsoft Teams Client Cache

When a user faces errors like the image is not showing in chat, presence information shows unknown, policies not applying, such issues are tied with the Teams client local cache. The Teams client maintains a local cache to provide faster service. You can clear the Teams desktop client cache with the following steps and then sign into the Teams client and test functionality.

It is a best practice to clear the Microsoft Teams client cache as the first step in troubleshooting if you discover user information mismatches, such as an incorrect display name, Teams presence information not showing correctly, Teams chat images not showing, or a Teams avatar not updating. Clearing the cache forces the client to immediately retrieve the latest data from the Teams service. Depending on which client is being utilized, there are different steps to follow to clear each client.

Clearing the Microsoft Teams Desktop Client Cache for Windows

The Microsoft Teams client cache is split into multiple directories and locations, so it is considered a clean start for the Teams app only after clearing these locations. Follow these steps to remove the Teams cache for the Teams windows client:

1. First, properly exit the Microsoft Teams client. Either right-click Teams from the icon tray and select Quit, or run Task Manager, select the Microsoft Teams process, and choose End Task.

2. Open File Explorer, and type in `%appdata%\Microsoft\teams`. Once in the directory, you must remove the files in the following folders (Figure 4-9 show the folder list):

   - Blob_Storage: `appdata%\Microsoft\Teams\Blob_Storage` (if present)

   - Web cache for images, JS files, cookies, profile photos: `%appdata%\Microsoft\Teams\Cache`

   - Databases: `%appdata%\Microsoft\Teams\databases`

   - GPU cache: `%appdata%\Microsoft\Teams\GPUCache`

   - IndexedDB: `%appdata%\Microsoft\Teams\IndexedDB`

- Local storage: `%appdata%\Microsoft\Teams\LocalStorage`

- Tmp: `%appdata%\Microsoft\Teams\tmp`

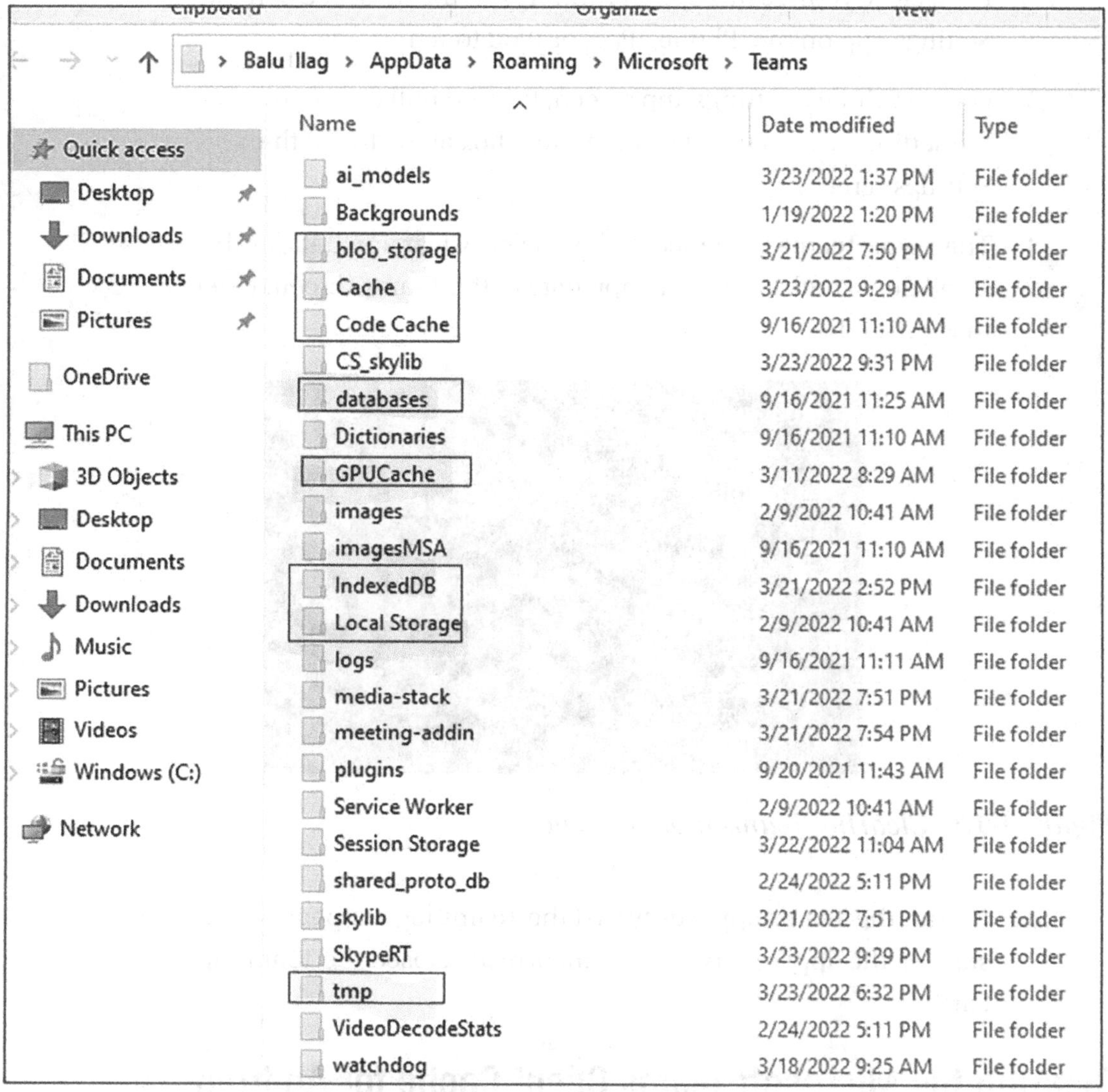

Figure 4-9. *Teams desktop client cache*

3. Restart the Teams client.

Clear the cached for Microsoft Teams iOS client: Follow these steps to clear the Teams client cache for iOS devices:

1. First, close your Teams app (if running) on the device. Open the Settings app on the iPhone, iPad, or iPod touch.

2. On the primary Settings app screen, tap and pull down on the settings screen to reveal the Search box at the top of the Settings screen.

3. Then type Teams in the search box, select Clear app data, and scroll down and select Clear app data in the Teams screen. Refer to Figure 4-10.

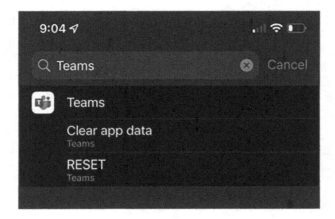

Figure 4-10.   *Clearing Teams mobile cache*

4. Restart the Teams app. Verify that the Teams logo appears when starting the app; otherwise, you incorrectly closed the Teams app earlier.

Clearing the Microsoft Teams Client Cache for Android

1. Close your Teams app (if running) and open the Settings device with the cogwheel.

2. Then select Apps and Apps again and then search for the Teams app from the app list and select it.

3. Then select Storage, and below Cache, select CLEAR CACHE.

4. Finally, restart the Teams app.

The Virtual Camera Has Stopped Working on a macOS Teams Desktop Client

This is a known issue, so Microsoft is aware of it. This issue occurs after security fixes are applied in the Teams client for macOS. Virtual camera apps may stop functioning.

The resolution is already fixed in Teams client for macOS version 1.4.00.8872 and later versions. If you or your user is running an older version of Teams client, upgrade to the latest version to resolve this issue.

Microsoft Teams Is Stuck in a Login Loop in the Browser

Suppose you are trying to sign into a Microsoft Teams web-based app in Microsoft Edge. In that case, using Internet Explorer, Google Chrome, Mozilla Firefox, or Safari, the site may continually loop, and you can never sign in. This issue occurs if your organization uses Trusted Sites and doesn't enable the URLs for Microsoft Teams. Therefore, the Teams web-based application is not able to sign in.

To resolve the issue, you can change the settings for your browser using administrator rights or work with your Windows administrator to update Group Policy Object (GPO) to allow Teams URLs. Here is the additional information to resolve the issue for each browser.

For Google Chrome: In the Chrome Settings window, select *Cookies and other site data* on the Privacy and Security tab. Under *Sites that can always use cookies*, select Add, and select the *Including third-party cookies on this site* check box.

Add the following Teams-related sites:

- [*.]microsoft.com

- [*.]microsoftonline.com

- [*.]teams.skype.com

- [*.]teams.microsoft.com

- [*.]sfbassets.com

- [*.]skypeforbusiness.com

If you want to modify the setting for all users, use the Chrome Administrative template. Download and install it from `https://support.google.com/chrome/a/answer/187202/set-chrome-browser-policies-on-managed-pcs`. Add the sites listed above to the Content settings ➤ CookiesAllowedForUrls setting.

Microsoft Edge Browser

In the Edge Settings window, select *Cookies and site permissions*, then select *Manage and delete cookies and site data* under *Cookies and data stored*.

Turn on *Allow sites to save and read cookie data (recommended)* and make sure *Block third-party cookies* is turned off. In the same window, under Allow, select Add to add these Teams sites:

- `[*.]microsoft.com`
- `[*.]microsoftonline.com`
- `[*.]teams.skype.com`
- `[*.]teams.microsoft.com`
- `[*.]sfbassets.com`
- `[*.]skypeforbusiness.com`

Figure 4-11 shows cookies and site permissions in the Edge browser.

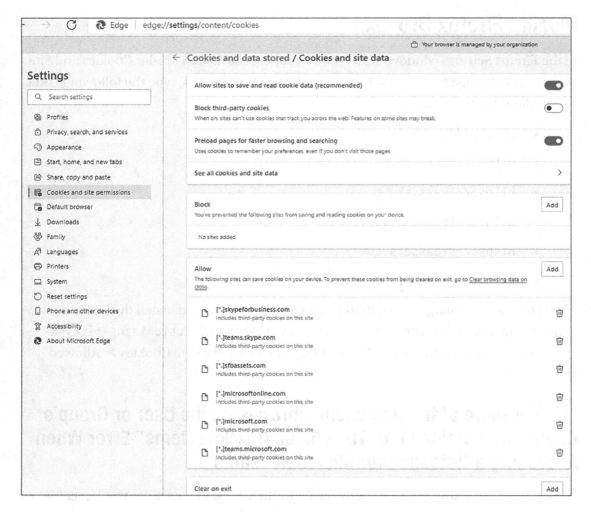

Figure 4-11. *Cookies and site permission in Edge*

Suppose you want to change the settings by using GPO. You need to download and install the Microsoft Edge Administrative Template (`https://docs.microsoft.com/en-us/deployedge/configure-microsoft-edge#1-download-and-install-the-microsoft-edge-administrative-template`). Then add the above-listed sites to the Content settings ➤ CookiesAllowedForUrls setting, either with a mandatory or recommended policy.

Mozilla Firefox Browser

In the Firefox Settings window, select the Privacy & Security tab. Under Cookies and Site Data, select Manage Exceptions. In the website text box address, type the following URLs, select Allow, and select Save Changes:

- `https://microsoft.com`

- `https://microsoftonline.com`

- `https://teams.skype.com`

- `https://teams.microsoft.com`

- `https://sfbassets.com`

- `https://skypeforbusiness.com`

If you want to change the settings using GPO, download and install the Firefox administrative template (`https://support.mozilla.org/kb/customizing-firefox-using-group-policy-windows`). Then add the above listed to the Cookies ➤ Allowed Sites setting.

"One or More of the Document Libraries on the User or Group's OneDrive Contains More Than 5,000 OneNote Items" Error When Accessing a Notebook for Microsoft Teams

You can't access a notebook for Microsoft Teams in Microsoft OneNote. You'll receive the following error message: "One or more of the document libraries on the user or group's OneDrive contains more than 5,000 OneNote items (notebooks, sections, section groups) and cannot be queried using the API. Please ensure that none of the user or group's document libraries contains more than 5,000 OneNote items. Please follow the link below for instructions on how to remedy this situation."

This error occurs if the document libraries contain more than 5,000 OneNote items. This is a known OneNote limitation in Microsoft Teams.

Microsoft is researching this problem and will post more information when it becomes available. There is no resolution yet, but you can use a workaround to reduce the number of items in OneNote.

Microsoft Teams Is Slow During Video Meetings on laptops Docked to 4K/UHD Monitors

Sometimes a user may see that the overall Microsoft Teams performance on laptops is affected during meetings that use video. This issue can occur if a computer is docked to an external 4K or ultra-high-definition (also known as ultra-HD or UHD) display.

The workaround is to minimize the resource requirements for your laptop to improve the Teams experience during the meeting and try these best practices:

a. The first thing you can do is update the Teams client and ensure that the latest update is installed. The newest performance fixes were released in June 2021, available in version 1.4.00.16575 or earlier.

b. Check and close any applications or browser tabs that you are not using.

c. Turn off the video in the meeting. Turn off your own video by selecting Turn camera off in the meeting controls. Also, if you want to turn off the incoming video, select *More actions ➤ Turn off the incoming video* in the meeting controls.

d. The next thing you do is to disable GPU hardware acceleration in Teams. To disable this function, select the Settings and more menu next to your profile picture at the top right of Teams, and then select the *Disable GPU hardware acceleration* option. Refer to Figure 4-12.

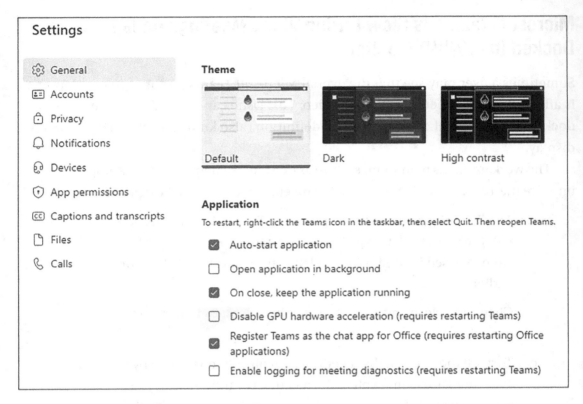

Figure 4-12. *Disabling GPU hardware acceleration*

e. Another thing you can do is disconnect your monitor from the port replicator or docking station and directly connect it to the video port on the laptop, if available.

f. Sometimes Teams clients keep resources connected; restarting Teams will help to release resources.

g. Higher display resolution requires more resources; it helps change the resolution of your 4K or UHD monitor to 1920 x 1080.

h. USB-C is faster but uses more resources from other connections; hence, use DVI or HDMI instead of USB-C to connect your monitor.

i. Sometimes disabling full-screen mode in the meeting helps. To do so, select More actions ➤ Fullscreen.

Unable to Create a Team

Sometimes users are unable to create a team in Microsoft Teams. The admin may have set a policy restricting who can create Office 365 groups or teams. You need to check with your Teams admin to understand your company's policy for creating groups and teams.

The Removed User Appears as an "Unknown User" in Microsoft Teams

When a user leaves the company or is removed from Teams, that user's name appears in Teams as "Unknown user." The conversation tab also displays "Unknown user has been added to the team." This is currently an open issue. Microsoft is researching this problem and will post more information when the information becomes available. Always check the Teams known issue article link (`https://docs.microsoft.com/en-us/MicrosoftTeams/troubleshoot/teams-welcome`).

Unable to See Dial Pad or Dial Pad Is Missing in Teams

The Microsoft Teams dial pad allows users to make a PSTN phone call to external phone numbers, and the dial pad shows the phone number assigned to the user. However, sometimes Teams users can't make outbound calls because the dial pad in the Calls screen in Teams is missing. There are multiple reasons for this. The following are the most common causes.

a. The user can log into Teams, but no dial-pad means the user has not been assigned a Teams Phone System license. Make sure that the user has been given a Teams Phone System license.

b. The user has not been assigned a Calling Plan license assign. Make sure that the user has been given a Calling Plan license.

c. Another common reason is that the user does not have Enterprise Voice (EV) enabled. Enable the user for EV.

d. The Teams dial pad shows only when the user is in Teams-Only mode. If the user is in Islands mode, this might be the cause.

e. Make sure the user has a Teams OnlineVoiceRoutingPolicy assigned with appropriate policy value. Use this command to do so:

```
Grant-CsOnlineVoiceRoutingPolicy -Identity "Balu llag"
-PolicyName $Null
Grant-CsOnlineVoiceRoutingPolicy -Identity "Balu Ilag"
-PolicyName "USA-CA-VoiceRoutingPolicy"
```

These actions force an update of the policy in the back-end environment of Teams. After this change is made, the user should see the dial pad appear under Calls within four hours.

f. You can use the self-diagnostic automated tool (`https://aka.ms/ TeamsDialPadMissingDiag`) to find the missing dial pad cause.

Unable to Dial Out Using Teams

Sometimes a user will be unable to dial out even though they have a line URI (phone number) assigned, a voice routing policy, a dial plan assigned, etc. However, the user is still unable to dial out.

This issue mainly happens in Teams Direct routing scenarios where phone numbers are coming from on-premises. When running the `Get-CsOnlineUser` commandnmm ++++ for the affected user, it shows the `OnlineDialOutPolicy` properties as blank. If you check for an active user account and find that the online dialout policy has a default policy assigned (`OnlineDialOutPolicy : DialoutCPCandPSTNInternational`), this says something is missing for the affected user.

Technically, the affected user account has policies and a line URI in Microsoft 365 cloud (Teams); however, the affected user might lack the msRTC attribute on on-premises Active Directory Domain Services (AD DS). Table 4-2 shows the msRTC attribute that might be missing.

Table 4-2. *MSRTC Attributes and Required Values*

msRTCSIP-DeploymentLocator	sipfed.online.lync.com
msRTCSIP-FederationEnabled	TRUE
msRTCSIP-InternetAccessEnabled	TRUE
msRTCSIP-Line	tel:+<1234567890>
msRTCSIP-PrimaryUserAddress	sip:username@domain.com
msRTCSIP-UserEnabled	TRUE

Update these attributes and wait for a couple of hours to sync the on-premises attribute to the cloud and test outbound calls. The outbound call should be working.

Error When Signing into Teams: "You're Missing Out! Ask Your Admin to Enable Microsoft Teams for <Company/SchoolName>"

Users may see an error message when they sign into Microsoft Teams, like "You're missing out! Ask your admin to enable Microsoft Teams for <CompanyName>." To resolve the issue of Office 365 Education tenants, Microsoft Teams isn't enabled by default. You will have to turn it on. Here's how to enable Microsoft Teams for your school.

Validating Teams Client Connectivity

The Microsoft Remote Test Connectivity Analyzer is a powerful tool used to diagnose the sign-in experience of user accounts hosted on the Teams environment. This allows you to analyze the specific network's login form to troubleshoot Teams calendars, recording, and delegation issues for desktop clients. While this tool is primarily designed to simulate the connectivity behavior of a Teams client, it provides valuable information for desktop client meeting-related issues. The Microsoft Remote Connectivity Analyzer for Teams (https://testconnectivity.microsoft.com/tests/teams) are tests from a service in a Microsoft datacenter and they can be helpful when trying to fix problems with an end user's machine and/or network.

Checking the Connectivity of a Microsoft Teams Workload

Microsoft provides a tool called Test Connectivity which helps test different Teams scenarios. You can access the Test Connectivity Tool by visiting `https://testconnectivity.microsoft.com/tests/teams`. Figure 4-13 shows the Microsoft Remote Connectivity Analyzer.

Here is the list of scenarios that the Test Connectivity Tool tests:

- **Teams Calendar Tab:** This test verifies that the Teams back-end service can connect to an Exchange mailbox.

- **Teams Meeting Delegation:** This test verifies if your account meets the requirements to schedule a Teams meeting on behalf of a delegator.

- **Teams Meeting Recording:** This test verifies if your account meets all requirements to record a meeting in Teams.

- **Teams Presence Based on Calendar Events:** This test verifies that Teams presence can be updated based on calendar events set in Outlook.

- **Teams Channel Meeting:** This test verifies if your account meets the requirements to schedule a channel meeting. If your mailbox is hosted, on-premises is verified if your Exchange on-premises inbound receive connector is appropriately configured.

- **Teams Voicemail:** This test verifies if your account meets the requirements to access your voicemail and that the Teams client can retry and display voicemail messages.

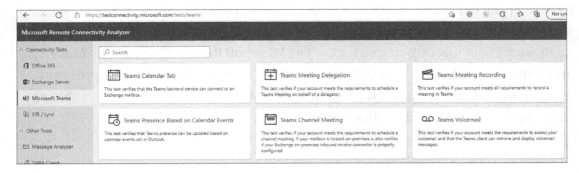

Figure 4-13. *Remote Connectivity Analyzer for testing Teams scenarios*

Microsoft Support and Recovery Assistant Tool

This is the automation tool you can install and use to resolve user-facing Teams issues. Visit the support site, get the assistant tool, and install the tool on the local machine where the Teams client is installed.

Issues with Teams User Presence in Outlook

The Teams User Presence for Outlook tool gives you the ability to check a Teams user's presence information correctly in Outlook. Go to `https://aka.ms/SaRA-TeamsPresence-sarahome`.

If you don't want to close Outlook and Teams, click Skip and perform the steps given in this article: `https://docs.microsoft.com/en-us/MicrosoftTeams/troubleshoot/teams-im-presence/issues-with-presence-in-outlook?tabs=64`. Figure 4-14 shows the Teams Presence Test result.

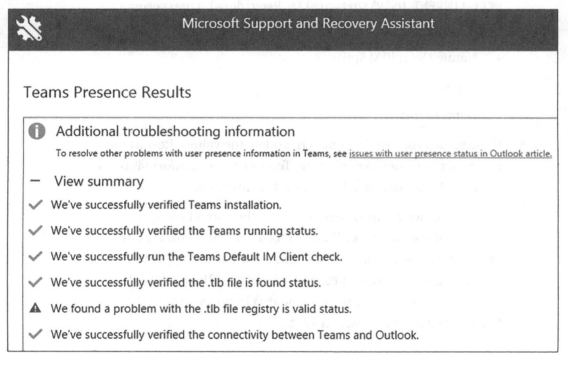

Figure 4-14. Teams Presence results

Additional Troubleshooting Information

1. You must have the Microsoft Teams app installed on your computer, running, and configured to display presence information.

2. For the contact whose presence you can't see, verify that their email address and Teams sign-in address are the same. If they are not, the contact should correct the addresses as necessary, sign out of Teams, and then sign back in.

3. Check the registry settings on your computer to verify that Teams is registered as the default instant messaging (IM) app. Note that improper editing of the registry may severely damage your computer. To check and update the registry, start the Registry Editor (you can search "registry" and locate subkey `HKEY_CURRENT_USER\Software\IM Providers`). Then verify these values:

   - Name: DefaultIMApp

   - Type: REG_SZ

   - Data: Teams

4. If the values you see don't match, update the values. Restart the computer and check whether the Teams presence information is working. If the issue persists, follow the next step.

5. Check whether the .tlb file is present in the correct path. The location of the .tlb file is different for 64-bit and 32-bit versions of Office. For 64-bit Office: `C:\users\<username>\appdata\local\microsoft\teamspresenceaddin\uc.tlb`. For 32-bit Office: `C:\users\<username>\appdata\local\microsoft\teamspresenceaddin\uc.win32.tlb`.

Note   The name of the .tlb file is different for each version.

---

6. If the issue persists, then uninstall and reinstall Teams.

Adding the Teams Meeting Add-in to Outlook

The Teams Meeting add-in for Outlook gives you the ability to create a Teams meeting from an Outlook meeting invite. You can use SARA automated tool to check and resolve the issue.

You can access the tool via a remote connectivity analyzer or by directly browsing the website `https://aka.ms/SaRA-TeamsAddin-sarahome`.

Teams Microphone Captures Background Noise

Multiple things can affect Teams and microphones can capture background noise. The following are the most common things that contribute to background noise:

- Your computer's fans or spinning hard drive is too close to the microphone. They shouldn't be close to the microphone.

- You may be sitting near a fan or air conditioning unit producing static noise. Do not sit next to a fan or air conditioning.

- If you are using a noise-canceling microphone, make sure it is positioned close to the mouth, approximately 2 centimeters or less than 1 inch away from the mouth. This filters out unwanted background noise, so you must place it correctly to avoid audio issues.

- When using the speaker on your phone, make sure that the phone is placed on a flat surface. Also, make sure that there is no obstruction between the phone and your mouth.

- If there is physical damage to the device, try using a different device.

- Make sure that the device you are using is optimized for Microsoft Teams.

The Audio Device Is Causing an Echo in Teams Meetings or Calls

If other people complain that they hear an echo when they are on an audio call with you, it might be caused by the audio device.

- You can turn down your speaker volume to reduce the echo.

- If your microphone or audio device is near a wall or other reflective surface that does not absorb sound, consider moving the microphone or changing its direction away from the reflective surface to reduce potential echoes.

- Using your webcam's microphone or computer speakers, try using a different audio device such as a headset, handset, or standard microphone.

- If possible, try placing the microphone as far away as possible from the computer speakers because the audio output from the speakers may feed into the microphone and produce echoes.

- If you are using a laptop with an integrated sound card that supports Microphone Boost, try disabling Microphone Boost to isolate the issue:

  - Click Start, and then click Control Panel.

  - In Control Panel, click Hardware and Sound, and then click Sound.

  - In the Sound dialog box, on the Recording tab, select your microphone, and then click Properties.

  - In the Microphone Properties dialog box, on the Levels tab, uncheck the Microphone Boost check box (if available).

- Make sure the device you are using is optimized for Microsoft Teams Apps.

Removing Contact Information from Teams

Sometimes Teams users may want to remove a contact from a Teams client. However, they may not see the option to remove a contact as it is under Calls ➤ Contacts. Follow these steps to remove contacts: Go to the Teams app and click Calls ➤ the Contacts tab, find the contact you want to remove, and click three dots (**...**) to expand the menu. Then you can click Remove Contact to remove the contact you don't want. Remember some contacts sync from your phone and Outlook. Some Teams contacts can be removed, but some contact phone numbers that sync from mobile phones cannot be remove. Figure 4-15 shows how to remove a contact.

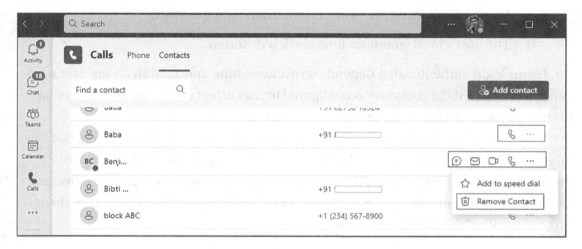

Figure 4-15. *Removing a contact from Teams*

Microsoft Teams Sign-in Issues

Common Teams sign-in problems can be broken down into the following categories:

- **Authentication**: Users enter the wrong username or password.

- **Provisioning**: Users may not be enabled for Teams or be allowed but not authorized to sign in. Another common reason is that directory synchronization has not occurred.

- **End-user configuration**: Software installed on the user's machine may be causing issues reaching the Microsoft 365 services.

- **Networking**: Validate that end users can reach the Microsoft 365 service from their location without an on-premises networking device impeding the communication path.

- **Service-related**: Typically, during service-related issues, all users in a tenant are affected, but not always. Service-related issues can affect certain users (for example, users in a geographic region or on a specific Teams Online Service).

Teams authentication: Teams authentication problem comes down to one of two things:

a.   Users are inputting the wrong user account and password.

b.   The user's local computer time clock is distorted.

Teams login authentication depends on accurate time information on the user's computer. Check if the computer is configured to the correct time zone and verify that the computer clock is no more than +/- 5 minutes off.

If the issue persists, capture basic user information to start troubleshooting. Use this information to identify the user and verify the user's configuration. Capture the user's username/user principal name (UPN). Make sure that the user is using the UserName@Domainname.com format to sign in. Remember that Microsoft (Office) 365 apps do not support the user\domain name format.

User Account Provisioning

The following things needs to check for user provisioning; follow these steps to verify that the user is enabled for Teams. If the user still cannot sign in, continue with the steps outlined in the next sections.

a.   **Verify user enablement for Teams:**

1.   Log into the Microsoft 365 admin center, navigate to Users and search for the username.

2.   Once found, click the name and check that the license is assigned/enabled. Make sure a Teams license is allowed.

3. Make sure the sign-in status is set to sign-in allowed, and verify that the username specified in the Teams client matches with the username shown in the Microsoft 365 admin center. (Admin ➤ active user ➤ user details ➤ Product licenses)

4. If the user is not login-enabled or not licensed, follow your organization's process to re-enable or provision the user for Teams.

b. **Verify directory synchronization including user account:**

1. Verify that the user account was created on Microsoft 365 via Dirsync/Azure AD Connect (if local Active Directory synchronization is in place) and there are no issues with DirSync.

2. The directory synchronization status can be accessed either by clicking on the DirSync Status tile or selecting Health/Directory Sync Status.

3. If there is an issue with the directory synchronization, you might see an error message indicating the problem. Access the Directory Synchronization Errors Report by clicking the *We found DirSync object errors* message or selecting Settings/DirSync Errors on the Admin navigation pane.

c. **End-user configuration:**

To isolate Teams app side problems, you can do a quick test login to the Teams web client (`https://teams.microsoft.com`).

Troubleshooting Using Teams Client Sign-In Logs

After a failed sign-in attempt, one of the first logs to look at is the Sign-in Log incorporated into the Teams client. You can read the log using any text editor; however, the human-readable sign-in logs feature is only on Windows-based desktop clients. You can revisit the section "Collecting Teams Diagnostic Logs."

Note   The firewall or proxy that the user is connected to the Internet through must allow access to Microsoft 365 URLs. You can refer to "Office 365 URLs and IP address ranges" (`https://docs.microsoft.com/en-us/microsoft-365/enterprise/urls-and-ip-address-ranges?view=o365-worldwide#skype-for-business-online-and-microsoft-teams`).

If the issue persists, delete the Teams cache folder and then try to sign in again to the Teams client. Review the logs with a text editor and engage Microsoft support as appropriate.

Service Health: Please reference the Service Health SOF Asset for detailed information on validating Service Health.

End User Audio/Video Quality

Microsoft Teams provides optimal call quality, but sometime a user may experience poor call quality. Most Teams call quality issues are tied to network connections. If a user reports a poor quality issue, follow these steps to troubleshoot:

1. **Verify the network conditions**: A good quality call depends on good network conditions. The client will highlight network connectivity issues during the call. It is always a best practice to switch connectivity (e.g., wireless to wired) if possible because end user will get higher quality on a managed corporate network than on an unmanaged network like public Wi-Fi.

2. **Verify the end user device**: Avoid using built-in audio for better audio and video quality. Always use a USB device listed on the Teams device link at `www.microsoft.com/en-us/microsoft-teams/across-devices/devices/category/headsets/36`. These devices are certified for the best audio and video quality. Connect the device to a different USB port and connect the device directly to the computer; avoid a USB hub for the headset or camera. Also, installing the latest device driver might remediate some audio and video quality issues. Using a headset on your computer's mic/line-in port is not a suitable replacement for a USB device as these devices are dependent on the computer's audio devices.

Troubleshooting Issues with Public and Private Channels

Teams is the central collaboration workspace in Microsoft 365 and it provides the cost and agility benefits of cloud-based chat, presence, audio, video call, and meetings without losing the business-class capabilities of Skype for Business Server. With Teams, Microsoft deploys and maintains the required server infrastructure, and it handles ongoing maintenance, security updates, and upgrades. You can selectively enable users for a Teams subscription in a Microsoft 365 tenant.

Channels in Teams let users manage their work by subject, project, or the most appropriate way to the Team. Figure 4-16 shows the team named Demo Team1 and the channels General and Test. The General channel automatically gets created whenever you create a new team, and it cannot be renamed or removed.

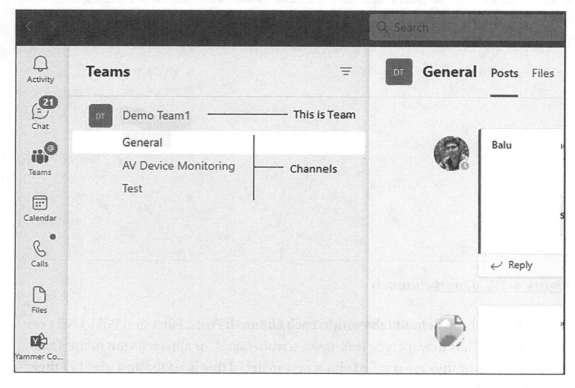

Figure 4-16.   *Team and channel*

Teams Channel Types

- **General channel**: All Teams have a General channel. This cannot be deleted and includes all members of the Team. Figure 4-17 shows the General channel.

- **Public channels** are added for specific purposes and include all Team members. Figure 4-17 shows the public channel as the Test channel.

- **Private channels** are added for specific purposes but only include certain Team members. Private channels display a padlock symbol. Figure 4-17 shows the private channel named Troubleshooting Book.

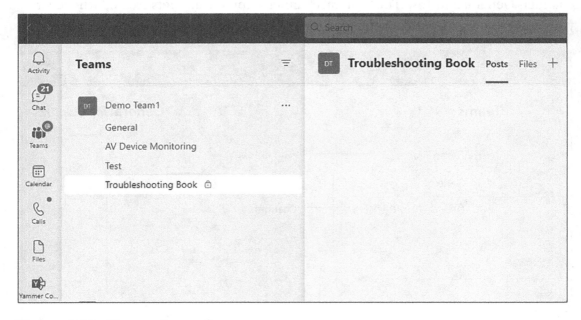

Figure 4-17. *Teams channels*

There are three default tabs within each channel: Posts, Files, and Wiki. Users can also add a tab. Tabs may include lists, tasks, a whiteboard, or apps relevant to the Team. Users can set how they are notified about new material that is added and whether they show or hide channels.

Differences Between the Capabilities of Public and Private Channels

As an admin or support engineer, you must know the different capabilities provided by public and private channels. Public channels are the default, and you must be a Team owner to set a channel as private or be assigned permission to create a private channel in both.

Select Your Team ➤ Manage Team ➤ Settings ➤ Member Permissions ➤ Allow members to create private channels in the Teams client. See Figure 4-18 for member permissions.

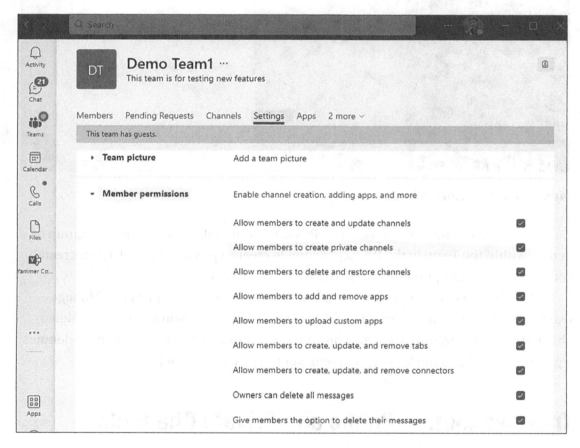

Figure 4-18. *Channel permissions*

The option is enabled in the Team Policy from the Teams admin center. Go to Microsoft Teams admin center ➤ Teams ➤ Teams Policy ➤ Create private channels = On.

Figure 4-19 shows the Teams policies.

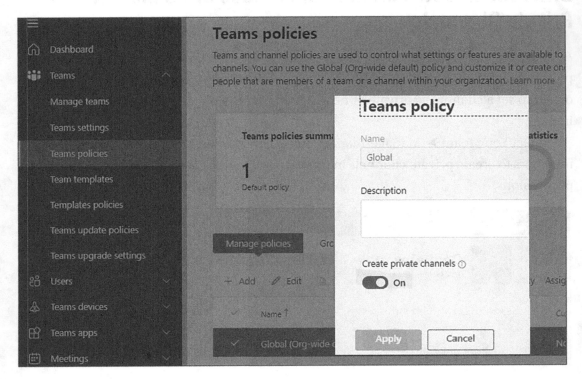

Figure 4-19. *Teams admin center*

In the Create team dialog box, select Private – Accessible only to a specific group of people within the Team in the Privacy section to create a private channel. Once created, you cannot change a public channel to private or vice versa.

Select the three dots for more options next to the team name and select Manage team. From the top navigation, choose Channels to display existing channels, deleted channels, and the option to add another channel. Under type, the globe symbol denotes a public channel and the lock symbol represents a private channel.

Troubleshooting Public and Private Channels

Teams and Channels Have Disappeared from a User's List

For lost channel: Open the Teams client, scroll to the end of the list of channels, select Hidden channels, select the "lost" channel, and then select *Show*. The channel will now be displayed in the user's list of channels.

For hidden Teams: Open the Teams client, scroll to the end of the list of teams, select Hidden teams, expand the list, select the lost teams and then select Show. See Figure 4-20.

Figure 4-20. *Hidden Teams and channels*

Users Unable to Create Private Channels

If the user cannot create a private channel, they have to contact you, as the Teams admin, to check the Teams policy assigned to them and validate if that policy allows private channel creation. Policy modification can be achieved by logging into the Teams admin center and selecting Teams ➤ Teams policies to check whether the policy allows private channels to be created.

A Team Owner Cannot Change a Public Channel to a Private Channel

Microsoft Teams, by design, does not allow public channels to be changed to private channels and private channels to be changed to public channels.

Limitations of Private Channels

Teams private channels are handy for keeping things private. However, there are some limitations to private channels:

- The first limitation is in private channel creation. Teams can create a maximum of 30 private channels.

- Another limitation is member count. Each private channel can have up to 250 members.

- Private channels do not support all apps integration.

- Users can add tabs to a private channel, but not Stream Planner or Forms.

- If a team is created from an existing team, the private channels are not also duplicated.

- Another significant limitation is that the private channel notifications are not included in missed activity emails.

- The retention policies do not support messages in private channels specific to compliance.

Note   The Teams admin can use the Microsoft Graph API to manage private channels.

Managing Permissions, Teams Policies, and Tenant Policies

How a user's account interacts with Teams is influenced by the user's permissions, Teams policies, and tenant policies. These settings work in combination with Teams policies. As a Teams admin, you can set the user permission policies that are assigned to users. And you can assign a policy package to users. These policies determine whether sent messages can be deleted or altered or whether read receipts will be sent for messaging policies.

Troubleshooting and Verifying Teams Channel Email Settings

Users can send emails to the Teams channel. However, before a user can send an email to a Teams channel, the admin must check the email integration settings in the Microsoft Teams admin center. To do so, the first log into the Microsoft Teams admin center, select Teams settings ➤ Email integration, and set *Allow users to send emails to a channel email address* to on. You can define allowed domain names for channel email in the same section. See Figure 4-21.

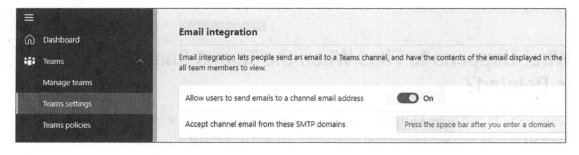

Figure 4-21. *Email integration*

Users can find the channel email address by selecting the three dots for more options at the top right of the channel screen. Select *Get an email address* and select *Copy to copy the email address to the clipboard*. Select Advanced settings to define how the channel email address can be used, such as *Anyone can send emails to this address, Only members of this Team, Only email sent from these domains*, or *Remove email address*.

Alternatively, select the three dots next to the channel name for more options in the channels list and then select Get email address.

Troubleshooting Replication Issues in Teams and Channels

Sometimes users may report problems adding one or more new users to a team or channel so you must verify that the users have been successfully added to the Teams Azure Active Directory. Basically, when users are added or modified, they are automatically added to various active directories. Sometimes there may be a delay in replicating the data into the different Microsoft 365 Active Directories. Use PowerShell to query and validate the data to verify whether a user has been successfully synchronized with the Teams Azure Active Directory. Install the Teams PowerShell module and then connect to it and use these commands to query and validate the data:

- `Get -TeamUser` to verify users belonging to a Team

- `Get -Team` to retrieve teams with a particular property, such as teams that a user belongs to

- `Get-TeamChannelUser` to return users of a particular channel

You can additionally check the status of a new user in the Microsoft admin center. Log into the Teams admin center, and then from the left-hand navigation, select Users ➤ Active Users to display all active users. You can search within the list of users to find the status of a particular user.

What Happens to Files When the Teams Channel Is Deleted?

Team owners can delete any channel in the Team. When a public channel is deleted, the files stay in SharePoint. When a private channel is deleted, the SharePoint files and folders are also deleted.

Private and public channels are also known as "soft deletions" because the deleted channel can be restored within 30 days, including the channel's files.

Restoring a Channel That Was Deleted by Mistake

In Teams, channels are not entirely deleted until 30 days after they were deleted. The team owner can restore the channel by select the three dots next to the team name, then Manage Team ➤ Channels ➤ Deleted. Select Restore next to the channel that was deleted by mistake. Figure 4-22 shows channel restoration.

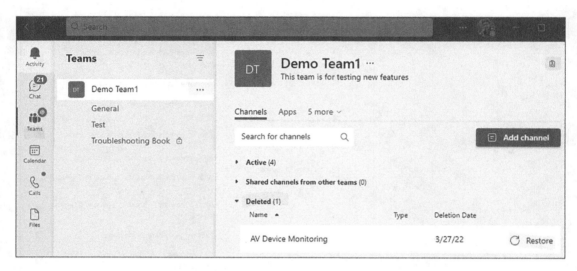

Figure 4-22. *Restoring a deleted channel*

It is essential to prevent users from unintentionally deleting channels. Select the three dots next to the team name, select Manage Team ➤ Settings ➤ Member permissions, and deselect *Allow members to delete and restore channels,* as shown in Figure 4-23.

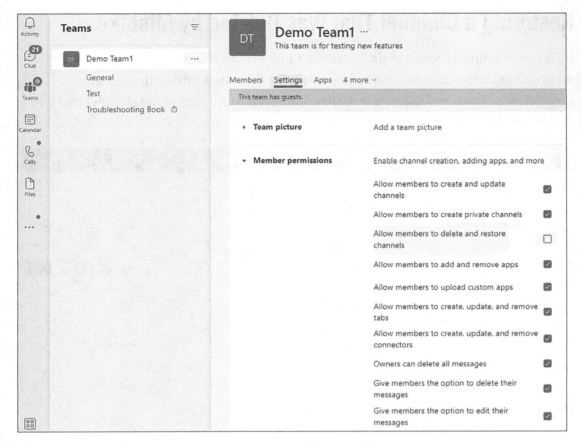

Figure 4-23. *Disallowing members the ability to delete channels*

A User Has Deleted a Private Channel and Cannot Now Create a Public Channel with the Same Name

This is a sync issue. If an error message is displayed stating that the channel already exists, wait 24 hours for the change to populate through the tenant and then try again.

Deploying and Updating Teams Client Software

The Microsoft Teams client provides multiple functionalities, including instant messaging, audio/video calls, meetings, audio conferencing, content sharing, and app integration. As a Teams admin, you must know how to install and update Teams clients.

Installing and Updating Teams Client Software

The installation of the Teams desktop client is a straightforward procedure, and most users can complete this procedure without administrative intervention. One way for users to install the client is to connect to the Download Microsoft Teams website (`www.microsoft.com/en-us/microsoft-teams/download-app`) and select the client they want to install.

However, in most organizations, administrators will want to use more control over the process to ensure users don't experience problems. This section covers Teams client installation and update management with a basic troubleshooting process.

Note   When you install Teams, the Teams installer logs the sequence of events to `%LocalAppData%\SquirrelTemp\SquirrelSetup.log`. Review this log if you experience problems during installation.

Managing Installation and Update Options for a Teams Desktop Client

Apart from downloading the desktop client from the Download Microsoft Teams website, users can initiate an automated installation process from the Office portal. To do so, users can install the Microsoft 365 apps (formerly Office 365 ProPlus), including the Teams desktop client, by using the following process:

1. They can log into Office 365 portal (`https://portal.office.com/`) with their Microsoft 365 account.

2. After login, they can select the Install Office shortcut and then

    - Select Office 365 apps to install the standard Microsoft 365 apps, including Teams.

    - Select Other install options to choose to open their account page. Both options are displayed in Figure 4-24.

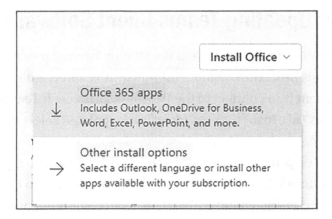

Figure 4-24. *Office installation options*

3. If users select the second option, they can decide to install the
    standard Microsoft 365 apps or specific apps.

Troubleshooting Teams Client Updates

Updates are applied periodically after installing the Teams client according to the update
channel you selected.

If you experience problems when updating, you should collect and review available
logs. After installing Teams, the log location is located in the %LocalAppData%\
Microsoft\Teams folder. In this folder, you'll find two log files:

- SquirrelSetup.log: This file is written by Update.exe, an executable
  that services the Teams app.

- Logs.txt: This file is used by the Teams app (specifically Teams.exe)
  to record significant application events. It could contain updated
  failure information.

Important   Because these log files contain personally identifiable information,
they're not sent to Microsoft.

If the update failure logs don't give helpful insights, consider collecting and
analyzing application and system logs using Windows Sysinternals. Use the procedure in
the "Collect and explore application and system logs" document to learn more.

Note   You can also manually update Teams from within the Teams client. Select the ellipsis button, and then select Check for updates.

Troubleshooting Teams Client Startup and Configuration

Teams have clients for all the platforms, including Windows, macOS, mobile (iOS and Android), and web. Most users use the Teams desktop and mobile clients to connect to Teams. This is why a Teams admin must know how to troubleshoot client startup and configuration.

Teams Desktop Client Startup

If a user reports trouble when they start the Teams desktop client, first decide if the issue is related to the desktop client or the Teams back-end service. To isolate the problem, have the user open Microsoft Edge or Google Chrome and use the Teams web app to sign in. If they can successfully use Teams in their browser, the trouble is related to the desktop client. If the user experiences problems connecting with a browser, check service health in the Microsoft 365 admin center to tell you if the Teams service has any issues.

Here are the high-level steps to troubleshoot the Teams desktop client:

1. Analyze the `SquirrelSetup.log` file in the `%LocalAppData%\Microsoft\Teams` folder. Go to the end of the file and validate if any errors are displayed.

2. Delete the Teams client cache. To do this, follow these steps:

    1. Close the Teams client completely, and if required, use Task Manager to ensure all Teams processes are ended.

    2. In File Explorer, navigate to `%appdata%\Microsoft\Teams`.

    3. Open the `Cache` folder and delete its contents.

    4. Restart Teams and try to sign in.

5. If that doesn't resolve the issue, in `%appdata%\Microsoft\Teams`, consider deleting the contents of the following subfolders:

   a) `\application cache\cache`

   b) `\blob_storage`

   c) `\databases`

   d) `\GPUcache`

   e) `\IndexedDB`

   f) `\Local Storage`

   g) `\tmp`

6. Restart Teams and try to sign in again.

3. If clearing the Teams cache doesn't help, consider installing the latest updates.

4. If the issue does not resolve, think about reinstalling the Teams desktop client.

Troubleshooting Audio and Video Devices

Teams provides optimal audio/video call quality in 1:1 calls or meetings; however, sometimes, call quality may be impacted due to the audio device user is using, their computer, the operating system, their network, or the Teams service. So, multiple things may cause call quality. One of the most common causes is audio and video devices, so using a Teams device is crucial for optimal call quality and a better user experience. However, users can occasionally experience problems with audio and video device configuration.

Here are the most common things that need to be verified.

First, validate Teams policy settings: Sometimes Teams policy settings that are applied to a set of users or single users may affect the audio/video call ability. For example, a policy may prohibit the use of audio/video calls. It is a good practice to verify policy settings before you inspect device configuration. An excellent place to start for difficulties in meetings is by reviewing the audio and video policy settings.

To verify the settings, log into the Microsoft Teams admin center (`https://admin.teams.microsoft.com/`) and review the Audio & video section of the appropriate meeting policy. Figure 4-25 shows the modes of the IP audio and video. Make sure that IP video is set to On. If video quality is poor, increasing the Media bit rate (Kbs) value helps.

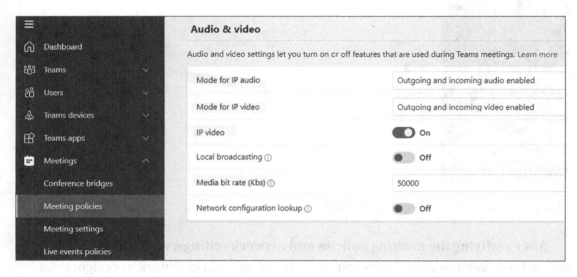

Figure 4-25. *IP audio and video are enabled.*

The next thing to check is network settings: Teams require specific network ports to be accessible. They can be assessed or controlled in the Meeting settings page in the Microsoft Teams admin center. It is essential that the audio and video ports are available and allowed on your organization's network environment. Additionally, for optimal call quality, you must have set up and inserted Quality of Service marks for real-time media traffic. Figure 4-26 shows the QoS and the audio, video, and sharing port numbers.

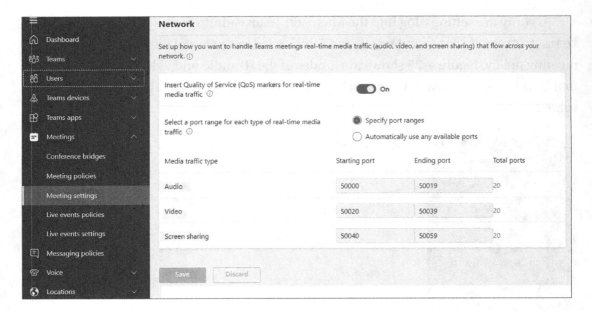

Figure 4-26. *Teams meeting settings*

After verifying the meeting policies and network settings, verify audio and video device (speaker/mic) configuration: The next thing to check is device configuration. Begin by confirming if the audio and video Teams certified device is correctly connected and installed on the user's computer. If not, then start by troubleshooting the devices in Windows.

1.   Log into the Teams client, click on (**...**), select Settings, and then select Devices. Select the appropriate audio device, speaker, or microphone.

2.   You can test the audio device by making a call under *Automatically adjusted mic sensitivity.* Figure 4-27 shows the device settings.

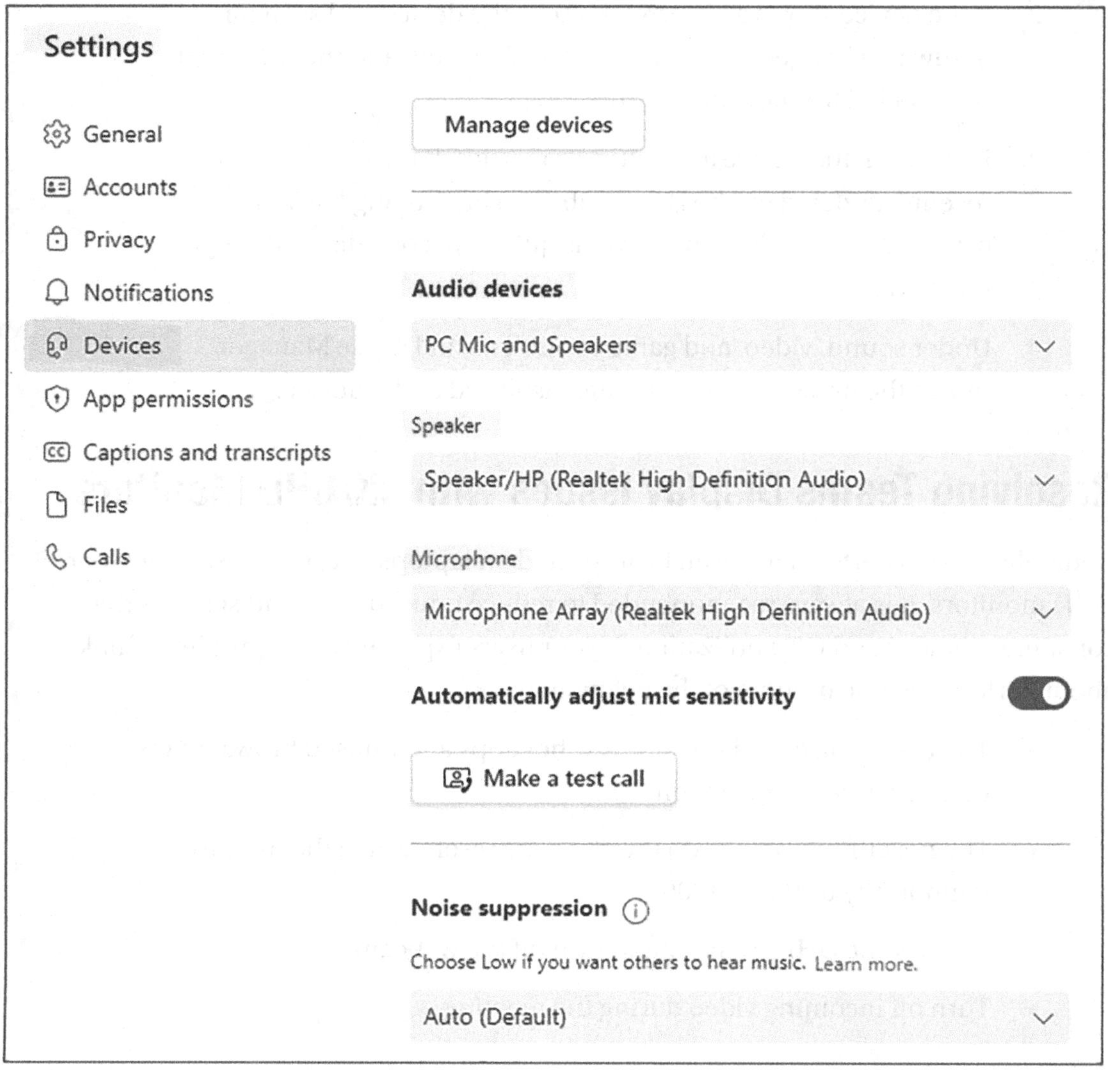

Figure 4-27. *Device settings*

3. You can check the camera under the device settings by select the appropriate camera device and check if it shows correctly.

If your devices don't show properly in Settings, consider advanced troubleshooting in Device Manager. Follow these steps to troubleshoot audio and video devices in Device Manager:

1. Right-click Start and select Device Manager, locate Cameras, and select your camera in the device list.

2. If the device shows as In error, remove the device and scan for hardware changes. The device will be detected, and the driver will be installed from the driver store.

3. Right-click the device and select Properties. If the driver has been recently updated on the Driver tab, consider rolling back the driver. Alternatively, if the driver is quite old, consider updating the driver.

4. Under sound, video, and game controllers, in Device Manager, repeat the preceding steps for the displayed audio device.

Resolving Teams Display Issues with 4K/UHD Monitors

Generally, Teams performance can be impacted on laptops docked to external 4K or UHD monitors. It is always recommended to reduce unused apps and services that consume memory and CPU utilization. If your users experience this problem, think about performing one or more of the below steps:

- The first thing to do is close any other apps and unused browser tabs that may reduce utilization.

- The next thing you can do is reduce the resolution of the monitor temporarily to 1920 x 1080.

- Undock the UHD monitor and turn off the webcam.

- Turn off incoming video during the meeting.

Troubleshooting Teams Desktop Client Performance Issues

Usually, the Teams client performs well and provides better call quality. Teams client performance is dependent on multiple things, which is why it can be challenging to identify the cause of performance-related problems. However, if your users complain about performance issues in Teams, you can start the investigation by reviewing resource usage.

Open Task Manager and check the CPU and memory usage; if you see high use, try to close apps and consider further investigating. Figure 4-28 shows the task manager.

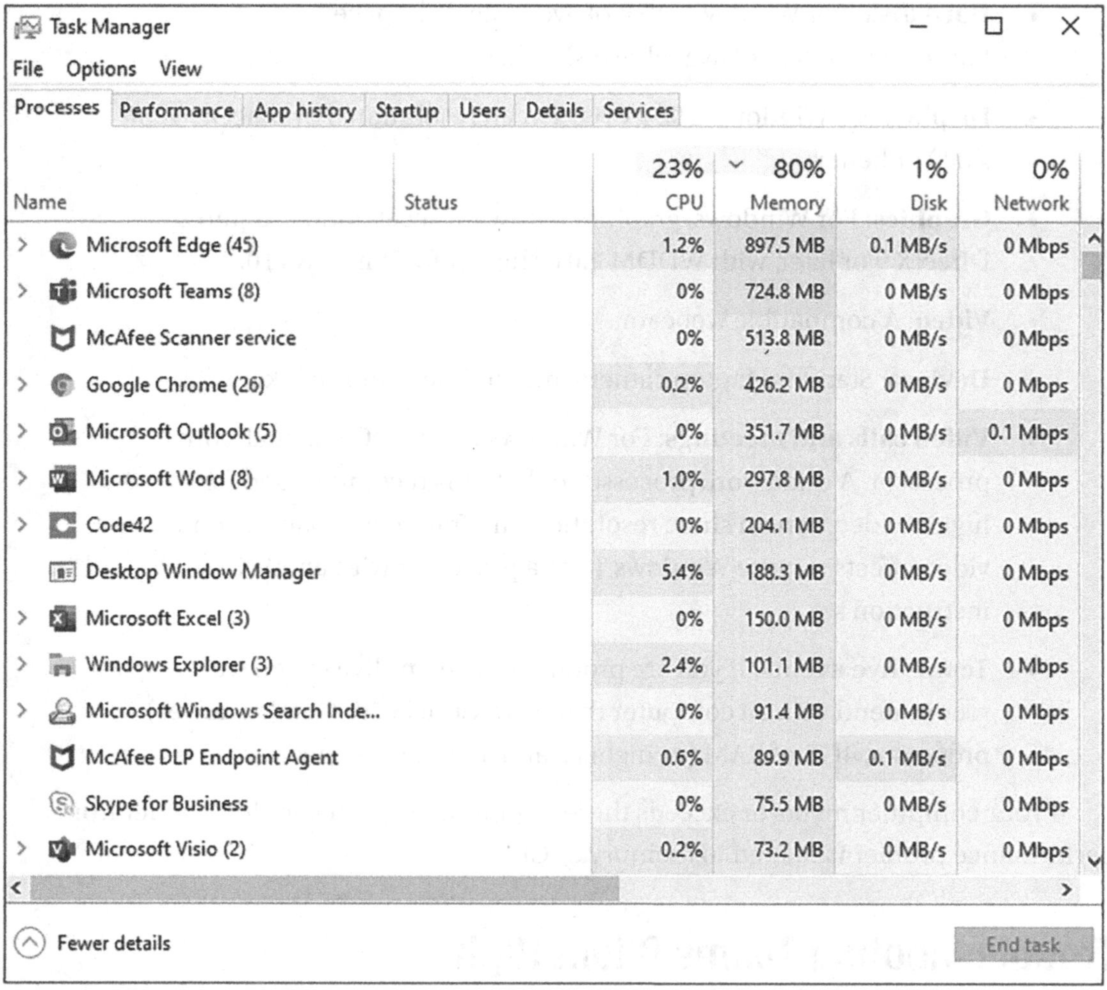

Figure 4-28. *Task manager showing app names*

Hardware Requirements for Teams Clients

It's essential to ensure that your computer meets the recommended hardware requirements to properly support the needs of the Teams client. These requirements are summarized here:

- **CPU**: For Windows, a minimum 1.6GHz (or higher) dual-core processor. For macOS, an Intel Core Duo processor.

- **Memory**: For both Windows and macOS, 4GB of RAM.

- **Hard disk**: For Windows, 3GB of available disk space. For macOS, 1.5GB of available disk space.

- **Display**: For Windows, 1024 x 768 screen resolution. For macOS, 1280 x 800 or better.

- **Graphics**: For Windows, graphics hardware acceleration requires DirectX 9 or later, with WDDM 2.0 or higher for Windows 10.

- **Video**: A compatible webcam

- **Devices**: Standard laptop camera, microphone, and speakers

- **Video calls and meetings**: For Windows and macOS, a dual-core processor. A quad-core processor or better is recommended for higher video/screen share resolution and frame rate. Background video effects require Windows 10 or a processor with an AVX2 instruction set.

- **Teams live events**: If you are producing a Teams live event, we recommend using a computer that has a Core i5 7th Gen (or newer) processor, 4GB of RAM (or higher), and a hardware encoder.

If your computer meets or exceeds these requirements, you shouldn't suffer from performance problems related to memory or CPU.

Troubleshooting Teams Client High Resource Consumption

Sometimes the user may see that the Teams client is using resources at a high rate of consumption, which impacts overall performance. Basically, a Teams client requires a dedicated 4GB of RAM over and above any other system requirements, so a user's computer requires 8GB of RAM as a minimum. If that's not the case, the user might struggle to optimize the Teams' performance.

Fundamentally, the Teams client is adjusted to only make use of memory when it's accessible. In other words, when the user's computer has more memory, Teams utilizes that memory. If a computer has insufficient available memory, Teams will use less. If users face Teams performance issues due to insufficient memory on their computer to run workloads, adding memory or reducing the application workloads is recommended.

You need to keep in mind that not all modern computers support the installation of additional memory. So, if users frequently see performance issues, they might need to switch to different devices to isolate performance issues with their computers. Once the problem is isolated, refresh their computer.

For the CPU, if you determine that Teams is degrading system performance because of excessive CPU usage, there are some minor changes to the Team client configuration that could help:

- **Disable hardware acceleration in Teams**: In Settings, select *the Disable GPU hardware acceleration (requires restarting Teams)* check box on the General tab. Then restart Teams.

- **De-register Teams as the chat app for Office**: In Settings, on the General tab, clear the *Register Teams as the chat app for Office (requires restarting Office applications)* check box. Then restart Teams. Figure 4-29 shows disabling hardware acceleration and reregistering team chat apps for Office.

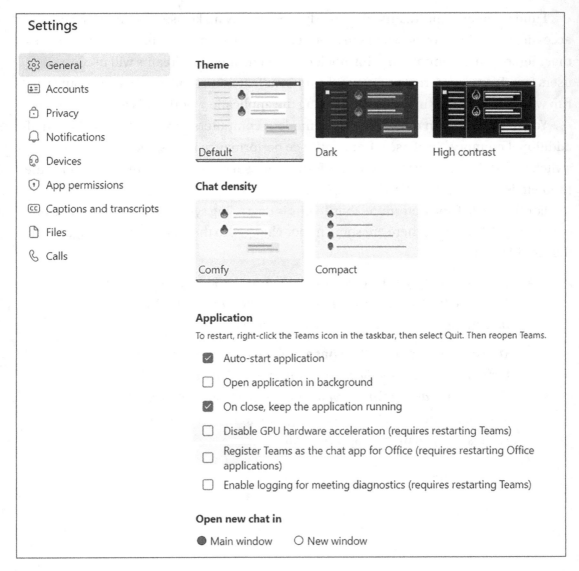

Figure 4-29. *Disable hardware acceleration and reregister Teams apps for Office*

It is a best practice to remove workloads by closing unused apps and browser tabs. Additionally, considering clearing the Teams cache help with performance issue.

Exploring Network Issues and Optimizing Network Performance

Teams call quality issues are pretty difficult to troubleshoot and can be tied with multiple things. One of the common causes of poor Teams client performance and call quality can be networking issues. When troubleshooting network-related problems, it's essential to take a logical, step-by-step approach. You can follow these steps to identify the cause of network latency, poor audio call quality, file upload delays, and slow chats:

1. **Test Microsoft 365 network connectivity:** From the Microsoft 365 admin center, select Health and then choose Network connectivity. Launch the Network Connectivity Test to measure the connectivity between your device and the Internet to Microsoft's network. Insights from these measurements can help you discover and understand connectivity problems for individual office locations and how you can update your network architecture to improve connections to Microsoft 365. This can dramatically increase productivity and satisfaction for people in your organization. Figure 4-30 shows network connectivity.

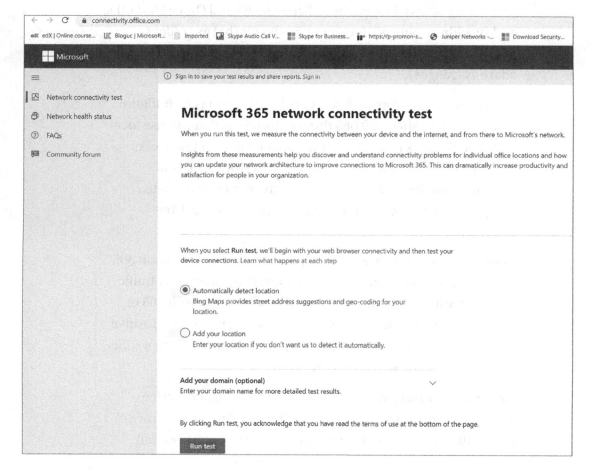

Figure 4-30. *Microsoft 365 network connectivity*

2. **Utilize the Teams network planner:** A network planner helps you determine and organize network requirements for connecting people who use Teams across your organization in a few steps. Provide your networking details, such as sites, subnets, and WAN and ExpressRoute connections. Then enter your estimated Teams usage, and the Network planner calculates your network requirements for Teams and cloud voice across your organization. Launch the Network Planner tool from the Microsoft Teams admin center.

3. **Verify external DNS name resolution:** Verify that all Teams clients can resolve external DNS queries for services provided by Microsoft 365 or Office 365. Ensure that your firewalls are not preventing access. Review the "Microsoft 365 and Office 365 URLs, and IP address ranges" document for details (`https://docs.microsoft.com/en-us/microsoftteams/office-365-urls-ip-address-ranges`).

4. **Verify routing to Microsoft data centers:** Ensure you configure connectivity to Microsoft 365 through locations that can use local or regional egress points to connect to the Microsoft network. Review the "Microsoft 365 network connectivity overview" document for details (`https://docs.microsoft.com/en-us/microsoft-365/enterprise/microsoft-365-networking-overview`).

5. **Configure a split-tunnel VPN:** Bypass the VPN for Microsoft 365 traffic by using split tunneling. Split tunneling means that traffic for Microsoft 365 or Office 365 goes directly to Microsoft 365 or Office 365 and avoids the VPN. Split tunneling has a very positive impact on Teams performance and quality. To implement a split-tunnel VPN, work with your VPN vendor.

6. **Implement QoS:** Consider implementing Quality of Service to configure packet prioritization for Teams. This will improve team call quality and help you monitor and troubleshoot call

quality. You should implement QoS on all segments of a managed network. Review the "Implement Quality of Service (QoS) in the Microsoft Teams" document for additional details (`https://docs.microsoft.com/en-us/microsoftteams/qos-in-teams`).

Evaluate Teams Web Traffic and Review HTTP Status Codes

Consider using a network analyzer if you want to analyze the details of communications between your Teams client and the Microsoft 365 services it connects to, one that can capture and display HTTP status codes. These codes help you to identify and troubleshoot Microsoft 365 traffic.

Installing and Troubleshooting the Teams Meeting Add-In

The Microsoft Teams Meeting add-in in Outlook allows users to schedule meetings from Outlook. When the add-in is installed in the Calendar feature in Outlook, it displays two tiles in the ribbon, such as Meet Now and New Teams Meeting. Users can use this option to schedule Teams meeting.

Installing the Teams Meeting Add-In

In Outlook, the Teams Meeting add-in is automatically installed for users with Microsoft Teams and Office 2013 or newer installed on their Windows 10 computer. There is no specific and different installation method for the Teams Meeting add-in. The Teams Meeting add-in isn't supported if users deployed Office Outlook from the Microsoft Store. If users can't see the Teams Meeting add-in, follow these steps:

1. First, completely close both Outlook and Teams. You can end the process through Task Manager.

2. Restart the Teams client and sign into Teams.

3. Restart the Outlook client.

If you cannot install the Teams meeting add-in, you might need to check the Teams meeting policy, which can control add-in deployment.

Configuring Teams Meeting Policy Settings

To configure the necessary meeting policy setting, you can use the Microsoft Teams admin center.

1. Log into the Teams admin center, select Meetings, and select Meeting policies.

2. In the details pane, select the appropriate policy. Enabling the Outlook add-in meetings setting enables the deployment of the add-in. Refer to Figure 4-31 for meeting policies.

3. When you've configured the desired settings, select Save.

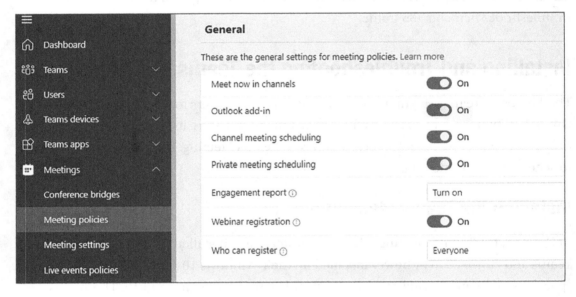

Figure 4-31. *Allowing the Outlook add-in setting*

- **Outlook add-in**: Defines if a user can schedule meetings from Outlook using the add-in.

- **Private meeting scheduling**: Determines if users can schedule private meetings in Teams. A meeting is private if it's not published to a channel in a team.

Note The Teams client installs the correct add-in by deciding if users need the 32-bit or 64-bit version.

Troubleshooting the Teams Meeting Add-In

If users experience problems with utilizing the add-in after making the necessary policy changes, verify that the add-in is installed and not disabled:

1. From Outlook, select File ➤ Options ➤ Add-ins.

2. Verify the presence of the Microsoft Teams Meeting add-in for Microsoft Outlook in the Active Application Add-ins list.

3. If the add-in appears in the Disabled Application Add-ins list, in Manage, select COM Add-ins and then choose Go.

4. Set the checkbox next to Microsoft Teams Meeting Add-in for Microsoft Office.

5. Select OK on all dialog boxes and restart Outlook. Figure 4-32 shows how to enable Teams Outlook add-ins.

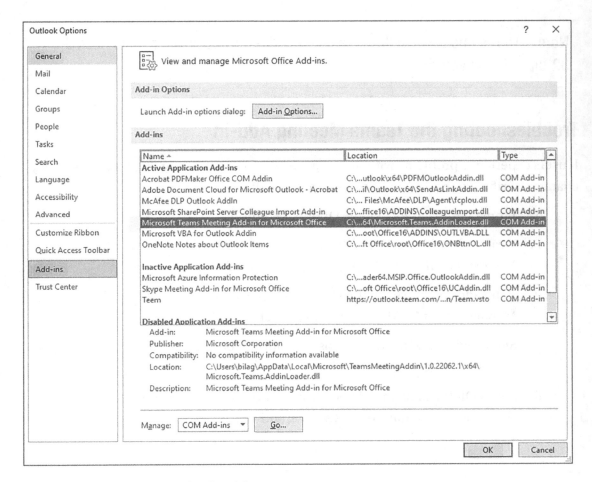

Figure 4-32. *Teams Outlook add-ins*

If the add-in is not installed, consider running the Microsoft Support Recovery Assistant. This tool will check for common problems and make appropriate suggestions to resolve issues it discovers. If you prefer, you can perform the following tasks instead of running the Microsoft Support Recovery Assistant:

1. Verify that the user is assigned a policy that allows the Outlook add-in and allows scheduling private meetings.

2. Verify that the user has permission to execute `regsvr32.exe`.

3. Check that all available updates for the Outlook desktop client have been applied.

4. Complete the following steps:

a. Restart the Teams desktop client.

b. Sign out and then sign back into the Teams desktop client.

c. Restart the Outlook desktop client.

Understanding Teams External and Guest Access and Troubleshooting Any Issues

Microsoft Teams provides internal as well as external communication and collaboration functionalities. Microsoft Teams lets users work with people inside and outside your organization, including collaborators, vendors, providers, or consultants. Teams provide two choices to collaborate and communicate with authenticated users outside of their organization when using Teams.

1. **External (federated) access**: External access enables access permission to users of an entire external domain. External access is a type of federation that allows users to find, call, chat, and set up meetings with people in other organizations. This external/federated communication is peer-to-peer and does not need group or channel.

2. **Guest access**: Guest access provides access permission to an individual. Guest access lets users invite people from outside your organization to join a team. Invited people get a guest account in Azure Active Directory.

When comparing guest access and external access, the critical thing to remember is that guest access grants access permission to an individual. In contrast, external access grants access permission to an entire domain.

Guest access: Guest access in Teams lets people outside your organization access teams and channels inside your organization. A guest isn't an employee, student, or member of the organization and doesn't have a school or work account with your organization. For example, guests might include partners, vendors, suppliers, or consultants.

Anyone can be added as a guest in Teams. Anyone with a business (with an Azure AD account) or consumer email account can participate as a guest in Teams and have full access to team chats, meetings, and files.

Organizations utilizing Teams can offer this external access while maintaining complete control over their own corporate data. All guests in Teams are covered by the exact compliance and auditing protection as the rest of Microsoft 365 and can be managed securely within Azure AD.

Before you get involved in fine-tuning and troubleshooting guest access within specific services, it's good to make sure guest access and external access are enabled at an organizational level.

Verifying External and Guest Access Settings

Both external access and guest access are tenant-level settings in Teams and are turned off by default. To verify if external and guest access are enabled, log into the Microsoft Teams admin center, select Users, and then choose external access or guest access.

Configuring External Access

External access allows communicating with other users outside of your organization. Your users can add apps when they host meetings or chats with external users. Teams enables external access for your Teams and Skype for Business users, allowing or blocking communication with users who are outside of your organization. You can also choose to allow or block communications on a per-domain basis. Figure 4-33 shows external access options.

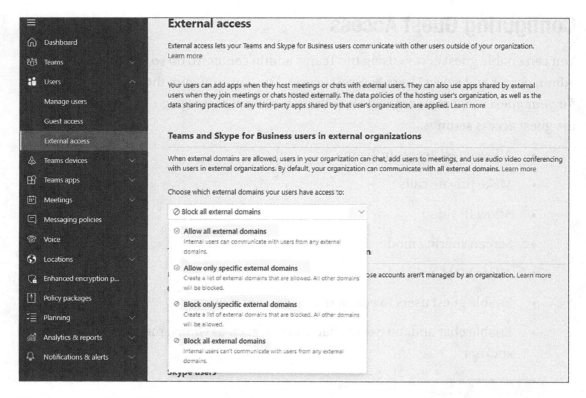

Figure 4-33. *Enabling external access*

External access can be configured in four ways, as follows:

- **Allow all external domains:** This option allows all internal users to communicate with users from any external domains. This option allows all domains.

- **Allow only specific external domains:** This option is more secure/ restricted, allowing for you to create a list of allowed external domains. All other domains will be blocked. Most organization chooses this option.

- **Block only specific external domains:** This option allows you to create a list of blocked external domains. All other domains will be allowed.

- **Block all external domains:** This option does not allow any external communication. This means internal users can't communicate with users from any external domains.

Configuring Guest Access

You can enable guest access using the Teams admin center. To do so, log into the Teams admin center and select Users ➤ Guest access. You can configure the following settings for your guest users at an org-wide level from the Guest access page. Figure 4-34 shows the guest access settings.

- Allow guest access in Teams

- Make private calls

- Allow IP video

- Screen sharing mode

- Allow Meet Now

- Enable guest users to edit or delete the sent message

- Enable chat and the use of chat features, such as Giphy, memes, and stickers

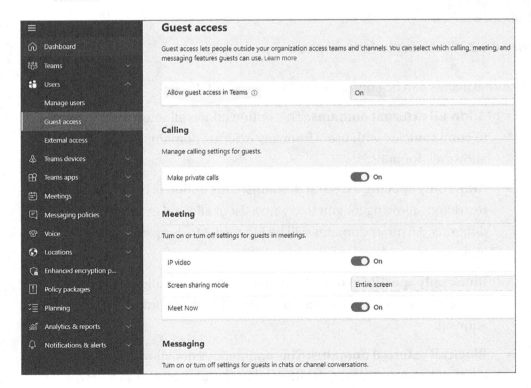

Figure 4-34. *Enabling guest access*

Troubleshooting Teams External Access

Using Microsoft Teams External access, Teams users can participate in chats and calls to users in other domains. Specifically, external access allows users to find, call, and send you instant messages and set up meetings with other domain users.

Use External Access When…

- You have users in different domains in your business. For example, your user `bilag@bloguc.com` can initiate a chat/call with another domain user named `Balu@abc.com`. You cannot search for an external user using a display name; you must use a complete email address like `bilag@bloguc.com`.

- You want the people in your organization to use Teams to contact people in specific businesses outside of your organization.

- You want anyone else in the world who uses Teams to be able to find and contact you using your email address.

If users from outside your organization are unable to collaborate with users within your organization, then follow these steps:

1. First, check whether you have enabled and configured external access in your organization.

2. Confirm that you have allowed the external domain in your Teams admin center under External domain and that the external domain administrator has also allowed your domain on their Teams tenant. You may need to wait for multiple hours to sync these settings.

3. Determine whether the type of collaboration sought is supported by external access because external allows one-to-one communication, including chat, call file share, and meetings.

4. Always use a complete email address to initiate the chat with an external user. Make sure they share the proper email address.

5. External access enables you to communicate with users from other domains already using Teams. Therefore, they must provide their own licenses to make use of Teams.

Troubleshooting Guest Access

If you want users from outside your organization to access teams and channels, guest access is the only way to make that happen. A team owner in Microsoft Teams can add and manage guests in their teams via a web, mobile, or desktop client. Anyone with a business or consumer email accounts, such as Outlook, Gmail, or others, can participate as a guest in Teams, with full access to team chats, meetings, and files. People outside your organization, such as partners or consultants, can be added as guests, and people from within your organization can join as regular team members.

If guests from outside your organization are unable to collaborate with users within your organization, you must follow these steps:

1. First, verify whether you have enabled guest access for Teams.

2. Determine whether the type of collaboration sought is supported by guest access.

3. Verify that the appropriate meeting, messaging, and call policies are configured correctly for guest access.

4. Verify that the guest users have available licenses in your organization.

5. Guest access utilizes your existing licenses when using certain features. Teams doesn't restrict the number of guests you can add. The total number of guests that can be added to your tenant is based on what your Azure AD licensing allows (usually five guests per licensed user).

Verifying Guest Meeting Configuration Policies

If you have supported and configured guest access at an organizational level, you might need to verify the settings for policies for meetings. If guest users experience issues when creating meetings, review the meeting policy settings for participants and guests. Figure 4-35 shows the meeting policy settings for participants and guests.

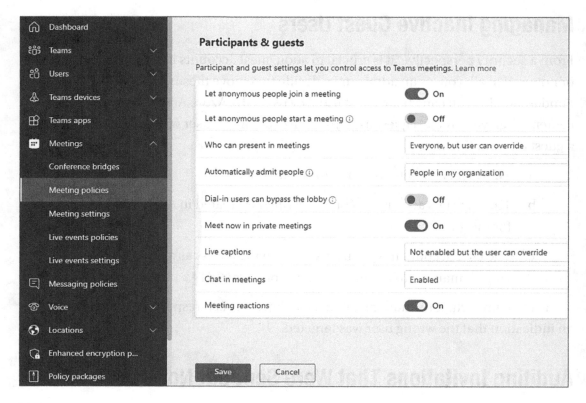

Figure 4-35. Teams meeting policy for guests

- **Let anonymous people start a meeting:** Enables an unauthenticated user to start a meeting. A user might connect anonymously when they connect to a meeting using their phone.

- **Allow Meet now in private meetings:** Determines if a user can start an unplanned private meeting.

- **Automatically admit people:** Determines who can automatically enter a meeting. For guests, you can select *Everyone, People in my organization and guests,* or *People in my organization, trusted organizations, and guests.*

Managing Inactive Guest Users

From a security perspective, it is crucial to audit guest accounts if they are intermittently or not used at all; you, as an admin, may decide to remove these accounts. Fundamentally, you can create guest users by using the Azure Active Directory admin center. When you create a guest user, you utilize the Invite user option. When you create a guest account this way,

a. The user is sent an invitation to collaborate.

b. Then a user's account of *User type: Guest* is created in Azure AD for the guest.

c. The user account has the user's own email address as a prefix to your domain suffix. Example: balui_abc.com#EXT#@bloguc.com

It's also important to audit invitations that haven't been responded to. This might be an indication that the wrong user was targeted.

Auditing Invitations That Were Sent but Not Used

Sometimes you invite guest users, but they may not respond or accept the invite, so it is essential to identify such users to remove their invitations or reinvite them. Guest user accounts created with an invitation are marked with *Creation type: Invitation*. To find out which users were invited as guests, filter the list of displayed users in the Azure Active Directory admin center by *Creation type: Invitation*.

Add the Invitation state column to the display to validate whether users have accepted the invite. Those users who have accepted their invites are displayed with an Invitation state of *Accepted*. Those that have not displayed *Pending acceptance*. You can now choose whether to remove the users with pending invitation states. To access this information, log into the Azure Active Directory admin center, select the appropriate user, and select the Sign-ins tab. Then set the date to the crucial period (the most extended period is one month) and review the activity.

Auditing Inactive Accounts

Inactive accounts present a security risk. You should periodically check which accounts are not being unused. One approach is to review the sign-in history of a user account.

If a user hasn't signed in over the last month, consider deleting the user account. If you'd like to go further back than one month, consider using Windows PowerShell or Microsoft Graph. You can find out more by reviewing the "How To: Manage inactive user accounts in the Azure AD" document.

Troubleshooting Issues with Teams Apps (First and Third Party)

Teams have one or more channels to focus on specific tasks. This is where people chat, hold meetings, share files, and add apps to improve their productivity. When users have problems with channels or working with apps, their efficiency is reduced. This section covers Teams app management and basic troubleshooting information.

Teams Admin Center App Management

The admin center has added admin app discovery and user requests for apps and has simplified the policy setup. The new interface for the Manage App page, which shows the app category list and editorial banners, supports the discovery of relevant apps for an admin.

Admin app discovery: In the Teams admin center, there is an enhanced app details page that shows the category of apps that helps you browse different types shorted by popularity. Furthermore, it offers a banner on top with an image and description to provide a recommendation to admins.

Users can request apps: As of April 2022, if apps are blocked in the Teams admin center, the end user cannot discover them in the Teams client. To improve this experience, Microsoft is creating improvements for app management. One of the improvements is that end users can request to add an app that they discovered as a blocked app in the Teams client app marketplace. Additionally, as a Teams admin, you will get insights about apps desired by the end users on the Manage apps page.

App setup policy enhancement: There are improvements to the in-app setup policy, such as messaging extensions apps can be pinned in the app setup policy for the admin and apps available in both personal and messaging extension contexts are suggested in both contexts. The admin can control lists by changing the order, appearance, and pinged apps sections. User-pinned apps render after admin pinned apps.

Additionally, it allows group assignments such as a setup policy to be assigned to a group or a distribution list. Also, existing precedence rules and rankings are applied.

From a security and compliance angle, the apps discovery capabilities are vast components of security hygiene. Across the security landscape, we discuss many risks and shadow IT because unknown apps or services within our environment are approved and regulated by IT.

Troubleshooting Issues with Apps

Teams allow users to do more than host meetings and chat. Out-of-the-box functionality includes file sharing, Wikis, and tabs; however, this functionality can be extended by allowing users to add apps, either developed by Microsoft, third parties, or the organization's own custom apps. This enables someone joining a new team to have everything they need to be productive together in one place. There are times when Teams apps don't work as expected. That is where the apps troubleshooting approach helps.

Configuring Teams to Allow or Block an App

The Teams admin center is where administrators can actively manage which apps users can add to their channels. From the left-hand navigation in the Teams admin center, select Teams apps. This shows the different options, including *Manage apps by defining which apps users can add, Define Permission policies, Defining set up policies*, and *Customize store*.

Manage apps: Allows management of which apps users in your organization can add to Teams, including custom apps developed by your organization. Log into the Teams admin center and select Teams apps ➤ Manage apps. Org-wide app settings control the performance for all users and override any other app permission policies assigned to users. You can make use of them to control problematic apps. The org-wide settings page is divided into several parts: tailored apps, third-party apps, custom apps, and external access.

- **Tailored apps:** Users with F licenses will get customized apps pinned on their behalf when signing into Teams. You can allow tailored apps using the admin center.

- **Third-party apps:** You can control which third-party apps can be installed in your organization. You can allow third-party apps.

- **New third-party apps published to the store:** Allow any new third-party apps posted to the store by default. This allows users to install new third-party apps published to the store for your organization, based on their Teams apps permission policy.

- **Custom apps:** You can control custom apps. Allow users to add custom apps developed as app packages and uploaded. Select *Save* if you make changes.

- **External apps:** Your users can add apps when they host meetings or chats with external users. The data policies of the hosting user's organization and the data-sharing practices of any third-party apps shared by that user's organization are applied. Go to External access to allow or block external domains. Figure 4-36 shows org-wide options.

Permission policies: As a Teams admin, use app permission policies to specify which categories of apps are available to users. You can either modify the Global policy applied to everyone in your organization or add specific (custom) policies and assign them to users or groups of users. There are three categories of apps: Microsoft apps, third-party apps, and custom apps. For each type, you *can Allow all, Allow specific apps, Block all*, or *Block particular apps*.

You should modify the Global policy first, defining settings appropriate to most users in your organization. If the Global policy does not meet your needs, create policies for specific groups of users. If you have created one or more app permission policies, you must assign them to individuals or groups of users. Figure 4-36 shows all options for Teams apps, including managing apps, permission policies, setup policies, customize store, and org-wide app settings.

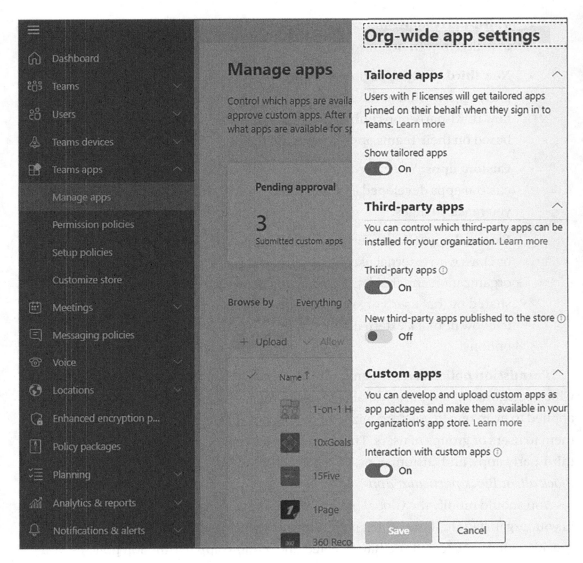

Figure 4-36. Managing apps

The setup policies enable you to control how users interact with Teams apps. Setup policies allow you different options like allowing user pinning and installing apps, which will you to install apps for users to ensure they have the software they need. You can also determines the order in which apps appear in the Teams navigation bar.

The Customize store option allows you to customize the Teams app store with your organization's logo, corporate colors, background, and text color.

Troubleshooting Issues Interoperating with Skype for Business

Microsoft Teams and Skype for Business (On-premises) can collaborate within the same organization. Interoperability is the word used for communication between Teams and Skype for Business when both systems are installed. While the two systems coexist, a user can be assigned a coexistence mode (sometimes called an upgrade mode), either by default or by an administrator.

Island: Each client application, either Skype for Business or Teams, operates as a separate island. Skype for Business clients communicate with other Skype for Business clients. Teams clients talk to other Teams clients. This is the default mode and requires users to have both clients always open. Federated users (people outside your organization) have their messages delivered to Skype for Business. Island mode does not provide interoperability; each system communicates only with clients of the same design.

Teams Only: Users upgrade to Teams and use Teams for most of their communication. They use Skype for Business only to communicate with users who have not yet upgraded. Teams Only mode makes Teams the default SIP/Tel protocol app. Links in a user's contact card in Outlook for calling or chat are handled by Teams.

Skype for Business Only users only use Skype for Business for chat, meetings, and calls, and do not use Teams. You can use this mode while planning your deployment of Teams.

Skype for Business With Teams Collaboration: This mode introduces users to Teams in a controlled way. This mode leaves Skype for Business unchanged for chat, calling, and meeting capabilities and adds Teams collaboration capabilities such as Teams and channels, access to files in Microsoft 365, and applications that include Teams communications capabilities, such as private chat, calling, and scheduling meetings. As an admin, you must note that the Teams private chat, calling, and scheduling meetings are off by default in this mode.

Skype for Business With Teams Collaboration and Meetings: This mode is also known as Meetings First because it accelerates the adoption of the Teams meeting capability. This coexistence mode benefits organizations with Skype for Business on-premises deployments with Enterprise Voice. These organizations are likely to take some time to upgrade to Teams and want to benefit from the special Teams meetings as soon as possible.

To assign the upgrade mode for users, log into the Microsoft Teams Admin center. Select Teams, then select the *Teams to upgrade settings,* and set the appropriate coexistence mode in the left navigation. Figure 4-37 shows the Teams upgrade settings with available coexistence modes.

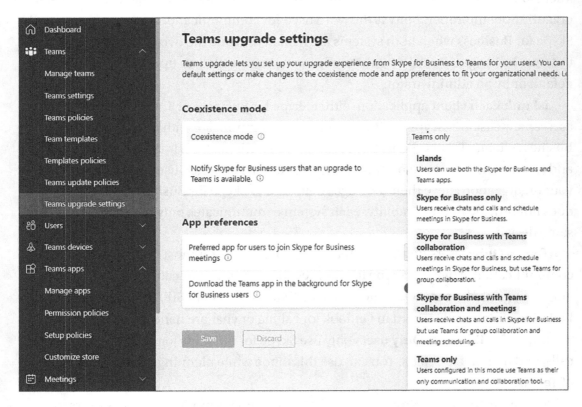

Figure 4-37. *Teams upgrade settings*

Troubleshooting Federation Issues Between Teams and Skype or Skype for Business

Microsoft Teams users can federate with Skype for Business on-premises users using external access. External access uses the SIP Interoperability gateway of Skype for Business. This allows Teams users to chat and join audio or video meetings with external Skype for Business users.

If someone cannot reach a Skype for Business user in another tenant, go to the Teams admin center, then Users, and then select External access and make sure using your Skype for Business domain is allowed.

Native Interop and Interop Escalation

Native and interop escalation are used depending on the coexistence modes assigned to users. A native interop experience occurs within the client when one user is in Skype for Business and the other is in Teams. Native interop does require users to start another client but lets them chat with the client they're currently using.

Native interop allows Skype for Business users to chat one-on-one with Teams users and vice versa. An interop chat goes through an interop gateway, part of Teams cloud service. Interop chats are plain text; rich text and emoticons are not supported. Users are notified when their conversation is an interop conversation.

An interop escalation experience occurs when a user performs an advanced action, such as sharing their desktop. The client facilitates the creation of a meeting that users can join to continue the experience. The conference is created on the platform of the initiator of the action, and those not on that platform receive a meeting join link. When they select the link, they join the meeting in a compatible client such as a browser, web app, or full client, depending on the configuration.

Both Skype for Business and Teams clients are supported in interoperability experiences in-tenant and cross-tenant (federated) communication.

Troubleshooting Interop Chat Scenarios

You are working in Microsoft Teams, and messages from an external contact are not being delivered. Check whether you are in Island or Teams Only mode. If you are in Island mode and the external contact is using Skype for Business, messages will be delivered to Skype for Business and not Microsoft Teams. To solve this problem, upgrade to Teams Only mode to provide all messages and calls from outside your organization to Teams.

You Are Unable to Start a Chat Conversation Using Skype for Business

Check the user's upgrade mode. The Teams Only method does not allow users to initiate a Skype for Business chat, call, or meeting.

Summary

You can only support users when you know how to troubleshoot the client side. This chapter provided the information you need to know. You learned about network connectivity and optimizing the connectivity for Teams workloads, Azure Active Directory, and conditional access policies for security controls. You learned about Teams account sign-in issues and how to capture and analyzing Teams diagnostic logs. You explored many resolutions to common problems. You know how to validating Teams client connectivity, troubleshoot issues with public and private channels and Teams client deployment and management. Additionally, you learned methodologies for Teams audio and video devices, Teams client performance, Teams external and guest access, and interop issues.

References

"How a web browser works step by step [latest]— navigation phase (part 2)." https://cabulous.medium.com/how-does-browser-work-in-2019-part-ii-navigation-342b27e56d7b

"Conditional Access service dependencies - Azure Active Directory." https://docs.microsoft.com/en-us/azure/active-directory/conditional-access/service-dependencies

"INTRODUCTION TO AZURE." http://mcsa15.biz/Introduction%20to%20Azure%20AD.pdf

"Use log files in troubleshooting Microsoft Teams." Microsoft Teams, https://docs.microsoft.com/en-us/microsoftteams/log-files

"Troubleshooting signing into Microsoft Stream (Classic)." Microsoft, https://docs.microsoft.com/en-us/stream/troubleshooting-sign-in

"Allow cookies for LMS URLs in your browser." Microsoft Docs, https://docs.microsoft.com/en-us/microsoft-365/lti/browser-cookies

"Issue when you access a notebook for Microsoft Teams." Microsoft Teams, https://docs.microsoft.com/en-us/microsoftteams/troubleshoot/teams-onenote-integration/issue-access-notebook

"Teams is slow during video meetings on laptops docked to 4K/UHD," https://docs.microsoft.com/en-us/microsoftteams/troubleshoot/teams-conferencing/teams-slow-video-meetings-laptops-4k

"Dial pad in missing in Teams." Microsoft Teams, https://docs.microsoft.com/en-us/microsoftteams/troubleshoot/teams-conferencing/no-dial-pad

"You're missing out, Ask your admin to enable Microsoft Teams." www.thewindowsclub.com/ask-your-admin-to-enable-microsoft-teams

"User presence status issues in Outlook." Microsoft Teams, https://docs.microsoft.com/en-us/microsoftteams/troubleshoot/teams-im-presence/issues-with-presence-in-outlook

"Your microphone is capturing too much noise." https://support.microsoft.com/en-us/office/your-microphone-is-capturing-too-much-noise-504d4c56-82cc-48b0-b414-e73a9b296149

"Your audio device may cause an echo." https://support.microsoft.com/en-us/office/your-audio-device-may-cause-an-echo-124e3b6c-6d01-4db2-94a3-75c0ecc289c3

"25 Free MS-740 Exam Questions: [Troubleshooting Microsoft Teams]." Whizlabs, www.whizlabs.com/blog/microsoft-ms-740-exam-questions/

"Microsoft Teams - Troubleshoot Teams client startup." https://www.linkedin.com/pulse/microsoft-teams-troubleshoot-client-startup-rene-vlieger

"Microsoft Teams Essentials for Small Businesses." Microsoft Teams, www.microsoft.com/en-us/microsoft-teams/essentials

"Manage external meetings and chat." Microsoft Teams, https://docs.microsoft.com/en-us/microsoftteams/manage-external-access

"Microsoft Teams Frequently Asked Questions (FAQs)." MessageOps, https://messageops.com/microsoft-teams-frequently-asked-questions-faqs/

"Understand Microsoft Teams and Skype for Business coexistence and …." https://docs.microsoft.com/en-us/microsoftteams/teams-and-skypeforbusiness-coexistence-and-interoperability

CHAPTER 5

Troubleshooting Microsoft Teams Call Quality Issues

Microsoft Teams is a cloud-only service that constantly evolves to provide optimal call quality to end users. Microsoft Teams supports all communication needs across the spectrum in the hybrid workplace, from one-to-one meetings to virtual events. Additionally, people can join meetings with different kinds of clients. For example, users can attend meetings from regular phones by dialing into the meeting using audio conferencing.

This chapter provides detailed information that helps you deliver an excellent call quality experience over an existing infrastructure. Additionally, this chapter covers information about different troubleshooting scenarios, including troubleshooting Teams meeting creation and recording issues, examining Teams content sharing and attendee access problems, Teams live events troubleshooting and management, and troubleshooting Teams messaging and reporting problems.

After reading this chapter, you should be able to explain how to get good performance for Teams calling and a good meeting experience even under not-so-optimal network conditions and how to troubleshoot Teams meeting and live event scenarios.

Understanding Teams Signaling and Media Flow for Troubleshooting

Microsoft Teams supports real-time media for audio/video calls and desktop sharing. To support real-time media, Teams use signaling and media traffic. This section examines the Teams media and signaling traffic flow to help you troubleshoot Teams call connectivity and quality issues.

© Balu N Ilag and Arun M Sabale 2022
B. N. Ilag and A. M. Sabale, *Troubleshooting Microsoft Teams*, https://doi.org/10.1007/978-1-4842-8622-7_5

Media traffic: Basically, data is compressed within the Real-time Transport Protocol (RTP) that facilitates audio, video, and screen sharing capabilities; this is the real-time media traffic. Fundamentally, Teams media traffic is very latency-sensitive; this is why, as a Teams admin, you want media traffic to take the shortest and most direct path possible and to use UDP versus TCP as the transport layer protocol, which is the best transport for interactive real-time media traffic from a call quality perspective. Sometimes Teams uses TCP, which is the last resort. Media can use TCP/IP and be tunneled within the HTTP protocol, but this is not recommended due to poor call quality consequences. RTP flow is secured utilizing SRTP, in which only the payload is encrypted.

Signaling traffic: This is the Teams connectivity and communication link among the Teams client and Teams cloud service (server) or other clients used to control activities, such as when a call is initiated and delivers instant messages. Most signaling traffic uses the HTTPS-based REST interfaces, although, in some scenarios like the connection between Microsoft 365 and a session border controller, it utilizes the SIP protocol. It's crucial to understand that this traffic is less sensitive to latency but may cause service outages or call timeouts if latency between the endpoints exceeds several seconds.

Microsoft 365 connectivity: Teams requires connectivity to the Internet. The Teams endpoint URLs and IP address ranges are listed in "Office 365 URLs and IP address ranges" at `https://docs.microsoft.com/en-us/office365/enterprise/urls-and-ip-address-ranges`. (Note that open connectivity to TCP ports 80 and 443 and UDP ports 3478 through 3481 is required.) The Teams media flow connectivity is implemented using standard IETF Interactive Connectivity Establishment (ICE) procedures.

The Teams Media Flow Requires ICE, STUN, TURN, and TR

Media flow is the term utilized for Microsoft Teams' real-time audio, video, and desktop sharing traffic between devices. For optimal call quality and user experience, Teams tries to establish a peer-to-peer connection over UDP. However, that isn't always feasible as Teams client devices are frequently on different networks, behind firewalls, and use Network Address Translation (NAT) servers. To provide an optimal call quality experience, Teams utilizes transport relays (TRs) to enable users to connect using UDP, TCP, or HTTP each time. The TR is a cloud server delivering ICE, Session Traversal Utilities for NAT (STUN), and Traversal using Relays around NAT (TURN) services.

ICE is the interactive connectivity establishment standard that allows peer-to-peer communication between devices on different networks. STUN and TURN are part of ICE and act as transport relay servers to allow packets with an additional source address to provide the media information inside. TURN is a protocol that assists in traversing network address translators or firewalls for multimedia applications like Microsoft Teams. Teams also use the Transmission Control Protocol (TCP) and User Datagram Protocol (UDP).

How Do ICE, STUN, and TURN Work?

First, a signaling connection gets established. Teams uses a REST API via HTTPS and WebSocket to establish the signaling connection to the Teams cloud service. Once Teams has a connection to the cloud, the STUN and TURN servers relay the packets. The STUN and TURN servers enable a device behind a firewall to set up a UDP connection and send and receive data through intermediary servers. By utilizing the signaling connection, which all Teams client devices can establish, the STUN and TURN servers ensure the media packets flow to their intended destination.

Understanding Teams Media Connectivity Using Transport Relays

Microsoft Teams connects to transport relay server media. It translates between various protocols so that everyone can speak together. Ideally, everyone talks via UDP over at least port 3478. UDP is great for audio and video because it is more efficient than TCP. However, in initiations like Figure 5-1 shows, if the client cannot use UDP, they may have to use TCP or HTTP. The TR can translate between TCP and HTTP and UDP. So, depending on what is allowed to do on one side of a network versus another, this dictates what the transport relay will receive. For instance, if there are five people on the call and four people can connect via UDP and the fifth can only connect via TCP, that TCP connection has no direct impact on the other four attendees. The other four continue to use the most optimal UDP, and the fifth attendee uses TCP. Because it is a slower protocol which is not suitable for real-time audio and video, the fifth attendee may have poor audio and video, but they still can join the meeting and won't impact how the others connect to the transport relay.

Figure 5-1 shows the optimal connectivity between endpoints as a direct UDP connection. When the direct connection is not possible, then a TR is used as fallback to establish the connection to the second endpoint. Also, an endpoint to a TR can be used as UDP, TCP, or native HTTP for proxy support.

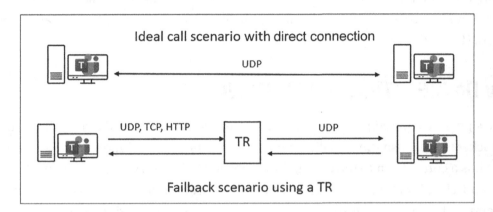

Figure 5-1. *Direct and failback scenarios*

How Do Teams Clients Find a Transport Relay?

A TR has an Anycast IP address; it is a single IP address assigned to geographically dispersed servers. Anycast IP is beneficial: you connect to an IP address, and it routes you to the closest instance. So, when you start up a Teams client, Teams always looks for one IP address across the globe. However, based on where the user is, it will connect to a location close to the user who is trying to log into Teams.

Transport Relay Discovery Plus Candidate Allocation

So, it is Anycast that will direct you to the closest Microsoft data center or Azure Front Door. The client connects to the transport relays Anycast IP address of 52.113.192.2, which is the global Anycast IP address. However, the user connection is then routed to the closest transport relay, and then an available transport relay answers and redirects from Anycast to an actual individual IP address. Figure 5-2 shows client TR discovery.

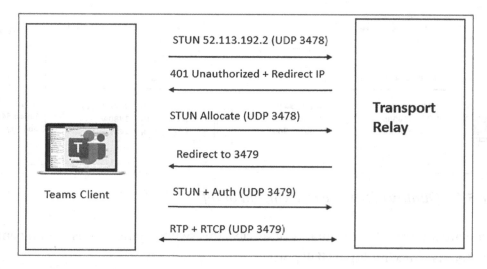

Figure 5-2. *Transport relay discovery and port allocation*

How UDP Ports Are Used in Teams Media

Microsoft has multiple transport relay servers deployed worldwide, but not all have the same IP address; it's the Anycast with the same IP address. All these transport relay servers are behind the Anycast IP address. So UDP 3478 is always used for initial communication with transport relays. Figure 5-3 shows the UDP port 3478 used for discovery, and the same port (3478) is used for audio, video, and desktop sharing. So, in all cases, by default Microsoft Teams and Teams rooms use UDP 3478 for all media communication. This port usage is controlled by the Insert Quality of Service ON /OFF switch found in the Teams admin center under the Meeting setting shown in Figure 5-3. If the Teams admin doesn't turn on the QoS setting, everything stays on UDP 3478; if they turn this switch on, then Teams will use 3478 for initial media negotiation and discovery. It will then use 3479 for audio, 3480 for video, and 3481 for desktop sharing. The reason for this is QoS: now that you are using four ports and three specifics for media, it helps to apply different priorities to different media. Audio is almost always chosen to be the highest priority (expedite forwarding or EF), video the second-highest (assured forwarding or AF41), and desktop sharing is the third-highest priority (assured forwarding or AF21). Refer to Table 5-1. So given a situation where you are out of bandwidth, the audio would be given the first chance to make it through the network.

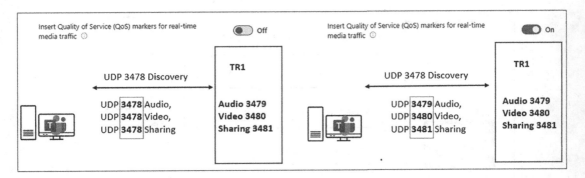

Figure 5-3. *Quality of Service marking on or off*

If you are interested in the quality of service, this switch in the Teams admin center enables Teams to use multiple UDP ports.

Table 5-1. *QoS Recommended Ports*

Media traffic type	Client source port range	Protocol	DSCP value	DSCP class
Audio	50,000–50,019	TCP/UDP	46	Expedited forwarding (EF)
Video	50,020–50,039	TCP/UDP	34	Assured forwarding (AF41)
Application/screen sharing	50,040–50,059	TCP/UDP	18	Assured forwarding (AF21)

What Happens If UDP Ports Are Blocked on One Side?

In a Teams meeting, if a UDP is blocked for one of the attendees, they can use TCP or HTTP to connect to the transport relay. The other attendee or attendees all have UDP and its transport relay translates between TCP or HTTP and UDP. This is also the case if you are in the same building. But if you are in building 1 and have a firewall that blocks UDP, and someone else is in building 2, which is behind the firewall that does not block UDP, to communicate you must go to a transport relay. In this scenario, you will not be able to have that peer-to-peer communication. If the user cannot reach his TR via UDP, it falls back to TCP or HTTP, and the allocated candidates remain on UDP and the call leg to the TR remains on UDP, as shown in Figure 5-4. Also, Figure 5-4 shows user1 and user2 peer-to-peer communication through a transport relay.

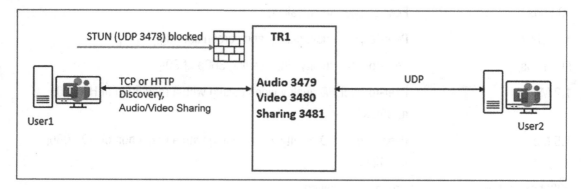

Figure 5-4. *UDP is blocked and a client falls back to TCP or HTTP.*

Why and When to Use Bandwidth Control in Teams

You can control how much bandwidth is used in the Teams meeting organizer, and it only applies to the meeting organizer. The meeting organizer defines how much bandwidth will be used in that meeting. For example, suppose you are in a low-bandwidth situation and you join a conference hosted by someone in a high-bandwidth situation. The meeting host has plenty of bandwidth. In that case, your bandwidth will not be limited even though you are in a low-bandwidth location because the meeting organizer is the one whose policy gets used for the meeting. Microsoft doesn't recommend changing this from the default value. Microsoft Teams codecs dynamically adjust to the available bandwidth. They lower the bandwidth requirement, video quality, or audio quality dynamically when there is a low-bandwidth environment. This can be set or used based on the use cases.

Bandwidth consumption set in the Teams admin center is the combined bandwidth consumption including audio, video, and sharing. The Teams meeting media stack optimizes for the end user experience under given conditions and there is no direct control over codecs and such. The limit is, on average consumption, not peak. Table 5-2 shows different scenarios with the bandwidth up or down.

Table 5-2. *Teams Calling Scenarios and Bandwidth Required*

Bandwidth (up or down)	Different calling scenarios
30 kbps	Peer-to-peer audio calling
130 kbps	Peer-to-peer audio calling and screen sharing
500 kbps	Peer-to-peer quality video calling 360p at 30fps
1.2 Mbps	Peer-to-peer HD quality video calling with a resolution of HD 720p at 30fps
1.5 Mbps	Peer-to-peer HD quality video calling with a resolution of HD 1080p at 30fps
500kbps/1Mbps	Group video calling
1 Mbps/2Mbps	HD group video calling (540p videos on 1080p screen)

Tips for Optimal Call Quality Between Teams Clients and Devices

- The first thing is to use local internet breakouts to ensure that the internet access is as close to the user as possible. This will reduce latency and loss and thus improve call quality.

- Make sure to open UDP ports 3478 to 3481 to allow communication with the TRS from the Teams client.

- In the Teams admin portal, select Quality of Service in the Meeting settings. This will open the ports between the client and its allocated TR, as shown in Figure 5-3.

- Make sure Teams traffic bypasses HTTP proxy servers.

- Prevent sending Teams media traffic through a VPN. Think about implementing VPN split tunneling to force Teams' media traffic via the local internet instead of the VPN tunnel.

- In the meetings policies, set the maximum bandwidth for users. This is an average limit, not a peak limit, and it stops high-usage clients from using too much bandwidth and reducing quality for others.

- Lastly, check that packet shaper or packet inspection devices are not installed between the Teams client and the Teams media TR server. Remember that any packet snipper, packet inspection, or packet shaper devices will drastically degrade the Teams media traffic quality.

Troubleshooting Teams Peer-to-Peer and Multi-Party Call Flow Problems

You have reached this topic, which means you understand how Teams media gets set up and a call is established. This section explains how to do troubleshooting specific to peer-to-peer calls. The Call Analytics tool can assist admins in troubleshooting call and connection problems with Microsoft Teams. Call Analytics reveals detailed information about the Teams client, devices, networks, and connectivity for the calls and meetings of each user in an organization's Microsoft 365 tenant. If Call Analytics includes building, site, and tenant information, this information will additionally be shown for each call and session. Detailed information available through Call Analytics can help a Teams admin to determine why a user had a poor call or meeting experience.

Viewing Call Analytics for a User

To view the call analytics for an individual user, follow these steps:

1. Log into the Teams admin center and from the left-hand navigation pane, select Users, and then search and select a user.

2. On the User Information page, choose *Meetings & calls*.

3. Call analytics will show all calls and meetings for that user for the past 30 days and recent meetings (real-time call quality information). Figure 5-5 shows poor and good calls.

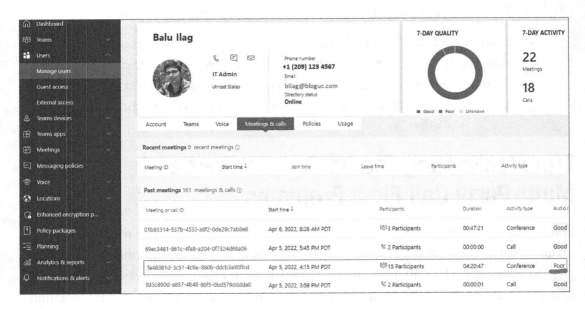

Figure 5-5. *Call analytics for the individual user*

4. You can view other information about a given session by choosing it, including detailed media and networking statistics.

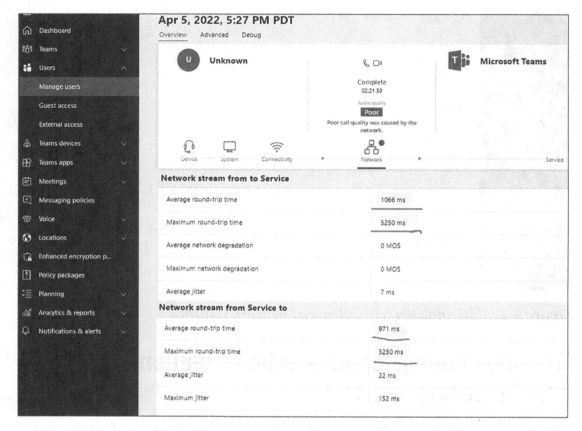

Figure 5-6. *Network statistics*

Figure 5-6 shows poor call statistics due to network latency. Figure 5-5 shows the details for each call or meeting; minor issues appear in yellow. A point highlighted in red indicates it's outside the normal range and may be contributing to the poor calls, but it's doubtful to be the only cause of the trouble. An issue highlighted in red (round-trip time) indicates it's a substantial latency problem, and it's likely the leading cause of the poor call quality for the session, as shown in Figure 5-6.

Advanced Call Analytics: In the Call Analytics page, on the top you can see the Overview, Advanced, and Debug tabs. You can select different phrases for more detailed information on the Overall Call Analytics page. Select the Advanced or Debug tabs, and then look for yellow and red items that indicate poor call quality or connection problems. Figure 5-7 shows the Advanced tab, which shows the outbound audio stream, system, connectivity, inbound network, and more information. The round trip time shows high latency, which marks the call as poor.

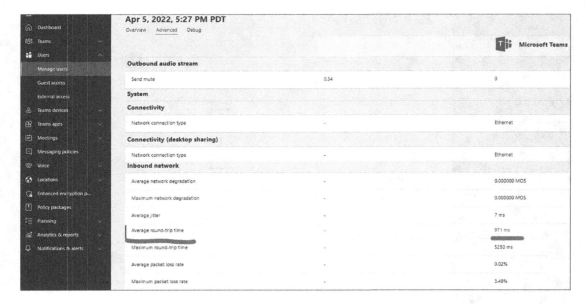

Figure 5-7. *Call Analytics with advanced network statistics*

Troubleshooting Teams Meeting Creation and Recording Issues

Microsoft Teams provides multiple features for communication and collaboration; one of the most used features is Teams meetings, and today it is a critical service within an organization. As a Teams admin, you must be able to configure Teams meetings and troubleshoot any problems that occur. Since moving to Microsoft 365, users have accepted the benefits offered by Teams meetings and live events. It's consequently essential that you, as the admin, can troubleshoot problems with conferences and live events to help optimize your users' experiences.

Troubleshooting Teams Meeting Creation

Teams meetings are one of the central Teams functionalities. Understanding how to configure the appropriate policies and their settings can help prevent the most common problems with meeting creation.

Implementing meeting policies: You can use meeting policies to manage the ability to create a Teams meeting. There is a default policy called the Global (org-wide default) meeting policy; you can use this policy or create custom policies for more complex environments. The global policy can be modified but cannot be deleted, and it automatically applies to all users unless the user has a custom policy assigned. After creating a policy, you can assign a policy to users using Teams admin center or PowerShell. Teams meeting policies get applied to the user based on per user and per organizer policy. The policy that applies to the user controls the features, such as

- **Per-organizer:** All meeting participants inherit the organizer's policy when implementing a per-organizer policy.

- **Per-user:** When you implement a per-user policy, only the per-user policy applies to restrict certain features for the organizer and/or meeting participants.

- **Per-organizer and per-user:** When you implement a combination of a per-organizer and per-user policies, certain features are restricted for meeting participants based on their policy and the organizer's policy.

Understanding Policy Precedence Is Essential for Troubleshooting

As an admin, you must make the policy precedence and decide what policy is assigned to which user because this will help you when you are troubleshooting any issues. Where there are multiple policies, you must understand which policy takes precedence. The following is the policy precedence order:

1. If a user is assigned a policy directly, that policy takes precedence.

2. If a user is not assigned a policy directly, then a policy set to a group of which they are a member takes precedence.

3. If a user belongs to multiple groups, each of which has an assigned policy, the group with the highest rank takes precedence.

4. If the user has no assigned policy and doesn't belong to groups with assigned policies, then the Global (org-wide default) policy applies.

243

You can use the Microsoft Teams admin center or PowerShell commands to verify which policies are applied to a user. Follow these steps to check a policy using the Teams admin center.

1. Log into the Teams admin center and then select Users.

2. Search the user by name or email address and select the user you want to review.

3. Select the Policies tab to see what policy is assigned. If you want to change the assigned policies, select Edit.

4. Change the policy assignments, and then select Apply.

If you want to use PowerShell, use the command `Get-CsUserPolicyAssignment` to review the assigned policies.

Note   It is essential to know that the policy assignment changes can take several hours to process. It is good practice to reapply the policy and check after 24 hours to see if the intended issue resolves.

Verifying Meeting Policy Settings

Once you have confirmed which policies affect a user, you can check and configure the specific policy settings. Use the Teams admin center to configure the meeting policy settings for the organization. Follow these steps to do this using the Teams admin center:

1. Log into the Teams admin center, select Meetings, and select Meeting policies.

2. In the details pane, select the appropriate policy and then review and modify the required settings.

3. When you have configured the desired settings, select Save. If your users are unable to create meetings, review the policy settings in the General section of the meetings policy displayed in Figure 5-8.

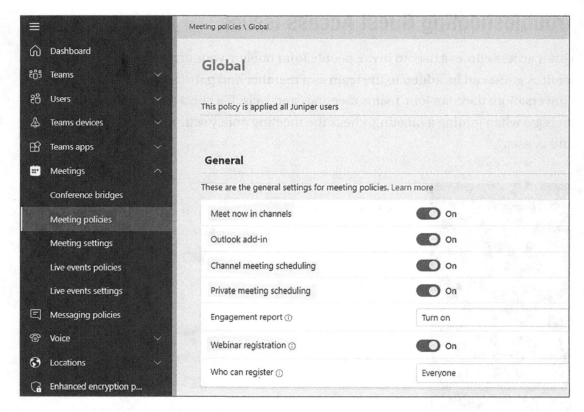

Figure 5-8. *Meeting policies*

The following are the general policy settings. All these settings are per-user policies that apply before a meeting starts.

- **Allow Meet now in channels:** Determines if a user can start unscheduled meetings in a Teams channel

- **Allow the Outlook add-in:** Determines if a user can schedule meetings from Outlook

- **Allow channel meeting scheduling:** Determines if users can schedule a meeting in a Teams channel

- **Allow channel meeting scheduling:** Determines if users can schedule a meeting in a Teams channel

- **Webinar registration:** Enables users to use Teams webinar registration

Troubleshooting Guest Access Issues

Guest access allows a user to invite people from outside your organization to join a team. A guest can be added to the team as a member and participate in a channel conversation; they can join Teams meetings and calls. If a guest user experiences an issue when joining a meeting, check the meeting policy settings for participants and guests.

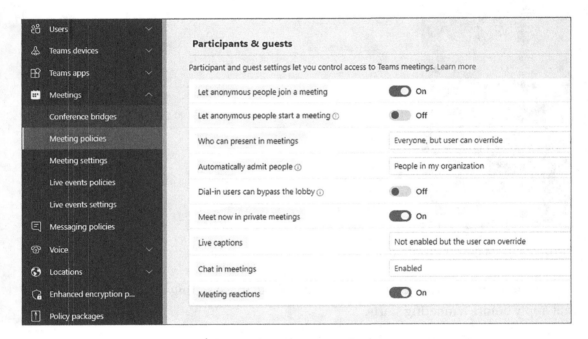

Figure 5-9. *Meeting policies for guest access*

Figure 5-9 shows participant and guest access general policy settings, including the following:

- **Let anonymous people start a meeting:** Enables an unauthenticated user to create a meeting. A user may anonymously connect when connecting to a meeting using their phone.

- **Allow Meet now in private meetings:** Determines if a user can start an unplanned private meeting

In addition to policy settings, you should check the Guest access settings. Log into the Teams admin center, select Users, and then Guest access. Then verify that *Allow Meet Now* is enabled. Meet Now allows guests to meet now in a channel.

Additionally, verify the setting *Allow guest access in Teams* is on and that *Make private calls*, *Meeting sharing*, and *IP video* are all enabled for guests. If guest access is not working for all users, this is the first thing you can check. Refer to Figure 5-10.

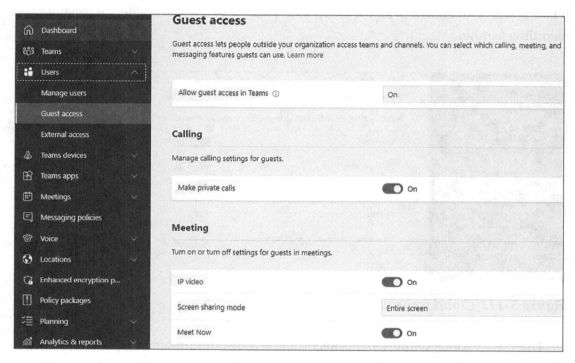

Figure 5-10. *Guest access settings*

Note that meeting participants that don't have any policies assigned (such as anonymous and federated participants) inherit the policy of the meeting organizer.

Troubleshooting Recording Issues

Teams provides a recording feature that allows users to record the session for future reference. Sometimes users can experience problems initiating a recording. The most common reason relates to incorrect policy settings. If the user has a policy assigned that does not allow meeting recording, that's a problem. The first thing to check is the policy set to the user.

Checking Audio and Video Policies

An excellent place to start is by reviewing the audio and video policy settings for the assigned policy for the user experiencing the issue. Remember to verify which policies are assigned to the user.

To do so, login to the Microsoft Teams admin center, click on Meetings, select Meeting policies, and review the *Recording & transcription* section of the appropriate meeting policy; as shown in Figure 5-11, *cloud recording* must be enabled to use the recording feature.

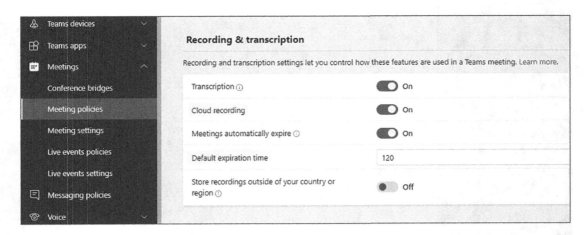

Figure 5-11. *Cloud recording*

There are various settings in this Recording & transcription section, but the one relevant to recordings is cloud recording. This setting is a per-organizer and per-user policy. The setting determines whether a user's meeting can be recorded. Depending on the settings, the recording can be started by the meeting organizer or another meeting participant.

For a participant to be able to start recording, the policy setting must be enabled for the participant, and the user must be an authenticated user from the same organization. This is why the guest cannot start recording.

Note   Guest users, and federated and anonymous users, can't start a recording.

Requirements for Recording

Meeting recordings are stored either in OneDrive or in SharePoint Online. Note that Teams meeting recordings are no longer saved to Microsoft Stream. All recordings are now saved to OneDrive and SharePoint. Recordings are available in different places depending on the type of meeting. The recording is processed and saved to SharePoint if it was a channel meeting or OneDrive if it was any other type of meeting.

The meeting recording shows up in the meeting chat or channel conversation (if you're meeting on a channel). Remember that for now, guests and external attendees can view the recording only if it's explicitly shared with them.

It is essential to check whether a user meets the Teams meeting recording test requirements by visiting `https://testconnectivity.microsoft.com/` and then selecting *Microsoft Teams* ➤ *Teams meeting recording*. Enter the account details of the user experiencing a problem with the recording, and then choose *Verify* and then *Perform Test*. Figure 5-12 shows the Microsoft Remote Connectivity Analyzer with Teams meeting recording testing.

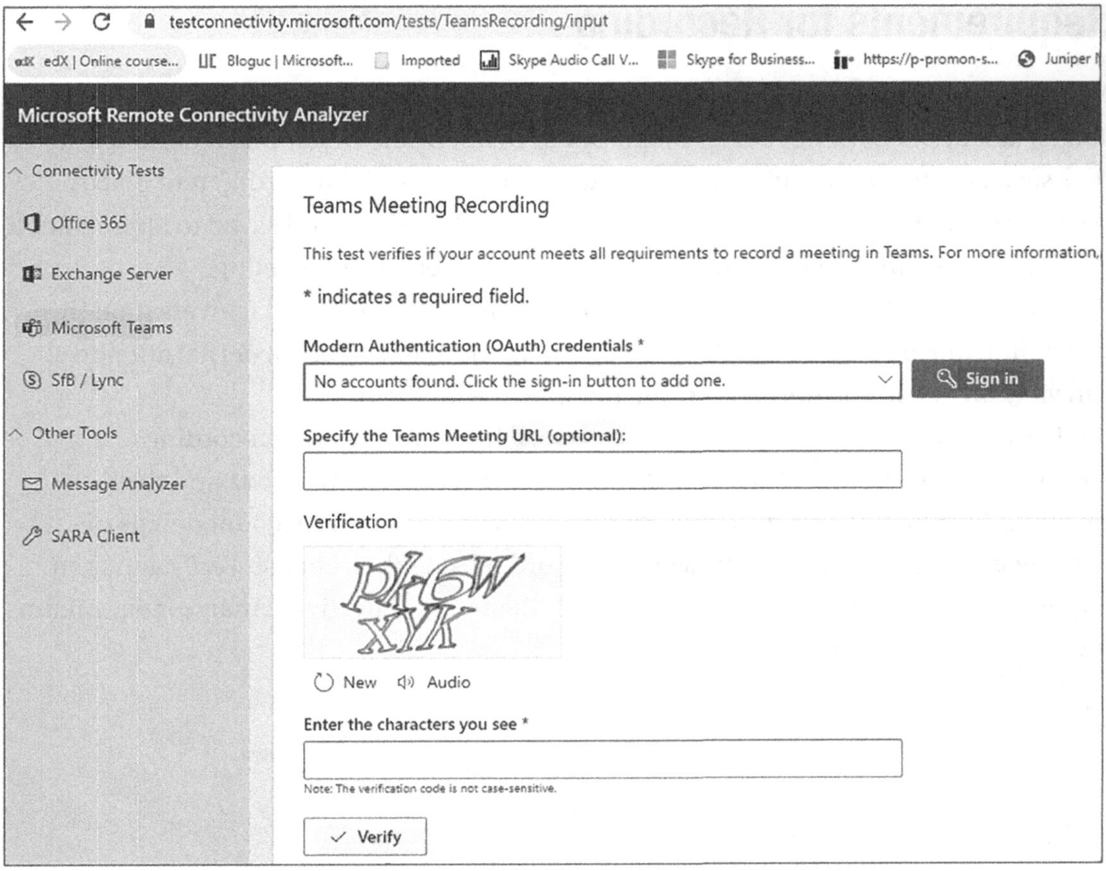

Figure 5-12. *Testing meeting recording*

You must check whether the user has a required Teams license, the tenant is configured correctly, and the user is enabled for cloud meeting recording. If the issue persists, keep reading.

Running the Meeting Recording Support Diagnostics

If you're still experiencing problems, you can additionally use the Teams meeting recording support diagnostics. Follow these steps:

1. Log into the Microsoft 365 admin center as a global admin, select Help from the menu bar, and enter Diag: Meeting Recording.

2. In the User Principal Name (UPN) box, enter the UPN of the user experiencing recording problems and then select Run Tests.

Any issues with the user's configuration are displayed. In addition, other insights and support documentation links are revealed.

Examining Teams Content Sharing and Attendee Access Problems

Microsoft Teams provides optimal quality for audio/video meetings with application sharing capabilities. But sometimes a user may have issues when using the Sharing feature. This section describes content sharing and attendee access issues.

Troubleshooting Sharing Issues

In Teams meetings, application sharing is frequently used. The meeting organizer, or another authorized participant, might want to share the following components:

- An entire screen (whole desktop)

- A single application (individual apps)

- PowerPoint slides (just the presentation)

- Whiteboard

- Shared notes

When users experience a problem with initiating shared content in a meeting, check the meeting policies assigned to the organizer and participants. Also, review the meeting settings.

Check content sharing policy settings: To check the content sharing settings, log into the Teams admin center and review the content sharing section of the appropriate meeting policy, as shown in Figure 5-13.

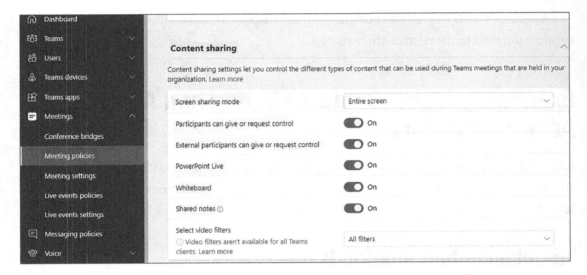

Figure 5-13. *Teams content sharing capabilities*

This list shows the content sharing policy setting options:

- **Screen sharing mode:** Enables you to define the screen sharing mode. Options are *the Entire screen* or *a single application*. Ensure that *Disabled* is not selected. This is a per-organizer and per-user setting.

- **The participant can give or request control:** Determines whether a user can provide control of the shared desktop to other participants in the meeting. This per-user setting determines whether the *Give Control* button is accessible during a meeting.

- **External participants can give or request control:** Determines whether external participants can be given control or request control of the sharer's screen. This is a per-user setting.

- **PowerPoint Live:** Determines if a user can share PowerPoint slide decks in a meeting. External users, including anonymous, guest, and federated users, inherit the policy of the meeting organizer. This is a per-user setting.

- **Whiteboard:** Determines if users can use and share the whiteboard during their meetings.

- **Shared notes:** Determines if a user can create and share notes in a meeting. External users, including anonymous, B2B, and federated users, inherit the policy of the meeting organizer. This is a per-user setting.

Per-Organizer and Per-User Policies

When considering the effect of policies, remember that per-organizer and per-user policies can sometimes be confusing. The following are a few instances:

Screen sharing instance: Screen sharing mode is a per-organizer and per-user policy. Say your global meeting policy allows for entire-screen sharing. However, user Balu is assigned a policy with disabled screen sharing. Anyone who joins the meeting can share their screens or apps if user Chanda schedules a meeting. If user Balu joins, he cannot share his screen or apps. If Balu schedules an appointment, no one can share their screen or apps.

Give or request control instance: The *Participants can give or request control* setting is per-user only. Say that your global meeting policy has this value on. However, user Balu is assigned a policy where this value is off. If user Chanda schedules a meeting, she can give control of the shared desktop to other participants. If user Balu schedules a meeting, he cannot provide control of the shared desktop to other participants. However, if user Chanda attends that meeting, he can give control.

Note   You can use the `Set-CsTeamsMeetingPolicy` PowerShell cmdlet to configure these policy settings.

Checking Network Settings

Specific to the network setting, different ports are used for Teams audio, video, and sharing media that must be accessible from your network. Network settings can be evaluated or managed in the Meeting settings page in the Teams admin center. For sharing, the default network ports are 50040 to 50059. Figure 5-14 shows audio, video, and screen sharing port ranges.

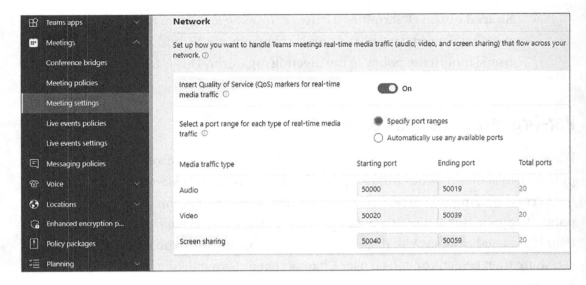

Figure 5-14. *Network settings*

Also, there may be an issue in network latency, packet loss, and jitter. So, checking network stats and speed is highly recommended.

Troubleshooting Meeting Attendee Access

When users attempt to join meetings, they may experience problems. These problems are often related to policy settings.

Review attendee access settings: To verify the settings for attendee access, open the appropriate meeting policy and navigate to *Participants & guests*. These settings let you control access to Teams meetings. See Figure 5-15.

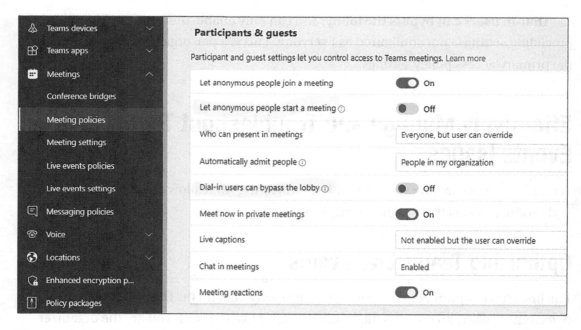

Figure 5-15. *Teams access policy settings*

The following are some of the settings for access policies that some companies allow and some do not. It depends on their requirements.

Let anonymous people start a meeting: Enables an unauthenticated user to create a meeting. This is a per-organizer setting. For security reasons, most companies keep this setting as off.

Automatically admit people: This setting determines who can be automatically admitted to a meeting. It defaults to *People in my organization and guests*. This is a per-organizer setting. You can choose from the following options:

- Everyone

- People in my organization and guests

- People in my organization, trusted organizations, and guests

- People in my organization

- Organizer only

- Invited users only

Dial-in users can bypass the lobby: You can only enable this setting when the preceding setting is not configured as Everyone. This is a per-organizer setting. These are the primary access policy settings.

Effectively Manage and Troubleshoot Teams Live Events Issues

Teams live events are an expansion of Teams meetings that allow the user to schedule and produce events that stream to large online audiences.

Optimizing Teams Live Events

The first step in optimizing live events is to properly plan them. This starts with determining who can create, schedule, and attend live events. If you are the organizer of a live event, you can schedule it in Teams the same way you organize a regular Teams meeting. This procedure will add the live event to your event group's calendars. Later, you will need to invite the attendees. Attending a live event is straightforward; as attendees of a live event in Teams, they can watch live events and participate in the moderated Q&A. However, they cannot share audio or video during the live event.

Deciding Who Can Schedule and Attend Live Events

In order to schedule a live event, users must meet the following license requirements. Technically, users need a Teams license assigned to organize the live event. Users don't need a license to attend a live event.

The organizer requires one of these licenses:

- A Microsoft 365 Enterprise E1, E3, or E5 license

- A Microsoft 365 Education A3 or A5 license

The producer or presenter requires one of these licenses:

- A Microsoft 365 Enterprise E1, E3, or E5 license

- A Microsoft 365 Education A1, A3, or A5 license

Note that the exception to these requirements is that guest users can present without a license if the other criteria for guest users are met. After verifying who can create, schedule, and attend live events, you can configure the related settings.

Suppose a guest user is part of another organization. In this case, they must ensure that they switch organizations to avoid joining the live event as an attendee and not as a presenter. It's recommended that you create a private team and channel to add the guest users that will attend the meeting.

Configuring Live Event Policies and Settings

Admins can configure or manage Teams Live Event settings and policies using the Teams admin center. As the Teams admin, you can use live event policies, live events settings, and manage live events policies to control access and functionality of your live events. By default, a single Global (org-wide default) policy exists. You can create and configure more custom policies as your needs determine.

Log into the Teams admin center and navigate to *Live events policies* under *Meetings*. Refer to Figure 5-16 for the Global policy; however, transcription for attendees is not enabled by default.

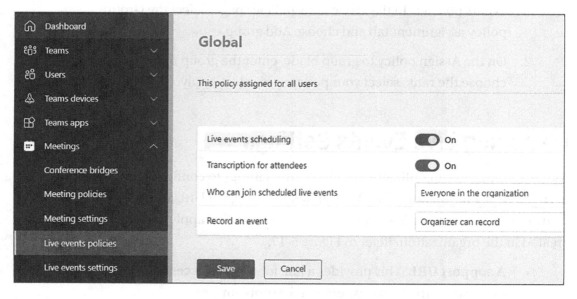

Figure 5-16. *Live event policies*

The following list shows available options for the live event policy:

- **Live events scheduling:** Enables users to organize live events

- **Transcription for attendees:** Enables users to see live captions during an event

- **Who can join scheduled live events:** Choose between *Everyone, Everyone in the organization,* and *Specific users or groups.* The default is *Everyone in the organization.*

- **Record an event:** You can select options *Always record, Never record,* and *The organizer can record. Always record* is the default.

After you have updated the live event policy and saved it, the next thing to do is assign your policy to the users. All users will be assigned to the global policy unless you assign a different policy. Live events are large events, so not every user schedules such events; this is why you cannot set the global policy to off for live events scheduling and create a custom policy and assign a newly created policy to the user group required to schedule live events. Follow these steps to assign the policy to the user group:

1. Log into the Teams admin center, select Meetings, and select Live events policies. In the Live events policies page, select the Group policy assignment tab and choose Add group.

2. On the Assign policy to group blade, enter the group name, choose the rank, select your policy, and select Apply.

Managing Live Events Settings

As the admin, you can utilize Teams live events settings to configure settings for live events within your organization. You can define a support URL and third-party video distribution provider in a live event setting. These settings apply to all live events that are created in the organization. Refer to Figure 5-17.

- **A support URL:** This provides a link for users to access during an event when they have experienced a problem.

- **A third-party video distribution provider:** Enables you to define a software-defined network solution or enterprise content delivery network solution through a Microsoft video delivery partner.

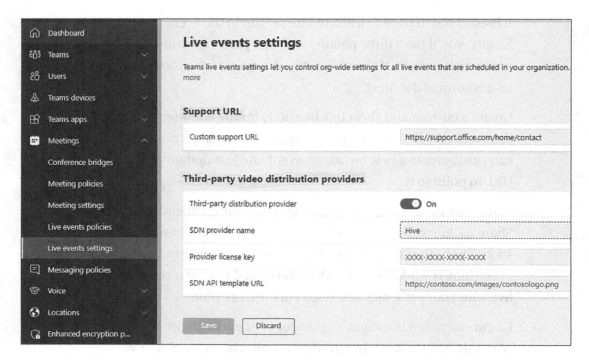

Figure 5-17. *Live event settings*

Figure 5-17 shows the third-party video distribution as Hive. If you opt to use a third-party video distribution partner, you must define the following settings:

- **Use a third-party distribution provider**: Enable this setting to use a third-party video distribution provider.

- **SDN provider name**: Select the provider you're using.

- **Provider license key**: Enter the license ID from your provider.

- **SDN API template URL**: Enter the API template URL from your provider.

Planning and Creating Your Event

- Testing is critical in running a successful live event. Conduct multiple events as preparations and watch the attendee experience live and on-demand. Learn the system well so producers don't have to solve problems during the live event.

- It is essential to have more than one person in the event group. Ideally, you'll have three people, with one person outside the presentation room. If there's a network outage in the room, you don't lose control of the meeting.

- Create a custom and short link like bit.ly for the attendee join link. In the event of any tragic event, or if a producer makes a mistake, you can easily create a new broadcast event and just update your custom URL to point to it.

- Make sure the event group joins about 30 minutes ahead of time. Share a slide with a nice intro, indicating that the event will begin soon. Then, start the live broadcast about 10 minutes early to ensure everything is working. Leave all audio muted until you're ready to go live with your presenter at the start of the live event.

- Communication is critical, so plan for your event group communication. Real-time communication is essential for live events. The event chat (available for the organizer, producers, and presenters) is a good way to stay in touch.

- Distribute work based on the assigned roles and responsibilities. Know who is responsible for each operation step, from camera operators, presenters, and Q&A moderators to your overall producer or director.

Troubleshooting Teams Messaging and Reporting Problems

This section provides information about Teams chat messaging problems and their resolutions.

Troubleshooting Messaging Issues

Microsoft Teams chat is controlled through the creation and assignment of messaging policies. If users experience problems with messaging, the first place to start is by reviewing these messaging policies. You can create, configure, and assign these policies using the Teams admin center or PowerShell.

Checking Messaging Policies

To verify the messaging policy, log into the Teams admin center, select the Messaging policies node, and open the appropriate policy. You can use only the built-in Global (org-wide default) policy. The default settings for the Global (org-wide default) policy are displayed in Figure 5-18. There are multiple things you can check and modify as per your requirements for your messaging policy.

Here is a list of settings available in the messaging policy:

- **Owners can delete sent messages:** When you turn on this setting, channel owners can remove all sent messages in a channel.

- **Delete sent messages:** Users can delete their own messages by turning on this setting.

- **Edit sent messages:** Users can edit their own messages when turning on this setting.

- **Read receipts:** Select which users can use read receipts. Choose between the following:

  - User-controlled (default value)

  - Turned off for everyone

  - Turned on for everyone

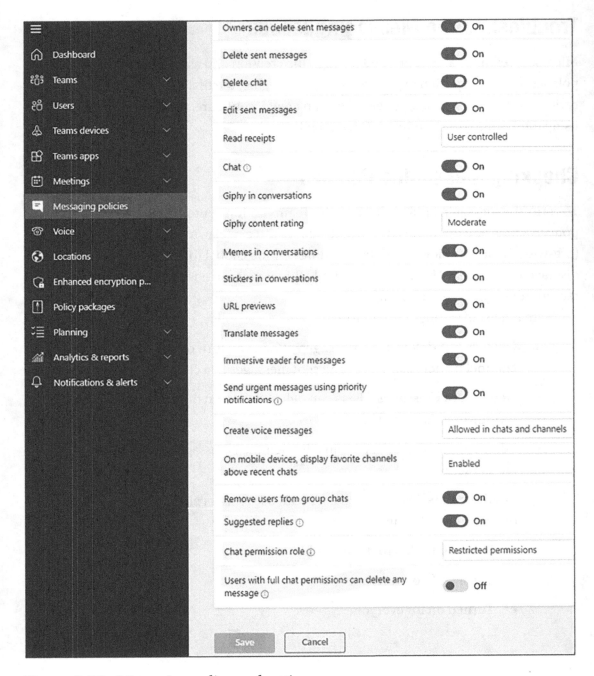

Figure 5-18.   *Messaging policy and settings*

- **Chat:** Enables or disables chat

- **Giphys in conversations:** When you turn on this setting, users can use animated pictures within the conversations.

- **Giphy content rating:** When you turn on the setting for sharing animated images, you can use this setting to apply the content rating to restrict the type of animated images that can display in conversations. Available content rating options are the following:

  - No restriction

  - Moderate (default value)

  - Strict

- **Memes in conversations:** Users can use internet memes when they turn on this setting.

- **Stickers in conversations:** When you turn on this setting, users can post images with editable text to get channel members' attention.

- **URL previews:** Enables a preview of a pasted URL to be visible in a message

- **Translate messages:** Translates messages

- **Immersive reader for viewing messages:** Enables users to hear posts, chat messages, and assignments read aloud. The immersive reader also includes grammar tools such as Parts of Speech and Picture Dictionary.

- **Send an urgent message using priority notifications:** When enabled, users can send messages marked as critical.

- **Create voice messages:** Enables users to use voice messages. You can choose between the following:

  - Allowed in chats and channels (default value)

  - Allowed in chats only

  - Disabled

- **On mobile devices, display favorite channels above recent chats:** Choose between Disabled and Enabled.

- **Remove users from group chats:** Enables users to remove other users from group chats

- **Suggested replies:** Provides quick and straightforward responses to inbound messages

- **Chat permission role:** If role-based chat permissions are enabled, you can choose the permission role:

  - Restricted permissions (default value)

  - Limited permissions

  - Full permissions

- **Users with full chat permissions can delete any messages:** Users with full permissions can delete any group or meeting chat message in their tenant.

If users see messaging issues and you as an admin have reviewed policies and still have messaging issues, consider collecting the chat ID. You can do this by accessing Teams through a web browser and containing the link that shows up as part of the URL when accessing the chat.

Troubleshooting File Sharing in Person-to-Person Private Chats

File sharing is another necessary functionality that Teams offers, but sometimes it doesn't work the way it should work. This section can help you.

Troubleshooting File Sharing Issues

In organizations, users use Microsoft Teams to share project files between colleagues and guests. As a Teams admin, you are commonly asked to troubleshoot file sharing problems. This section provides information and discusses how to troubleshoot file sharing problems such as private troubleshooting chat (P2P) file issues, file issues for private channels, and file issues for public channels.

Troubleshooting File Sharing in Person-to-Person Private Chats

Chat is an essential feature that users use every day. Users can chat one-to-one or in groups by choosing *New chat* at the top of the chat list and sending a message to start the chat. Users then enter the names of people they would like to add in the To field, up to 250 people. Refer to Figure 5-19 for chat functionality.

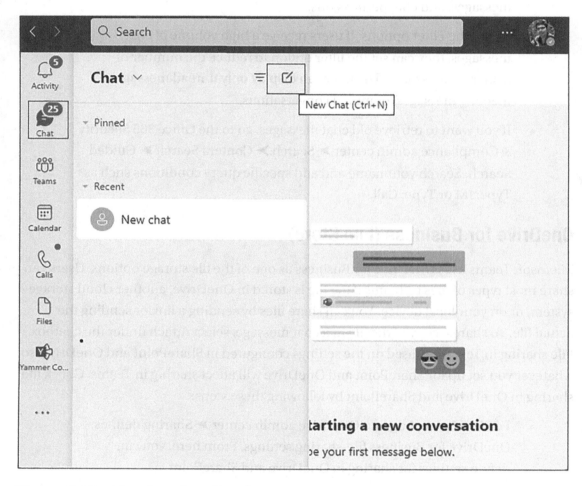

Figure 5-19. *Chat functionality*

Teams save all the chat history from the first message, even if someone leaves the group.

Common Troubleshooting Steps for Chat Issues

- The first thing to do is have users restart Teams to force a refresh.

- Check Messaging policies. From the Teams admin center, select *Messaging policies*. Messaging policies control behavior such as whether Giphy can be used in chats, whether users can delete sent messages, and chat permissions.

- Check the Filter options. If users receive a high volume of chat messages, they can set the filter option to reduce the number of displayed messages. The filter can display only unread messages, meeting messages, or muted conversations.

- If you want to retrieve old chat messages, go to the Office 365 Security & Compliance admin center ➤ Search ➤ Content Search ➤ Guided Search. Search your name and add specific query conditions such as Type: IM or Type: Call.

OneDrive for Business (File Store)

Microsoft Teams uses OneDrive for Business as one of the file storage options. Users can share most types of files in Teams if the file is stored in OneDrive, another cloud storage system, or on your local device. You can share files by sending a link or sending the actual file. To share a copy of the file in a chat message, select Attach under the chatbox. File sharing in Teams is based on the settings configured in SharePoint and OneDrive, so whatever you set up for SharePoint and OneDrive will affect sharing in Teams. Check file sharing in OneDrive and SharePoint by following these steps:

- **For OneDrive**: Log into OneDrive admin center ➤ Sharing defines OneDrive for Business file-sharing settings. From here, you can define settings for sharing in OneDrive and SharePoint.

- **For SharePoint**: Log into SharePoint admin center ➤ Policies ➤ Sharing defines SharePoint file-sharing settings.

Troubleshooting Sharing Files Using OneDrive

OneDrive is mainly used for file store and sharing purposes. Sometimes a user may have a problem accessing OneDrive for Business. Here are common troubleshooting steps:

A user cannot access OneDrive: When the user is unable to access OneDrive, the first thing to check is that the user has a license for OneDrive. A license to use OneDrive is included in Microsoft 365 E3 and E5 subscriptions. Check whether the user has access to SharePoint; if they can access SharePoint, they will also have access to OneDrive.

Sometime there may be a sync issue. So, it is best practice to allow up to 24 hours for a user to be able to access OneDrive after the correct license has been assigned. If you are pre-provisioning OneDrive for many users using PowerShell scripts, it can take several days for OneDrive to be provisioned for all users.

A user is having trouble sharing a file in their Personal Vault: This is expected as files in a user's Personal Vault cannot be shared. Personal Vault is a BitLocker encrypted vault designed to store personally sensitive documents. Move the file to another folder in OneDrive and then share it.

Microsoft account needs validating: File sharing problems may be due to a Microsoft account validation issue. Go to `https://account.live.com/reputationcheck` to validate your Microsoft account.

Your sharing limit has been reached: File sharing is limited in OneDrive. You can wait before sharing a file because sharing limits are reset after 24 hours. Alternatively, upgrade to a premium subscription.

OneDrive desktop app is not installed: When a user has the OneDrive desktop app installed on their computer, files in OneDrive will have the Share option available when they right-click on a file or folder. If the OneDrive desktop app is not installed, the Share option is not shown. OneDrive is automatically provisioned the first time a user browses to OneDrive.

OneDrive will not sync files correctly: Reinstalling Microsoft OneDrive can sometimes resolve sync issues and reset all OneDrive settings. OneDrive will perform a full sync after the reinstallation. Users will not lose any data by uninstalling OneDrive. Any files or data in OneDrive are still available when the user signs in at OneDrive.com. See the "Learn more" section for more information.

Troubleshooting file sharing in person-to-person chat: When you share a file in a person-to-person chat, the file is stored in a SharePoint document library and can be viewed in the Files tab. When a used deletes a shared file, it is also deleted from the SharePoint document library.

Troubleshooting File Sharing Issues

File sharing issues are more common, and there are different reasons for file sharing not working. Here is a list of the most common issues and their resolutions:

A user does not have file access permissions: You can set and check how users can share files in the SharePoint admin center ➤ Policies ➤ Sharing and Access control.

A user cannot share a file: If the user cannot share a file, check whether file sharing has been switched off for that file type in the Teams admin center ➤ Org-wide settings ➤ Teams settings ➤ Files.

The storage limit has been reached: This issue occurs when the user's storage limit is reached. Use the SharePoint admin center to amend the site storage limits for SharePoint and OneDrive. From the SharePoint admin center, select Settings ➤ SharePoint Site storage limits. This can be set to

- **Automatic**: Lets sites use as much of your organization's storage as needed.

- **Manual**: Sets specific limits for each location.

An external user does not have permission to share a file:

External sharing settings are set at the

- Organization level in the Azure Active Directory admin portal

- Site level in the SharePoint admin center

From SharePoint admin center ➤ Policies ➤ Sharing, select how you want external users to share files:

- Who can view a file or folder link? These settings apply to SharePoint and OneDrive, but include Teams because Teams inherits permissions:

    - People that the user specifies

    - People within the organization

    - Anyone

- What people can do with a link:

    - View

    - Edit

- The number of days after which a link will expire

- Link permissions for files and folders

    - **Files**: View and Edit or View

    - **Folders**: View, Edit, and Upload or View

- Other settings

    - Audit settings including showing owners the names of people who viewed their files in OneDrive

    - Allowing site owners to display the names of people who viewed files or pages in SharePoint

    - Using short links for sharing files and folders

Also, check access control for unmanaged devices and network location settings.

Someone from outside your organization is having difficulty sharing a file: This is by design; file sharing is not available in Teams to chat with external users.

Managing SharePoint and OneDrive Settings

You can use the SharePoint admin center to view and modify SharePoint and OneDrive settings as an admin. Here are some common issues and resolutions.

Validate That the SharePoint Site for the Channel Is Accessible

A SharePoint team site is automatically created for you when you create a team. Shared files are stored in the SharePoint document library and can be viewed in Teams and SharePoint. Teams owners can check who has permissions for the channel by selecting the three dots next to the channel name and selecting *Manage channel*. The owner and members of the private channel are listed.

To verify that the SharePoint site for the channel is accessible for a user, from SharePoint, select My Sites ➤ See more, if necessary. All the SharePoint sites for Teams channels will be displayed.

Validating SharePoint Access Permissions

To verify the SharePoint access permissions, in SharePoint, go to Settings (gear icon) ➤ Library settings ➤ Permissions and Management ➤ Permissions for this document library.

If this is a document library created by Teams, a warning is displayed: *This library inherits permissions from its parent*. Permission levels are displayed for team owners, members, and visitors.

Confirming That the SharePoint Site Collection Link Is Intact

A SharePoint site collection link is in the site URL. If you have problems with file storage, check that the SharePoint site collection link is intact and hasn't been corrupted.

Select Copy Link from the top navigation bar in the Teams Files tab. The Get Link dialog box is displayed. Select the SharePoint tab to view the SharePoint link.

Troubleshooting File Issues for Public Channels

This section discusses file sharing and public channel troubleshooting.

Verifying SharePoint Access Permissions

To verify SharePoint access permissions for public channels, select a public channel and select the Files tab in Teams. From the top navigation bar, choose Open in SharePoint to open the relevant SharePoint document library. In SharePoint, from the top navigation, select Settings (the gear icon) and then choose Site permissions. In the Permissions blade, you can invite people to collaborate in this group and view site owners, site members, and site visitors.

Select the *Change how members can share* to open the Site sharing settings blade. In the *Site sharing settings* blade, you can define sharing permissions, turn access requests on or off, and define whether or not access requests can be sent by email. You can also add a custom message to the request access page.

Select *Advanced permissions settings* to view the SharePoint permissions page for the site.

Determining Whether the Name for a Channel or Team Has Been Changed

Owners and team members can change the name of a channel by selecting More options next to the Channel name ➤ Edit this channel.

If *Edit this channel* is not visible, the team owner has changed the member's permissions.

Teams Channel Troubleshooting

Here are some general tips.

A user can't change the name of the General channel: This is by design. The General channel cannot be amended or deleted.

A user changed a channel name and cannot find shared files: This should not happen. Users should be able to change a channel name without affecting shared files. Try renaming the channel back to its original name. Alternatively, search for the old channel name in SharePoint.

Confirm that the SharePoint site collection link is intact: You can check that the SharePoint site collection link is correct. In Teams, select the Files tab of a public channel, and in the top navigation bar, select the Copy link. Select the SharePoint tab in the Get link dialog box and either copy the link or check the link.

Troubleshooting File Synchronization Issues and Missing Files

A user has shared a file in Teams, but it is not visible in the Files tab: All Teams files are stored in a SharePoint document library. From the top navigation, select Open in SharePoint to find out if the file is visible in SharePoint. Check the SharePoint folder name; it should be the same as the Teams channel name. Also, check whether you have reached the shared file limit.

A user has set up file sync but cannot sync shared files in Teams with their OneDrive: Check that OneDrive is running and the user has signed into OneDrive. OneDrive will show a padlock icon if the file or folder has settings that prevent it from syncing. Check that the sharing limit has not been reached or that the file is not too large. See "Learn more" for details of current restrictions and limitations in OneDrive and SharePoint.

Summary

Microsoft Teams provides optimal audio/video call quality; however, sometimes network impairment causes call setup and quality issues. After reading this chapter, you now know all about Teams signaling and media flow so you can troubleshoot Teams performance issues. You also learned Teams one-to-one and multi-party call flow troubleshooting, Teams meeting creation and recording problems and resolutions, and Teams content sharing and attendee access problems and solutions.

References

"After reading this chapter you should be able to make …." www.coursehero.com/file/p5qirc0a/After-reading-this-chapter-you-should-be-able-to-make-inferences-about-Timothy/

"Microsoft Teams call flows." https://docs.microsoft.com/en-us/microsoftteams/microsoft-teams-online-call-flows

"Cost Estimating Methods and How To Calculate Cost Estimations." www.indeed.com/career-advice/career-development/cost-estimating-methods

"Deactivating a user account or group account." https://rubrik-docs.s3-us-west-1.amazonaws.com/en-us/5.3/ug/cdm_user_guide/deactivating_a_user_account_or_group_account.html

"Frequently Asked Questions · bcgit/bc-java Wiki." https://github.com/bcgit/bc-java/wiki/Frequently-Asked-Questions

"About your 2019 Goals - Mid-year review - MC's Perspective." www.mariechristinanthony.com/blog/about-your-2019-goals-mid-year-review

"Record a meeting in Teams." https://support.microsoft.com/en-us/office/record-a-meeting-in-teams-34dfbe7f-b07d-4a27-b4c6-de62f1348c24

"Here are some ways to protect your privacy while video conferencing." CBC, www.cbc.ca/news/canada/nova-scotia/ways-to-protect-privacy-video-conferencing-zoom-1.5517928

"Inviting External Users to Meetings as Guest." Kellogg. https://help.kellogg.edu/inviting-external-users-to-meetings-as-guest

"How to Schedule a Teams Live Event." Instruction, UH, www.instruction.uh.edu/knowledgebase/how-to-schedule-a-teams-live-event/

"Attend a live event in Teams." https://support-uat.microsoft.com/en-us/office/attend-a-live-event-in-teams-a1c7b989-ebb1-4479-b750-c86c9bc98d84

#FWNSummit 2019: Full Schedule. https://fwnsummit2019.sched.com/list/descriptions/

"Configure live event settings in Microsoft Teams." https://docs.microsoft.com/en-us/MicrosoftTeams/teams-live-events/configure-teams-live-events

"Best practices for producing a Teams live event." https://support.microsoft.com/en-us/office/best-practices-for-producing-a-teams-live-event-e500370e-4dd1-4187-8b48-af10ef02cf42

"DD2 crashes during races." Fanatec Forum, https://podium.fanatec.com/discussion/21553/dd2-crashes-during-races

"Audiobooks - Archives: Audible.com & ISBN." Goodreads, www.goodreads.com/topic/show/410686-audible-com-isbn

"Best Google Drive Alternatives [Top 8 providers]." NordVPN, https://nordvpn.com/blog/google-drive-alternatives/

"1 Perfect How To Unlock A Spreadsheet In Teams," Ginasbakery, https://ginasbakery.com/how-to-unlock-a-spreadsheet-in-teams/

"How can I get a files Id on Onedrive using the graph api?" Stack Overflow. https://stackoverflow.com/questions/69114015/how-can-i-get-a-files-id-on-onedrive-using-the-graph-api

"OneDrive Slow to Sync." Microsoft Community, https://answers.microsoft.com/en-us/msoffice/forum/all/onedrive-slow-to-sync/7aaec89e-488c-4864-aff0-019c95335c2c

"MS Teams and SharePoint." Microsoft Community, https://answers.microsoft.com/en-us/msoffice/forum/all/ms-teams-and-sharepoint/e4860225-596d-41d4-90e2-072a401d3009

"Chat box visible but can't write." Microsoft Community, https://answers.microsoft.com/en-us/msteams/forum/all/chat-box-visible-but-cant-write/8ca0ae10-148f-43e2-b039-ee5a3144ae9d

CHAPTER 6

Troubleshoot Microsoft Teams Phone System (Calling Plan and Direct Routing) Issues

As a Teams admin, you must configure and troubleshoot Microsoft Teams Phone System problems. After completing this chapter, you will be able to deploy, configure, and maintain Teams Phone System. You will also be able to troubleshoot Teams Direct Routing and call plan issues. You will also learn how to enable voice services for users to make and receive calls. You will learn how to facilitate voice services when using Teams Phone System with calling plans and facilitate voice services for users when Direct Routing is configured. This chapter provides the necessary information that you need to troubleshoot Microsoft Teams Phone System issues.

Understanding Microsoft Teams Phone System

Before even troubleshooting the Teams Phone System issue, you need to know some basic terminology. This section provides the required information to get prepared for solving Phone System problem.

Phone System Basics

Before knowing Teams Phone System troubleshooting, you must understand VoIP, PSTN network, PBX, SIP trunk, PRI line, and Microsoft Phone System.

© Balu N Ilag and Arun M Sabale 2022
B. N. Ilag and A. M. Sabale, *Troubleshooting Microsoft Teams*, https://doi.org/10.1007/978-1-4842-8622-7_6

Public Switched Telephone Network: The PSTN is the whole global telephone network operated by different national, regional, and local telephone companies. The PSTN offers the infrastructure and services for public telecommunications, including all telephone lines, mobile networks, communication satellites, fiber optic cables, microwave transmission links, and underwater telephone cables, all of which are interconnected with switching centers.

Voice over Internet Protocol (VoIP): VoIP or IP phone service allows voice and video calling and conferencing through an internet connection or a dedicated Internet Protocol (IP) network instead of dedicated voice transmission lines (traditional phone service). VoIP utilizes Voice over IP technology to transform signals from analog to digital before transmitting them over the Internet. VoIP phones and devices work with voice or video calling applications. For example, the calls between Teams clients are the VoIP calls.

Teams calls between your organization's users are handled internally within Phone System. They never go to the PSTN. This design applies to calls between users in your organization located in different countries/regions. VoIP removes long-distance costs on internal calls.

Private branch exchange: A PBX is a telephone exchange or switching system that operates in a private organization. It allows sharing of central office trunks between internally installed telephones. It offers intercommunication between those internal telephones within the organization without the help of external lines. The main office lines provide connections to the PSTN, and the PBX enables the shared use of these lines between all the organization's stations.

Session Initiation Protocol trunks: A SIP trunk facilitates an endpoint's PBX phone system to send and receive calls through the Internet. SIP trunking is a service offered by communications service providers that use the SIP to provision streaming media services and VoIP connectivity between an on-premises phone system and the PSTN. SIP trunks enable internet telephony service providers to deliver telephone services and unified communications to customers equipped with SIP-based IP PBX and unified communications facilities.

Microsoft Phone System: Phone System is a Microsoft technology for enabling call control and PBX capabilities in the Microsoft 365 or Office 365 cloud with Microsoft Teams. Calls between users in your organization are handled internally within Phone System. They never go to the PSTN. This design applies to calls between users in your organization located in different geographical areas, removing long-distance costs on these internal calls.

Microsoft Teams Phone System

Teams brings together calling, meetings, chat, collaboration, phone calls, and apps, helping you easily stay connected right in your workflow. With capabilities like spam identification, you can feel more confident answering your most important calls, and it's easy to take calls with you anywhere you go. Stay connected from wherever you're working with reliable devices, from headsets and speakers to modern desk phones, to new form factors like Teams displays for rich and productive calling experiences.

Teams Phone System is a robust calling platform that every part of the business can feel confident running on. With voice-enabled channels, departments can add calling to the channels where they chat and collaborate to help solve problems as a team. For the most critical customer service needs, Microsoft is expanding Dynamics 365 Customer Service into an all-in-one digital contact center solution, building on the power of Microsoft Teams. This brings chat, voice, and video connectivity from Dynamics 365 to Teams for a truly integrated experience. Stay up to date on customer, call, and case details right in Teams. With flexible calling service options like Operator Connect, it's simple to bring the connectivity you need to Teams with the reliability and support you expect. Build personal connections and stay in touch with colleagues and customers with Teams Phone.

Specifically, Teams Phone provided calling services to Teams. Now, the phone has evolved into many forms, but it remains an innovative tool as a concept. It's quick. It doesn't have to be a meeting. It allows for straightforward, spontaneous connections to build trust and get work done. Microsoft has shared the newest developments from Microsoft Teams Phone to help customers embrace the future of calling. Nearly 80 million people in over 180 countries rely on Teams Phone to make more prosperous and more productive calls. From experience, the world has rapidly shifted to virtual meetings.

Teams Phone System Types

Teams Phone system connectivity methods: Teams Phone System with Operator Connect is another option for providing PSTN connectivity with Teams and Phone System.

Operator Connect provides multiple functionalities such as allowing you to leverage existing contracts or find a new operator. It's an operator-managed infrastructure, so you need to keep your on-premises infrastructure. It offers enhanced support and reliability as carriers themselves manage it, and it offers faster and easier deployment.

Teams Phone System with Teams calling plans: Phone System with Teams calling plans is the Microsoft all-in-the-cloud voice solution for Teams users. In this solution, Microsoft acts as a carrier, and it is designed and managed by Microsoft. This design is the most straightforward option to connect Microsoft Phone System to the PSTN. This configuration enables calls to landlines and mobile phones around the world. However, calling is not available everywhere, so you must check if Teams calling plans are available in your country/region.

Teams calling plans provide domestic or international calls that enable calling to phones worldwide (depending on the type of service being licensed). Another advantage is that deployment or maintenance of an on-premises deployment isn't necessary because calling plans operates out of Microsoft 365.

Teams Phone System Direct Routing: Direct Routing allows Phone System to connect through an organization's on-premises SBC to the PSTN using its own telephony carrier. Direct Routing also enables an organization to connect its SBC to a telephony trunk using third-party hardware. It can configure interoperability between its on-premises telephony equipment, including PBX and analog devices, and Phone System.

Direct Routing provides multiple features. For example, the organization can reuse its existing investment by connecting its own supported SBC to Microsoft Phone System without the need for other on-premises software, it can use any telephony carrier with Teams Phone System, and an organization can configure interoperability between Microsoft Phone System and its telephony equipment, such as a third-party PBX and analog devices. Additionally, an organization can choose to configure and manage this option, or it can be configured and managed by its carrier or partner (assuming the carrier or partner provides this option).

There are some requirements for Direct Routing, such as organizations must have an uninterrupted connection to Microsoft 365, organizations must deploy and maintain a supported SBC, and they must have a contract with a third-party carrier (unless it's deployed as an option to provide a connection to third-party PBX, analog devices, or other telephony equipment for users who are on Phone System with a calling plan.)

Teams Phone System Direct routing is a popular connectivity mechanism because it is available in almost all countries and virtually any telephony carrier supported with Teams Phone System with supported SBC. You can refer to Chapter 3 for the configuration information for Teams calling plans, Operator Connect, and Teams Direct Routing. This chapter covers the troubleshooting aspect of Teams Direct Routing.

> **Note**   Teams calling plans are managed services from Microsoft so Microsoft manages and controls them.
>
> Teams Operator Connect, a managed infrastructure service, controls (PSTN calling services and SBCs) services from certified carriers.

Teams Phone Number Types

Microsoft Teams make use of different kinds of telephone numbers depending on the purpose for which the phone number will be used.

User phone numbers: These numbers can be assigned to users in an organization for calling purposes. There are two kinds of user numbers: geographic numbers and non-geographic numbers.

Service numbers: These numbers are assigned to services such as audio conferencing, auto attendants, and call queues. Service phone numbers have a higher concurrent call capacity than user numbers and will vary by country/region and the type of number (whether it's a toll or toll-free service number).

Troubleshooting Microsoft Teams Phone System

This section teaches you how Teams Phone System works, best practices, and the actual scenarios that you may encounter in your environment plus troubleshooting steps.

Troubleshooting Direct Routing Issues

Direct Routing (DR) allows an organization to connect its SBC to a telephony trunk using third-party hardware. It can configure interoperability between its on-premises telephony equipment, including PBX and analog devices, and Phone System.

When To Use Direct Routing

You can use DR when you want to connect Teams with a phone system. DR allows you to keeping your current PSTN carrier when you want to mix routing, with some calls going through a Microsoft calling plan and some through your carrier.

Microsoft Phone System Direct Routing connects an on-premises telephony system to Microsoft Teams. This section covers troubleshooting the common issues with Direct Routing.

First, make sure Teams Direct Routing is configured, SBC with PSTN connectivity is up and running, and SIP options inbound and outbound are working to a Teams SIP proxy and PSTN service provider device. You can refer to Chapter 3 for setup information.

1. Check the license assignment:

   - The first thing to check is whether the user has a Teams license assigned.

   - The user can have a Phone System license assigned as an add-on or part of the E5 license suite.

   - Optionally, the user may require an Audio-Conferencing license if they want to dial into meetings.

2. Check the policy assignment:

   - The user must be enabled for Enterprise Voice with a voice routing policy and dial plan policy assigned to make phone calls.

3. Check the phone number assigned to the user account. Use the following command to check and assign the phone number to the user account.

   You can run the below command to check that the user has an on-premise phone number.

   ```
   Get-CsOnlineUser -Identity "<User name>" | fl OnPremLineUri,LineUri
   ```

   The below comment enables users for Enterprise Voice when using on-premise phone numbers.

   ```
   Set-CsPhoneNumberAssignment -Identity "<User name>"
   -EnterpriseVoiceEnabled $true
   ```

   The below command assigns a phone number to the user account with the phone number type as DirectRourting.

   ```
   Set-CsPhoneNumberAssignment -Identity "<User name>" -PhoneNumber
   <phone number> -PhoneNumberType DirectRouting
   ```

4. If the issue persists, run Teams Direct Routing diagnostics.

    You can run Teams Direct Routing-specific diagnostics by
    explaining the problem. Log into the Microsoft 365 admin center
    as an administrator to run the diagnostic first. Select Show all ➤
    Support ➤ New service request in the navigation window.

    On the new service request page, describe the issue in natural
    language. You will be prompted to enter more information to help
    diagnose the problem. As you enter the case, possible matches
    are displayed together with recommended articles for you to read.
    After the diagnostic tool has finished searching, it shows steps you
    can take to resolve the problem. Direct Routing is one of several
    scenarios currently supported in Teams diagnostics.

Troubleshooting Dial Pad Problems

Sometimes the user doesn't see the dial pad in the Teams client. If a user has stated
that the dial pad is missing from the Calls screen in Teams and the user cannot make
outbound calls, check the following things:

- Verify the license assignment and check if the user has a Teams
  license and Phone System license assigned.

- If the user is set up for a calling plan, check if the user has a calling
  plan assigned.

- Check if Enterprise Voice is enabled; if it's not allowed, allow
  Enterprise Voice for the user account.

- The Teams dial pad will not know when the user is in Islands mode.

- The user must have a voice routing policy (policy
  OnlineVoiceRoutingPolicy value set policy name). PowerShell
  command example:

  ```
  Grant-CsOnlineVoiceRoutingPolicy -Identity "Balu Ilag"
  -PolicyName $Null
  Grant-CsOnlineVoiceRoutingPolicy -Identity "Balu Ilag"
  -PolicyName "USA-CA-Tracy-International"
  ```

- After a few hours, the user should see the dial pad on the Calls screen.

Note   If the `OnlineVoiceRoutingPolicy` value is set incorrectly, then the
admin should select the correct value for the policy to force an update.

Troubleshooting Phone Number Issues

Sometimes admins assign a phone number to the user account, but it doesn't show;
because of the latency between Microsoft 365 and Teams, it can take up to 24 hours
for users to be allowed. Contact Microsoft support if the phone number isn't assigned
correctly after 24 hours.

Unable to Find Direct Routing Phone Numbers in the Teams Admin Center

This is expected behavior. Teams Direct Routing numbers can only be assigned with
PowerShell. Here is the PowerShell command:

```
Set-CsPhoneNumberAssignment -Identity "baluilag@bloguc.com" -PhoneNumber
"+14081234567;ext=1001" -PhoneNumberType DirectRouting
```

How Do Microsoft Teams Use Reverse Number Lookup?

Reverse number lookup (RNL) is the method that is mainly used for translating phone
numbers to calling parties' names. In Teams, when the user receives external phone
(PSTN) calls in their Teams client, RNL will show the display name of the calling party
instead of the actual phone number. Along with RNL, the Teams system converts the
number calling the user to a name configured in their Teams contacts, Outlook contacts,
or even an Azure Active Directory account.

Investigating RNL Issues

When you receive PSTN calls in your Teams client, RNL will show the display name of
the calling party instead of the actual phone number. The following order will be applied
to check for a match in sequence with the last match being shown:

1. SIP Invite From Header

2. Azure Active Directory

3. Outlook contacts

4. Teams contacts

Teams call display names will also appear in your activity feed, call history, and voicemail. If the display name is not being displayed, or the display name is not what you would expect, follow the below steps until you have found the issue. Check the user's personal Teams contacts or Outlook contacts for a match. This is the most common reason for an "incorrect" display name appearing.

It is essential to review Azure Active Directory users and contacts for a match with PowerShell.

```
Get-User |ft DisplayName, *phone*
Get-Contact |ft DisplayName, *phone*
```

Review the output for a match. If a match is found, correct the display name. If no match is found, add or edit a contact as appropriate.

If the issue persists and you are utilizing Direct Routing, check the SBC syslog (SIP logs) for the SIP Invite From Header and check its display. Below, the example invite shows the from and to name coming from the carrier. If these names are correct, then the issue is with local contacts only.

```
INVITE sip:+14081234567@12.9.10.190;user=phone SIP/2.0
Via: SIP/2.0/UDP 12.3.51.12:5060;branch=z9hG4bKe2gc2o20b02kjfibaig0.1
From: "Balu N Ilag"<sip:+14082345678@15.88.39.7;user=phone>;t
ag=763225069-1649211816987-
To: "Chanda B Ilag."<sip:+14081234567@12.9.10.190;user=phone>
Call-ID: BW022336987060422197536154l@152.188.39.7
CSeq: 1045929486 INVITE
```

Identifying and Troubleshooting Direct Routing Issues

Teams Direct Routing allows an organization to utilize its existing PTSN infrastructure and its existing PBX. Direct Routing is used in situations where no calling plans are available. Teams Direct Routing presents unique capabilities for troubleshooting that are not accessible for calling plans or Operator Connect.

Troubleshooting Certificate Issues for Direct Routing

Teams Direct Routing requires your SBC to have a valid TLS certificate. The certificate must have the SBC FQDN as the common name (CN) or the subject alternative name (SAN) field. The certificate should be issued directly from an external certification authority, not an intermediate provider.

The Teams admin can check the TLS connectivity status for each SBC under the Teams admin center. To check, log into Teams admin center ➤ Voice ➤ Direct Routing, which shows the SBC list with TLS connectivity status, SIP Option status, concurrent calls capacity, and more. TLS handshake monitoring will flag if a certificate is invalid or expired. Figure 6-1 shows the SBC list. Note that sbc1 – sbc4 have TLS connectivity status as Active, but SBC (sbc5.bloguc.com) shows that the TLS connectivity status is Inactive and has a certificate that has expired.

Figure 6-1. *Teams DR SBC TLS connectivity status*

Basically, Phone System has several mechanisms to detect the health of the connected SBCs. Together with TLS handshake monitoring, SIP options help detect the issues on the application level. Imagine you have a trunk that can be reached on the network level by a ping, but a certificate has expired or the SIP stack doesn't work. To identify the issues early, Microsoft recommends enabling sending SIP Options to the Teams SIP proxy server. You may need to consult with your SBC manufacturer documentation to configure sending the SIP options.

The direct routing dashboard will warn if a certificate expires within 30 days. You can renew the certificate before the service is disrupted. By selecting the Warning message, you can see a detailed issue description in a pop-up window on the right and recommendations for how to fix an issue.

Alert message: Teams DR monitors trunk connectivity every 15 seconds using a TLS handshake and SIP options monitoring. To troubleshoot and fix, check your SBC certificate validity, check the trunk availability, check your network environment and firewall, and make sure that sending SIP options on the trunk is turned on.

Troubleshooting SIP Options Issues

Teams Direct Routing utilizes SIP Options sent by the SBCs to monitor SBC health. It will monitor trunk connectivity every 15 seconds using a TLS handshake and SIP options monitoring. SIP options is a SIP method; it lets a User Agent (UA) query another UA or a proxy regarding its capabilities. In this case, the Teams Service is a UA and the SBC is a UA.

There are no actions required from the tenant admin to enable the SIP options monitoring because it's enabled by default. You, as admin, can turn SIP Option requests on or off for an individual SBC. Direct Routing takes the regular one-minute interval options three times. If options were sent during the last three minutes, the SBC is considered healthy. If the SBC is not sending SIP options, the SBC is deemed to be unhealthy. Figure 6-1 shows the SIP options status as Active for sbc1 to sbc4, which is healthy, but sbc5 shows a SIP options status as a warning, which means it's unhealthy.

As an admin, you can review the health of SIP options in Teams admin center ➤ Voice ➤ Direct Routing. It is recommended that your SBC be configured to send SIP options. If it cannot, or you do not want to send SIP Options, you can turn off this monitoring in the SBC config on the Teams admin center. Log into the Microsoft Teams admin center at https://admin.teams.microsoft.com. Then click Voice and select Direct Routing. Then select the relevant SBC to troubleshoot. Then go to the settings tab and set Send SIP options to off. Refer to Figure 6-2 to enable or disable the Send SIP Option request. This figure shows that the Send SIP Option is enabled, which can be disabled by toggling the switch from on to off.

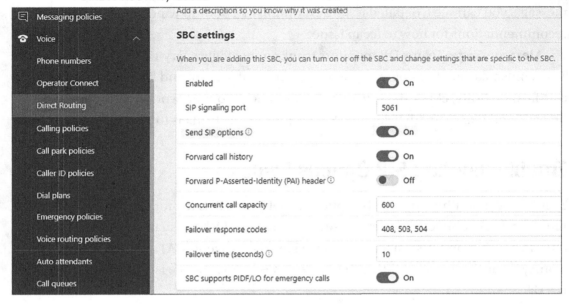

Figure 6-2. *SIP options*

If you turn off SIP Options, the SBC will be excluded from the Teams monitoring and
alerting system. Calls may continue to be routed to this SBC even if it is offline.

Troubleshooting Direct Routing SBC Connectivity

Sometimes you may see connectivity issues between your SBC and the Teams SIP
proxy service; you can check the network performance between the SBC and the
service in the Teams admin center. Log into the Teams admin center at https://
admin.teams.microsoft.com and select Voice and Direct Routing. Then select the SBC
in question. Under Usage, look at Network parameters. You have options to choose 7
days, 30 days, or 60 days. Figure 6-3 shows that the SBC sbc7.bloguc.com displays the
network effectiveness (call) as 88.3% because network parameters show high latency,
contributing to call quality degradation. Also, you can see the average latency, jitter,
packet loss, and any peaks.

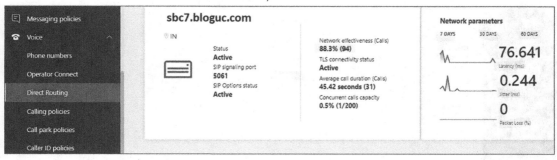

Figure 6-3. *Network parameters*

Apart from network parameters, Microsoft additionally calculates a network effectiveness ratio for each SBC. This is an ITU-T recommended parameter to measure the ability of the network to deliver calls. It is calculated based on this formula:

$NER = Answered\ calls + UserBusy + Ring\ no\ Answer + Terminal$
$RejectSeizures\ x\ 100$

The ratio calculates how many calls were sent. It ignores user-related errors, such as unanswered calls or user-rejected calls. If the value decreases, it indicates that the network has a problem that requires investigation.

Examining the PSTN Usage Reports for SIP Call Failures

It is essential to analyze the PSTN usage report. There is a wealth of Direct Routing troubleshooting information in a place you might not expect. To see these reports, log into the Teams admin center, go to Analytics & reports, and select Usage Reports.

- Select the dropdown below Report and select PSTN and SMS (preview) usage.

- Select a date range; the last 28 days is fine for this troubleshooting.

- Select Run report.

- Select the Direct Routing tab. Refer to Figure 6-4, which shows DR PSTN and SMS usage reports.

Figure 6-4. *PSTN and SMS (preview) usage*

Here is the list of parameters you will see in the Direct Routing call log with all the usual call details for each call:

- **Invite time (UTC)**: The time when the initial Invite was sent on an outbound call from a Teams user or bot call to the SBC or received on an inbound call to a Teams or bot call by the SIP Proxy component of Direct Routing from the SBC.

- **Failure time (UTC)**: The time the call failed. For failed calls only. Final SIP Code, Final Microsoft subcode, and Final SIP Phrase explain why the call failed and can help with troubleshooting.

- **End time (UTC)**: The time the call ended (for successful calls only).

- **Success**: If the call was successful or not.

- **Azure region for media**: The data center is used as a media path in a non-bypass call.

- **Azure region for signaling**: The data center is used for signaling bypass and non-bypass calls.

- **Final SIP code**: The code with which the call ended

- **Final SIP phrase**: The description of the SIP code and Microsoft subcode

- **Media bypass**: Indicates whether the trunk was enabled for media bypass

Checking and Validating SBC Connections

When you use Teams DR for connecting your on-premises telephony infrastructure to
Microsoft Teams, an on-premises SBS is used to communicate to Phone System Direct
Routing. One or more SBCs may be installed depending on the volume of calls and high
availability needs within your organization.

It is recommended to check that the SBC is on the list of paired SBCs and validate
the SIP options. This will verify that the SBC connection has been made. Also, see the
PowerShell script to test Direct Routing SBC connections (`https://docs.microsoft.
com/en-us/microsoftteams/sip-tester-powershell-script`).

Using the Teams Direct Routing Dashboard
for a Health Check

The Health Dashboard for Direct Routing allows you to monitor the interface between
the SBC and Direct Routing. The Health Dashboard provides high-level information
about the connected SBCs and detailed information. You must be logged in as an
administrator to access the health dashboard. Figure 6-5 shows the Direct Routing
dashboard, in that sbc5.bloguc.com offers enabled status as off and all SBCs are enabled
status On.

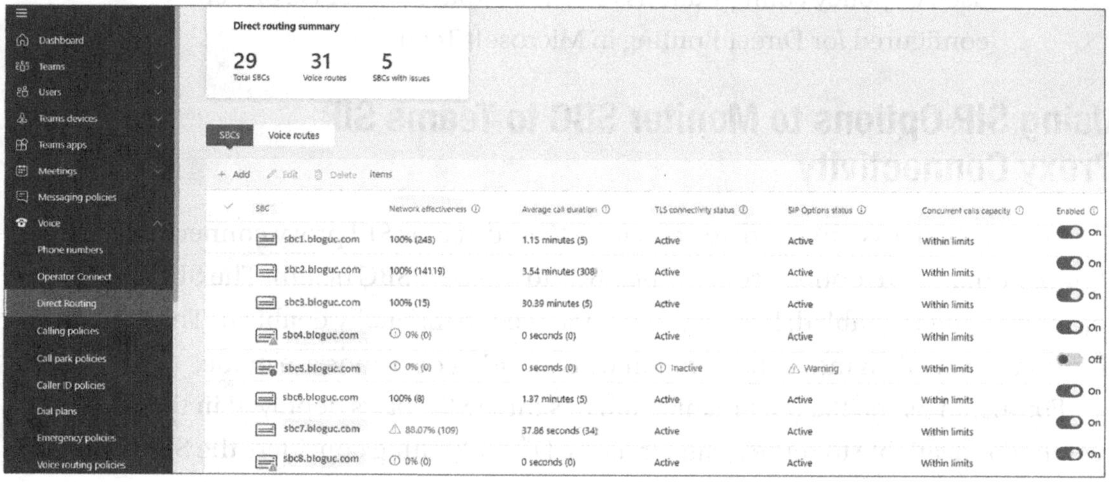

Figure 6-5. *Teams DR Dashboard*

Troubleshooting Direct Routing Configuration

Teams Direct Routing provides inbound and outbound call capability that requires different components, such as SBCs, Direct Routing components in the Microsoft cloud, and the telecom trunks. These components are supported by other vendors: SBCs are supported by SBC vendors, Teams DR components are supported by Microsoft, and telecom trunks are supported by the telecom provider. You may have to open a support case with the respective vendor.

Here are a few tools that help in Teams DR troubleshooting.

Teams Direct Routing Diagnostic Tool

This tool help validate that a user is correctly configured for Direct Routing:

1. First, select Run Tests, which will populate the diagnostic in the Microsoft 365 Admin Center.

   Run Tests: Direct Routing (https://aka.ms/TeamsDirectRoutingDiag)

2. Enter the user's email you want to test in the Username or Email field in the Run diagnostic pane, and then select Run Tests.

3. The tests will return the best next steps to address any tenant, user, or policy configurations to validate that the user is correctly configured for Direct Routing in Microsoft Teams.

Using SIP Options to Monitor SBC to Teams SIP Proxy Connectivity

SIP options is an essential tool to validate SBC and Teams SIP proxy connectivity. Direct Routing utilizes SIP options sent by the SBCs to monitor SBC health. The SIP option for monitoring is enabled; hence, you do not need to manually enable it. The collected information is taken into consideration when routing decisions are made.

For instance, the Bloguc organization has three SBC pairs deployed in the USA region. It is available to route a call for users. Direct Routing considers the SIP options information received from each SBC to determine routing.

Teams Direct routing routes call to the SBC, which is healthy. An SBC is considered healthy if statistics at the moment of sending the call show that the SBC sends options every minute. Direct Routing takes the regular interval options three times (the normal interval is one minute). If options were sent during the last three minutes, the SBC is considered healthy.

Analysis of the SBC Syslog

As the admin, you may encounter issues like outbound calls not working even though the Teams user account has the correct voice policy assigned or inbound calls not reaching Teams users. In these situations, the SBC syslog comes handy to validate that the outbound call is getting to the SBC and its route to the carrier or inbound call reaches SBC from the carrier and it routes to Teams DR.

The SBC syslogs offer information about the issues related to the pairing of the SBCs and the Direct Routing service. In addition to the Call Quality Dashboard, you can also use SBC syslogs to view the descriptive error codes stored in the logs. They can help you identify the root cause of direct-dialing call issues.

Issues with SBC pairing or where the SIP "Invite" was rejected (such as when the name of the trunk FQDN is misconfigured) can be identified from the SBC logs. Direct Routing sends a detailed description to the SBCs recorded in the SBC logs. Refer to the SBC vendor instructions for further details.

Inbound or Outbound Call Troubleshooting Using SBC Syslog

This section discusses inbound and outbound call routing and connection issues with SBC logs, so use it as a pointer and find actual causes.

Before an incoming or outbound call can be handled, OPTIONS messages are exchanged between the Teams SIP Proxy server and the SBC device. These OPTIONS messages allow the Teams SIP Proxy to provide the permitted capabilities to the SBC. OPTIONS negotiation needs to be successful (200 OK response), allowing for further communication between the SBC and Teams SIP Proxy for establishing calls.

When you encounter an inbound or outbound call issue, you need to capture the SBC syslog with helpful information. To capture the SBC syslog, refer to your SBC vendor instructions. Typically, you get a tool that you can install on your computer. You add your computer IP address inside the SBC under logging configuration so that the SBC can send the log to your computer.

Here is additional information for each call process step:

- INVITE: Call Invite

- 100 Trying:

- 180 Ringing: Call progress – converted by the SIP proxy to the SIP message 180. On receiving message 180, the SBC must generate local ringing.

- 183 Session Progress: Media answer, converted by the SIP proxy to message 183 with media candidates in Session Description Protocol (SDP). On receiving message 183, the SBC expects to connect to the media candidates received in the SDP message.

- 200 OK: Call accepted, converted by the SIP proxy to SIP message 200 with SDP. On receiving message 200, the SBC is expected to send and receive media to and from the provided SDP candidates.

- ACK:

- BY:

Inbound Calls Media Flow Details

The SIP proxy needs to find the tenant to which the call is destined and find the specific user within this tenant on an incoming call. The tenant administrator might configure non-DID numbers, like +1001, in multiple tenants. Therefore, finding the particular tenant to perform the reverse number lookup is essential because the non-DID numbers might be the same in various Microsoft 365 or Office 365 organizations.

Note   Microsoft recommends consistently applying the user=phone parameter to simplify the call setup process.

Request-URI: For all incoming calls, the Request-URI matches the phone number of a user. Here is the example request: URI, INVITE sip:+14081234567@sip.pstnhub.microsoft.com:5061;user=phone SIP/2.0

From Header: For all incoming calls, the From Header matches the caller's phone number against the callee's blocked phone number list.

From: "Office"<sip:+14081234567@sbc1.bloguc.com:5061;user=phone>;tag=428 1ef6c-19fef6;sgid=15

SBC, Teams proxy, internal and external phone numbers:

- SBC FQDN = sbc1.bloguc.com

- Teams SIP proxy IP: *52.114.148.0*

- From external number: Balu Ilag (4081234567)

- To Teams number: +12091234567

Successful Inbound Call Session Information

Sending To 52.114.148.0:5061 from 60.12.230.108:28547 via TLS

CALL-ID: call-E3426BE9-0700-0010-0014-3AA93@60.12.230.108

GCID: 154337

Message found at line: 8275

INVITE sip:+14081234567@sip.pstnhub.microsoft.com:5061;user=phone SIP/2.0

Allow: INVITE, ACK, CANCEL, BYE, NOTIFY, OPTIONS, REFER, REGISTER, INFO, UPDATE, PRACK

Call-ID: call-E3426BE9-0700-0010-0014-3AA93@60.12.230.108

Contact: <sip:+12091234567@sbc1.bloguc.com:5061;transport=TLS;mad dr=60.12.230.108>

Content-Length: 429

Content-Type: application/sdp

CSeq: 2 INVITE

From: "Office" <sip:+14081234567@sbc1.bloguc.com:5061;user=phone>;tag=4281 ef6c-19fef6;sgid=15

Max-Forwards: 69

Min-SE: 600

P-Asserted-Identity: "Office" <sip:+14081234567@sbc1.bloguc. com:5061;user=phone>

Session-Expires: 3600

Supported: replaces,update,timer,100rel

To: <sip:+14081234567@sip.pstnhub.microsoft.com:5061;user=phone>

User-Agent: SONUS SBC2000 9.0.3v584 Ribbon

Via: SIP/2.0/TLS 60.12.230.108:5061;branch=z9hG4bK-UX-4281-ef6c-2c57dc

X-Sonus-Diagnostics: SBCInternal;cid=154337;media-mode="audio:DSP video:N/
A";tdmchannel="b:0 t:15 g:1 c:1"

X-MS-SBC: Ribbon/2000/9.0.3v584

Figure 6-6 shows the successful inbound call with all the steps involved in the process.

```
[2022-04-17 16:35:12:602]  ---------------->  INVITE
[2022-04-17 16:35:12:639]  <----------------  100 Trying
[2022-04-17 16:35:12:640]  <----------------  100 Trying
[2022-04-17 16:35:12:753]  <----------------  INVITE
[2022-04-17 16:35:12:777]  ---------------->  100 Trying
[2022-04-17 16:35:14:581]  ---------------->  180 Ringing
[2022-04-17 16:35:14:590]  <----------------  180 Ringing
[2022-04-17 16:35:14:591]  <----------------  180 Ringing
[2022-04-17 16:35:15:042]  ---------------->  180 Ringing
[2022-04-17 16:35:15:088]  ---------------->  180 Ringing
[2022-04-17 16:35:15:572]  ---------------->  183 Session Progress
[2022-04-17 16:35:15:592]  <----------------  183 Session Progress
[2022-04-17 16:35:15:594]  <----------------  183 Session Progress
[2022-04-17 16:35:17:285]  ---------------->  180 Ringing
[2022-04-17 16:35:18:267]  ---------------->  180 Ringing
[2022-04-17 16:35:19:261]  ---------------->  200 OK
[2022-04-17 16:35:19:283]  <----------------  ACK
[2022-04-17 16:35:19:307]  <----------------  200 OK
[2022-04-17 16:35:19:308]  <----------------  200 OK
[2022-04-17 16:35:19:763]  ---------------->  ACK
[2022-04-17 16:35:19:839]  <----------------  INVITE
[2022-04-17 16:35:19:915]  ---------------->  100 Trying
[2022-04-17 16:35:20:815]  ---------------->  200 OK
[2022-04-17 16:35:20:829]  <----------------  ACK
[2022-04-17 16:35:24:515]  ---------------->  BYE
[2022-04-17 16:35:24:524]  <----------------  200 OK
[2022-04-17 16:35:24:525]  <----------------  200 OK
[2022-04-17 16:35:24:533]  <----------------  BYE
[2022-04-17 16:35:24:672]  ---------------->  200 OK
```

Figure 6-6. *Call setup process steps*

The Teams Direct routing PSTN call media flow ladder diagram is shown in
Figure 6-7.

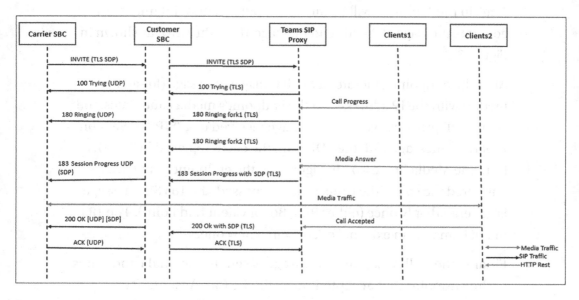

Figure 6-7. *Teams DR PSTN call media setup*

Process Teams SIP Proxy

This call process ladder diagram shows the inbound call setup from the carrier to the
SBC to the Teams SIP proxy to the endpoints.

- On receiving the first Invite from the SBC (60.12.230.108), the Teams
  SIP proxy (52.114.148.0) sends the message "SIP SIP/2.0 100 Trying"
  and notifies all end user endpoints about the incoming call.

- After the notification is received, each Teams endpoint will start
  ringing and sending "SIP/2.0 180 Ringing Call progress" messages to
  the SIP proxy. Because a Teams user can have multiple endpoints, the
  SIP proxy may receive multiple Call Progress messages.

- The SIP proxy converts the Call Progress message to the SIP message
  "SIP SIP/2.0 180 Ringing" for every Call Progress message received
  from the clients. The interval for sending such messages is defined
  by the interval of the receiving messages from the Call Controller.
  In Figure 6-6, there are two 180 messages generated by the SIP
  proxy. These messages come from the two Teams endpoints of the

user. The clients each have a unique Tag ID. Every message coming from a different endpoint will be a separate session (the parameter "tag" in the "To" field will be different). But an endpoint might not generate message 180 and send message 183 right away, as shown in Figure 6-6.

- After the endpoint generates a Media Answer message (for actual media) with the IP addresses of the endpoint's media candidates, the Teams SIP proxy converts the message received to a "SIP 183 Session Progress" message with the SDP from the client replaced by the SDP from the Media Processor. In Figure 6-7, the endpoint from Fork 2 answered the call. If the trunk is non-bypassed, the 183 SIP message is generated only once (either Ring Bot or Client End Point). The 183 might come on an existing fork or start a new one.

- Finally, the Call Acceptance message is sent to the final candidates of the endpoint that accepted the call. The Call Acceptance message is converted to SIP message 200 OK. This message goes from the Teams SIP proxy to the SBC to the carrier device. At this media, a session was established, and call audio media started flowing. Refer to Figure 6-7.

Teams Call Media Flow in a Media Bypass Scenario

In a media bypass scenarios, similar messages are used like 100 Trying, 180, 183 progress. In this call, media candidates can come from different endpoints. Refer to Figure 6-8.

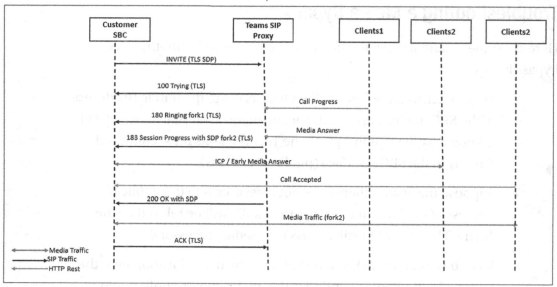

Figure 6-8. Teams PSTN call media flow with a media bypass

Media Bypass with Direct Routing

Media bypass allows you to shorten the path of media traffic to improve performance and call quality. In a bypass, scenario media stays between the SBC and the Teams client instead of being sent to the Microsoft Phone System (SIP proxy). The SBC and the Teams client must be in the exact location or network for configuring the media bypass. Without media bypass, media will flow to Microsoft data centers and back to the SBC. With media bypass, the media is kept between the Teams user and SBC, as shown in Figure 6-9.

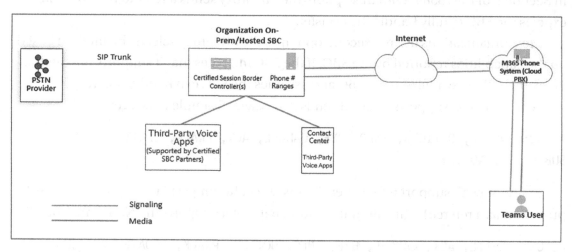

Figure 6-9. Teams DR with media bypass

Troubleshooting a Media Bypass

Here are some essential considerations that help in troubleshooting media
bypass issues:

- First, check that the Teams client has access to the public IP address
  of the SBC, including from the organization's internal network. This
  is known as "hair-pinning." All the Teams clients must communicate
  directly to the SBC interface (public IP address).

- Suppose the Teams client does not have access to the public IP
  address of the SBC. In that case, the media will be relayed by the
  Teams TR servers but still bypass the media processors.

- It is a best practice to keep the SBC and the users' location near the
  Microsoft TR servers to optimize the media bypass configuration.

- Additionally, allow internal users to connect directly to the SBC
  interface (public IP address) but block the external users.

How Do Teams Call Transfers Work?

Teams supports two options for call transfers. In the first option, SIP proxy processes
refer to the client locally and act as a referee as described in section 7.1 of RFC 3892. The
SIP proxy terminates the transfer and adds a new invite with this option. In the second
option, the SIP proxy sends the refer to the SBC and acts as a transferor as described
in Section 6 of RFC 5589. With this option, the SIP proxy sends a refer to the SBC and
expects the SBC to fully handle the transfer.

Most organizations use the second option as the SIP proxy selects the method based
on the capabilities reported by the SBC. If the SBC indicates that it supports the method
Refer, the SIP proxy refers to the SBC and assumes the SBC can handle the transfer fully.

When the SBC supports refers, it sends a message. Example message:

```
ALLOW: INVITE, OPTIONS, INFO, BYE, CANCEL, ACK, PRACK, UPDATE, REFER,
SUBSCRIBE, NOTIFY
```

If SBC doesn't support refers, then Teams Direct Routing will use Option 1 (the SIP
proxy acts as a referee). The SBC must also signal that it supports the Notify method:

```
ALLOW: INVITE, ACK, CANCEL, BYE, INFO, NOTIFY, PRACK, UPDATE, OPTIONS
```

How Does the Failover Mechanism Work for SBC Connections to the Teams SIP Proxy?

Microsoft has multiple Direct Routing servers (FQDNs) deployed in different datacenters; if a Direct Routing datacenter is busy, the SIP proxy service can send a Retry-After message with a one-second interval to the SBC. When the SBC receives a 503 message with a Retry-After header in response to an INVITE, the SBC must terminate that connection and try the next available Microsoft data center.

The User Receives Multiple Missed Calls for the Declined Incoming Call

It is crucial to handle retries (603 responses). Suppose an end user observes several missed calls for one call after declining the incoming call. This means that the SBC or PSTN trunk provider's retry mechanism is misconfigured. The SBC must be reconfigured to stop the retry efforts on the 603 responses.

Troubleshooting Teams Call Routing and Normalization Issues

Phone number normalization plays a critical role in Teams phone calls. This section provides detailed information about inbound and outbound call translation rules with Teams numbers and PSTN numbers.

Using the Inbound or Outbound Number Translation Rule for Teams Calls

You, as an admin, must know the inbound and outbound phone number translation rules, which help ensure interoperability between the SBC and Phone System Direct Routing and create a Number Translation Rules policy using PowerShell. This rule translates numbers to the correct format. Number Translation Rules policies convert inbound calls from a caller to a Teams client or convert outbound calls from a Teams client to a PSTN endpoint (the person being called). Each policy can include multiple translation rules, which are applied in sequence.

- Inbound calls mean calls from a PSTN endpoint (caller) to a Teams client (callee)

- Outbound calls meaning calls from a Teams client (caller) to a PSTN endpoint (callee)

You can use a PowerShell command for creating, modifying, displaying, and deleting number manipulation rules, such as the `New-CsTeamsTranslationRule`, `Set-CsTeamsTranslationRule`, `Get-CsTeamsTranslationRule`, and `Remove-CsTeamsTranslationRule` cmdlets.

For example, the following command shows the number translation rule that adds + in front of a called number:

```
New-CsTeamsTranslationRule -Identity 'AddPlus1' -Pattern
'^(\d{10})$' -Translation '+1$1'
```

See Table 6-1 for rules with patterns.

Table 6-1. *Normalization Rules and Patterns*

Name	Pattern	Translation
AddPlus1	^(\d{10})$	+1$1
AddE164TracyCAAreaCode	^(\d{4})$	+1209123$1
AddTracyCAAreaCode	^(\d{4})$	408123$1
StripPlus1	^+1(\d{10})$	$1

Once the number translation rule is created, it must be assigned to the SBC configuration to make that rule in the number translation process. The following command shows the new SBC configuration with an add +1 rule and E164 with area code. The inbound PSTN number rule adds +1 and the outbound PSTN number translation rule adds the area code and strips +1.

```
New-CSOnlinePSTNGateway -Identity sbc1.bloguc.com -SipSignalingPort
5061 -InboundTeamsNumberTranslationRules 'AddPlus1', 'AddE164Tracy
CAAreaCode' -InboundPSTNNumberTranslationRules 'AddPlus1' -Outbound
PSTNNumberTranslationRules 'AddTracyCAAreaCode','StripPlus1'  -Outbound
TeamsNumberTranslationRules 'StripPlus1'
```

Note   The maximum number of translation rules is 400, the full translation
parameter name length is 100 symbols, the maximum translation parameter
pattern length is 1024 symbols, and the maximum translation parameter
translation length is 256.

Applying Number Translation Rules

It is essential to know how the translation rules get applied because you may have
multiple rules created. Number Translation Rule policy rules are applied in sequence
(top to bottom fashion).

For the troubleshooting aspect, the first thing to do is understand what rule you will
set for inbound calls; you want to normalize Teams inbound calls, PSTN inbound calls,
or outbound calls.

The next thing to check is the sequence of your rules and, if necessary, change the
policy's order. Another thing to check is the pattern and translation in the rule.

Troubleshooting Dial Plans (Normalizing
the Phone Number)

A dial plan translates a short number like an extension number into a unique number
that adheres to an international dialing standard, usually E.164. Dial plans are
implemented in the Microsoft Teams admin center using regular expressions to create
a set of normalization rules. These rules allow users to keep numbers they are familiar
with, which are then translated into internationally unique numbers.

Note   Before creating dial plans and normalization rules, decide on an organization-wide naming convention. This will decrease errors and enhance understanding when troubleshooting problems. Names should be descriptive so that anyone can understand their purpose. For example, NA-CA-Tracy-International.

There are three different types of the dial plans, which are used in order. This means that if you haven't modified any dial plan, the service dial plan will be used. If you modify the tenant global dial plan, it will be used in combination with the user dial plan. Finally, the user dial plan is used.

- **Service dial plan**: The service dial plan contains standard normalization rules and cannot be changed. The scope is everyone within the country assigned to a user record.

- **Global**: The global dial plan contains organization-wide rules customized to your organization. The scope is all users in your organization.

- **User**: The user dial plan normalization rules are customized for a specific group of users. Their scope is a group of users.

How Do Normalization Rules Work?

A dial plan is a set of rules. Each dial plan must have one or more normalization rules created using regular expressions. Normalization rules are used in sequence. The first matching rule will be used when a number is dialed, and all other rules will be ignored. Create the most restrictive rules first, followed by less restrictive rules.

Note   You can create PowerShell scripts to create dial plans. Scripts let more than one person check the rules before the script is run. You can add comments to a script to make it more understandable. Scripts are also easier to update without introducing other errors. To create dial plan scripts, you need the Teams PowerShell module.

Troubleshooting Normalization Rules

When Teams phone numbers are not normalized, you, as the admin, need to check that the normalization rules are in the correct dial plan. Dial plans are used in sequence and merged with the plan above in the hierarchy. If you have modified the global dial plan, this will be combined with the service dial plan. If you have created one or more user dial plans, they will be merged with the global dial plan.

Note   You aren't required to add a country code because it is already added in the service dial plan.

It is a best practice to test each dial plan by entering a phone number and selecting the Save & Test button. Figure 6-10 shows the dial plan testing. When you dial any six digit number, it normalizes it with the E.164 format.

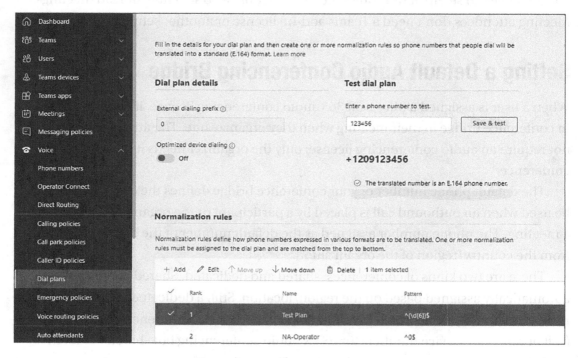

Figure 6-10. *Testing a dial plan*

Sometimes users are forced to type in five or more digits, even though a dial plan normalization rule is in place to allow short digit dialing. Users should type the whole number instead of the shortened number to isolate the dial plan issue as a workaround.

Configuring and Troubleshooting Audio Conferencing

Teams audio conferencing provides an alternate way to join a meeting through a dial-in conference bridge number. Sometimes people in your organization want to use a mobile phone or landline to call into a Teams meeting instead of their computer.

Microsoft Teams audio conferencing enables people to use a phone to join a meeting. Audio conferencing is only available in some countries, and users must have a Teams Add-on license. Not all users will require audio conferencing capabilities; you only need to set up audio conferencing for people who schedule or lead meetings. Meeting attendees don't need a Teams add-on license or another setup.

Setting a Default Audio Conferencing Bridge

When a user is assigned a Microsoft 365 audio conferencing license, it enables a dial-in conference bridge in their meeting when they organize one. The attendee does not require an audio conferencing license; only the organizer needs it to schedule a conference.

The default phone number of your conference bridge defines the caller ID that will be used when an outbound call is placed by a participant or the organizer from within a meeting. The phone number assigned as the default number of the bridge will be one from the country/region of the organization.

There are two kinds of conferences: shared and dedicated. Shared conferences are automatically assigned based on the region/location. Still, a dedicated conference bridge needs to manually be acquired from Microsoft. A dedicated conference bridge can be (toll or toll-free) service numbers for PSTN audio conferencing but shared conference bridges are always toll service numbers for PSTN audio conferencing.

Note   You will need to set up communication credits (prepared buckets of credit) for the toll-free conference bridge to work.

You, as an admin, can set up or change the default audio conferencing bridge number for your organization. Log into the Teams admin center, navigate to Meetings/Conference bridges, select a bridge number, and select "Set as Default."

Setting Up Audio Conferencing

1. First, determine whether audio conferencing is available in your region.

2. Then acquire and assign licenses for users who need them.

3. The next thing is to get service numbers for your conferencing bridges. They can be toll or toll-free numbers. You can get service numbers from the Microsoft Teams admin center in some regions. Or you can port your existing service numbers. In other cases, you may have to request a number from Microsoft.

4. Then assign a service number to the conferencing bridge.

5. Set the default and alternate languages for a conferencing bridge.

6. Set your conferencing bridge settings.

7. Then assign dial-in phone numbers for users who lead meetings.

8. Optionally, set up meeting invitations.

9. Optionally, purchase communications credits.

All these settings you can do in the Teams admin center. Here is the list of settings for audio conferencing that can be customized:

- **Audio conferencing:** To turn audio conferencing on or off for the user, select Edit (next to Audio Conferencing), and then in the Audio Conferencing pane, toggle Audio conferencing on or off.

- **Send conference info in the email:** Select this link only if you want to immediately send an email to the user with their conference ID and phone number. (This email does not include the PIN.)

- **Conference ID:** Select *Reset conference ID* if you need to reset the conference ID for the user.

- **PIN:** Select Reset PIN if you need to reset the PIN for the user.

- **Default conferencing toll phone number (required):** These are numbers set on the audio conferencing bridge. Format the numbers as you want them to appear in Microsoft Teams meeting requests. To change the default toll number, select Edit (next to Audio Conferencing). In the Audio Conferencing pane, pick a number under Toll number.

- **Invites from this user can include a toll-free number:** To change this setting, select Edit (next to Audio Conferencing), and in the Audio Conferencing pane, toggle *Include toll-free numbers in meeting requests from this user* on or off.

- **Unauthenticated users can be the first person in the meeting:** To change this setting, toggle *Unauthenticated users can be the first person in the meeting* on or off.

- **Dial-out permissions:** To change this setting, click Edit (next to Audio Conferencing), and in the Audio Conferencing pane, choose an option under *Dial-out from meetings*.

Communications Credits

Consider purchasing communications credits. Communications credits are used to pay for audio conferencing and calling plan minutes. They ensure that users can always

- Add toll-free numbers with audio conferencing meetings, auto attendants, or call queues. Toll-free calls are billed per minute and require a positive communications credits balance.

- Dial out from an audio conference meeting to add someone else from anywhere in the world.

- Dial out from an audio conference meeting to a mobile phone with the Microsoft Teams app or Skype for Business app installed to destinations that aren't already included in your subscription.

- Dial any international phone number when you have domestic calling plan subscriptions.

- Dial international phone numbers beyond what is included in a domestic and international calling plan subscription.

- Dial out and pay per minute once you have exhausted your monthly minute allotment.

Suppose you do not set up communications credits. Users may run out of minutes depending on your calling plan, audio conferencing plan, and country or region. This results in users not being able to make calls or dial out from online audio-conferencing meetings.

Troubleshooting Phone System, Numbers, Dial Plans, Voice Routing, and Emergency Call Routing Policies

Microsoft's technology that allows call control and PBX capabilities is called Phone System. This section covers voice and end user-level troubleshooting for how users dial phone numbers. Teams provides the cloud voice capabilities delivered from Microsoft 365; these functionalities include PBX functionality and options for connecting to the PSTN.

Teams Phone System allows users to place and receive calls, transfer calls, and mute or unmute calls. Phone System features include call answering and initiating (by name and number) with an integrated dial pad, call holding and retrieving, call forwarding and simultaneous ringing, call history, voicemail, and emergency calls.

Additionally, users can use different devices to establish calls, including mobile devices, a headset connected to a computer, and IP phones.

Managing and Troubleshooting Phone Number Assignment Issues

You must first get phone numbers before assigning phone numbers to your organization's users or services. There are three ways to get phone numbers:

1. Get new numbers for users using the Teams admin center; select countries/regions for the phone number.

2. Use the port option. Port your existing numbers. You can port or transfer existing numbers from your current service provider or phone carrier.

3.   Use a request form for new numbers. Depending on your country/
     region, you may not be able to get your new phone numbers using
     the Microsoft Teams admin center, or you will need specific phone
     numbers or area codes. You download a form, complete it, and
     return it to Microsoft.

How Many Numbers Can You Get?

The number of phone numbers for users (subscribers) equals the total number of
domestic calling plan and/or domestic and international calling plan licenses you have
assigned multiplied by 1.1, plus 10 additional phone numbers. For example, if you have
50 users in total with a domestic calling plan and/or domestic and international calling
plan, you can acquire 65 phone numbers (50 x 1.1 + 10).

What Kind of Phone Numbers?

Teams use different telephone number types depending on the purpose for which the
phone number will be used:

1.   **User numbers:** You can assign these numbers to users in your
     organization for calling purposes.

2.   **Service numbers:** You can assign these numbers to services such
     as audio conferencing, auto attendants, and call queues.

Note   Service phone numbers, which have a higher concurrent call capacity than
user numbers, vary by country/region and the type of number (whether it's a toll or
toll-free number).

How Do You Assign Phone Numbers to Users?

Once you get the phone numbers, assign them to users and create calling plans. You can
use the Microsoft Teams admin center to give a phone number to a user and later change
or remove the phone number if needed. To assign a number:

1.   Log into the Teams admin center and in the left navigation, select
     Voice, and then select Phone numbers.

2. Select an unassigned number on the list on the Phone numbers page, and then select Edit.

3. Under Assigned to, search for the user by display name or username in the Edit pane and select Assign.

4. To assign or change the associated emergency location, under Emergency location, search for and then select the location and finally select Save.

Assigning a phone number using PowerShell: To establish a remote PowerShell session with Teams, you first need to install the module and connect to Microsoft Teams. To install the Teams PowerShell module, use the following command:

```
Install-Module MicrosoftTeams
```

After you install the module, you can establish a remote session with your tenant with the following command:

```
Connect-MicrosoftTeams
```

Before assigning a phone number and emergency location, you can retrieve a list of phone numbers and locations available. This makes finding free numbers to assign easier and ensures you specify the correct location ID for emergency services. To retrieve a list of phone numbers and their respective activation state, use the following command:

```
Get-CsOnlineTelephoneNumber | ft Id,ActivationState
```

To retrieve a list of emergency locations that are validated, use the following command:

```
Get-CsOnlineLisLocation -ValidationStatus Validated
```

After selecting a phone number and emergency location, use the Set-CsOnline VoiceUser command in a format like the following one to enable the user for Teams Voice:

```
Set-CsOnlineVoiceUser -Identity "<User name>" -TelephoneNumber
+12091234567 -LocationID b42m21t-10d7-95b0-9ddb-5432d29d606b
```

Here is newly introduced command for phone number assignment:

```
Set-CsPhoneNumberAssignment -Identity baluilag@bloguc.com -PhoneNumber
"+12091234567" -PhoneNumberType CallingPlan
Set-CsPhoneNumberAssignment -Identity "baluilag@bloguc.com" -PhoneNumber
"+12091234567" -PhoneNumberType DirectRouting
```

Assigning a Dial Plan, Voice Routing, Emergency Call Routing, and Calling Policies to a User

Multiple policies can be assigned to Teams users to enable different features like allowing the user to dial out. Still, two essential policies for Voice are dial plans and calling policies. You can refer to Chapter 3 for policy creation information.

A dial plan is a named set of normalization rules that translate dialed phone numbers by an individual user into an alternate format (typically E.164) for call authorization and voice routing purposes. They describe how phone numbers expressed in various formats are translated to an alternate format. Another important policy is the calling policy, which controls the available features for the user. To assign policies and dial plans to a user, follow these steps:

1. Log into the Teams admin center (`https://admin.teams.microsoft.com`) with an account that has the Teams Administrator role.

2. Select Users and search for a user's name in the left navigation on the Teams admin center page.

3. Select the user you want to assign the policy to by checking the space in front of the user's name and then choose Edit Settings.

4. In the edit pane on the right, scroll down to Dial plan and select Global (**o**rg-wide default) or any other policy you want to assign from the dropdown menu.

5. Still in the edit pane on the right, navigate the Calling policy and then select AllowCalling or any other calling policy you want to assign from the dropdown menu. Review the different policy types you can assign through this dialogue and then select Apply.

Assigning Policies Through the Teams PowerShell Module

Using PowerShell, an admin can assign each policy type to individual users. Each policy type comes with its own set of commands for managing it. The `Grant-` command will allow you to assign existing policies.

For a dial plan, use the `Grant-CsTenantDialPlan` command with the following format:

```
Grant-CsTenantDialPlan -Identity baluilag@bloguc.com -PolicyName
NAM-CA-Tracy
```

For a Voice policy, use the `Grant-CsonlineVoiceRoutingPolicy` command with the following format:

```
Grant-CsonlineVoiceRoutingPolicy -Identity baluilag@bloguc.com -PolicyName
NA-CA-International
```

For an emergency policy, use the `Grant-CsTeamsEmergencyCallRoutingPolicy` command with the following format:

```
Grant-CsTeamsEmergencyCallRoutingPolicy -Identity baluilag@bloguc.com
-PolicyName NA-CA-Emergency
```

For a calling policy, use the `Grant-CsTeamsCallingPolicy` command with the following format:

```
Grant-CsTeamsCallingPolicy -Identity "baluilag@bloguc.com" -PolicyName
"India-LBR_Policy"
```

There are additional policies for apps, meeting policies, live event policies, and more.

Note   A location-based routing (LBR) policy requires you to be compliant with Indian Telecom regulations. This helps to prevent toll-bypass.

Enabling Users for Direct Routing with Teams Phone

Before you can enable Direct Routing for users, the admin needs to have configured it at
the organization level. This includes configuring an on-premises SBC or using settings
provided by a telephony provider offering a Direct Routing service, and then configuring
voice routing, emergency calls, and, if required, high-availability functionality. Refer
to Chapter 3 for detailed configuration information. After configuring Direct Routing,
perform the following steps to enable functionality for end users:

1. First, assign the required licenses for Teams with Direct Routing
   (Teams and Phone system licenses).

2. Then enable a user for Enterprise Voice services and assign a
   telephone number to that user.

3. Enable voicemail for the user and then assign a Voice routing
   policy, dial plan, or emergency call routing policy for that user.

Note   The user's policy, license, and phone number assignments take up to 24
hours because of the latency between Microsoft 365 and Microsoft Teams.

Enabling Voice and Voicemail Services with Direct Routing

After you have assigned the correct licenses, the next step is to configure the user's
online phone settings. Perform the following steps using the Teams PowerShell module.
First, establish a remote session using this command (you need to install the Teams
PowerShell module):

```
Connect-MicrosoftTeams
```

To enable a user for Enterprise Voice functionality and voicemail, use the following
command:

```
Set-CsUser -Identity baluilag@bloguc.com -EnterpriseVoiceEnabled
$true -HostedVoiceMail $true
```

To assign a phone number, use the following command:

```
Set-CsPhoneNumberAssignment -Identity "baluilag@bloguc.com" -PhoneNumber
"+12091234567" -PhoneNumberType DirectRouting
```

It's recommended, but not required, that the phone number you use is configured as a full E.164 phone number with the country/region code. It is supported to configure phone numbers with extensions, which will be used to look up users when the lookup against the base number returns more than one result. This allows companies to configure phone numbers with the same base number and unique extensions. The next thing to assign is a Voice routing policy.

Assigning a Voice Routing Policy

After configuring a phone number for the user and enabling the user for voicemail, you will assign a Voice routing policy to the user. This will allow the user to dial out and receive calls by associating them with a specific Direct Routing configuration. Use this command to assign a Voice routing policy:

```
Grant-CsOnlineVoiceRoutingPolicy -Identity baluilag@bloguc.com -PolicyName
NAM-CA-International
```

The audio conferencing license is not available separately; it is incorporated with the enterprise licenses. As the admin, after assigning an audio-conferencing license to a user, you can edit an individual user's settings. You might want to do this to set the default audio bridge number, conference ID, or PIN.

Group Call Configuration

Group call is a highly useful feature, enabling users to manage who they want to be notified when they get a call. Group call pickup is less disruptive to recipients than other forms of call sharing, such as call forwarding or simultaneous ringing. Group call pickup is less invasive because users can configure how they want to be notified of an incoming shared call (through audio and visual notification, visual only, or a banner in the Teams app). They can decide whether to answer it.

To share calls with others, a user must create a call group and add the users they want to share the calls with. The user can also configure simultaneous rings or forwarding. The admin doesn't have to configure these features for their users since the call group creation and notification settings are available for configuration on the user side. However, administrators can use the Teams PowerShell module to modify the `AllowCallGroups` parameter in the `TeamsCallingPolicy` to enable or disable call groups.

To create a policy that prevents the use of call groups, use this PowerShell command:

```
New-CsTeamsCallingPolicy -Identity "AllowCallingPreventCallgroups"
-AllowCallGroups $false
```

After creating a policy, assign the new policy to a user using this PowerShell command:

```
Grant-CsTeamsCallingPolicy -Identity baluilag@bloguc.com -PolicyName
AllowCallingPreventCallgroups
```

A user can be enabled to use call groups by either changing their policy using the `Set-CsTeamsCallingPolicy` cmdlet or granting a different policy to the user.

You can use the Teams client to add a call group by completing the following steps:

1. In the upper right corner of the Teams client, select … ➤ Settings
   ➤ Calls.

2. Below *Call answering rules*, select *Forward my calls*, and open
   the dropdown menu by selecting Voicemail for voicemail
   features. Select the call group to open a Call group new window.
   Figure 6-11 shows the call forwarding options.

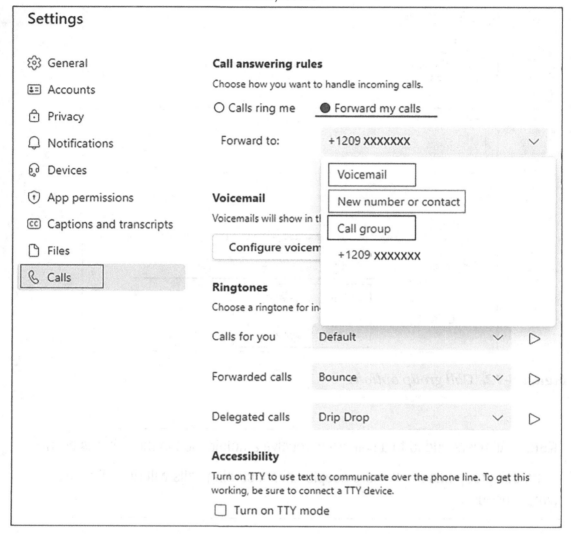

Figure 6-11. *Call settings*

3. Use the search field called *Add people* and select the users you
want to add to the call group.

In the Ring order menu, you can select to ring *All at the same time* or *In the order
above* to call people in order in 20-second intervals. See Figure 6-12.

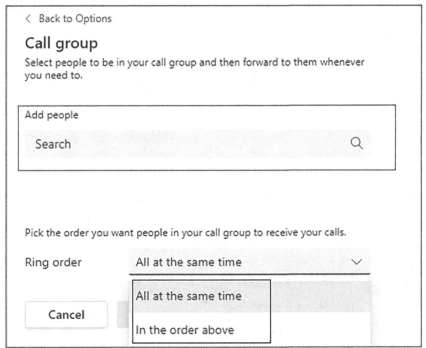

Figure 6-12. *Call group options*

Note   All users added to a call group receive a notification in their Teams client.

If the call group has six or more people, then incoming calls will ring all of them simultaneously.

When an admin turns off group calling for a user after the user has already set up a call group, the call group relationships for the user in the Teams admin center must be cleaned up to avoid incorrect call routing.

To clean up or modify the call group for a user, complete the following steps:

1. Log into the Teams admin center at `https://admin.teams.microsoft.com`.

2. In the left-hand navigation pane in the Teams Admin Center, select Users, select the user's name, and then choose Edit.

3. Select the Voice tab and navigate to the Group call pickup section.

4. In the list of users, select the users you want to remove from the call group and choose Remove or Add users and then select Apply.

Troubleshooting and Managing Call Forwarding, Simultaneous Ring, and Delegation Issues

Teams Phone System provides multiple features, but some are more frequently used, such as inbound/outbound calls, call forwarding, simultaneous ring, and delegation. Sometimes these features don't work as expected. As a support engineer or admin, you need to validate how this feature is configured and its settings on the client side. Users can configure and update these feature settings within the Teams client when they log in to affect the changes. Refer to Figure 6-11.

Call forwarding, simultaneous, and delegation settings allow users to forward their calls to voicemail, another user, or a call group. Users can use the Teams client to make changes to these settings by following these steps:

- **For call forwarding:** Open the Teams client, and then select Settings and Calls in the upper right corner of the client. Under *Call answering rules,* choose *Forward my calls.* Select if you want your forwarded calls to go to voicemail, another person, or a call group.

- **For simultaneous ring:** The call rings both in the user's Teams clients and also in another user or a call group. To configure a simultaneous ring, select Settings and Calls in the upper right corner of the client. Under *Call answering rules*, select *Calls ring me*. Then choose a ring and select where else you want your calls to ring: another person, no one, or a call group.

- **Call delegation:** This allows another user to make or receive calls on behalf of the user who configures the delegation. To configure delegation, select Settings and General in the upper right corner of the client. Select Manage delegates and then select your delegates and type the person's name to assign delegate rights to. Then select the permissions to give them, and select Add.

Troubleshooting Calling Policy Features

In Teams, calling policies control what calling features are available to users. Suppose a user doesn't have the required call settings. In that case, the first thing to verify is if they have been assigned a calling policy and that it contains the appropriate settings. Specific to the calling policy, the admin can utilize the Global (org-wide default) policy and a custom policy that has been created as per organization needs. Here is the list of available options in a calling policy:

- **Make private calls:** Controls all calling capabilities in Teams. Turn it off to disable all calling functionality in Teams.

- **Cloud recording for calling:** This controls cloud recording.

- **Call forwarding and simultaneous ringing to people in your organization:** Determines whether incoming calls are forwarded to other users or can ring another person simultaneously.

- **Call forwarding and simultaneous ringing to external phone numbers:** Determines whether incoming calls can be forwarded to an external number or ring an external number simultaneously.

- **Voicemail is available for routing inbound calls:** Enables inbound calls to be sent to voicemail. Valid options are Enabled (voicemail is always available for inbound calls), Disabled (voicemail is not available for inbound calls), and User-controlled (users can determine whether they want voicemail to be known).

- **Inbound calls can be routed to call groups:** Determines whether incoming calls can be forwarded to a call group.

- **Delegation for inbound and outbound calls:** Determines whether incoming calls can be forwarded to a call group.

- **Prevent toll bypass and send calls through the PSTN:** When this setting is on, calls are sent through the PSTN and incur charges rather than sending them through the network and bypassing the tolls.

- **Music on hold:** This enables the music-on-hold option. It can be set as enable or not enable, or the user can control it.

- **Busy on busy is available when in a call:** Lets you configure how incoming calls are handled when a user is already in a call or conference or has a call placed on hold. New or incoming calls can be rejected with a busy signal or routed according to the user's unanswered settings.

- **Web PSTN calling:** Enables users to call PSTN numbers using the Teams web client.

- **Real-time caption in Teams calls:** Turn it on or off. By default, it's on.

- **Automatically answer incoming meeting invites:** This allows a user to automatically answer meeting invites.

- **Spam filtering** can be turned on, turned off, or turned on without IVR.

- **SIP devices can be used for calls:** it enables SIP devices for calls; by default, it's off.

Configuring a Calling Policy Using Teams Admin Center

1. Log into the Teams admin center, expand the Voice section, and select Calling policies.

2. Select the appropriate policy, configure the required settings, and select Save.

3. Select the Group policy assignment tab on the Calling policies page and select Add group.

4. Enter the group name on the Assign policy to the group blade, select the rank, and select your policy.

5. Select Apply. See Figure 6-13.

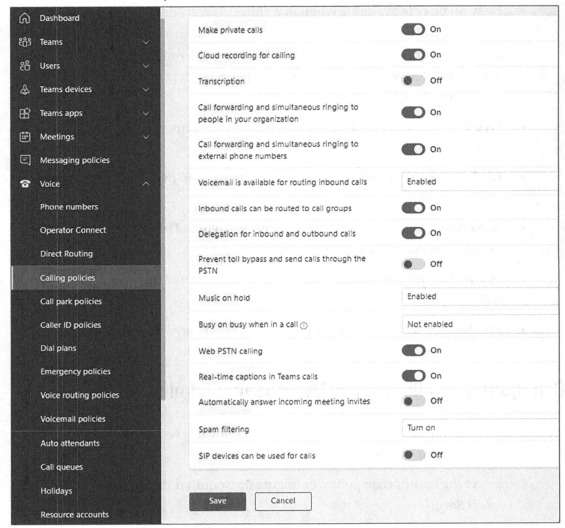

Figure 6-13. *Calling policy setting*

Another way to create a calling policy is by using the PowerShell command
line. The command that you can use to configure the calling policy settings is Set-
CSTeamsCallingPolicy.

Troubleshooting Phone System Issues

Microsoft Teams Phone System provides PBX abilities without requiring you to deploy
complex and expensive equipment. Phone System allows organizations to replace
their existing on-premises PBX system with features delivered from Microsoft 365 that

are tightly integrated into the cloud experience. For Teams users, an organization can connect their on-premises telephony infrastructure to Phone System by using Direct Routing. For Direct Routing configuration information, refer to Chapter 3.

You can connect Phone System to the PSTN in two ways: purchase a Microsoft calling plan and use your existing telephony infrastructure for on-premises PSTN connectivity. You can use Teams Phone System to support these services:

- **Auto attendants:** Used to create a menu system for your organization. Enables callers to move through the system to locate and place or transfer calls to organization users or specific departments.

- **Call queues:** Provides the greetings used when someone calls a phone number in your organization. Includes the ability to automatically put calls on hold and the ability to find the next available call agent to handle the call.

- **Voicemail:** Enables licensed users to access voicemail that has been left by callers. After you assign a Phone System license and a phone number to a user, cloud voicemail is automatically set up and provisioned.

Validating Phone System Setup and Configuration

The majority of issues happen due to misconfiguration. So before troubleshooting Teams Phone System issues, you, as an admin, must be aware of how to set it up. Multiple steps must be performed for Phone System setup. Here are the high-level steps to set up Phone System.

- First, check if Phone System is available in your country or region. Verify availability by reviewing the "Country and region availability for Audio Conferencing and Calling Plans" document.

- Buy an assigned Phone System and Calling Plan license. The steps to set a Phone System and Calling Plan license for a single user are the same as assigning a Microsoft 365 license.

- Then get phone numbers for your users.

- Get service phone numbers for audio conferencing, call queues, and auto attendants if required.

- Set up your calling plans and audio conferencing, if needed.

- Set up a cloud call queue and auto attendant, if needed. Refer to Chapter 3 for detailed steps.

- Assign service phone numbers for audio conferencing, call queues, and auto attendants.

- Set up communications credits for your organization if you'd like to use toll-free numbers with Microsoft Teams. Refer to Chapter 3.

You can refer to Chapter 3 for creating call queues and auto attendants.

Troubleshooting Auto Attendants and Call Queues

For Teams call queue or auto-attendant troubleshooting, you must use the Teams admin center to identify, open, and verify each setting. If users are experiencing auto attendant or call queuing issues, you should check the following standard things:

- First, check the resource accounts that are allocated to a Phone System virtual license.

- Then validate if Enterprise Voice is enabled for the resource accounts.

- Using Direct Routing, verify that call queues are allocated a Direct Routing phone number. The command to use for phone number assignment is `Set-CsOnlineApplicationInstance`.

- Validate your call routing plan and voice routing policy. The command to use for assigning a call routing policy is `Grant-CsOnline VoiceRoutingPolicy`.

- Once you have verified all of the above attributes, review the configuration of your auto attendants or call queue and their call flow.

- If the issue persists, gather Microsoft Teams logs and the SBC syslog for further analysis. You may open a case with Microsoft for a deeper log analysis.

Microsoft Teams Room System

Microsoft Teams Rooms offers a complete meeting experience that brings high-definition video, audio, and content sharing to meetings of all sizes, from small huddle areas to large conference rooms. When you start a Microsoft Teams Rooms device, a Windows 10 IoT Enterprise instance starts up.

After Windows starts, Teams Rooms signs in using a local account called Skype or a default account, and the password is admin/admin. However, when the device connects to Teams, you must enable and configure modern authentication. You can learn more about this procedure by reviewing the "Authentication in Microsoft Teams Rooms" (`https://docs.microsoft.com/en-us/microsoftteams/rooms/rooms-authentication`) document.

Each Teams room requires a resource account to sign in, and each account requires Teams license and a Phone System license (optional). Since there are multiple licenses, it is best to use the Teams Room Standard or Premium license with all essential features combined.

Troubleshooting Teams Rooms System Sign-In Issues

Sometimes a user may experience problems connecting to Teams from a Teams Room; this connection issue is tied with the account, authentication, and conditional access applied to the resource account.

- The first thing to check is the Room account; this resource account must have a Teams license assigned with an additional add-on feature or a single Teams room standard or premium license.

- Ensure that the account is correctly set up with a password-never-expire policy, as it's not a human account to manage passwords periodically.

- Validate the current authentication configuration for the account.

- Check and review conditional access policies in Azure AD.

- Check sign-in login in Azure AD and see what is affecting it.

- Collect and review logs on the Teams Room device.

Analyzing Log Data from Teams Rooms Devices

The Teams Rooms device log provides detailed information about the login process, app version, and media log. You must invoke the log collection script that ships with the Microsoft Teams Rooms app to collect logs. In Admin mode, start an elevated command prompt, and then issue the following command:

```
PowerShell -ExecutionPolicy unrestricted c:\rigel\x64\scripts\provisioning\
ScriptLaunch.ps1 CollectSrsV2Logs.ps1
```

After the script is executed, logs get collected in the `C:\rigel` folder, which you can examine later. You can also perform these steps by using the Microsoft Teams PowerShell module.

Managing and Troubleshooting Microsoft Teams Phone Devices and Room Systems

Manage Microsoft Teams phones: Microsoft Teams Phones are designed for users who require a traditional phone experience. Teams-certified phones provide the best experience with Microsoft Teams and support the broadest range of features. In addition to Teams-certified phones, you can choose lower-cost phones designed for Teams or utilize generic SIP phones via a gateway.

Teams-certified phones provide a Teams app experience for calling and meetings. A SIP phone via a gateway offers no specific Teams functionality. It will usually have a traditional LCD display for calling. Low-cost Teams phones do not provide the full range of capabilities of Teams-certified phones but benefit from the ability to connect directly to Microsoft Teams. Teams-certified phones have a broad array of features to help your users do their jobs and help you manage their usage. You can refer to Chapter 3 for detailed information.

Managing and Troubleshooting Microsoft Teams Rooms Systems

Microsoft Teams Rooms are the native meeting room system solution for Teams. They include functionality supporting traditional meeting room experiences, such as audio, video, and screen sharing. Microsoft Teams Rooms also support advanced capabilities,

including multi-screen support, meeting transcription, smart room speakers that
identify who is speaking, and meeting views, such as Together Mode, and receiving
regular updates to functionality from Microsoft. Microsoft Teams Rooms scale to
different room sizes. Teams Rooms use a wide variety of certified audio and video
peripherals based on the size and use of the room. By selecting the suitable core device
and console, combined with microphones, speakers, cameras, and displays appropriate
for the space, you can deploy Microsoft Teams Rooms into areas of any size, from small
huddle spaces to large conference spaces and boardrooms.

Microsoft Teams devices are designed to help people maximize the power of Teams
and bridge the gap between remote and shared workspaces. Through a combination
of Teams meetings features, people-centric room experiences, and industry-leading
hardware, users benefit from low-friction, inclusive, and interactive meetings, whether
they join remotely or in the meeting room.

There are two types of Microsoft Teams Room systems, Windows and Android.
Microsoft Teams Rooms on Windows (MTRoW) run Windows 10. They typically include
a Surface Pro device or a certified PC device and a center room touchscreen. MTRoW
devices are usually designed for larger meeting spaces, such as medium and large
meeting rooms, and support usage with a wide range of certified Teams devices.

Microsoft Teams Rooms on Android (MTRoA) devices run similar software to
Microsoft Teams Phone and Displays and are managed using similar concepts. They are
typically designed for smaller meeting spaces, including huddle rooms or small meeting
rooms. They are also suitable for personal meeting room devices dedicated to a specific
user. Like MTRoW devices, these devices can also have a center room touchscreen
attached and HDMI ingests for screen sharing and support multiple screens.

Licensing Requirements

Microsoft Teams Room Systems require a license. Two dedicated SKUs are available for
licensing meetings and calling on a per-device basis for meeting room devices (Microsoft
Teams Rooms, Microsoft Surface Hub, and collaboration bars for Microsoft Teams).
Table 6-2 shows the Microsoft Teams Room Standard and Premium licenses that include
Teams, Phone System, audio conferencing, Intune, Azure AD P1, and more. The table
shows the differences between the two SKUs.

Table 6-2. *Teams Room License Requirements*

License include	Microsoft Teams Rooms Standard	Microsoft Teams Rooms Premium
Microsoft Teams	Yes	Yes
Phone System	Yes	Yes
Audio conferencing	Yes (with additional billing)	Yes (with additional billing)
Microsoft Intune	Yes	Yes
Azure Active Directory P1	Yes	Yes
Worldwide availability	Yes (without sovereign clouds)	Yes (without sovereign clouds)
Channel availability	EA, EAS, CSP	EA, EAS, CSP
	Web Direct	Web Direct
Managed services	No	Yes

Teams Room Management Options

There are two core options for managing Microsoft Teams Rooms: unmanaged and
managed. An unmanaged option allows an IT administrator to manage devices
without Microsoft or partner assistance. Managed options include Microsoft Teams
Room Premium, Microsoft Endpoint Manager, and Azure Monitor. All options include
capabilities to manage device settings, collect statistics, and collect logs using the Teams
admin center.

The easiest way to manage Teams Rooms is to let it manage itself. All Windows
updates and Teams Rooms application updates come directly from Microsoft when
run in an unmanaged configuration. Teams Rooms runs a scheduled task nightly at
2:00 a.m. to download and install any pending updates. The Teams Rooms compute
module needs access to the Microsoft update servers on the Internet. You use the local
administrator account to sign into the machine when necessary.

Using Microsoft Endpoint Manager Configuration Manager, you can deploy
operating software for Microsoft Teams Rooms to multiple devices and utilize Operating
System Deployment (OSD) functionality, packages, and task sequences. Using this
approach requires the creation of defined packages and task sequences. It allows the
deployment of the monitoring agent to managed devices. This approach is validated for
Surface Pro-based Microsoft Teams Rooms by Microsoft. It requires vendor guidance for
non-Surface Pro-based devices.

Azure Monitor allows you to leverage cloud-based integrated end-to-end
management of Microsoft Teams Rooms devices, using Log Analytics within Azure
Monitor to provide basic telemetry and alerts. This allows configuration of a dashboard
view of device heartbeat status, hardware status, operating system details, deployed
Microsoft Teams Rooms application software versions, application errors, and other
information, including device restarts.

Microsoft Teams Rooms Premium consists of multiple features such as inventory
management, update management, troubleshooting and remediation, and many more.
These features and services make up the Microsoft Teams Rooms managed service. In
addition to the managed services, Teams Rooms Premium includes the Teams Rooms
standard license. The Microsoft Teams Rooms managed service is for organizations to
improve their meeting room experience and rapidly scale their footprint by offering
proactive management for Microsoft Teams Rooms devices.

Teams Room Troubleshooting

When the Teams Room is not functioning correctly, there is a problem in setup or the
Teams back-end service. It is essential to properly configure the Teams account and
other policies for an optimal Teams room experience. The following information will
help you set up the Teams resource account correctly, which is the first step in the
troubleshooting workflow.

Creating a Rooms account: A Microsoft Teams Rooms account "resource account"
needs to be built in Azure AD and Exchange so that the account can be used to access its
meeting calendar and establish Microsoft Teams connectivity. Additionally, the device
account must be configured/assigned with a Microsoft Teams Rooms System Standard
or Premium license (or equivalent) and enabled with an Exchange Rooms Resource
Mailbox. The device account must be configured in Microsoft Teams as a room resource.

In hybrid situations, the account used for Microsoft Teams Rooms must have
password sync enabled in Azure Active Directory (AAD) Sync because Microsoft Teams
Rooms authentication requires Microsoft 365 or Office 365 authentication. When setting
up the account, ensure that the account's SIP address matches its User Principal Name
(UPN) in AAD.

It is a best practice to create a Teams Rooms account using PowerShell. Refer to
Chapter 3 for resource account creation.

After resource account creation, enable it for Enterprise Voice so that the Rooms account can make and receive phone calls. If you don't allow Voice services, users will not be able to dial out from a Microsoft Teams Room. A standard or premium Meeting Rooms system license includes a Phone System license; however, unless Direct Routing is in use, a Calling Plan license will also need to be applied. Below is the sample command that enables a room for Enterprise Voice. After enabling Enterprise Voice services for a device account, the Microsoft Teams Room will display a dial pad.

```
Set-CsMeetingRoom -Identity "MicrosoftTeamsRoom@bloguc.com" -Enterprise
VoiceEnabled:$True
```

Microsoft Rooms Policy Options

The Microsoft Teams admin center is the best place to create and assign any policy to the room account. You can perform the following tasks using the Teams admin center. Log in and open the Microsoft Teams admin center to manage Teams Rooms devices and go to Devices ➤ Teams Rooms.

- Device management like restarting devices and downloading device logs

- Apply Teams-specific settings

- Check the health status of Microsoft Teams Rooms devices and their peripherals, including cameras, displays, and microphones

- Review current and past meeting activity (such as details about call quality, network health and connectivity, and number of participants)

- See peripherals (such as cameras and projectors) connected to a Microsoft Teams Rooms device

Suppose you are seeing a problem in Teams Rooms functionality. In that case, you can change settings on one or more devices in your organization. Select the device or devices you want to manage and then select Edit Settings to change settings. Table 6-3 shows the settings you can change using the Microsoft Teams admin center.

Table 6-3. *Teams Account Settings Available*

Teams Rooms setting	Accepted values	Supports bulk edit
Email	Email address	No
Supported meeting mode	Skype for business (default) and Microsoft Teams/ Skype for Business and Microsoft Teams (default)/ Skype for Business Only	Yes
Modern authentication	On/Off	Yes
Exchange address	Email address	No
Domain\username (optional)	Account domain and username	No
Configure domain	Comma-separated list	Yes
Meetings	**Accepted values**	**Supports bulk edit**
Automatic screen sharing	On/Off	Yes
Show meeting names	On/Off	Yes
Automatically leave if everyone else left the meeting	On/Off	Yes
Device	**Accepted values**	**Supports bulk edit**
Dual monitor mode	On/Off	Yes
Bluetooth beaconing	On/Off	Yes
Automatically accept proximity-based meeting invitations	Selected/Unselected	Yes
Send logs with feedback	On/Off	Yes
Email address for logs and feedback	Email address	Yes

(continued)

Table 6-3. (*continued*)

Teams Rooms setting	Accepted values	Supports bulk edit
Peripherals	**Accepted values**	**Supports bulk edit**
Conferencing microphone	List of available microphones	No
Conferencing speaker	List of available speakers	No
Default volume	0-100	No
Default speaker	List of available speakers	No
Default volume	0-100	No
Content camera	List of available cameras	No
Content camera enhancements	On/Off	No
Rotate content camera 180 degrees	On/Off	No
Theming	**Accepted values**	**Supports bulk edit**
	Default/No theme/Custom/List of built-in themes	Yes

Using Remote Provisioning and Sign In for Teams Phones

Teams admins can remotely provision and sign into a Teams Android device. This is useful when deploying devices to many desks and reducing the end users need for a first sign-in and set up. It enables technicians to provide device information and verification codes to IT admins, who can then ensure the device is ready to use once a device is allocated to the user. To provision a device remotely, you must upload the MAC IDs of the devices being provisioned and create a verification code. The entire process can be completed remotely from the Teams admin center.

After you have successfully completed the provisioning of a device, it is now ready to work.

Updating Microsoft Teams Devices Remotely

Using the Teams admin center, you can remotely update Teams devices, such as Teams phones, Teams panels, and collaboration bars. You can choose device firmware automatic update behavior. Here is a list of updates that can be updated through the Teams admin center:

- Teams app and teams admin agent

- Company portal app

- OEM agent app

- Device firmware

Device firmware updates can be applied automatically or scheduled for a future date and time. Other available device updates aren't applied automatically but can be applied manually or scheduled for a future date and time. This can be useful when you need to test new device updates and document features before deploying them to users or when scheduling updates to devices outside of business hours.

Teams Rooms Device (Automatic) Updates

Sometimes Teams Rooms functionality problems are tied with the device or Teams client version, so it is essential to understand the device updates. Teams device firmware updates are applied automatically. You, as an admin, can decide whether to use updates as soon as they are released (if you choose this option, updates are applied on the first weekend after an update is released) or 30 or 90 days after an update is released. By default, device firmware updates are applied 30 days after release. For detailed information, refer to Chapter 3.

Managing Teams Devices Effectively

Teams have different devices, and as an admin, you need to manage these devices. One of the effective ways to manage these devices is the device tag. Device tags in Teams allow you to group, organize, and simply manage the devices you have deployed in your organization. Device tags are frequently used in large organizations to organize and filter devices based on something meaningful to the organization, such as a tag for security devices, executive devices, contact center devices, or specific types of meeting rooms you have planned. Using Teams admin center, you can add one or more tags to devices,

331

utilize filters to view devices that match the tag you specify, and then perform actions on the devices with that tag. You can manage identification with role permissions of Global admin, Teams Service admin, or Teams Device admin.

Managing device tags: Using the device tag management panel in the Teams admin center, you can perform management tasks such as seeing all of your device tags, creating multiple device tags easily and then assign them to devices later, and removing device tags that are no longer needed. Before you can remove a device tag, you need to remove it from all the devices it has been added to. Additionally, you can rename device tags. When you rename a device tag, that change is reflected on all the devices it's been added to. Tags can be up to 25 characters.

Discovering tagged devices: After creating a tag and assigning it to devices, you can find the tagged device. You can use the tag to filter the device list to return only the devices with a specified tag added to them. This can be helpful if you just want to view all the devices in a specific room, all the devices of a particular type, or any other criteria you used when adding your tags. If you need to perform bulk actions against all phones in a contact center, ensuring they have a tag set will allow you to do this quickly and not apply those changes to executives or receptionists. You can also perform bulk actions on returned devices, such as applying updates in waves or setting different configuration policies depending on the groups of devices identified using device tags.

1. Log into the Teams admin center (`https://admin.teams.microsoft.com`) with an account that is a member of one of the required privileged roles.

2. Click Devices and select the device pane containing the devices you want to filter. Then select the Filter icon.

   a. If you only want to specify a single tag, or if you're going to find devices that have all the tags you specify, select *match all of these conditions*.

   a. If you want to find devices that match one or more device tags, select *match any of these conditions*.

3. Select the Tag field and specify a device tag name in the *Enter a value* field.

   b. If you want to add more device tags, select Add more and repeat step 6 for each tag you want to add.

4. Select Apply.

Once you have filtered the devices in your device list, you can perform actions on them as you usually would. For instance, you can select them and then assign configurations, edit their settings (if they're Teams Rooms devices), and more. When you are done, you can remove the filter by selecting the *X* next to the Tag filter entry or selecting *Clear all* on the right side of the list.

Troubleshooting Unexpected Sign-Out Issues

There are different reasons for a Teams device to unexpected sign out like a Teams authentication password policy, conditional access policy, Teams back-end service, network, and so on. This information applies to all device types:

- Teams Rooms on Android

- Teams phone devices

- Teams panels

- Teams displays

If you see Teams device sign-out issues, follow these below steps:

- You, as an admin, will need to sign into the affected Android devices. Manually sign into the affected device.

- If a manual sign-in is not an option, perform a remote sign-out and sign-in operation using the Teams admin center.

  - Log into the Microsoft Teams admin center.

  - Select Devices in the navigation menu on the left and choose your Android device.

  - On the page for the Android device, select Actions ➤ Sign out to sign out of the device.

- After sign-out, log in to Teams device again by selecting the Sign-in option in the Teams admin center.

- You will see a pop-up window; wait between 2-5 mins, and the window will be populated with a URL, a code, and instructions to sign in. Use the information provided to sign into the device.

- If this does not work, perform a remote device restart through the Teams admin center using the Restart option on the device page. Once completed, perform a remote sign-in operation.

  - Log into the Microsoft Teams admin center.

  - Select Devices in the navigation menu on the left and choose your Android device.

  - On the page for the Android device, select Restart to restart the device.

  - After the device restarts, select sign in.

  - A pop-up window will display. After a wait time of two to five minutes, the window will be populated with a URL, a code, and instructions to sign in. Use the provided information to sign into the device.

- If this does not work, perform a manual restart of the device and then a manual sign-in or remote Teams admin center sign-in.

- If this does not work, perform a factory reset of the device, then a manual sign-in or remote Teams admin center sign-in.

  - Perform a factory reset from the OEM device settings or by using the specific key combination to the OEM model.

  - Use remote sign-in or remote restart and sign into the device.

- Performing a sign-in will refresh the authentication, and no further action will be required.

Best Practices for Teams Android Devices Setup and Management

- Always use the Resource account for Teams devices and remove password expiration. This is required because Teams shared devices use an Exchange resource mailbox. Creating these mailboxes generates a report automatically. These accounts can either be synced to Azure AD from Active Directory or created directly in Azure AD. Any password expiration policies for users will also apply to accounts used on Teams shared devices; therefore, to avoid disruptions caused by password expiration policies, set the password expiration policy for shared devices to never expire.

- Check the conditional access policies and see if they applied to Teams devices. Azure AD conditional access sets additional requirements that devices must meet to sign in. For Teams devices, review the guidance that follows to determine if you have authored the policies that will allow shared device users to do their work.

- Do not use multi-factor authentication for Teams shared devices. Accounts for shared devices are linked to a room or physical space rather than to an end user account. Because shared devices don't support multi-factor authentication, exclude shared devices from any multi-factor authentication policies.

- You may utilize location-based access with named locations. Suppose shared devices are provisioned in a well-defined location that can be identified with a range of IP addresses. In that case, you can configure conditional access using named locations for these devices. This conditional access will allow these devices to access your corporate resources only when they are within your network.

- Always prevent Teams shared devices from sign-in frequency condition policies. In conditional access, you can configure sign-in frequency to require users to sign in again to access a resource after a specified period. If the sign-in frequency is enforced for Rooms accounts, shared devices will sign out until they are signed in again by an admin. Microsoft recommends excluding shared devices from any sign-in frequency policies.

Troubleshooting Teams Apps Access

Teams Apps help customize, streamline, and optimize how users work in Microsoft Teams to make collaboration more effective.

- Apps in chat allow taking action directly in a conversation.

- Apps in the channel allow you to share content and keep your team informed.

- Apps in meetings allow driving real-time collaboration as you come together.

Controlling the Apps

Teams have different kinds of apps like Microsoft Apps (first-party apps), organization builds (custom apps), and third-party apps. The admin can use app permission policies to control what apps are available to Microsoft Teams users in your organization to manage these apps. You can allow or block all apps or specific apps published by Microsoft, third parties, and organization build apps. When you block an app, users who have the policy cannot install it from the Teams app store. You must be a global or Teams service admin to manage these policies.

The Teams admin center is the central place to manage app permission policies. You can use the Global (org-wide default) policy or create and assign custom policies. Users in the organization will automatically get the international policy unless you create and assign a custom policy. After you edit or assign a policy, it can take a few hours for changes to take effect.

For Teams apps management, the admin can use policies to control users' permissions, install apps, and upload custom apps created within the organization.

Allowing or Blocking Teams Apps

Sometimes you need to allow or block an app as per the organization's need. Log into the Teams admin center, click Teams apps ➤ Manage apps, then select Allow or Block. See Figure 6-14 for allowing or blocking apps. When you block an app, all interactions with that app are disabled. The app doesn't appear in Teams for any users in the organization.

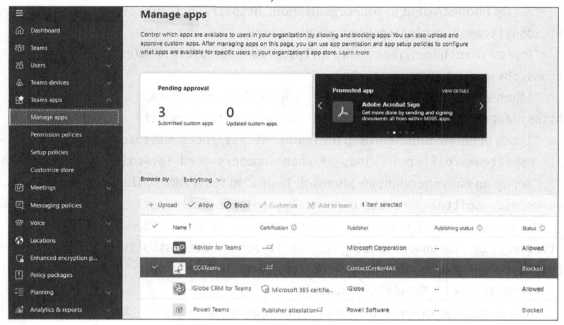

Figure 6-14. Teams app allow or block

Summary

You learned how to configure and troubleshoot Microsoft Teams Phone System
problems. You now understand the Microsoft Teams Phone System and different
troubleshooting scenarios such as troubleshooting Teams Direct Routing and SBC
connectivity issues; troubleshooting Teams PSTN call routing and phone number
normalization issues; configuring and troubleshooting audio conferencing;
troubleshooting phone number, dial plan, voice routing, and emergency call routing
policies; and troubleshooting the Microsoft Teams Rooms system.

References

"Chapter 1 Data models - After completing this chapter, you will be able …."
www.studocu.com/en-za/document/university-of-pretoria/informatics/
chapter-1-data-models/16151807

"SIP Trunk Service | Welcome to Sri Lanka Telecom." https://slt.lk/en/business/
products/sip-trunk-service

"Set up Phone System in your organization." `https://docs.microsoft.com/en-us/ microsoftteams/setting-up-your-phone-system`

"Private Branch Exchange (PBX)." `https://www.microsoft.com/en-us/microsoft- teams/pbx-private-branch-exchange`

"Microsoft Teams Operator Connect – Digital Transformations." `https://agarwalronak.com/microsoft-teams-operator-connect/`

"Types of phone numbers used for Teams." `https://docs.microsoft.com/en-us/ microsoftteams/different-kinds-of-phone-numbers-used-for-calling-plans`

"Set up an auto attendant for Microsoft Teams." `https://docs.microsoft.com/ en-us/microsoftteams/create-a-phone-system-auto-attendant`

"Understanding Microsoft Teams Administration: Configure, Customize, and ...." `https://ebin.pub/understanding-microsoft-teams-administration- configure-customize-and-manage-the-teams-experience-1st- ed-9781484258743-9781484258750.html`

"Assign, change, or remove a phone number for a user." `https://docs.microsoft. com/en-us/microsoftteams/assign-change-or-remove-a-phone-number-for-a-user`

"Azure direct routing infrastructure requirements." `https://docs.microsoft.com/ en-us/azure/communication-services/concepts/telephony/direct-routing- infrastructure`

"Health Dashboard for Direct Routing." `https://docs.microsoft.com/en-us/ microsoftteams/direct-routing-health-dashboard`

"Monitor and troubleshoot Direct Routing." `https://docs.microsoft.com/en-us/ microsoftteams/direct-routing-monitor-and-troubleshoot`

"How to Hide an Element on a Specific Viewport." Webflow, `https://discourse. webflow.com/t/how-to-hide-an-element-on-a-specific-viewport/19786`

"FPSMC Install Error 1722." `https://social.technet.microsoft.com/Forums/ scriptcenter/en-US/08fbc9d7-fd19-4d02-8fb7-756986e228e9/fpsmc-install- error-1722`

"Phone System Direct Routing." `https://docs.microsoft.com/en-us/ microsoftteams/direct-routing-protocols-sip`

"Change phone numbers on Audio Conferencing bridge." `https://docs. microsoft.com/en-us/MicrosoftTeams/change-the-phone-numbers-on-your-audio- conferencing-bridge`

"Phone numbers for Audio Conferencing." `https://docs.microsoft.com/en-us/ microsoftteams/phone-numbers-for-audio-conferencing-in-teams`

"Manage Audio Conferencing settings for users." https://docs.microsoft.
com/en-us/MicrosoftTeams/manage-the-audio-conferencing-settings-for-a-
user-in-teams

"What are Communications Credits?" https://docs.microsoft.com/en-us/
microsoftteams/what-are-communications-credits

"Sahara Net Has 10." Sahara Net, https://sahara.com/cloud/sahara-net-has-10/

"Getting phone numbers for your users." https://docs.microsoft.com/en-us/
microsoftteams/getting-phone-numbers-for-your-users

"Microsoft 365 Business." https://answers.microsoft.com/en-us/msoffice/
forum/all/microsoft-365-business/8991e590-d29d-4181-8e7a-eb1e12f86c15

"I'm struggling with Microsoft Teams asking for a phone number when ...."
https://answers.microsoft.com/en-us/msteams/forum/all/im-struggling-with-
microsoft-teams-asking-for-a/4d4b5402-2b3a-48e7-8fd8-4ba104615252

"RM Unify - How to block and unblock users in Microsoft 365." https://support.
rm.com/technicalarticle.asp?cref=tec5030148

"Configure Skype for Business hybrid." https://docs.microsoft.com/en-us/
skypeforbusiness/hybrid/configure-federation-with-skype-for-business-online

"Teams Phone System - Remove Country Code?" https://techcommunity.
microsoft.com/t5/microsoft-teams/teams-phone-system-remove-country-code/
td-p/2022571

"Assign phone number to user in teams powershell." https://migration.
firstimpressionsbook.com/ttxef/assign-phone-number-to-user-in-teams-
powershell

"Call forwarding, call groups, and simultaneous ring in Teams." https://support.
microsoft.com/en-us/office/call-forwarding-call-groups-and-simultaneous-
ring-in-teams-a88da9e8-1343-4d3c-9bda-4b9615e4183e

"Plan for Busy Options for Skype for Business Server - Skype for ...." https://docs.
microsoft.com/en-us/skypeforbusiness/plan-your-deployment/enterprise-voice-
solution/busy-options

"Plan for Microsoft Teams Rooms." https://docs.microsoft.com/en-us/
MicrosoftTeams/rooms/rooms-plan

"Microsoft Teams Rooms maintenance and operations." https://docs.microsoft.
com/en-us/MicrosoftTeams/rooms/rooms-operations

"Microsoft Teams Rooms requirements." https://docs.microsoft.com/th-th/
MicrosoftTeams/rooms/requirements

"Manage Microsoft Teams Rooms." https://docs.microsoft.com/en-us/microsoftteams/rooms/rooms-manage

"Release notes for Microsoft Teams - Office release notes." https://docs.microsoft.com/en-us/officeupdates/teams-admin

"Update Microsoft Teams devices remotely." https://docs.microsoft.com/en-us/microsoftteams/devices/remote-update

"Signed out of Teams on Android devices." https://docs.microsoft.com/en-us/microsoftteams/troubleshoot/teams-rooms-and-devices/signed-out-of-teams-android-devices

"Authentication best practices for Microsoft Teams shared device ...." https://docs.microsoft.com/en-us/microsoftteams/devices/authentication-best-practices-for-android-devices

CHAPTER 7

Real-World Troubleshooting

This chapter primarily focuses on day-to-day issues and troubleshooting them. Microsoft Teams communication involves multiple components to provide different capabilities. It is recommended to read the Teams overview chapter to understand each part involved in Teams communication. Before troubleshooting the problem, you, as an admin, must gather enough information to understand the issue and review it. Here is the simple troubleshooting process flow:

1. Gather issue information by calling the end user or over email, including when and what the issue is, any error message, an error screenshot, and more.

2. Check if this issue is with a single user or multiple users to scope the problem. If there is an issue with a single user, check the user-specific information. If various users are affected, check the service. For instance, if users cannot dial out, check the SBC, Teams Direct Routing configuration, voice routing policy, and so on.

3. For individual user issues, inspect the information such as the policy assigned to the user, the phone number, and the profile, Correlate the problem with the user's profile information and correct if anything is incorrect.

4. If the issue persists, get diagnostic logs and examine them.

5. You may need to open a support case with the Microsoft support team with all the issue information and diagnostic logs.

© Balu N Ilag and Arun M Sabale 2022
B. N. Ilag and A. M. Sabale, *Troubleshooting Microsoft Teams*, https://doi.org/10.1007/978-1-4842-8622-7_7

Common Issues and Troubleshooting Tips

Unable to Add a Member to the Team

"We couldn't add members. We ran into an issue. Please try again later."

Sometimes the user cannot add internal or external members to the Team and gets the above error message.

Resolution

As a workaround, users can add members to the Microsoft 365 group. This issue occurs when the value `UsersPermissionToReadOtherUsersEnabled` is set to `False` in Azure AD. To correct the problem, change this setting to `True`.

Unable to Add a Guest User to the Team

By default, guest access in Teams is turned off. Until guest access is enabled, the user cannot invite a guest to Teams for external collaboration. To allow guest access in Teams, follow these steps:

1. Log into Microsoft Teams admin center and navigate to users.

2. Select Guest Access and then set Allow guest access in Microsoft Teams to on. See Figure 7-1.

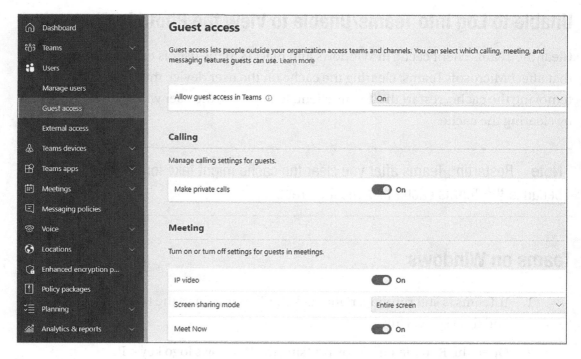

Figure 7-1. *Guest access enabled*

Note   In addition to enabling guest access in the Teams admin center, you may need to check guest access in Azure AD and SharePoint external access.

Enabling Archiving or Increasing the Mailbox Quota for a Microsoft 365 Mailbox Used by Teams

Enabling archiving and increasing the Microsoft 365 Group mailbox quota aren't supported. Messages for every channel within a Microsoft Teams team are stored in the Microsoft 365 Group mailbox that's associated with that Team.

Unable to Send Chat Messages to a Group Chat in Teams

In Teams, the chat creator receives the error message (Failed to send) if more than 200 members are added concurrently to a group chat. This behavior is by design. Although group chats can have up to 250 members, no more than 200 members can be added simultaneously.

Unable to Log into Teams/Unable to View the Photo in Chat

Clear the Teams client cache in Windows and macOS. If the user is experiencing issues that affect Microsoft Teams, clearing the cache on the user device may help. After removing the cache, restart the Teams client. Remember, the user will not lose any data by clearing the cache.

Note   Restarting Teams after you clear the cache might take longer than usual because the Teams cache files must be rebuilt.

Teams on Windows

1. If Teams is still running, right-click the Teams icon in the taskbar and then select Quit.

2. Open the Run dialog box by pressing the Windows logo key + R.

3. In the Run dialog box, enter `%appdata%\Microsoft\Teams`, and then select OK.

4. Delete all files and folders in the `%appdata%\Microsoft\Teams` directory.

5. Restart Teams.

Teams on macOS

1. If Teams is still running, right-click the Teams icon in the dock, and then select Quit, or press Command (⌘)-Q.

2. In the Finder, open the `/Applications/Utilities` folder and then double-click Terminal.

3. Enter the following command, and then press Return.

    `rm -r ~/Library/Application\ Support/Microsoft/Teams`

4. Finally, restart the Teams client.

Including or Exclude Teams from Antivirus or DLP Applications

Sometimes third-party antivirus and data loss prevention (DLP) applications can interfere with the Microsoft Teams app, preventing the application from starting correctly. We have seen multiple occasions where antivirus software causes Teams app startup and performance issues. It is essential to avoid any interference caused by non-Microsoft antivirus or DLP apps in computer clients. Additionally, Teams apps exclusion helps enhance performance and mitigate the effect on security.

To prevent any interference of Teams, add the following items to the "exclusion list" process in the antivirus software:

- `C:\Users\*\AppData\Local\Microsoft\Teams\current\teams.exe`

- `C:\Users\*\AppData\Local\Microsoft\Teams\update.exe`

- `C:\Users\*\AppData\Local\Microsoft\Teams\current\squirrel.exe`

Figure 7-2 shows the McAfee Endpoint antivirus exclusion list with additional Teams-specific files.

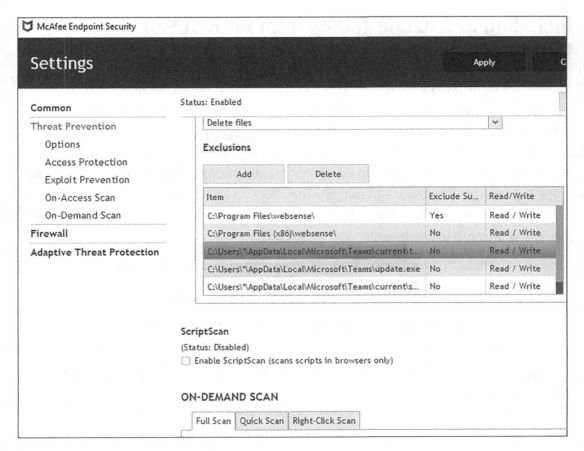

Figure 7-2. Antivirus exclusion

Or, you can add the items to the "safe" ("allow listed") programs list in the DLP application. The method to accomplish this varies. You may contact the antivirus or DLP application manufacturer for more precise steps.

Microsoft Teams Automated Diagnostic Scenarios

Microsoft has created multiple Teams related self-service diagnostic scenarios that cover various support topics and the most common tasks for which admins request configuration support. It is essential to note that while these diagnostics cannot make modifications to a Teams tenant, they do offer an understanding of known issues and guidelines for an admin to fix the problems promptly.

Accessing Self-Service Support Scenarios

To access Teams-specific support self-service scenarios, log into the Microsoft 365 admin center (`https://admin.microsoft.com/`).

Once logged in, navigate to Support ➤ New service request. After you briefly describe your issue (for instance, "Teams dial-pad missing"), the system determines whether a diagnostic scenario matches your problem. Refer to Figure 7-3.

After writing the issue description ("Teams dial-pad missing"), enter the username or email address of the affected user, say `bilag@bloguc.com`.

Then finally, click the Run Test button. Figure 7-3 shows New service request page.

If a diagnostic detects an issue, and you've implemented a fix based on the results, consider rerunning the diagnostic to ensure the issue is entirely resolved.

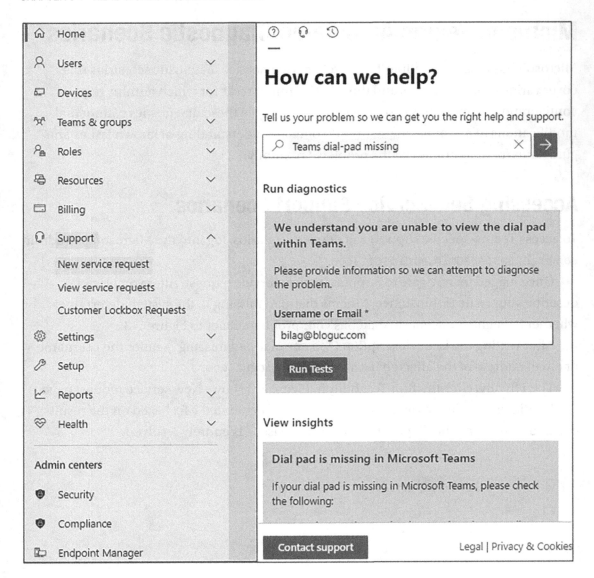

Figure 7-3. *Self-service scenarios*

Table 7-1 has all of the self-service supported procedures crested by Microsoft for Teams.

Table 7-1. *Self-Service Diagnostics Scenarios*

Scenario category	Diagnostic	Description	Access link	Support article
Authentication	Teams sign-in	Validates that a user can sign in to the Teams app	https://aka.ms/ TeamsSignInDiag	https://docs.microsoft. com/en-us/microsoftteams/ troubleshoot/teams-sign-in/ resolve-sign-in-errors
Authentication	Teams Federation	Validates that the Teams user can communicate with a federated Teams user	https://aka.ms/ TeamsFederationDiag	https://docs.microsoft.com/ en-us/microsoftteams/manage- external-access#federation- diagnostic-tool
Authentication	Unable to invite guest users to Teams	Validates that a specific guest can sign into Teams	https://aka.ms/ TeamsGuestAccessDiag	https://docs.microsoft.com/ en-us/microsoftteams/guest- access
Files	Teams files guest access	Validates that guest users can be added to Teams and the Team is shared with the user	https://aka.ms/ TeamsFilesGuestAccessDiag	https://docs.microsoft. com/en-us/microsoftteams/ troubleshoot/files/guests- cannot-access-files
Files	Unable to upload files to Teams chat	Validates if the specified user can upload files in Teams chat	https://aka.ms/ TeamsUploadFilesInChat	https://docs.microsoft. com/en-us/microsoftteams/ troubleshoot/files/cannot- upload-files-or-access- onedrive

(continued)

349

Table 7-1. (*continued*)

Scenario category	Diagnostic	Description	Access link	Support article
Files	Unable to access files shared in Teams chat	Validates that a specified user is unable to access files shared by another user in chats	https://aka.ms/ TeamsSharedFilesInChat	https://docs.microsoft. com/en-us/microsoftteams/ troubleshoot/known-issues/do- not-have-access-to-this-file- teams
Files	Unable to access files in a team	Validates that a specified user has access to files in the Team	https://aka.ms/ TeamsAccessFilesInChat	https://docs.microsoft. com/en-us/microsoftteams/ troubleshoot/files/access- files-tab-errors
Files	We can't get your files	Validates that a Team is provisioned and accessible by the specified user	https://aka.ms/ TeamsCannotGetFiles	
Meetings	Teams Calendar App	Validates that the prerequisites are properly configured for the Microsoft Teams calendar app to function	https://aka.ms/ TeamsCalendarDiag	

Meetings	Meeting recording missing	Attempts to locate a missing Teams meeting recording	https://aka.ms/ MissingRecordingDiag	https://docs.microsoft.com/ en-us/microsoftteams/cloud-recording#meeting-recording-diagnostic-tools
Meetings	1:1 Call Recording	Checks a user's policy for 1:1 call recording capability	https://aka.ms/ Teams11CallRecDiag	
Meetings	Teams add-in is missing in Outlook	Validates that a user has the correct policies to enable the Teams Outlook add-in	https://aka.ms/ TeamsAdd-inDiag	
Meetings	Teams live events	Validates that a user can schedule Teams live events	https://aka.ms/ TeamsLiveEventsDiag	
Meetings	Teams meeting recordings	Validates that the user is properly configured to record a meeting in Teams	https://aka.ms/ MeetingRecordingDiag	https://docs.microsoft.com/ en-us/microsoftteams/cloud-recording#meeting-recording-diagnostic-tools
Presence	Teams presence	Validates that a user's Teams presence can be correctly displayed	https://aka.ms/ TeamsPresenceDiag	https://docs.microsoft. com/en-us/microsoftteams/ troubleshoot/teams-im-presence/presence-not-show-actual-status

(continued)

351

Table 7-1. (*continued*)

Scenario category	Diagnostic	Description	Access link	Support article
Voice	Teams Direct Routing	Validates that a user is correctly configured for direct routing	https://aka.ms/ TeamsDirectRoutingDiag	https://docs.microsoft. com/en-us/microsoftteams/ direct-routing-monitor-and- troubleshoot
Voice	Teams call queue	Validates that a call queue is able to receive calls	https://aka.ms/ TeamsCallQueueDiag	https://docs.microsoft. com/en-us/microsoftteams/ create-a-phone-system-call- queue#call-queue-diagnostic- tool
Voice	Teams dial pad is missing	Validates that the dial pad is visible within Teams	https://aka.ms/ TeamsDialPadMissingDiag	https://docs.microsoft. com/en-us/microsoftteams/ troubleshoot/teams- conferencing/no-dial-pad
Voice	Unable to make domestic or international PSTN calls in Teams	Validates that a user has the ability to make or receive domestic or international PSTN calls	https://aka.ms/ TeamsPSTNDiag	

Voice	Unable to join or create a Teams conference call	Validates that a user has the ability to create or join a PSTN conference call	https://aka.ms/TeasConfDiag
Voice	Teams auto attendant	Validates that an auto attendant is able to receive calls	https://aka.ms/TeamsAADiag https://docs.microsoft.com/en-us/microsoftteams/create-a-phone-system-auto-attendant#auto-attendant-diagnostic-tool
Voice	Teams voicemail	Validates that a user is properly configured to use voicemail in Teams	https://aka.ms/TeamsVoicemailDiag
Voice	Teams call forwarding	Validates that a user is properly configured to forward calls to a specified number	https://aka.ms/TeamsCallForwardingDiag

Modern Authentication Failure in Microsoft Teams

Users receive an error when using multi-factor (or modern) authentication in Microsoft Teams forms. The resolution is to use the web app for authentication. Make sure the following switch is set:

```
Set-MsolDomainFederationSettings -DomainName yourdomainhere -Preferred
AuthenticationProtocol WsFed -SupportsMfa $False -PromptLoginBehavior
Disabled.
```

Microsoft Teams Stops Working When Joining from Edge or Internet Explorer

When trying to join Microsoft Teams using Edge or Internet Explorer, Teams will loop, stop working, or fail to sign in. The Teams web-based application will not correctly sign in if Teams URLs are not allowed as a trusted site.

To resolve this, you can add the following websites in trusted sites, IE, or Edge settings from the Control Panel, either with Administrator rights or a Group Policy Object:

1. Under Internet Options ➤ Privacy ➤ Advanced, accept first-party and third-party cookies and check the box for *Always allow session cookies*.

2. Select Internet Options ➤ Security ➤ Trusted Sites ➤ Sites, and add the following URLs:

   ```
   https://login.microsoftonline.com
   https://*.teams.microsoft.com
   ```

You Don't See Team Members After Your Account Is Re-enabled

When a Teams account is disabled for signing in, by design, the account is automatically removed as a member from all teams in this situation. However, even after your account is re-enabled and you still don't see the teams of which you were previously a member, wait for 24 to 48 hours for your account memberships to be automatically restored. However, your membership won't be restored for private channels in Teams. You must make new requests for membership to each private channel that you want to rejoin.

Unblocking a phone number in Teams

Sometimes you will find that a phone number is blocked in Teams. This happens when you delete the resource account before removing the phone number. Today there is a way to unblock the phone number; the admin can contact Microsoft support to release the telephone number.

The Attendee Maximum for Meetings Is Capped at 1,000

When you set up a Microsoft Teams meeting for a large group of people but find it only allows a maximum of 1,000 attendees, to resolve the issue, create the meeting using live events in Teams, which can host up to 10,000 users.

Microsoft Teams Rooms Can't Open PowerPoint Presentations After Disabling TLS 1.0 and TLS 1.1 in Skype for Business Server 2019 and Skype for Business Server 2015

When another user shares a PowerPoint presentation, you may receive this error message on the Microsoft Teams Rooms device: *"We can't connect to the server for sharing right now."*

Microsoft Teams Rooms (formerly called Skype Room System v2) devices are running versions 4.0.64.0 to 4.3.42.0 (inclusively) and still use TLS 1.0 to send a Client Hello to the front-end web conferencing service. If TLS 1.0 and TLS 1.1 are disabled on the Skype for Business Server 2015 or 2019, the TLS handshake will fail. Install the March 31, 2020, update for Microsoft Teams Room version 4.4.25.0.

Teams Requires Five or More Digits to Dial Out

Users dialing out from a meeting in Teams are forced to type in five or more digits, even though a dial plan normalization rule is available to normalize short digit dialing to E.164.

Dial out by typing the whole DID number or local number format instead of the internal extension number.

The Dial Pad Is Missing in Teams

In Teams, the missing dial pad is a prevalent issue. If the dial pad is missing, Teams users can't make outbound calls. Here are possible causes of this issue:

- The user hasn't been assigned Teams and Phone System licenses.

- The user hasn't been given a calling plan.

- The user hasn't enabled Enterprise Voice.

- The user is in Islands mode.

- The `OnlineVoiceRoutingPolicy` value isn't set correctly for the user.

To solve the issue, follow these steps:

- Ensure that the user has been assigned Teams and Phone System licenses.

- Make sure that the user has been assigned a calling plan.

- Enable the user for Enterprise Voice.

- For more information about Islands mode, see "Understand Microsoft Teams and Skype for Business coexistence and interoperability."

- Teams administrators should remove the user's `OnlineVoiceRoutingPolicy` value and set the correct value for the policy:

```
Grant-CsOnlineVoiceRoutingPolicy -Identity "Balu Ilag"
-PolicyName $Null
Grant-CsOnlineVoiceRoutingPolicy -Identity "Balu Ilag"
-PolicyName "CA-Tracy-International"
```

These actions force an update of the policy in the back-end environment of Teams. After this change is made, the user should see the dial pad appear under Calls within four hours.

Self-diagnostics tool: Microsoft 365 admin users have access to diagnostic tools that they can run within the tenant to verify possible issues that affect the dial pad.

Select the Run Tests link (`https://aka.ms/TeamsDialPadMissingDiag`). This will populate the diagnostic in the Microsoft 365 admin center.

The Organizer Is Unable to Start an Outlook Meeting and Is Stuck in the Virtual Lobby

Sometimes the organizer of a conference created in Outlook may find they cannot begin the meeting and may be unable to proceed from the virtual lobby. This issue might occur if your Outlook client is signed into an account different than your Teams client. When you join the meeting, make sure your Outlook client and Teams client are signed into the same account from which the meeting was scheduled.

PSTN Callers with the Same "From" Number Are Shown As the Same User

When multiple PSTN callers join a meeting in Teams, and their caller IDs are masked as a single number, they show up as a single caller in the meeting roster rather than as individual callers. This is a known issue, and Microsoft is researching this problem. Keep checking Microsoft's known issue list to get more information.

Static Conference ID Not Supported for Microsoft Teams Meetings

Suppose the admin overrides the default setting from dynamic conference ID to static conference ID. In that case, the setting may not affect Microsoft Teams meetings. This is currently a known issue, and Microsoft is researching the problem. Keep checking Microsoft documentation to get updated information.

Microsoft Teams Meetings Are Not Available

If you try to join a meeting in Teams but find it is not available, you might be using a legacy Exchange on-premises server. Meeting functionality is unavailable when Exchange Mailbox is hosted (homed) on-premises in versions older than Exchange 2016 CU3. You, as an admin, have to upgrade to Exchange 2016 CU3 or later for the on-premises deployment.

Unable to Hear Audio While Sharing Content During a Live Event in Microsoft Teams

When you share content during a live event in Teams, audio from the shared content (such as a YouTube link or a saved video file) cannot be heard by participants. To share your system audio during a live event,

1. Open your meeting controls, and then select Share.

2. Select Include system audio.

Remember, you won't be able to include your computer's audio while you share a PowerPoint presentation or whiteboard. Currently, Microsoft supports this feature on Windows devices only.

Teams Is Slow During Video Meetings on Laptops Docked to 4K/UHD Monitors

Microsoft Teams' performance on laptops may be impacted during video meetings. This issue can occur if a computer is docked to an external 4K or ultra-high-definition (also known as ultra-HD or UHD) display. You may reduce the resource requirements for your laptop to improve the Teams experience during the meeting and try these common things to enhance the performance:

- It is always recommended to close any applications or browser tabs that you are not using.

- Turn off video in the meeting by turning off your own video; select Turn camera off in the meeting controls. Also, turn off the incoming video; select More actions ➤ Turn off incoming video in the meeting controls.

- Another thing that you can try is to disable GPU hardware acceleration in Teams. To disable this function, log into Teams and select the Settings and more menu next to your profile picture at the top right of Teams. Then, select the Disable GPU hardware acceleration option.

- It is a best practice to disconnect your monitor from the port replicator or docking station and directly connect it to the video port on the laptop.

- Sometimes the Teams client holds resources, so Restart Teams to release resources.

- Changing the resolution of your 4Kor UHD monitor to 1920 x 1080 will reduce resource use.

- Use DVI or HDMI instead of USB-C to connect your monitor.

- Disable full-screen mode in the meeting by selecting More actions ➤ Fullscreen.

- Update Teams and make sure that the latest update is installed. The newest performance fixes were released in June 2021, available in version 1.4.00.16575 or later.

Microsoft is continuing to improve the meeting experience by optimizing audio, video, and screen sharing when using a 4K monitor. These updates will become available in upcoming client releases.

Error "The following application instance is not present in BVD" When Assigning a Phone Number to a Resource Account

Sometimes you see the error "The following application instance is not present in BVD." It cannot assign a phone number to a resource account in Microsoft Teams. Allow 24 hours for the resource account to sync. If it has been more than 24 hours, remove the phone number assignment, delete the resource account, and create a new one with a different name.

Users with Exchange Online Mailboxes Can't Access Meetings or Connectors

You have actively blocked EWS from services within Exchange Online but need to have Microsoft Teams compliant with EWS policies and cannot access meetings or connectors. To make Microsoft Teams compliant, add the following user agent strings for Microsoft Teams within the EWS Allow List, including asterisks: `SkypeSpaces/*` and `MicrosoftNinja/*`.

The following command can also be used:

```
Set-organizationconfig -EwsAllowList @{Add="MicrosoftNinja/*","SkypeS
paces/*"}
```

External Federated Contacts Don't Appear in Teams Search

You have access to diagnostic tools that you can run within the tenant to verify possible issues that affect the federation. Select the Run Tests link (`https://aka.ms/TeamsFederationDiag`). This will populate the diagnostic in the Microsoft 365 admin center.

Suppose you have imported contacts from a federated partner tenant into Azure Active Directory (Azure AD) or Exchange Online. In that case, the connections might not appear in Microsoft Teams contact searches. This problem occurs because Teams uses contacts in your organization's Active Directory and contacts that are added to your Outlook default folder. Searching in Teams for external federated contacts is supported only under the following conditions:

- Your mailbox is hosted through Exchange Online, not Microsoft Exchange Server on-premises.

- The external contact phone number is included in the contact information.

- Your search for the external contact by email address, not the contact name.

Note   Although it is not supported, searching for an external federated contact might work if the contact is currently cached on the client's computer.

External federated contacts will appear in searches if these three conditions are met.

In Teams, you can communicate with anyone in your organization's Active Directory. You can add anyone as a contact in Teams by selecting Calls, selecting the Contacts tab, and selecting Add contact.

The Public Team List Does Not Display All Teams in Teams

The list of public teams is based on Microsoft Graph. If you don't see a team, try searching for it in the top right search box. Also, the team owners should communicate team names to colleagues since many Teams could show up in the search results.

Troubleshooting Teams Delegation Issues

In Teams, delegation is beneficial. Here are the practical steps.

Step 1: Verify That the Delegate Has Been Granted Editor Permission to Access the Delegator's Calendar

Open the Exchange Management Shell on one of the Exchange-based servers and then run this Exchange PowerShell command to verify that the Editor access right has been granted to the delegate:

```
Get-MailboxFolderPermission -Identity <delegator's UserPrincipalName>:\
calendar | Format-List
```

Check whether the `AccessRights` parameter contains a value of `Editor`. If not, run this command to grant the permission:

```
Set-MailboxFolderPermission -Identity <delegator's UserPrincipalName>\
Calendar -User <delegate'sUserPrincipalName> -AccessRights Editor
```

Step 2: Verify That the Delegate Has Been Granted "GrantSendOnBehalfTo" by the Delegator

Run this command to verify that the GrantSendOnBehalfTo permission was granted to the delegate:

```
Get-Mailbox -Identity <delegator's UserPrincipalName> | Format-List *grant*
```

Verify that the GrantSendOnBehalfTo parameter contains the delegate's alias. If not, run this command to grant the permission:

```
Set-Mailbox <delegator's UserPrincipalName> -Grantsendonbehalfto
@{add="<delegate's UserPrincipalName>"}
```

Step 3: Verify that Teams Isn't Blocked from Accessing EWS for the Entire Organization

Run this Exchange PowerShell command to check whether the EwsApplicationAccessPolicy parameter was set to EnforceAllowList for the entire organization:

```
Get-OrganizationConfig | Select-Object Ews*
```

If the parameter was set to EnforceAllowList, only clients listed in EwsAllowList are allowed to access EWS. An empty value EwsAllowList (EwsAllowList={}) prevents all users from accessing EWS.

Ensure that *SchedulingService* is listed as an array member of the EwsAllowList parameter. If not, run this command to add it:

```
Set-OrganizationConfig -EwsAllowList @{Add="*SchedulingService*"}
```

If the EwsEnabled parameter is set to False, you must set it to True or Null (blank). Otherwise, the Teams service will be blocked from accessing the EWS.

Step 4: Verify That Teams Isn't Blocked from Accessing EWS for the Delegator's Mailbox

Run this Exchange PowerShell command to check whether the EwsApplicationAccessPolicy parameter was set to EnforceAllowList for the delegator's mailbox:

```
Get-CasMailbox <delegator'sUserPrincipalName> | Select-Object Ews*
```

If the parameter was set to EnforceAllowList, only clients listed in EwsAllowList are allowed to access EWS.

Make sure that *SchedulingService* is listed as an array member of the EwsAllowList parameter. If not, run this Exchange PowerShell command to add it:

```
Set-CASMailbox <delegator'sUserPrincipalName> -EwsAllowList
@{Add="*SchedulingService*"}
```

If the EwsEnabled parameter is set to False, you must set it to True. Otherwise, the Teams service will be blocked from accessing the EWS.

Step 5: Escalate the Issue

If you have verified that there's no problem with the prerequisites or configurations mentioned in this section, submit a service request to Microsoft Support with this information:

- The UserPrincipalName for both delegator and delegate

- The Teams Meeting Add-in logs under the folder %appdata%\\ microsoft\\teams\\meeting-addin

- The time in UTC when the issue was reproduced

Teams client debugs logs are collected from the delegate's machine.

Troubleshoot Teams Calendar App Issues

The Microsoft Teams calendar app is very useful; however, sometimes this app is missing or not seen in the Teams client. Here are common troubleshooting steps.

Step 1: First, Verify That the Teams Calendar App Is Enabled by Following These Steps

1. Open the Microsoft Teams admin center, go to Users, and select View policies for the affected user.

2. Select the App setup policy assigned to that user. The Global (org-Wide default) policy is being used in this example, Confirm that the calendar app (ID ef56c0de-36fc-4ef8-b417-3d82ba9d073c) is displayed.

Step 2: Verify Teams Upgrade Coexistence Mode Allows Teams Meetings

1. Open the Microsoft Teams admin center and then go to Users and select the affected user.

2. Verify that the coexistence mode setting is a value other than Skype for Business only or Skype for Business with Teams collaboration. Figure 7-4 shows that the Teams coexistence mode is Teams Only.

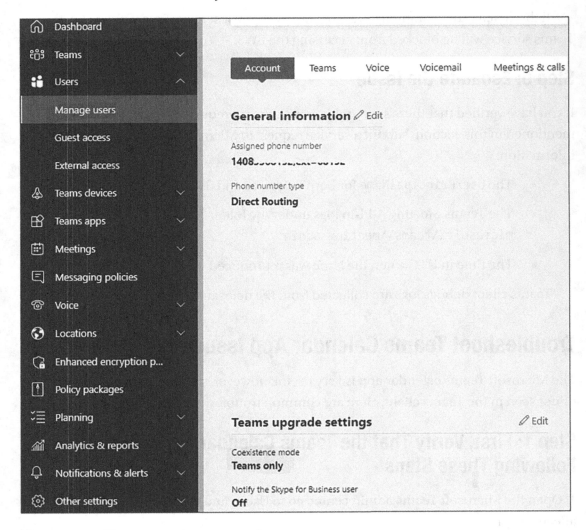

Figure 7-4. *Teams coexistence mode*

3. If the user coexistence mode was set to Use Org-wide settings, the default tenant coexistence mode will be used. Go to org-wide settings and select Teams Upgrade.

4. Verify that the default coexistence mode setting is a value other than Skype for Business only or Skype for Business with Teams collaboration.

Step 3: Verify That Teams Isn't Blocked from Accessing EWS for the Entire Organization

Run this Exchange PowerShell command to check whether the parameter `EwsApplicationAccessPolicy` was set to `EnforceAllowList` for the entire organization:

```
Get-OrganizationConfig | Format-List EwsApplicationAccessPolicy,Ews*List
```

If the parameter was set to `EnforceAllowList`, only clients that are listed in `EwsAllowList` are allowed to access EWS.

Make sure that `MicrosoftNinja/*`, `*Teams/*`, and `SkypeSpaces/*` are listed as array members of the `EwsAllowList` parameter. If they aren't, run this command to add them:

```
Set-OrganizationConfig -EwsAllowList @{Add="MicrosoftNinja/*","*Teams/*",
"SkypeSpaces/*"}
```

If the `EwsEnabled` parameter is set to False, you must set it to True or Null (blank). Otherwise, the Teams service will be blocked from accessing EWS.

Step 4: Verify That Teams Isn't Blocked from Accessing EWS for the Affected User

Run this Exchange PowerShell command to check whether the `EwsApplicationAccess Policy` parameter was set to `EnforceAllowList` for the user mailbox:

```
Get-CASMailbox <UserPincipalName> | Select-Object Ews*
```

If the parameter was set to `EnforceAllowList`, only clients that are listed in `EwsAllowList` are allowed to access EWS.

Make sure that `MicrosoftNinja/*`, `*Teams/*`, and `SkypeSpaces/*` are listed as array members of the `EwsAllowList` parameter. If they aren't, run this Exchange PowerShell command to add them:

```
Set-CASMailbox <UserPincipalName> -EwsAllowList @{Add="MicrosoftNinja/*","*
Teams/*","SkypeSpaces/*"}
```

If the `EwsEnabled` parameter is set to False, you have to set it to True. Otherwise, the Teams service will also be blocked from accessing EWS.

Step 5: Verify That the Microsoft Teams Calendar App Test Is Successful

1. Ask the user to go to the Microsoft Remote Connectivity Analyzer at `https://testconnectivity.microsoft.com/tests/TeamsCalendarMissing/input`.

2. Input the requested information and then select the Perform Test button to start the Microsoft Teams calendar app test. If the test fails, you should attempt to resolve the issue and rerun the test.

Step 6: Escalate the issue

If you have verified that there's no problem with the prerequisites and configurations mentioned in this article, submit a service request to Microsoft Support with this information:

- The `UserPrincipalName` of the affected user

- The time in UTC when the issue was reproduced

- Capture the Teams client debug logs and attach them to the service request.

Troubleshooting Teams Presence Issues

Teams presence information helps in getting real-time status with user-free/busy information.

Step 1: Locate the On-Premises Exchange EWS URL

Find the on-premises Exchange EWS URL for the user mailbox and change the URL format (replace `/EWS/Exchange.asmx` with `/API`) in this manner: `https://mail.contoso.com/EWS/Exchange.asmx` to `https://mail.contoso.com/api`. Try to access the REST API URL from a browser in the external network. The REST API URL has been published if you get a 401 response from the on-premises Exchange environment. Otherwise, contact the local network team to get the URL published.

It is essential to understand that the Teams presence service doesn't support the fallback to the EWS URL if the access to the Exchange REST API fails.

Step 2: Verify That the Teams Presence Based on the Calendar Events Test Is Successful

1. Ask the user to go to the Teams Presence Based on Calendar Events (`https://testconnectivity.microsoft.com/tests/TeamsCalendarPresence/input`) section of the Microsoft Remote Connectivity Analyzer.

2. Input the requested information and select the Perform Test button to start the Teams Presence Based on Calendar Events test. If the test fails, you should attempt to resolve the issue and rerun the test.

Step 3: Verify That Teams Is Not Blocked from Accessing EWS for the Entire Organization

Run this Exchange PowerShell command to check whether the `EwsApplicationAccessPolicy` parameter was set to `EnforceAllowList` for the entire organization:

```
Get-OrganizationConfig | Select-Object Ews*
```

If the parameter was set to `EnforceAllowList`, only clients that are listed in `EwsAllowList` are allowed to access EWS. An empty value `EwsAllowList` (`EwsAllowList={}`) prevents all clients from accessing EWS. Make sure that `*Microsoft.Skype.Presence.App/*` is listed as an array member of the `EsAllowList` parameter. If not, run this command to add it:

```
Set-OrganizationConfig -EwsAllowList @{Add="*Microsoft.Skype.Presence.App/*"}
```

If the `EwsEnabled` parameter is set to False, you have to set it to True or Null (blank). Otherwise, the Teams service will be blocked from accessing the EWS.

Step 4: Verify That Teams Is Not Blocked from Accessing EWS for the User's Mailbox

Run this Exchange PowerShell command to check whether the `EwsApplicationAccessPolicy` parameter was set to `EnforceAllowList` for the user's mailbox:

```
Get-CasMailbox <user'sUserPrincipalName> | Select-Object Ews*
```

If the parameter was set to `EnforceAllowList`, only the clients that are listed in `EwsAllowList` are allowed to access EWS.

Make sure `*Microsoft.Skype.Presence.App/*` is listed as an array member of the `EwsAllowList` parameter. If not, run this Exchange PowerShell command to add it:

```
Set-CASMailbox <user's UserPrincipalName> -EwsAllowList @{Add="*Microsoft.
Skype.Presence.App/*"}
```

If the `EwsEnabled` parameter is set to False, you have to set it to True. Otherwise, the Teams service will be blocked from accessing the EWS.

Step 5: Escalate the Issue

If you verified there's no problem with the prerequisites and configurations mentioned in this topic, submit a service request to Microsoft Support with this information:

- The `UserPrincipalName` of the affected user

- The time in UTC when the issue was reproduced

- With service requests, you can submit Teams client debug logs.

Error When Opening a File in Teams: You Don't Have Access to This File

In Microsoft Teams, you can share a file with another user in a chat window. The file is automatically stored on your OneDrive site. When the other user tries to open the file in Teams, the error message is displayed "You don't have access to this file." This issue occurs because the limited-access user permission lockdown mode feature is activated on your OneDrive site. This site collection feature helps prevent anonymous users from accessing application pages and is primarily helpful on classic, publishing-based SharePoint sites. Microsoft recommends that you do not enable this feature on OneDrive sites.

To resolve this issue, deactivate this feature in OneDrive.

1. Sign into your OneDrive site and select the Setting icon in the screen's upper-right corner.

2. Select OneDrive Settings ➤ More Settings.

3. Under Features and storage, select Site Collection Features.

4. Locate Limited-access user permission lockdown mode and select Deactivate.

Microsoft 365 admin users have access to diagnostics that can be run within the tenant to verify possible issues with accessing files shared in Teams chat. Select Run Tests, which will populate the diagnostic in the Microsoft 365 Admin Center. The diagnostic performs an extensive range of verifications.

"Attempted to Perform an Unauthorized Operation" Error When Accessing the Files Tab in Teams

When guest users try to use the Files tab to access shared files in Microsoft Teams, they receive the following error message: *"Something went wrong, Attempted to perform an unauthorized operation."* In Teams chat and channels, the file-sharing settings are based on the sharing settings for SharePoint and OneDrive in the SharePoint admin center. This issue occurs because these settings are not made correctly in the SharePoint admin center.

To solve this issue, configure the sharing settings in Teams and SharePoint as follows:

Enable group owners to add people outside the organization as guests: When you create a team, a Microsoft 365 group is designed to manage team membership. To let the group owners add people outside the organization to the group as guests, select the *Let group owners to add people outside the organization to groups* check box from Microsoft 365 Groups guest settings.

Enabling Guest Sharing from the SharePoint Admin Center

1. Sign into the SharePoint admin center as an administrator.

2. In the left navigation pane, select Policies ➤ Sharing.

3. Specify the sharing level for SharePoint and OneDrive to one of the options like Existing guests, Anyone, or New and existing guests

Users Cannot Send a Poll to External or Guest Users in Teams Private Chat

When sending a Forms poll to external users in a private federated chat between different Microsoft Teams tenants fails, this error is displayed: "Something went wrong; please try again later." When sending a Forms poll to anonymous users (guests), they can't respond. This error is displayed: "Something went wrong; please try again later." These are known Teams limitations.

A Contact's Presence Status Is Unknown in Teams

In Microsoft Teams, sometimes the presence status of a contact is displayed as status unknown, or the status doesn't update. A presence unknown issue occurs if one or more of the below conditions are true:

- The contact is offline (the contact hasn't signed into Teams).

- The contact set the presence status to appear offline.

- A network communication issue affects the unified presence service (UPS), or there is huge latency on the network.

- The contact is using Microsoft Skype for Business. Based on the presence in the coexistence scenario, this issue may be expected behavior.

To resolve the unknown presence issue, follow these steps:

1. First, verify that the contact has signed into Teams.

2. Check that the contact hasn't set the presence status to appear offline.

3. Validate the network connectivity to Teams endpoints.

4. Verify that the contact is currently using Microsoft Teams.

If none of these steps fix the issue, open a support ticket that contains the following information:

- The sign-in address of the user (also known as the observer) who sees that the presence of the contact is status unknown

- The sign-in address of the contact (also known as the publisher) whose presence shows as status unknown

- The desktop and debug logs from both the observer and publisher

- Use log files in troubleshooting Microsoft Teams

- The UTC time at which the publisher updated the presence and the time at which the observer noticed that the contact's presence status wasn't updated. Verify that the times are captured in all the log files.

Teams Presence Status Is Not Updating Correctly

In Microsoft Teams, sometimes the user's presence status is shown incorrectly. For instance, if your desktop is inactive for more than 5 minutes, the user presence status changes to Away. However, when you resume activity on your desktop, your presence status doesn't immediately switch to Available. The Teams app goes into an inactive mode when users lock their computer; the computer enters idle or sleeps mode. The Teams mobile app runs in the background. Mainly this issue occurs if the latest Teams updates aren't installed. Try the first resolution, and check whether the issue is resolved. If it isn't, go to the second option.

First, update the Teams app by selecting your profile picture at the top of the app, and then choose Check for updates.

After your desktop resumes from an inactive to an active state, wait three minutes and check whether your presence status is updated.

Note   Users whose mailboxes are hosted on-premises are expected to have presence delays with a maximum of an hour.

If the issue is not resolved, open a service request with Microsoft support and share detailed information with the diagnostic log.

External Users Appear As Unknown in Meeting Details

Sometimes when an external (federated) user joins meetings and calls using the Teams client, their name shows as unknown in Teams Call Analytics. In the Teams admin center, you access the Call Analytics information for the user:

1. Under Users ➤ Manage Users, select the user.

2. On the user's profile page, select the Meetings & calls tab. Then select a meeting ID to view the details. In this scenario, the username is displayed as unknown on the Overview page.

This behavior is by design. On the meeting details page, the Teams admin center UI uses the Microsoft Graph API to query the Azure AD tenant for user properties, such as displayName. Because external users aren't available for queries, the username is displayed as Unknown.

The Chat Option Is Missing in Teams Meetings

As an attendee in a Teams meeting, a user may experience one of the following issues when they try to access the meeting chat:

- The Chat icon is missing.

- The following error message when selecting the Chat icon: "You can't see the meeting chat history."

- The admin has disabled the chat.

These issues can have different reasons. Here are the most frequent causes.

1. The *Allow chat in meetings* setting is disabled in the meeting policy assigned to the user.

2. The number of attendees in the meeting exceeds 1,000 (the maximum number supported for chat).

3. You were added to the meeting as an attendee by using a meeting link such as one that's shared in a forwarded meeting invitation. However, you were not added to the original invitation. In this scenario, attendees will have access to chats, files, notes, and other meeting content only during the meeting. They will lose access to them after the meeting ends. If this is a recurring meeting, attendees will also not have access to the meeting chat in subsequent meetings.

Leave and rejoin the meeting to ensure that this isn't a transient issue. If the problem persists, try the following solutions:

- Enable the *Allow chat in meetings* setting. The Teams admin can enable and configure meeting policies. They can also update the meeting policy that's assigned to the user.

- Check if the number of attendees is not more than 1,000. The meeting organizer should make sure that the number of attendees in the meeting is less than the maximum limit.

- To enable access to the chat after the meeting is over, the meeting organizer should add the attendee to the original meeting invitation or to the original recurring meeting series, as appropriate.

- If the issue persists, open a support service request with Microsoft support and share the details of the problem.

Issues with Meeting Recordings

Sometimes a user may experience one of the following issues in Microsoft Teams related to meeting recordings:

- The meeting recording button is missing.

- The meeting recording link isn't included or visible in a chat window.

To determine if there's a problem with your account, run the Teams Meeting Recording Test (https://aka.ms/MRCA-TMR). These diagnostic checks if your account meets all requirements to record a meeting in Teams. If the issue persists, continue with the following information.

To troubleshoot the issue, begin by running the Meeting Recording Support Diagnostic available in the Microsoft 365 admin center. It checks these prerequisites for Teams meeting recordings:

- You must be assigned the correct license.

- You must have the proper meeting policies.

- You must have a supported storage location (Stream, OneDrive for Business, or SharePoint).

Resolution

To resolve the recording issue, you may run the Meeting Recording Support Diagnostic (`https://aka.ms/MeetingRecordingDiag`). Figure 7-5 shows the Teams meeting recording diagnostic.

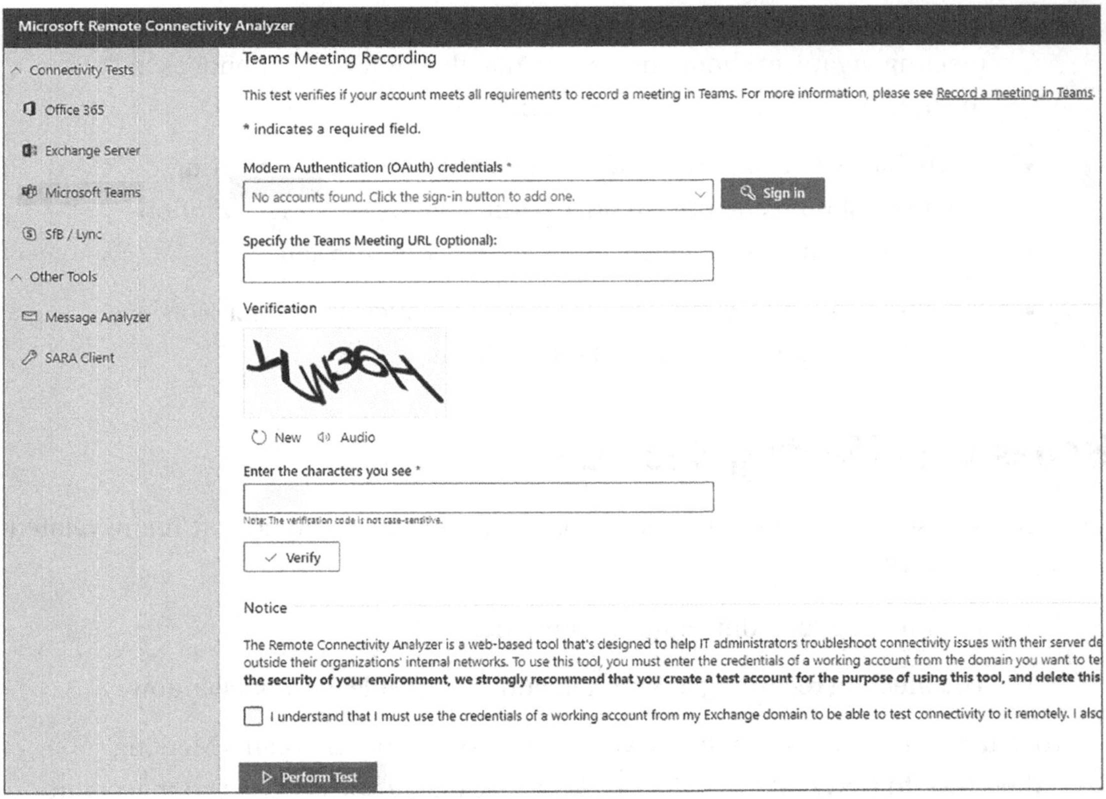

Figure 7-5. *Remote connectivity analyzer*

If the diagnostic reports that your organization is configured for Microsoft Stream storage, but you are in a country/region that isn't supported yet by the stream, use one of the following options:

- Replace the Stream storage with OneDrive for Business or SharePoint.

- Set the meeting policy to save recordings outside the local region using the `-AllowRecordingStorageOutsideRegion` attribute in the `Set-CsTeamsMeetingPolicy` cmdlet.

The Meeting Recording Button Is Missing

- The initial step is to leave and rejoin the meeting. This might restore the recording functionality.

- Use the Teams web client (`https://teams.microsoft.com/`) to join and record the meeting.

- Make sure you're trying to record a meeting and not a 1:1 call. Call recording is controlled by the `AllowCloudRecordingForCalls` parameter of Teams calling policies.

- Additionally, run the 1:1 Call Recording Diagnostic for an impacted user:

  - Sign into the Microsoft 365 admin center and type Diag: Teams 1:1 Call Recording in the Need Help? box.

  - Enter the SIP address and select Run Tests.

Then try again to record the meeting. If the issue isn't resolved, open a support ticket with Microsoft and the issue details.

The Meeting Recording Link Is Not Visible in the Chat Window Issue

In large meeting and chat sessions, a known issue prevents the meeting recording link from appearing for one or more users. Try scrolling up to the top of the chat window and then scrolling back to the bottom. This action might trigger a chat service event and restore the meeting recording link.

If the meeting recording link still isn't visible, use one of these methods to locate the recording, depending on your storage location. The location is provided in the diagnostic report.

Method 1: Meeting recordings are stored in Stream so sign into Microsoft Stream. Select My content ➤ Meetings to open the Meetings page in Stream. The options from the My content menu appear on a bar at the top of each page. You can pivot to Teams meeting recordings from any page by selecting the Meetings tab on the bar.

Method 2: Meeting recordings are stored on OneDrive for Business or SharePoint. For non-channel meetings, the recording is stored in the Recordings folder under My files (for instance, `<Recording user's OneDrive for Business>/My files/Recordings`). The recording is stored in the Teams site documentation library in the Recordings folder in SharePoint for channel meetings. To find the recording link in the Teams channel, select Files ➤ Recordings ➤ Open in SharePoint (for instance, in Teams, `<Teams channel name>/Files/Recordings`).

You can also find the recording link for users directly in SharePoint from the Recordings folder under `Documents` (for instance in SharePoint, `<SharePoint/Documents/Channel name>/Recordings`).

Known Issues That Affect Teams Webinars

Microsoft Teams recently unveiled the webinar feature as an alternative to formal meetings. See "Set up for webinars in Microsoft Teams" to learn how to manage webinars. This article discusses known issues that might occur when you use webinars and provides resolutions and workarounds that you can try.

The "For Everyone" Option Is Greyed Out or Missing

When creating a webinar, the *For everyone* option on the Require registration menu is unavailable (grayed out) or missing, even though the `WhoCanRegister` parameter value is set to Everyone by default. This issue occurs if there is a change in the meeting policy. Reset the `WhoCanRegister` parameter value to Everyone and wait 24 hours to solve the problem. To reset the `WhoCanRegister` parameter, run the PowerShell cmdlet: `Set-CsTeamsMeetingPolicy -WhoCanRegister Everyone`

Remember, if the "anonymous join" functionality is turned off in the meeting settings, anonymous users can't join the webinars.

Configuring Setting for Microsoft Teams with Apple CarPlay

Apple CarPlay allows users to safely make Teams audio calls on the road using Siri voice commands. But, if the user uses a Microsoft Intune-managed iOS device to make the calls, Siri can be blocked from use by the org admin. Suppose the user is unable to use Apple CarPlay in Teams. In that case, you, as an admin, must configure the following settings by using the Microsoft Endpoint Manager admin center.

First, Allow User Devices to Use Siri

The default setting for using Siri should allow the user to use CarPlay. If you have created a configuration profile that directs your device to block Siri, the setting must be updated.

1. Log into the Endpoint manager and then navigate to Devices ➤ Configuration profiles ➤ Your_Configuration_profile ➤ Properties ➤ Configuration Settings ➤ Built-in Apps.

2. Set the Block Siri option to Not configured.

Allow Data Transfer to Any App on Your Device

Suppose you have created an application protection policy that allows data transfer to only specific apps. In that case, that restriction must be removed to enable data transfer to all apps.

1. Log into the Endpoint manager and then navigate to Apps ➤ App protection policies ➤ Your_App_protection_policy ➤ Properties ➤ Data protection.

2. Set Send Org data to other apps to All apps.

Unable to See the Shared Image in Teams Chat

1. Sometimes when you share the image with others while doing chat, your image will not show in Teams chat. Instead, it shows the image icon. Even you will not see images shared by others.

2. The solution is straightforward. Simply exit the Teams client or delete the cache on your computer.

Microsoft Teams Phone System Issues and Resolutions

A Quick Recap About Teams Phone System

Microsoft Teams provide phone system capabilities through methods such as Teams calling plan (managed, implemented, and operated by Microsoft), Teams Operator Connects (managed by an operator), and Teams Direct Routing (implemented, organized, and operated by the organization).

The Phone System concept:

- Outbound call: A call initiated by a Teams user

- PSTN call: Any call to a phone number not within Teams. This may include other internal PBX, analog phones, or external numbers.

- Internal call: A call between two phones within the same company. Maybe a call between Lync and a PBX phone.

- Direct inward dial (DID) number: A PSTN phone number (also called DDI)

- RNL: Reverse number lookup

- NANP: North America Numbering Plan

- Dial Plans: Meant to "codify" dialing habits into E164 format and assign them to the user account

- Voice Rout Policy: Contains Voice usage, and limits or extends a user's telephony feature set

- PSTN usages: Contains Voice Route(s)

- Voice routes: Sends dialed numbers to the correct gateway(s) and controls which numbers a user is allowed to call

A Teams User Can't Make a Phone Call

1. The first thing to check is what type of call the user makes: Teams calls or dialing out to an external PSTN number. That means Teams outbound call routing is happening.

2. If the user is dialing an external phone number, check if the phone number is normalizing correctly in Teams.

3. To bypass normalization checks, you may ask the user to dial a number in E.164 format (example, +14081234567).

4. After the normalization check pass, Teams does a reverse number lookup to check if the dialed number is associated with a user account, conference room account, or resource account. Since it is an external phone number, no match is found, and the call moves on to the Teams online voice route policy.

5. The Teams online voice route policy includes PSTN usage and routes. So, Teams will check each PSTN usage and route for the match.

6. The call is processed to Teams Direct, routing the SBC to the PSTN provider as soon as the match happens. Finally, the external endpoint receives the call.

Searching for a New (Unused) Phone Number Using Teams Admin Center

If you have phone number ranges but don't know which phone numbers are assigned and which are not, you can use the filter option under Manage user in the Teams admin center. To search for unassigned numbers, log into the Teams admin center (`https://admin.teams.microsoft.com/users`), click Users ➤ Manage users ➤ and select the filter icon. On the filter page, select the phone number and condition "starts with" and type the phone number, like +1209, and click Apply. See Figure 7-6.

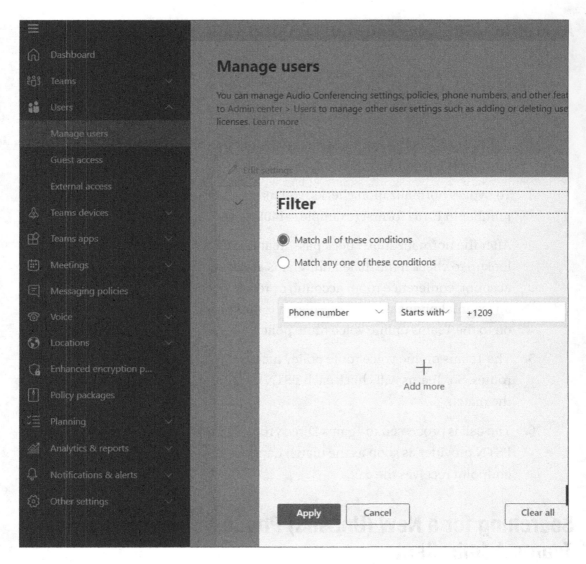

Figure 7-6. *A users filter for phone numbers*

When you click Apply, the result comes in ascending order to you can see a missing number that is not assigned to a user can be used as a free number. Remember, phone numbers can be set to analog devices, Teams room, or IP phones.

Unable to Manage Dial Plans

When you try to access a dial plan in the Microsoft Teams admin center, you may get this error message: "*We can't get the effective dial plan, so the dial plan can't be tested.*" You may receive another error message when you try to test a dial plan: "*Something went wrong while testing this phone number. If you continue to have problems, contact Microsoft customer support.*" There will be a third error message, "*Management object not found for identity OrgID_of_unlicensed_user,*" when you run the `Get-CsEffective TenantDialPlan` cmdlet in Teams PowerShell to see the details of a dial plan.

Basically, these errors trigger when a query looks up the value of the `EffectiveTenantDialPlanName` property. This property is used to populate the information in the dial plan. If the admin does not have an applicable product license, this query can't run. Because the value is not returned, an error occurs. To resolve the issue, the admin account must have a Teams license assigned.

Call Transfers Are Not Working in Microsoft Teams

The call transfer feature is handy. It allows users to call another Teams user or an external phone number. However, sometimes the call doesn't work the way it should. This section concentrates on troubleshooting issues related to call transfers initiated by Microsoft Teams. This does not apply to problems associated with calling transfers started from SBC or PSTN sources.

Call Transfers

Call transfers initiated by Microsoft Teams can occur in multiple scenarios, such as user-initiated call transfers, call transfers from an auto attendant, and call transfers from a call queue. Before you troubleshoot issues, understand the SIP-related information.

Different methods can be used for a call transfer. Here are the methods used primarily for call transfers.

1. Using a SIP Refer message

2. Using a SIP Invite message that has a Replaces header. This method is mainly used for call queue responses.

3. Using an internal Microsoft Teams infrastructure. This method isn't visible to the SBC. The technique is used only if the first two methods are not supported.

All transfers that use a SIP Refer message must go through the Microsoft Teams infrastructure. When the Microsoft SIP proxy sends a SIP Refer message to SBC, a SIP Invite message should be returned to the SIP proxy (Teams), not to PSTN or any other destination. Even if the call is transferred to an external PSTN number, this is true. SBC doesn't have to parse the SIP Refer message to look for the transfer target. The SBC should send the SIP Invite message together with the Request-URI (RURI) setting only to the contents of the Refer-To header.

It also should include the Referred-By header from the SIP Refer message. You, as an admin, have to make sure that the strings of the SIP Invite message are not changed and that they are sent as the same strings provided in the SIP Refer message (especially in the Referred-By header). These strings are used to identify calls, targets, and other essential parts of a call transfer. Note that the strings could be either x-* strings or custom strings in the Referred-By and Refer-To headers.

Auto Attendant Does Not Transfer Calls to an External PSTN Number

Auto attendant call transfer external phone number issues occur for different reasons, such as no or incorrect licenses assigned to the auto attendant resource account. If you can transfer a call to an internal user or a bot, but if you can't transfer a call to an external PSTN number, this might indicate a licensing issue.

The SIP Invite message may get sent to an incorrect device. For instance, the message is forwarded to a PSTN provider. By design, SIP Refer messages don't contain complete information about the target. For example, a PSTN number is normalized to the international format.

To resolve this issue, assign the correct license to the auto attendant resource account to enable it to make PSTN calls. If the problem persists, make sure that the SIP Invite message is sent to the SIP proxy that can transfer calls appropriately. The SIP proxy sends the SIP Invite message to the PSTN network according to settings like normalization rules, SBC routing, and caller ID.

The SIP Refer Message Doesn't Contain a Phone Number, or the Phone Number Is Incorrectly Formatted

This behavior is by design. To work around this behavior, ensure that the SIP proxy sends the SIP Refer message to the SBC. Then, configure the SBC to copy the Referred-By and Refer-To strings to the SIP Invite message that will be sent back to the SIP proxy.

No SIP Refer Comes from the SIP Proxy to the SBC

It is essential to get the SIP Refer from the Teams SIP proxy to SBC. To resolve this issue, follow these steps:

1. First, ensure that the SIP Refer method is supported for call transfers by SBC in the SIP Invite or "SIP 200 OK" response (depending on whether the call is initiated by the SBC or Microsoft). Suppose the SIP Refer method isn't supported. In that case, call transfers are made using SIP Invite with a Replaces header (if this method is supported). If the SIP Invite method doesn't work, the internal transfer hidden from the SBC is used.

2. Also, ensure that the firewall and SBC settings allow incoming connections from any Microsoft signaling IP address, not only specific addresses. SIP Refer can come from any IP address using a new TLS connection, even if the last part of the call came from another IP address.

If SBC receives SIP Refer messages after following these steps, make sure that the new SIP Invite is delivered to the SIP proxy, even if the call is transferred to an external PSTN number. If the call is transferred to an external PSTN number, the SIP proxy will forward the call and send a new SIP Invite to SBC.

In this case, make sure that the call doesn't fail on the SBC. If this call fails and generates an error, this error will be sent back to the SBC on the transferred call.

Teams Calls Get Dropped Before the Transfer Is Completed

Teams call drop issues may occur for different reasons: the SIP proxy doesn't receive the "202 Accepted" response or the "SIP Notify" messages from the SBC as a response to the SIP Refer message process timing out or the "SIP Bye" message arrives from SBC too early and the call ends before the message is fully transferred. To resolve this issue, make sure that the SBC sends the "SIP 202 Accepted" response and "SIP Notify" message to provide an update about the progress of the transferred call. When the SIP proxy receives a "SIP Notify" message that includes the "200 OK" response, it will safely end the original call by sending the "SIP Bye" response because it knows that the call was replaced with a new call.

No Ringing Sound When Transferring Calls

Sometimes the ringing sound doesn't happen when the call transfer happens. To resolve this issue, follow these steps:

1. Ensure that the SIP Refer method is supported by the SBC in the initial SIP Invite or "SIP 200 OK" response (depending on whether the call is initiated by the SBC or Microsoft). SIP Refer is required to successfully generate the ringing sound. It is because, currently, no simulated ringing sound is generated when you transfer calls internally.

2. If the SBC receives the SIP Refer message, but PSTN users still don't hear a ring tone, make sure that the SBC connects to the newly initiated transfer call and plays a ring tone that's based on the "SIP 180 Ringing" or "SIP 183 Session" response that's sent from the SIP proxy.

Local Media Optimization for Direct Routing Isn't Working As Expected

You might find that local media optimization (LMO) for Direct Routing doesn't work as expected. For instance, Microsoft Teams doesn't send the X-Ms-UserLocation and X-Ms-MediaPath headers, or the X-Ms-UserLocation header contains the wrong location, or the calls fail.

The X-Ms-UserLocation and X-Ms-MediaPath headers are required for LMO. One of the most common reasons these headers are not sent is that the gateway is not configured correctly for LMO. To check the gateway configuration, run the following Get-CsOnlinePSTNGateway cmdlet:

```
Get-CSOnlinePSTNGateway | Select Identity, Fqdn, Enabled, MediaBypass,
GatewaySiteId, ProxySbc, BypassMode
```

For LMO to be enabled, make sure that all the selected properties in this cmdlet are set. This is especially important for BypassMode. Here's an example of the output from this command:

```
Identity           : SBC1.bloguc.com
Fqdn               : SBC1.bloguc.com
Enabled            : True
MediaBypass        : True
GatewaySiteId      : California
ProxySbc           : Proxysbc.bloguc.com
BypassMode         : Always

Identity           : SBC2.bloguc.com
Fqdn               : SBC2.bloguc.com
Enabled            : True
MediaBypass        : True
GatewaySiteId      : India
ProxySbc           :
BypassMode         : Always
```

Wrong Location Sent in the X-Ms-UserLocation Header

Sometimes the network location information in the X-Ms-UserLocation header is listed as external, but you anticipate seeing an internal value; this means that the public IP address of the Teams client doesn't match any entry in the list trusted IP addresses. To resolve this issue, identify the client's public IP address used by Teams and add it to the trusted IP address list.

1. Capture and open Microsoft Teams log files and locate the public IP address listed for the client in the MS Teams Diagnostics Log [Date]__[Time]_calling.txt file. In the log, search for trustedIpMatchInfo. When the Teams client public IP doesn't match, it shows in the log like this:

    ```
    "ncsDebugInfo": {
        "trustedIpMatchInfo": {
          "publicIp": "110.190.180.13",
          "trustedIpAddress": "110.190.180.10",
          "maskBits": 27,
          "reason": "NotMatched"
        },
    ```

2. Run the `Get-CsTenantTrustedIPAddress` command to get the list of trusted IP addresses. Check the output and verify that the IP address shown in the Teams diagnostic log matches the trusted IP address. You will notice that the client's IP address identified in step 1 is missing from the trusted IP list.

3. Run the `New-CsTenantTrustedIPAddress` command to add the missing IP address to the list. Here is the example command:

```
New-CsTenantTrustedIPAddress -IPAddress 110.190.180.10 -MaskBits
27 -Description "California Site trusted IP"
```

You can see that the client's IP address has now been added to the list of trusted IP addresses.

4. Finally, immediately restart the Teams client to recognize the newly added IP address. Otherwise, the list can take up to 30 minutes to be updated. After the restart, Teams will find a match for the client's IP address in the list of trusted IP addresses and be shown in the Teams diagnostic log like this example:

```
"ncsDebugInfo": {
"trustedIpMatchInfo": {
"publicIp": "110.190.180.13"
"trustedIpAddress":"110.190.180.10",
"maskBits": 27,
"reason": "Matched"
}
```

Teams Incoming Calls Fail or Go to Voicemail If Both LMO and LBR Are Enabled

Teams incoming phone call failure occurs for several reasons. This issue happens when either the headers or the routing information are not configured correctly in the SBC from which the call is received. Check that the SIP message headers sent from the SBC contain the following information and update them if they are incorrect:

- The SIP URI contains the FQDN of the regional SBC.

- The Contact header contains the FQDN of the regional SBC.

- The Record-Route contains the FQDN of the proxy SBC.

Only the Record-Route is checked if a proxy SBC is not defined for the regional SBC. If the Record-Route is missing, then the Contact header is checked. If the headers are configured correctly, the issue might be caused by a misconfigured routing on the SBC.

Make sure that the SBC has location-based routing (LBR) enabled. The GatewaySiteLbrEnabled parameter must be set to True. Also, the SBC must be assigned to the same site as the client that's initiating the call. For the LBR work correctly, the Teams user who initiates phone calls and LBR-enabled SBC should be on the same site. It is not mandatory to allow the proxy SBC for LBR.

To determine whether the SBC assignment is correct, identify the user site that's registered in the Teams client logs and compare it with the assignment information for the SBC:

1. Log into the Teams client, capture the diagnostic log, and open the Microsoft Teams log files.

2. Identify the user site information listed in the MS Teams Diagnostics Log [Date]__[Time]_calling.txt file. For instance, the following log shows a user's network sites in Mumbai:

```
"siteMatchInfo": {
        "ipv4": "10.200.210.91",
        "subnetLengthIPv4": "23",
        "subnetId": "10.200.210.0",
        "maskBits": 23,
        "networkSiteId": "Mumbai",
        "enableLocationBasedRouting": true,
        "reason": "Matched"
```

3. Then check if the SBC is on the same site. To check the configuration of the SBC, run the Get-CsOnlinePSTNGateway command. See the example output. The user's site is in Mumbai but the SBC is in Bangalore and is thus mismatched, which is a call failure reason.

```
Identity     .  : SBC3.bloguc.com
Fqdn            : SBC3.bloguc.com
Enabled         : True
MediaBypass     : True
GatewaySiteId   : Bangalore
ProxySbc        : proxysbc.bloguc.com
BypassMode      : Always
```

4. To resolve the issue, update the site for the SBC (SBC3.
    bloguc.com). To update the SBC's configuration, run the Set-
    CsOnlinePSTNGateway command as follows:

```
Set-CSOnlinePSTNGateway -Identity "SBC3.bloguc.com" -GatewaySiteID
"Mumbai"
```

You can run the Get-CsOnlinePSTNGateway command to verify the SBC's updated configuration.

Teams Outbound Calls Are Not Working Using Direct Routing

Users may experience different issues when using Direct Routing to make outbound calls from a Teams client to a SBC. Here are the most common problems that Direct Routing users may encounter:

- A connection to the SBC is not established.

- Some users in a tenant are unable to make calls.

- No users in a tenant can make calls.

An Incorrect Caller ID Is Displayed to the Call Recipient

When you use Direct Routing, the caller ID information delivered to the call recipient is listed in the From and P-Asserted-Identity headers in the SIP options message. The From header contains any of the following items:

- The phone number assigned to the caller who is initiating the call. If the caller's phone number has to be hidden from the call recipient, it's replaced with "anonymous."

- A service number assigned to the caller by using the `CsCallingLineIdentity` command

- The phone number of the original caller if the call was forwarded

The P-Asserted-Identity header contains the user's phone number who is billed for the call. If `Privacy:id` is set, this indicates that the information in the header must be hidden from the call recipient.

If the information in the From and P-Asserted-Identity headers doesn't match, and if the PSTN prioritizes the P-Asserted-Identity header information over the From header information, then incorrect information will be displayed.

To resolve the problem, make sure that the correct caller ID is presented to the call recipient, and configure the SBC to either remove the P-Asserted-Identity header from the SIP options message or modify its contents.

A Connection to the SBC Is Not Established

Sometimes calls reach the SBC, but no connection is established. In this situation, when the SBC receives a SIP options message from the Teams SIP proxy, it returns a failure message that includes error codes in the range of 400 to 699.

Different causes may prevent a connection to the SBC. Here are the most common causes:

1. The SIP failure message is generated by another telephony device on the same network as the SBC. In this case, you need to troubleshoot the other device to fix the error. If you need support, contact the device vendor.

2. Your PSTN provider is experiencing some issues and is sending the SIP failure message. This is most likely the case if the failure error code is SIP 403 or SIP 404. For resolution, you can contact the PSTN provider for support in fixing the issue.

3. The issue is not caused by another device on the network or your PSTN provider. However, the cause is otherwise unknown. You can contact the SBC vendor for support in fixing the issue in this situation.

Unable to Make a Phone Call Using Teams

Sometimes users are unable to make an outbound call. Suppose the connection between the Teams client and the SBC is working correctly, but some users cannot make calls. The issue might be caused by incorrect settings, policy assignments, or incorrect provisioning of those users. Here are the most common reasons for the dial-out problem.

1. Users are missing the dial pad on the Calls tab in Teams. To resolve the issue, you need to ensure that the user has the correct license (E3 with Phone System or E5), Enterprise Voice, and all required policy settings (dial plan and voice routing policy). To check the settings, run the `Get-CsOnlineUser` command in Teams PowerShell, like so:

   ```
   Get-CsOnlineUser -Identity <UserId> | fl Identity,Enterprise
   VoiceEnabled,HostedVoiceMail,OnPremLineURI
   ```

2. There are no patterns available in the Online Voice Routing policy (OVRP) that match the number dialed by the user. To resolve the issue, make sure to assign an appropriate online voice routing policy to the affected user. Specific OVRP conditions must be true to place a phone call correctly.

   - Pattern available in the OVRP that matches the dialed number

   - The call's usage profile matches the one set up for the specific user.

   - The gateway that's specified for the SBC is enabled. If it's disabled, either enable it or select a different enabled gateway.

3. The user's OVRP contains invalid characters. Sometime, there will be a typo, and invalid, invisible characters can be inserted in the OVRP when you paste information into it from Microsoft Word or other editors. Although the characters are not displayed, they are considered when deciding the route the call should take. To fix the issue, remove the policy and recreate it by either rewriting it manually or copying it from an editor like Notepad.

Multiple Users Are Unable to Make Phone Calls using Teams

When multiple users cannot make calls, this means there is an issue in the system or device, or it's a connectivity issue, or the calls are not reaching the SBC. Here are the most common causes.

The Teams PSTN Gateway Is Disabled

The Teams admin center has a complete list of all the PSTN gateways and their status. You can check if each PSTN gateway used by Teams is available and enabled. You can also use Teams PowerShell to review and update the gateway. To check the status of the gateway, run the `Get-CsOnlinePSTNGateway` command. The output must show that the value of the `Enabled` parameter is set to True. The following command shows all of the PSTN gateways and their statuses:

```
Get-CsOnlinePSTNGateway | fl Identity,Fqdn,SipSignalingPort,MaxConcurrentSe
ssions,Enabled
```

If the intended SBC is not enabled, run the following command to allow the SBC with the true parameter:

```
Set-CsOnlinePSTNGateway -Identity "sbc3.bloguc.com" -Enabled $true
```

PSTN Gateway or SBC Not Responding for SIP Options

The gateway is not responding to SIP options messages because some device on the network, such as a firewall, is blocking the messages. Ensure that the SIP signaling IPs and FQDNs are allowed on all network devices that connect the SBC to the Internet. The IP addresses that must be allowed are listed at SIP signaling, and media from the SBC public IP to the Teams SIP proxy IPs and Teams SIP proxy to SBC public IP.

SBC Connectivity Issues

When you set up Direct Routing, you may experience SBC connectivity issues, such as SIP options not being received, TLS connection problems, the SBC doesn't respond, or the SBC is marked as inactive in the Teams admin portal.

These issues are most likely caused by a TLS certificate problem, or an SBC is not configured correctly for Direct Routing.

Overview of the SIP Options Process

SBC sends a TLS connection request that includes a TLS certificate to the SIP proxy server FQDN (`sip.pstnhub.microsoft.com`).

The SIP Proxy Checks the Connection Request

If the request is not valid, the TLS connection is closed, and the SIP proxy does not receive SIP options from the SBC. If the request is valid, the TLS connection is established, and the SBC uses it to send SIP options to the SIP proxy.

After receiving SIP options, the SIP proxy checks the Record-Route to determine whether the SBC FQDN belongs to a known tenant. The SIP proxy checks the Contact header if the FQDN information is not detected there. If the SBC FQDN is detected and recognized, the SIP proxy sends a 200 OK message using the same TLS connection.

The SIP proxy sends SIP options to the SBC FQDN listed in the Contact header of the SIP options received from the SBC. After receiving SIP options from the SIP proxy, the SBC responds by sending a 200 OK message. This step confirms that the SBC is healthy. As the final step, the SBC is marked as Active in the Teams Admin portal.

SIP Option Not Working

After the TLS connection is successfully established and the SBC is able to send and receive messages to and from the Teams SIP proxy, there might still be problems that affect the format or content of the SIP options.

- The SBC doesn't receive a 200 OK response from the SIP proxy.

- The SBC gets a 200 OK response but no SIP options.

- The SBC status is intermittently inactive.

- The FQDN doesn't match the contents of the CN or SAN in the provided certificate.

- The domain activation is not registered in the Microsoft 365 environment.

TLS Connection Issues

If the TLS connection is closed right away and the SIP options are not received from the SBC, or 200 OK is not received from the SBC, the problem might be with the TLS version. The TLS version configured on the SBC should be 1.2 or higher.

- The SBC certificate is self-signed or not from a trusted CA.

- The SBC doesn't trust the SIP proxy certificate.

- The SBC certificate is invalid.

- SBC certificates or intermediary certificates are missing in the SBC TLS "Hello" message.

- The SBC connection is interrupted.

Call Forwarding Is Not Working in Teams Direct Routing

In Teams Direct routing scenarios, first check if the SBC is enabled. The `ForwardCallHistory` value must be True to enable the PSTN gateway for call forwarding. Then check that the user correctly set call forwarding in the Teams client. In my case, everything was correctly configured; however, the call was going from the SBC to the carrier via a different SIP trunk, and the carrier was rejecting the calls.

Decoding a Microsoft Teams Meeting URL

Microsoft Teams meeting allows joining a meeting with a single click using a desktop client or web client. Teams meeting join URLs have multiple things tied together, such as the meeting ID, tenant ID, and organizer ID. Here is a sample meeting URL:

Click here to join the meeting (https://teams.microsoft.com/l/meetup-join/1 9%3ameeting_**NTcxOGM5YzQtOTFkMC0oMWY4LWE5ZmItNjY2YTVmMjk1NjZ**h%40thread.v2/0 ?context=%7b%22Tid%22%3a%22**abc345ca-4cdb-4130-854a-1d193232e9bn1**%22%2c%220 id%22%3a%22**e8183a6b-717f-4eca-812e-490096ca60c9**%22%7d)

To decode the Teams meeting, use `www.URLdecoder.org` to simplify the URL and the copy meeting ID, tenant ID, and organizer ID.

- Meeting ID: NTcxOGM5YzQtOTFkMC00MWY4LWE5ZmIt NjY2YTVmMjk1NjZh

- TID: Tenant ID **abc345ca-4cdb-4130-854a-1d193232e9bn1**

- OID: Organizer ID **e8183a6b-717f-4eca-812e-490096ca60c9**

No Notification When a Meeting Has Started

The first troubleshooting step is to validate that the notification is coming from different Teams clients, like if a meeting starting notification works when using a Windows laptop. The next step is to uninstall and reinstall the Microsoft Teams client from `https://teams.microsoft.com` or the app store. And then check if a notification is coming or not.

How Does Microsoft Teams Notification Work?

Notification is handy in knowing missing activities. Notifications are mainly used to carry information and updates, inspire end-users to engage with a Teams client, show reminders, assist as a step in the end-user journey, and much more. So, Teams provides different ways to access, receive, and manage notifications.

Microsoft Teams notifies end-users on different occasions and activities such as chats, meetings, file sharing, and project planning. Notifications help be more productive in Teams by taking action on each notification shown in the activity feed, like mentioned messages, missed calls, chat messages, etc.

Manage Teams Notification:

For managing notifications, you need to select the Settings and more (…) icon in the top right of Teams, then select the Settings button ➤ Notifications. End-user can easily turn-On or turn-Off notification sounds by switching the button "Play sound for incoming calls and notifications." There are three options to manage channel notification All activity, Mentions & Replies, or custom.

- All activity: To get notified about all your shown channels, select All Activity.

- Mentions & Replies: To be notified only when you are @mentioned or receive replies to your messages in channels, select Mentions & replies.

- Custom: For the most control over your channel notifications, select custom.

Tip   You can manage notifications for any Teams feature by clicking on the three dots (...) to see the notification option. Once you see the option, you can turn on or turn off the notification. Sometimes Teams notifications don't show due to different reasons. Below is the most common reason.

- Notification was stopped due to the end-user already being in a meeting with another client.

- Notification was stopped due to a transient network issue.

Why does the meeting start notification not shows in the Teams iOS app?

Basically, the Teams desktop client provides meeting started notifications without any restriction; however, the Teams iOS client cannot. It means the reliability may have been higher before Apple placed limitations on our non-VoIP notifications. As a result, the meeting started notifications may not be certain to be shown by the system itself, regardless of any Teams processing involved. It is one of the reasons for lower reliability. Another problem is the calendar syncing issue. The calendar sync does not reliably happen in the background, so the user needs to actively use the calendar on the calendar tab in the Teams iOS client.

In case the notification is not working, the most common troubleshooting is to turn off all the notifications, restart the Teams client, and then turn on the notification again. Between that and the calendar sync, we have a solid explanation of the observed behavior. The only thing left to test would be to consistently sync the calendar in the app and observe the behavior of the notification. If the issue persists, it is likely related to these new restrictions.

Determine why meeting start notifications in IOS no longer regularly occur in the system tray. The product group identified an issue stemming from restrictions imposed by Apple on notifications. This has affected the reliability of system notifications on IOS devices.

Microsoft Teams Call Quality Issues

Troubleshooting Teams call quality issues is always challenging because Teams call involves multiple components such as Teams client machine, Teams cloud service (transport relay), network, device, and so on. So, using the right tool for the right task will help troubleshoot issues. Say Bloguc Inc helpdesk users report poor call quality issues. To investigate the issue, the first thing to do is gather issue-related information, including when the issue happened, what the exact error message was, and whether the issue was reproducible. Additionally, collect information on the common things that impact Teams call quality and reliability issues.

When we talk about the audio quality issue, the first thing we need to define is what the user means by a poor audio call. Was it an echo in the call, noise, or one-way audio? For instance, echoes can be because of the network, devices, or the performance of Teams back-end service.

When the Issue Happens, Where Do We See It?

There are few places where you can see the issue; Teams Call Analytics is the best place to see single user call quality information. The Call Quality Dashboard shows overall call quality.

Call Analytics shows latency, packet loss, and jitter information. This report shows inbound and outbound call quality information. For example, user Balu's inbound stream shows a 50% packet loss, so it will be a poor quality call. The Call Analytics report shows individual user call quality, which offers five dimensions: packet loss greater than 10%, jitter more than 30%, round trip time greater than 500m, network MOS degradation greater than 1%, and concealed samples greater than 7%. So, check for the most impact, packet loss, and the time amount of the packet loss.

Capturing Network Traces Using the Wireshark Tool for Packet Loss Troubleshooting

When Teams users complain about poor audio/video call quality because of packet loss, how do you figure out where you are losing packets? Wireshark (`www.wireshark.org/download.html`) helps. To troubleshoot Teams call quality problems tied with packet loss, you need to capture network traffic and quantify the packets to see lost packets. To troubleshoot packet loss, here are some highly recommended steps:

- Capture simultaneous network traces on Teams endpoint (both endpoints).

- Filter network capture by RTP or RTCP ports to see the traffic you are most concerned about.

- Then identify RTCP sender/receiver Call Analytics report blocks where packet loss was reported. QoE data is collected from RTCP packet loss. The media stack is processed and then put in a Call Analytics report.

- Verify sequence numbers end to end to determine which segment has a network packet loss. Remember, the sequence is not packets arriving.

- Evaluate RTP payload types for packets immediately preceding the reported packet loss to determine causality.

How Does Microsoft Teams' "Spam Likely" Notification Work?

Microsoft Teams has a spam call notification to identify and notify the end user if an incoming phone call is spam. Teams' incoming PSTN call spam protection is a service that returns risk levels for a phone number based on data collected from third parties, internal call records, and user abuse reports. Each inbound PSTN call is sent to Team users and sent to Microsoft by a PSTN hub unless the user has opted out of spam protection.

Later, calls are marked as spam based on TeleSign and Microsoft's proprietary decision engine data. If TeleSign or Microsoft's proprietary decision engine flag the call as spam, the user sees the incoming call as "spam likely."

When an inbound call occurs, the incoming phone number is sent to the TeleSign Score API to be checked. TeleSign's Score API is like a credit check for phone numbers. When a phone number is submitted to the Score API, the phone number is evaluated. A score is returned, indicating how risky that user is. Note that, apart from the phone number, no other customer data is sent to TeleSign.

Microsoft Teams Shows the Wrong Display. Teams Meeting Shows the Incorrect Username. Teams Meeting Doesn't Show the Proper Picture of Users.

These issues are due to the Microsoft Teams cache that stores locally in users' machines. Teams cache stays there for 28 days. Teams stores the picture cache for 60 days before deleting it.

Microsoft Teams doesn't store users' account information in a separate directory. Teams use Azure Active Directory (Active Directory Domain Service) sync with Azure AD, which Teams uses.

When you make changes to a user account like new policy assignments and phone number changes, they take 24 hours to reflect. Usually, changes show in 2-3 hours but can take up to 24 hours.

Some data, such as display name and telephone number, can be cached for up to 28 days in the client; profile pictures can be cached for up to 60 days. To clear the cache for a Windows machine, follow these steps:

1. Exit Outlook and Microsoft Teams.

2. Go to `%appdata%\Microsoft\Teams`.

3. Delete all the files inside the `Teams` folder.

4. Relaunch Microsoft Teams and Outlook.

To clear the cache for a macOS, follow these steps:

1. Exit Outlook and Microsoft Teams.

2. Open Finder, click Go, and select Go to Folder `~/Library/Application Support/Microsoft`.

3. Move the `Teams` folder to Trash.

4. Delete the Microsoft Teams identities cache from the keychain if it is present.

5. Relaunch Microsoft Teams and Outlook.

Common Issues When You Use SIP Devices with Teams

The SIP gateway enables your organization to use any compatible SIP device (existing device) with Microsoft Teams. The next sections cover a few common issues.

Can't Onboard My SIP Device

Here are the everyday things that might affect device onboarding. Make sure to check each item.

1. The first thing to check is if the user is using a compatible SIP device. The compatible SIP list is at `https://docs.microsoft.com/en-us/microsoftteams/sip-gateway-plan#compatible-devices`.

2. Before using it, make sure to reset the device to the factory default settings.

3. Validate that the SIP gateway provisioning server's URL begins in HTTP, not HTTPS. For example, use `http://noam.ipp.sdg.teams.microsoft.com`, not `https://noam.ipp.sdg.teams.microsoft.com`.

4. Check whether the device can connect to the SIP gateway. Verify that the connection isn't blocked by your firewall or proxy server and that the required HTTPS endpoints and TCP/UDP ports are open. For more information, see the list of items that follows "Before you can configure the SIP Gateway" in Configure SIP Gateway `https://docs.microsoft.com/en-us/microsoftteams/sip-gateway-configure`.

Web App Authentication Fails When Trying to Sign In

Follow these steps to solve the authentication issue:

1. Check if you are using the correct credentials. Sign into the Teams web app (`https://teams.microsoft.com`) by using the same credentials to check whether the credentials are valid.

2. If an organization uses Conditional Access, make sure that the IP address of the SIP gateway is excluded.

A Device Doesn't Update After a Successful Sign-In

1. Check whether the requirements to use SIP gateway (`https://docs.microsoft.com/en-us/microsoftteams/sip-gateway-plan#requirements-to-use-sip-gateway`) are met. To use a SIP gateway, Teams users must have a phone number with PSTN calling enabled.

2. Check whether the SIP gateway policy is set correctly (`https://docs.microsoft.com/en-us/microsoftteams/sip-gateway-configure#enable-sip-gateway-for-the-users-in-your-organization`).

3. Check whether another user from a different tenant signed into the device but didn't sign out gracefully. Have that user sign in and sign out again if they didn't.

4. Check whether the device can connect to the SIP gateway. Verify that the connection isn't blocked by your firewall or proxy server and that the required HTTPS endpoints and TCP/UDP ports are open. (`https://docs.microsoft.com/en-us/microsoftteams/sip-gateway-configure`).

Teams on Android Devices Unexpectedly Signed Out

Sometimes Teams devices, including Teams Rooms on Android, Teams phone devices, Teams panels, and Teams displays, are signed out of Teams automatically. You can use one of the following options to sign into Teams.

Option 1: Sign In From the Teams Admin Center

Make sure that your device is running the following versions of the Teams app or a newer version before you begin:

- Teams Rooms on Android: 1.0.96.2021051904

- Teams phone devices: 1449/1.0.94.2021101205

- Teams panels: 1449/1.0.95.2021111203

1. Log into the Microsoft Teams admin center, select Devices in the navigation menu on the left, and select your Android device.

2. On the page for the Android device, select Actions ➤ Sign out to sign out of the device.

3. After you're signed out, select Sign in, and a pop-up window will display. After a wait time of two to five minutes, the window will be populated with a URL, a code, and instructions to sign in. Use the information provided to sign into the device.

Option 2: Restart the Device and Then Sign In from the Teams Admin Center

The next thing to try is to restart the Android device remotely from the Microsoft Teams admin center and sign in. To do so, follow these steps:

1. Log into the Microsoft Teams admin center, select Devices in the navigation menu on the left, and select your Android device.

2. On the page for the Android device, select restart to restart the device.

3. After the device restarts, select Sign in, and a pop-up window will display. After a wait time of two to five minutes, the window will be populated with a URL, a code, and instructions to sign in. Use the provided information to sign into the device.

Option 3: Generate a New Code on the Device to Sign In

To generate new code, follow these steps:

1. First, select the Refresh code on the device to generate a new code to sign in. If a new code is generated, use it to sign into the device.

2. Select *Sign in on this device* if a new code isn't generated.

3. The username will already be populated in the appropriate field. Enter the password to sign into the device.

4. If the sign-in is still unsuccessful, select Start over. This will sign you out of the device.

5. Select Refresh code to generate a new code to sign into the device.

Option 4: If You Still Can't Sign into the Device, Reset It to Its Factory Settings

1. Perform a factory reset from the OEM device settings or use the specific key combination to the OEM model.

2. Use options 1, 2, or 3 to sign into the device.

Summary

Microsoft Teams provides multiple features, including real-time conversation, content collaboration, audio/video calls with optimal call quality, conference calls, and app integration. While using these features, the user may encounter an issue. As a support engineer or admin, you must know and troubleshoot these issues to assist users. This chapter provided you detailed information on how to solve many common problems. By using this information, you can develop your own troubleshooting methodology. If you are not clear with the concept, we recommend reading Chapters 1-5 to understand each component before reading this chapter.

References

"OfficeDocs-Support/couldnt-add-member-error.md." https://github.com/ MicrosoftDocs/OfficeDocs-Support/blob/public/Teams/teams-administration/ couldnt-add-member-error.md

"Error (Failed to send) when sending messages to a group chat in Teams." https://docs.microsoft.com/en-us/microsoftteams/troubleshoot/teams- administration/unable-send-message-group-chat

"How to include or exclude Teams from antivirus or DLP applications." https://docs.microsoft.com/en-us/microsoftteams/troubleshoot/ teams-administration/include-exclude-teams-from-antivirus-dlp

"Self-help diagnostics for Teams administrators." https://docs.microsoft.com/ en-us/microsoftteams/troubleshoot/teams-administration/admin-self-help- diagnostics

"Can't see previous joined teams after your account is re-enabled." `https://docs.microsoft.com/en-us/microsoftteams/troubleshoot/channels/logon-reenabled-user-not-see-previous-joined-teams`

"Teams meetings are limited to 1000." `https://docs.microsoft.com/en-us/microsoftteams/troubleshoot/teams-conferencing/teams-meetings-capped-at-250`

"Microsoft Teams Room can't open PowerPoint presentations after ...." `https://docs.microsoft.com/en-us/microsoftteams/troubleshoot/teams-conferencing/teams-room-cant-open-powerpoint-presentations-tls`

"OfficeDocs-Support/no-dial-pad.md." `https://github.com/MicrosoftDocs/OfficeDocs-Support/blob/public/Teams/teams-conferencing/no-dial-pad.md`

"Guests can't access Files tab for shared files in Teams." `https://docs.microsoft.com/en-us/microsoftteams/troubleshoot/files/guests-cannot-access-files`

"Cannot hear sound when sharing content during a Teams live event." `https://docs.microsoft.com/en-us/microsoftteams/troubleshoot/teams-conferencing/no-audio-when-sharing-content-in-meeting`

"Teams is slow during video meetings on laptops docked to 4K/UHD." `https://docs.microsoft.com/en-us/microsoftteams/troubleshoot/teams-conferencing/teams-slow-video-meetings-laptops-4k`

"External federated contacts don't appear in Teams search." `https://docs.microsoft.com/en-us/microsoftteams/troubleshoot/exchange-integration/external-contacts-not-in-search`

"Troubleshoot Microsoft Teams and Exchange Server interaction issues." `https://docs.microsoft.com/en-us/microsoftteams/troubleshoot/exchange-integration/teams-exchange-interaction-issue`

"OfficeDocs-Support/teams-exchange-interaction-issue.md." `https://github.com/MicrosoftDocs/OfficeDocs-Support/blob/public/Teams/exchange-integration/teams-exchange-interaction-issue.md`

"Error (You don't have access to this file) when opening a file in Teams." `https://docs.microsoft.com/en-us/microsoftteams/troubleshoot/files/do-not-have-access-to-this-file-teams`

"External users shown as Unknown in meeting details." `https://docs.microsoft.com/en-us/microsoftteams/troubleshoot/meetings/external-user-shown-as-unknown`

"Chat issues in Teams meeting." `https://docs.microsoft.com/en-us/microsoftteams/troubleshoot/meetings/meeting-chat-issues`

"Issues with meeting recordings." https://docs.microsoft.com/en-us/
microsoftteams/troubleshoot/meetings/troubleshoot-meeting-recording-issues

"Issues with Teams webinars." https://docs.microsoft.com/en-us/
MicrosoftTeams/troubleshoot/meetings/issues-with-webinars

"Errors when trying to manage dial plans." https://docs.microsoft.com/en-us/
microsoftteams/troubleshoot/phone-system/dial-plans/errors-managing-
dial-plans

"Issues with call transfers." https://docs.microsoft.com/en-us/microsoftteams/
troubleshoot/phone-system/direct-routing/issues-with-call-transfers

"Issues with Local Media Optimization." https://docs.microsoft.com/en-us/
microsoftteams/troubleshoot/phone-system/direct-routing/issues-with-lmo

"Issues with Local Media Optimization." https://docs.microsoft.com/en-us/
microsoftteams/troubleshoot/phone-system/direct-routing/issues-with-lmo

"Issues with outbound calls." https://docs.microsoft.com/en-us/
microsoftteams/troubleshoot/phone-system/direct-routing/issues-with-
outbound-calls

"Can't establish a Remote Desktop session." https://docs.microsoft.com/en-us/
troubleshoot/windows-server/remote/cant-establish-remote-desktop-session

"SBC connectivity issues." https://docs.microsoft.com/en-us/microsoftteams/
troubleshoot/phone-system/direct-routing/sip-options-tls-certificate-issues

"Sbc ip 1 contact number." www.keyword-suggest-tool.com/search/
sbc+ip+1+contact+number/

"OfficeDocs-Support/sip-gateway-issues.md." https://github.com/
MicrosoftDocs/OfficeDocs-Support/blob/public/Teams/teams-rooms-and-devices/
sip-gateway-issues.md

"Common issues when using SIP devices with Teams." https://docs.microsoft.
com/en-us/microsoftteams/troubleshoot/teams-rooms-and-devices/sip-
gateway-issues

"Signed out of Teams on Android devices." https://docs.microsoft.com/en-us/
microsoftteams/troubleshoot/teams-rooms-and-devices/signed-out-of-teams-
android-devices

"Overview." https://developer.telesign.com/standard/docs/score-
api-overview

"Updated user information not displayed in Teams." https://support.lesley.
edu/support/solutions/articles/4000182940-updated-user-information-not-
displayed-in-teamss

CHAPTER 8

Teams Call Quality Dashboard for Call Quality Troubleshooting

Microsoft Teams is unified communication and collaboration tool that provides real-time conversation, presence, audio/video calls, and meetings with desktop sharing, phone calls, and content sharing. These features are highly critical and require constant monitoring to ensure users get good call quality. Also, call quality monitoring helps troubleshoot, manage, and enhance the call quality in Teams.

This chapter provides detailed guidance on Microsoft Teams call monitoring using an in-build report. You will also get an idea of how to create a PowerBI-based call quality dashboard.

The Essential Information for Optimal Call Quality

All clients that use Microsoft 365 (Office) cloud-based services, including Microsoft Teams, need to connect to the Office 365 endpoints. Office 365 endpoints represent a set of destination IP addresses, DNS domain names, and URLs for Office 365 traffic on the Internet.

Different Office 365 clients and devices connect to Office 365 services through multiple network paths and network equipment, including switches, routers, proxy servers, and firewalls. Therefore, to optimize the performance of Office 365 cloud-based services, the network admins should configure network equipment according to the Office 365 endpoint requirements.

© Balu N Ilag and Arun M Sabale 2022

B. N. Ilag and A. M. Sabale, *Troubleshooting Microsoft Teams*, https://doi.org/10.1007/978-1-4842-8622-7_8

For Teams to function correctly, you must open TCP ports 80 and 443 and UDP ports 3478 through 3481 from the clients to the Internet. The TCP ports connect to web-based content such as SharePoint Online, Exchange Online, and the Teams Chat services. Plug-ins and connectors also connect over these TCP ports. The four UDP ports are used for media such as audio and video to ensure they flow correctly. Refer to Table 8-1 for different scenarios and source/destination ports.

Table 8-1. *Teams Traffic Scenarios with Source and Destination Ports*

Scenario	Source IP/port	Destination IP/port
Non-real-time traffic	Client IP/high ports	Office 365/80, 443 TCP
Real-time media traffic	Client IP/50,000-50,059 UDP	Transport relays/3478-3481 UDP

Bandwidth Requirements for Teams Modality (Audio/Video/Sharing)

Microsoft Teams is meant to give an optimal audio, video, and desktop sharing experience regardless of your network environment. With that being said, when network bandwidth is not enough, Microsoft Teams prioritizes audio quality over video quality. Where bandwidth is not limited, Teams enhances media quality, including up to 1080p video resolution, up to 30fps for video, and 15fps for content, and high-fidelity audio (it must be enabled on Teams client, Settings ➤ Devices➤ High fidelity music audio).

Table 8-2 explains how Microsoft Teams uses bandwidth. It is always conservative on bandwidth utilization and can deliver HD video quality in under 1.2Mbps. The real bandwidth consumption in each audio/video call or meeting will differ based on various factors, including video layout, video resolution, and video frames per second. When additional bandwidth is offered, quality and usage will increase to provide a good quality experience.

Table 8-2. *Audio/Video/Sharing Scenarios with Required Up/Down Bandwidth*

Bandwidth (up/down)	Microsoft Teams audio/video/sharing scenarios
30 kbps	Peer-to-peer audio calling
130 kbps	Peer-to-peer audio calling and screen sharing
500 kbps	Peer-to-peer quality video calling 360p at 30fps
1.2 Mbps	Peer-to-peer HD quality video calling with the resolution of HD 720p at 30fps
1.5 Mbps	Peer-to-peer HD quality video calling with the resolution of HD 1080p at 30fps
500kbps/1Mbps	Group video calling
1Mbps/2Mbps	HD Group video calling (540p videos on 1080p screen)

Teams Call Quality Dashboard Use

In the previous section, you learned about Teams network ports/protocols and bandwidth requirements for optimal call quality. This section primarily focuses on the Teams Call Quality Dashboard (CQD). Microsoft Teams has two in-built tools that provide call quality information. The CQD shows overall call quality for the entire tenant and dashboard, whereas Call Analytics shows individual users' call quality information and report.

- **Call Quality Dashboard:** This dashboard helps analyze org-wide trends or problems and drive improvements for performance. However, you cannot drill down to individual user call quality.

- **Call Analytics:** This tool analyzes call and meeting quality for individual users. It is beneficial for troubleshooting individual users' call quality problems. However, you cannot see the overall call quality for the entire tenant.

Enhancing call quality requires Quality of Service (QoS) to be enabled. It is not enabled by default and requires additional configuration on your wired and wireless network devices to prioritize Teams latency-sensitive and essential network traffic.

Call Analytics with Reporting Labels

Call Analytics shows call and meeting quality for individual users in Teams. Location-enhanced Call Analytics reports contain the location names instead of just an IP subnet, making the reports easier to understand and use for remediating potential issues.

The Reporting labels page in the Microsoft Teams admin center lets you provide a text file containing a list of physical locations and their associated network subnets. Call Analytics uses this file for generating reports.

It is a best practice to upload the data report labels and locations to correlate data using Call Analytics. The report labels and location data you provide are a single data structure. There is currently no interface available to make individual edits to the data.

The file must be either a .tsv file (columns separated by a tab) or a .csv file (columns separated by a comma).

Configuring Reporting Labels

1. Log into the Teams admin center and then select Locations ➤ Reporting labels.

2. On the Reporting labels page, select Upload data.

3. In the Upload data pane, select a file, browse to and upload your edited .csv or .tsv file, and then select Upload. See Figure 8-1.

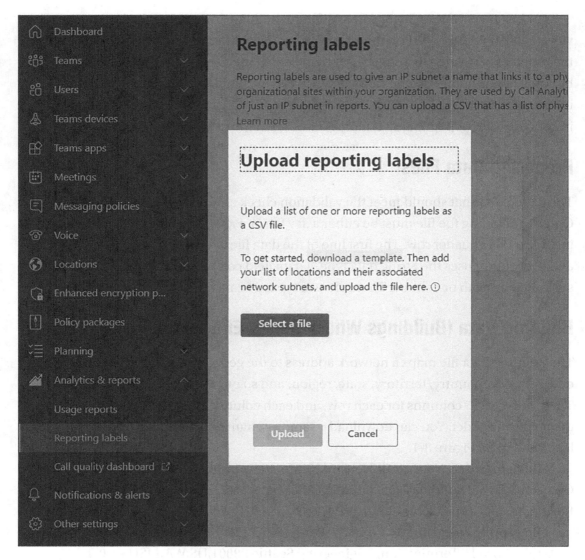

Figure 8-1.   *Uploading a reporting label*

Once the file is uploaded successfully, you can see the update in the locations summary pane. Sometimes location information takes a long time to populate.

Configuring Tenant Data for Location-Enhanced CQD Reports

The CQD provides valuable information about how users get audio/video call quality, but you will need to configure location information to see the call quality based on the location/site. Basically, location-enhanced CQD reports help the network engineer determine if the problem is a site-related issue.

For instance, you can incorporate different building locations or endpoint-specific views such as wired or WiFi-connected devices. The data can be assessed to decide if the problem is isolated to a single user or affects a larger segment of users. To turn on building or endpoint-specific views in CQD, you must upload building or endpoint information on the CQD Tenant Data Upload page as an admin. You get detail information about populating building data files in the next section.

Preparing Data Files

The data file format should meet the validation check criteria before uploading it. Criteria including the file must be either a .tsv file or a .csv file, and the data file does not include a table header row. The first line of the data file is expected to be actual data, and if a column uses the String data type, a data field can be empty but must still be separated by a tab or comma. There are two types of data files you can upload.

Building Data (Buildings Where Teams Endpoints Are Located)

The building data file maps a network address to the geographical information (building, city, ZIP code, country/territory, state, region, and so on) for a specific Teams tenant. There must be 15 columns for each row, and each column must have the appropriate data type and order. You can download a sample tenant data template from a reporting label, shown in Figure 8-1.

File field order: NetworkIP, NetworkName, NetworkRange, BuildingName, OwnershipType, BuildingType, BuildingOfficeType, City, Zipcode, Country, State, Region, InsideCorp, ExpressRoute, VPN

File sample row: 192.168.1.0,USA/Seattle/SEATTLE-SEA-1,26,SEATTLE-SEA-1,Contoso,IT Termination, Engineering,Seattle,98001,US,WA,MSUS,1,0,0

Note   There is a 1,000,000 expanded row limit per tenant data file. Data types in the file can only be String, Integer, or Boolean. For the Integer data type, the value must be numeric. Boolean values must be either 0 or 1.

Uploading Building or Endpoint Information

1. Open the CQD (from the Teams admin center or at `https://cqd.teams.microsoft.com`), select the gear icon in the upper-right corner, and choose Tenant Data Upload.

2. On the Tenant Data Upload page, select Building or Endpoint from the dropdown menu.

3. Select Browse to choose the data file, specify a Start date, and, optionally, specify an end date.

4. Select Upload to upload the file to CQD. Figure 8-2 shows the file upload option.

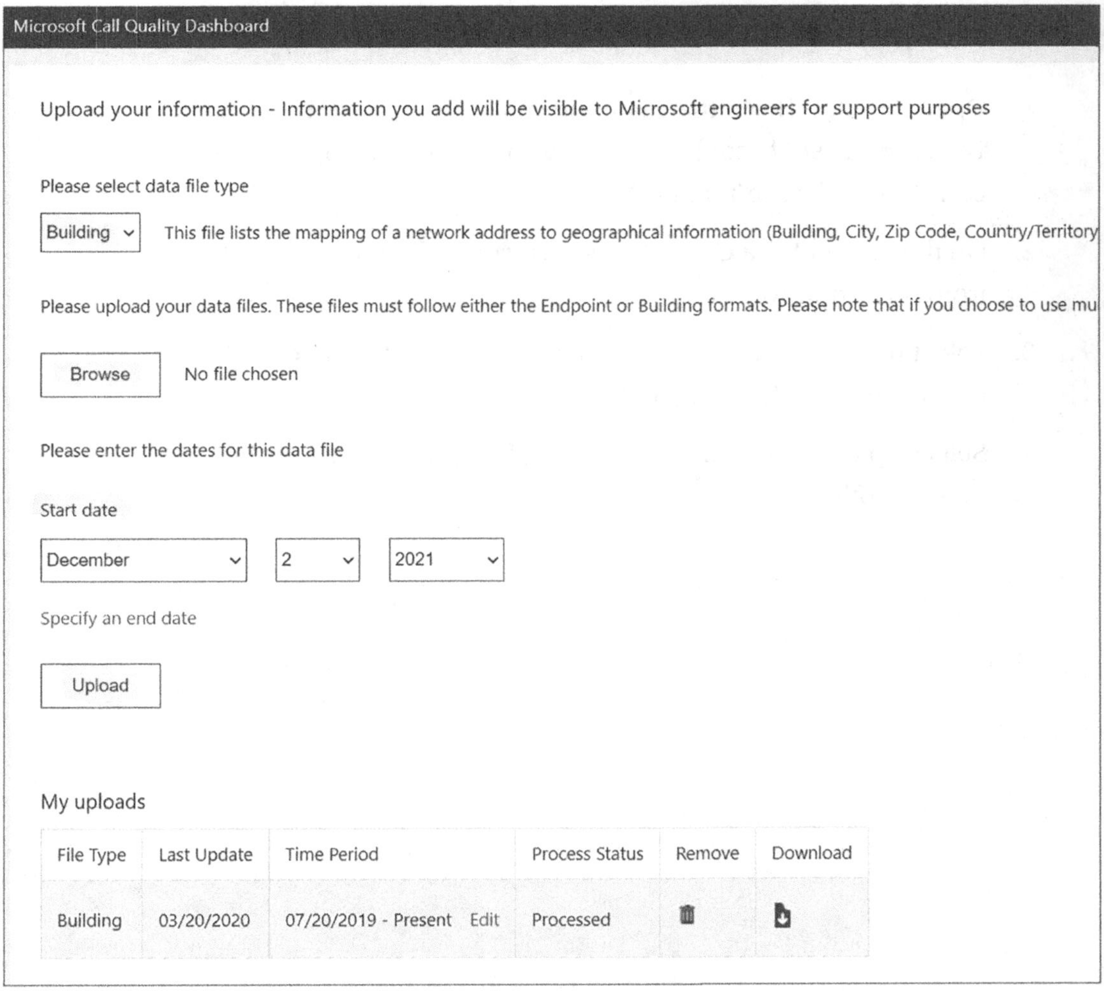

Figure 8-2. *Uploading building data*

It can take up to four hours to validate and finish processing the building file. If no errors occur during validation, you can see the uploaded data file in the My uploads table at the bottom of that page. The next section discusses troubleshooting any building file update issues.

Troubleshooting Building File Updates

Sometimes an admin is unable to upload the updated file. It is essential to understand that there can be only one active building data file in CQD. If you need to update the information, remove the current file, and upload the newly edited file. However, the start and end dates depend on the following scenarios.

1. **To add new subnets**: Edit the original building file and provide an end date that occurs at least one day before the new subnets were acquired. Upload the newly modified building file and set the start date for one day after the previous building file ends.

2. **To add missing subnets**: Be sure to set the start date to at least eight months prior so that the CQD will process the historical data.

   Review the Missing Subnet Report on the Quality of Experience Reports page in the CQD to find these missing networks. It presents all the subnets with ten or more audio streams that are not defined in the building data file and are marked as outside. Ensure that there are no managed networks in this list.

Identifying and Troubleshooting Issues with the CQD

The Teams CQD summarizes an organization's calls and meetings monthly, daily, or hourly. It allows an organization to investigate problems based on quality, failure, and in-product user feedback. The CQD is intended to help Microsoft Teams admins and network engineers to monitor call and meeting quality at an organization-wide level. The near-real-time data enables Teams admins to quickly resolve troubleshooting efforts by drilling down to find where issues originated and who was affected.

Note   The CQD data is not real-time call quality data. It shows after the call ends.

Suppose a user's poor call quality is because of a network issue affecting the other users on the same network, which will show in the CQD but not the individual user. The individual call experience is not visible in the CQD, but the overall quality of calls made using Teams is captured.

413

Who Can Access the CQD?

You know the CQD is beneficial for troubleshooting call quality issues. However, who can access the CQD? The CQD can be accessed by anyone who is assigned a Teams Administrator, Teams Communications Support Engineer, Teams Communications Support Specialist, or Reports Reader role. This is the full list of roles that can access the CQD:

- Global Administrator

- Global Reader

- Skype for Business Administrator

- Teams Service Administrator

- Teams Communications Administrator

- Teams Communications Support Engineer

- Teams Communications Support Specialist

- Reports Reader

Accessing the CQD

You can access CQD using different methods, such as logging into the Teams admin center (Teams admin center ➤ Call Quality Dashboard), directly visiting the CQD portal (https://cqd.teams.microsoft.com/spd), via the Graph API, and using Power BI. When you first sign into the CQD portal, you will see the summary reports. This report shows daily and monthly call quality trends. Call quality is classified as good, poor, or unclassified. When logging into CQD, select Microsoft Teams in the product filter. Select *Overall Call Quality*, *Server-Client*, or *Voice Quality SLA* using the tabs. Figure 8-3 shows the Client-Client report; it has wired inside monthly and wired inside subnets, outside reports, and many more reports.

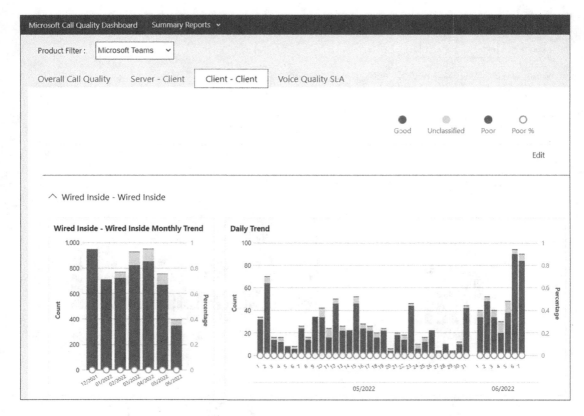

Figure 8-3.   *CQD summary report with Client-Client*

Reports Available in the CQD and Their Use

Multiple reports are available in the CQD; each report is detailed below.

Summary reports: Summary reports are displayed on the CQD when you first sign into it. They provide an at-a-glance look at quality trends with daily, monthly, and table reports to assist with identifying subnets that have poor quality. The following fields show in the summary report. Figure 8-4 shows the Overall Call Quality report.

- **Overall Call Quality**: Aggregate of the other three tabs

- **Server—Client**: Details of the streams between server and client endpoints

- **Client—Client**: Details of the streams between two client endpoints

- **Voice Quality SLA**: Info about calls included in the Skype for Business voice quality SLA

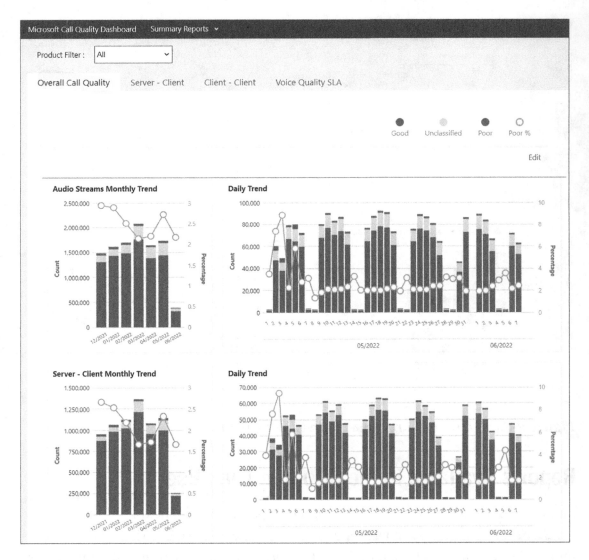

Figure 8-4. *The summary report*

Detailed Report: This is one of the best and most valuable reports. To access a detailed report, use the menu at the top to select other reports. For each type of report, you can filter and show different selections. Here is a list of reports with a short description:

- **Location-Enhanced Reports**: This report shows quality trends based on location information. This report appears only if you have uploaded your tenant (location) data.

- **Reliability Reports**: Includes audio, video, video-based screen sharing (VBSS), and app sharing reports

- **Quality of Experience Reports**: Audio quality and reliability for all clients and devices, including meeting rooms. These reports are a "slimmed-down" version of the downloadable CQD templates, focusing on critical areas for analyzing audio quality and reliability.

- **Quality Drill-Down Reports**: You can drill down dates by region, locations, subnets, hour, and users.

- **Failure Drill-Down Reports**: You can drill down dates by region, locations, subnets, hour, and users.

- **Rate My Call Reports**: Analyze user call ratings by region, location, or user. Includes verbatim feedback.

- **Help Desk Reports**: Help Desk Reports look at call and meeting data for individual users, groups of users, or everyone. Incorporating building and end-user personal information, these reports help identify possible system issues based on network location, conference details, devices, or firmware.

- **Client Version Reports**:

    - **Client Version Summary**: View the sessions and user counts for each client app version.

    - **Client Version by User**: View usernames for each client app version.

    - Pre-built filters for Product and Client Types help focus the versions on specific clients.

- **Endpoint Reports**: Shows call quality by machine endpoints (computer make and model)

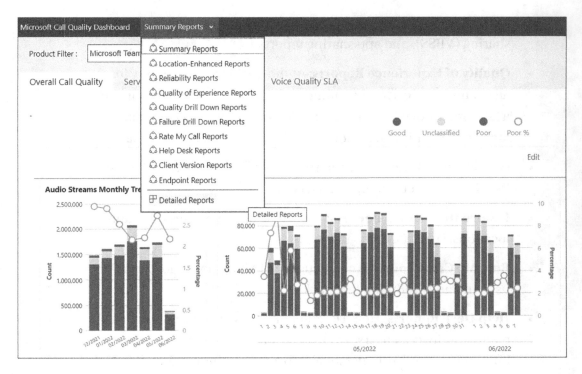

Figure 8-5. *Detailed report*

Figure 8-5 shows how to open a detailed report, which is highly critical for improving the call quality and experience in Teams.

Microsoft Call Quality Connector and PowerBI

Microsoft has created multiple PowerBI-based report templates that will help you know usage in the team, audio health, device usage, client version, phone system usage, and so on. This section covers PowerBI Teams connector connectivity and fundamental report analysis.

Using PowerBI to Analyze CQD Data

The Call Quality Dashboard also allows you to access Power BI reports. These reports include summary reports, help desk reports, user feedback reports, mobile device reports, and more.

Before you can use the Power BI query templates (PBIX files) for the CQD, you must download and install the Microsoft Call Quality connector for Power BI. The installation process uses the `MicrosoftCallQuality.pqx` file included in the download.

Installing the Microsoft Call Quality Power BI Connector

Follow these steps to download and install the Microsoft Call Quality connector for Power BI:

1. First, check if your computer already has a `[Documents]\Power BI Desktop\Custom Connectors` folder. If not, create this folder.

2. Download the Power BI Connector for Microsoft CQD from `www.microsoft.com/en-us/download/details.aspx?id=102291` (either a *.mez or *.pqx file) and place it in the `Custom Connectors` directory. Refer to Figure 8-6.

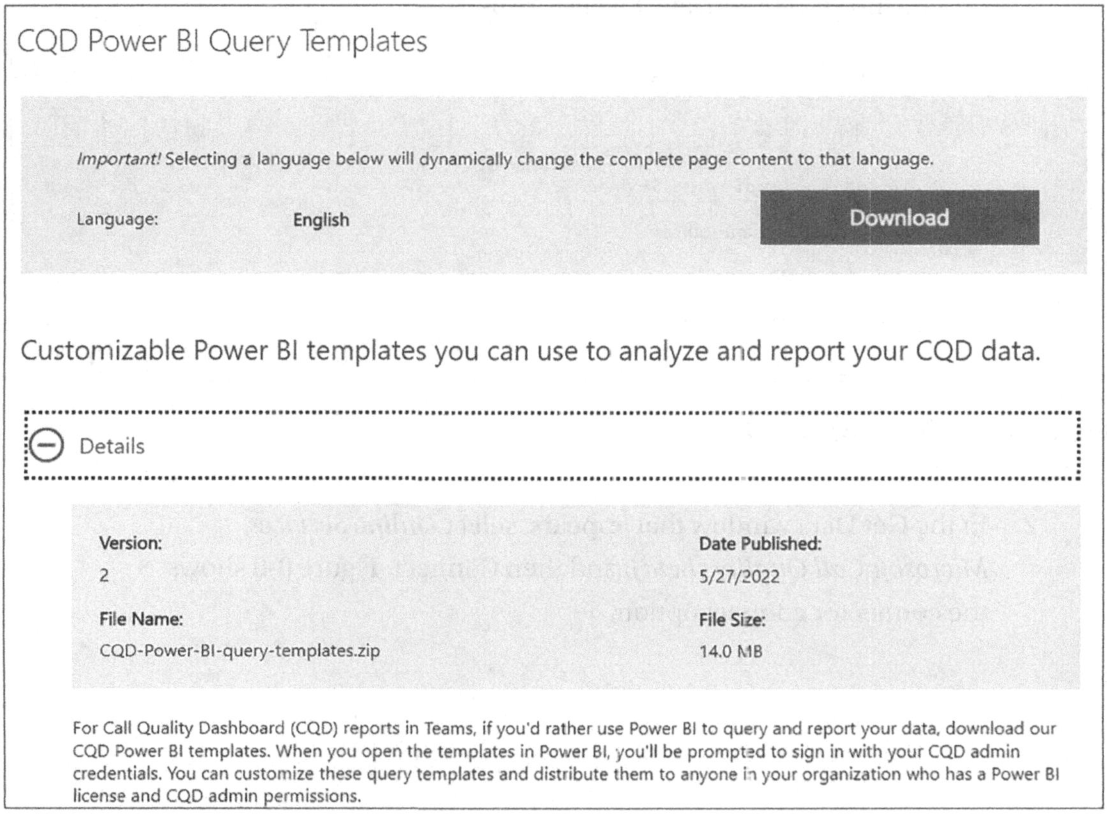

CQD Power BI Query Templates

Important! Selecting a language below will dynamically change the complete page content to that language.

Language: English   **Download**

Customizable Power BI templates you can use to analyze and report your CQD data.

⊖ Details

Version:	Date Published:
2	5/27/2022
File Name:	File Size:
CQD-Power-BI-query-templates.zip	14.0 MB

For Call Quality Dashboard (CQD) reports in Teams, if you'd rather use Power BI to query and report your data, download our CQD Power BI templates. When you open the templates in Power BI, you'll be prompted to sign in with your CQD admin credentials. You can customize these query templates and distribute them to anyone in your organization who has a Power BI license and CQD admin permissions.

Figure 8-6. *CQD Power BI query download*

3. If the connector file is a *.mez file, you must adjust your
    security settings as described in the custom connector setup
    documentation.

Note   If a new version of this Power BI Connector for Microsoft Teams is released,
replace the old connector file in the `Custom Connectors` directory with the
new file.

Configuring the Microsoft Call Quality Power BI Connector

To build the report and run queries, you must complete these steps to connect to the
CQD data source:

1. Open any PowerBI report, select the Home tab on the Power BI
    portal, and select Get Data. See Figure 8-7.

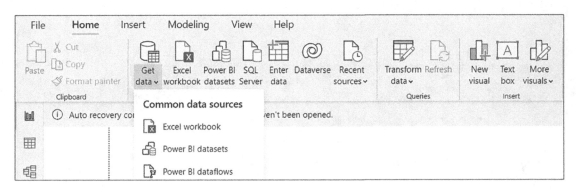

Figure 8-7. *PowerBI Get Data*

2. In the Get Data window that appears, select *Online Services,*
    Microsoft Call Quality (Beta), and then Connect. Figure 8-8 shows
    the connector connect option.

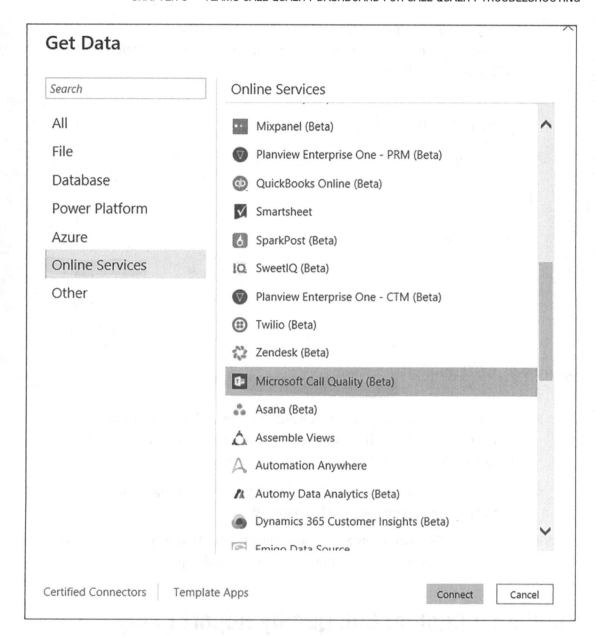

Figure 8-8. *Microsoft call quality connector*

3. You will get one warning about connecting to a third-party service. Click Continue. You will then be prompted to sign in. Use the same credentials you used to sign into the CQD.

4. Then you will get prompted to select between two data
    connectivity modes. Select DirectQuery and then select OK. Refer
    to Figure 8-9 for the connection setting.

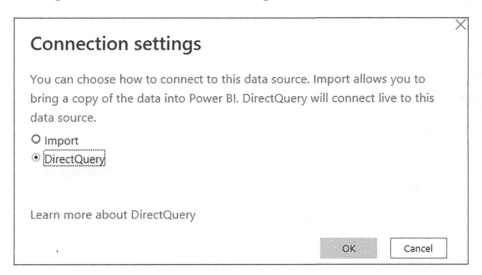

Figure 8-9. *CQD connection setting*

5. You will receive a final prompt showing you the entire data model
    for the CQD. No data will be visible at this point, only the data
    model for CQD. Select Load to complete the setup process.

6. At this point, Power BI will load the data model into the right side
    of the window. No queries will be loaded by default.

With the loaded CQD data sources, you are ready to build a query and display data.
Continue to the next section for instructions on how to build a query.

Building a Custom Call Quality Report Using PowerBI Connector

An in-built report is definably helpful but creating custom reports based on existing
templates is highly recommended. This section helps you build custom reports.

Building Your Custom Queries

The Microsoft Call Quality Power BI Connector enables you to build custom reports. You can use customizable Power BI templates that Microsoft has predefined as a starting point for a new report's layout, data model, and queries. When you download the report templates (`www.microsoft.com/en-us/download/details.aspx?id=102291`), you can use them as starting point to build a custom report. Here is a list of report templates available as part of the download:

- `CQD Teams Auto Attendant & Call Queue Historical Report.pbit`: This template provides the following three reports:

  - **Auto Attendant**: This report shows analytics for calls coming into your auto attendants.

  - **Call Queue**: This report shows analytics for calls coming into your call queues.

  - **Agent Timeline**: This report shows a timeline view of agents active in call queue calls.

- `CQD Helpdesk Report.pbit`: This report integrates building and end user personal information; this report is designed to let you drill up from a single user to find the upstream root cause of poor call quality for that user (for example, the user is in a building that's experiencing network problems).

- `CQD Location Enhanced Report.pbit`: One of the essential reports that includes nine reports, providing call quality, building Wi-Fi, reliability, and Rate My Call (RMC) information with other drill-throughs by building or by user. Make sure you upload the building data to maximize your reporting experience.

- `CQD Mobile Device Report.pbit`: This report provides insights fine-tuned towards mobile device users, including call quality, reliability, and Rate My Call. View mobile network, Wi-Fi network, and mobile operating system reports (Android, iOS).

- `CQD PSTN Direct Routing Report.pbit`: This report provides insights specific to PSTN calls that go through Direct Routing.

- `CQD Summary Report.pbit`: Another essential report that shows better visualizations, improved presentation, increased information density, and rolling dates. These reports make it easier to identify outliers. Drill into call quality by location with an easy-to-use interactive map. It offers nine new reports:

  - Quality Overall

  - Reliability Overall

  - RMC (Rate My Call) Overall

  - Conference Quality

  - P2P Quality

  - Conference Reliability

  - P2P Reliability

  - Conference RMC

  - P2P RMC

- `CQD Teams Utilization Report.pbit`: This report shows how users in your organization are using Teams and how often. Make sure you upload the building data to maximize your reporting experience.

- `CQD User Feedback (Rate My Call) Report.pbit`: This report shows Rate My Call data in a way you can easily use to help support calling in your organization. Cross-reference with feedback to identify end-user education opportunities.

Teams Phone System Direct Routing Health Dashboard

The Teams Direct Routing Health Dashboard allows you as an admin to monitor information about its SBC, the telephony service, and the network parameters between its SBC and the Direct Routing interface. This information can help identify issues, including the reasons for dropped calls. For instance, the SBC may stop sending calls if a certificate on the SBC has expired or there are network issues.

Finding Issues with the Teams Direct Routing Health Dashboard

Microsoft Teams provides different capabilities such as chat, Teams audio/video calls, meetings with app sharing, and content sharing as native features. In addition to the native features, Teams also provides the Phone System PSTN capability to make an external phone call and receive inbound calls. There are different ways to connect phone systems with Teams, such as calling plans (all in the cloud) offered and managed by Microsoft, Operator Connect (managed by the service provider), and Teams Direct Routing (deployed and managed by the organization). Teams Direct Routing (DR) is the most popular way to connect Teams with the phone system. When you decide to use your telephony carrier (service provider) for PSTN connectivity by using Teams Direct Routing, you can use Teams Phone System with virtually any telephony carrier. Microsoft Phone System Direct Routing enables your organization to connect its on-premises telephony infrastructure to Microsoft Teams. Once an organization has configured its Direct Routing environment, several components are required to ensure everything is running smoothly. For instance, you may have a SBC or multiple SBCs connected to Microsoft Teams and carrier connectivity. You may also have a third-party PBX system, as shown in Figure 8-10.

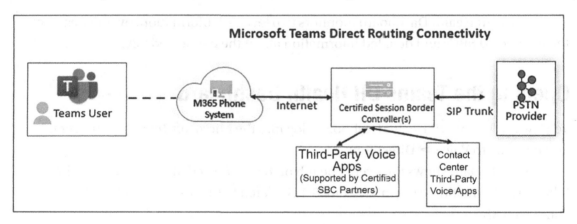

Figure 8-10. *Teams Direct Routing connectivity*

So, it is essential to monitor Teams DR connectivity. The following tools can be used to monitor and troubleshoot Direct Routing issues:

- **SBC syslog and PBX logs:** Your SBC could also be connected to other environments, giving you access to logs that help you troubleshoot or debug issues. If your SBC communicates with a third-party PBX, you can collect logs from there. You may need different tools to view the SBC log. Refer to vendor documentation. For example, you can use the LX tool for Ribbons SBC syslog and the Syslog Viewer for AudioCodes SBC log view.

- **PSTN provider:** You can also work with your PSTN provider to get more insight into issues that may arise from the PSTN side of your environment.

- **Teams Direct Routing Health Dashboard:** You can monitor the connection between your SBC and the Direct Routing interface with the Direct Routing Health Dashboard.

Teams Direct Routing Health Dashboard

The Teams DR Health Dashboard monitors two levels of information: overall health of the connected SBCs and detailed information about the connected SBCs.

Opening the Teams DR Health Dashboard

To view the Teams DR Health Dashboard, log into the Microsoft Teams admin center and navigate to Voice ➤ Direct Routing.

The dashboard shows the overall health of the connected SBCs. It provides the following information (shown in Figure 8-11) related to the overall health of the connected SBCs.

Figure 8-11. *Teams DR Dashboard*

- **Direct Routing summary:** This shows the total number of SBCs registered in the system. Registration means that the tenant administrator added an SBC using the New-CsOnlinePSTNGateway command. If the SBC was added in PowerShell but never connected, the Health Dashboard shows it in an unhealthy status.

- **SBC:** The FQDN of the paired SBC

- **Network Effectiveness Ratio (NER):** The NER measures the ability of a network to deliver calls by measuring the number of calls sent versus the number of calls delivered to a recipient.

  - **Detail information for an individual SBC:** When you click an individual SBC, you will see detailed information, including network effectiveness, TLS connection status, average call duration, and concurrent call capacity. Additionally, you can see usage and setting. Refer to Figure 8-12.

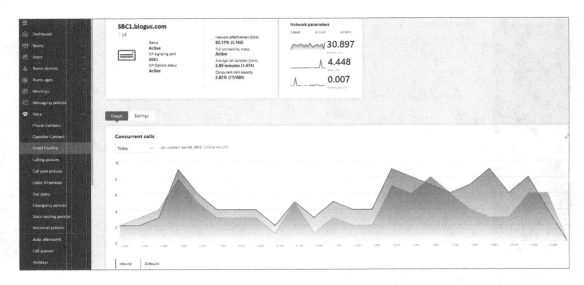

Figure 8-12. *SBC detailed information*

What Is NER and How Is It Measured?

The NER measures the ability of networks to deliver calls to the far-end terminal, excluding user actions resulting in call rejections. If the recipient rejects a call or sends the call to voicemail, the call is counted as a successful delivery. This scenario means that an answer message, a busy signal, or a ring with no answer are all considered successful calls.

For instance, assume Direct Routing sent a call to the SBC and the SBC returns SIP code *504 Server Time-out - The server attempted to access another server to process the request and did not receive a prompt response.* This response indicates an issue on the SBC side, which will lower the NER on the Health Dashboard for this SBC. Because the action you take may depend on the number of cells affected, the DR Health Dashboard shows how many calls were analyzed to calculate a parameter. If the number of calls is less than 100, the NER may be low but still be expected.

The formula used to calculate the NER is NER = 100 x (Answered calls + user busy + ring no answer + terminal reject seizures)/Total calls.

What is the average call duration? Information about average call duration can help an organization monitor the quality of its calls. The average duration of a 1:1 PSTN call is four to five minutes. However, for each company, this average can differ. Microsoft recommends establishing a baseline for the average call duration for your company.

If this parameter goes significantly below the baseline, it may indicate that your users are having issues with call quality or reliability and are hanging up earlier than usual. If you start seeing low average call duration, for example, 15 seconds, callers may be hanging up because your service is not performing reliably. Because your action may depend on the number of cells affected, the Health Dashboard shows how many calls were analyzed to calculate a parameter. Figure 8-12 shows the average call duration for SBC1. bloguc.com.

TLS connectivity status: TLS (Transport Layer Security) connectivity shows the status of the TLS connections between Direct Routing and the SBC. The Health Dashboard also analyzes the certificate expiration date and warns if a certificate is set to expire within 30 days. This notification enables administrators to renew the certificate before service is disrupted. By selecting the warning message, you can see a detailed issue description in a pop-up window and a recommendation for how to fix the issue. Figure 8-12 shows the TLS connectivity status.

SIP options status: By default, the SBC sends options messages every minute. This configuration can vary for different SBC vendors. Direct Routing warns if the SIP options are not sent or are not configured. Figure 8-12 shows the SIP option status as Active.

Validating the SIP Options Status

Besides showing an issue with SIP options flow, the Health Dashboard also provides detailed descriptions of the errors. You can access the description by selecting the warning message. A pop-up window will show the detailed error description. Possible values for SIP options status messages are as follows:

- **Active:** The SBC is active, indicating that the Microsoft Direct Routing service sees the options flowing regularly.

- **Warning, no SIP options:** The SBC exists in the database (you created it using the command New-CsOnlinePSTNGateway). It has been configured to send SIP options, but the Direct Routing service never saw the SIP options coming back from this SBC.

- **Warning, SIP Messages are not configured:** Trunk monitoring using SIP options is not turned on. The Microsoft Calling System uses SIP options and TLS handshake monitoring to detect the health of the connected SBCs at the application level. You will have problems if this trunk can be reached at the network level (by ping, but the certificate has expired, or the SIP stack does not work). To help identify such problems early, Microsoft recommends enabling sending SIP options. Check your SBC manufacturer documentation to configure sending SIP options.

Concurrent calls capacity: You can specify the limit of concurrent calls that an SBC can handle by using the New- or Set-CsOnlinePSTNGateway cmdlet in PowerShell with the -MaxConcurrentSessions parameter. This parameter calculates how many calls were sent or received by Direct Routing using a specific SBC and compares it with the limit set. If the SBC also handles calls to different PBXs, this number will not show the actual concurrent calls.

Network parameters: All network parameters are measured from the Teams Direct Routing interface to the SBC. Here is the list of network parameters that determine the Teams call quality:

- **Jitter:** This parameter is the millisecond measure of variation in network propagation delay time computed between two endpoints using RTCP.

- **Packet loss:** This parameter measures packets that failed to arrive, computed between two endpoints.

- **Latency:** Called round-trip time, this parameter is the length of time it takes for a signal to be sent and the length of time it takes to acknowledge that signal to be received. This time delay consists of the propagation times between the two points of a signal.

Microsoft Teams Reports

Teams analytics and reports will help you create different reports to get insights and information about teams usage. Teams Call Analytics and usage reporting provides insights into how Teams is used in the organization. It is constructive to understand how users use Teams chat, call, meeting, and PSTN phone call features; based on that, you can make informed decisions on which features need more focus and which don't.

To access the report, follow these steps:

1. Log into the Microsoft Teams admin center (`https://admin.teams.microsoft.com/`) with Teams Service Administrator permissions.

2. Then select Analytics & reports from the left navigation bar and then select Usage reports.

3. From the Usage reports screen, select the report and date range.

4. Then select Run *report* to generate the report.

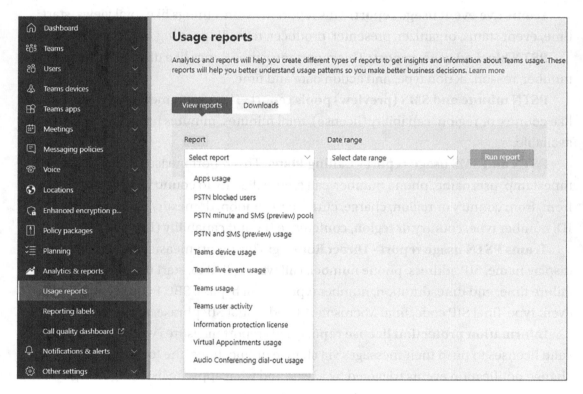

Figure 8-13. *Teams analytics & reports*

Figure 8-13 shows the list of reports that you can generate and analyze the data for usage for reporting purposes. To view a report, in the left navigation of the Microsoft Teams admin center, select Analytics & reports ➤ Usage reports. Then select any report and select the date range and run the report. After generating a report, select the Downloads tab to access downloaded reports when they are ready.

Teams usage report: This report measures things like active users, active users in teams and channels, active channels, messages, privacy settings of teams, and guests in a team.

Teams user activity report: This report measures the things like messages a user posted in a team chat; messages a user posted in a private chat; 1:1 calls a user participated in; number of meetings a user organized; number of meetings a user participated in; meetings audio, video, and screen sharing time; and last activity date of a user.

Teams device usage report: This report measures things like Windows users, Mac users, iOS users, and Android phone users.

Teams live event usage report: This report measures things like total views, start time, event status, organizer, presenter, producer, recording setting, and production type.

PSTN blocked users report: This report measures things like display name, phone number, reason, action type, and action date and time.

PSTN minute and SMS (preview) pools report: This report measures things like country or region, capability (license), total minutes, minutes used, and minutes available.

PSTN and SMS usage report - Calling Plans: This report measures things like timestamp, username, phone number, call type, called to, to country or region, called from, from country or region, charge, currency, duration, domestic/international, call-ID, number type, country or region, conference ID, and capability (license).

Teams PSTN usage report - Direct Routing: This report measures the timestamp, display name, SIP address, phone number, call type, called to, start time, invite time, failure time, end time, duration, number type, media bypass, SBC FQDN, Azure region, event type, final SIP code, final Microsoft subcode, final SIP phrase, and correlation ID.

Information protection license report: This report measures whether users have valid licenses to push their messages via change notifications, the total number of change notification events triggered by a user, and what apps are listening to org-wide change notification events. Figure 8-13 shows the report.

Teams virtual visits usage report: This report measures the things like the number of virtual appointments, number of bookings appointments, number of Teams electronic health records (EHR)-integrated appointments, average duration of an appointment, average lobby wait time of attendees, start time, meeting ID, lobby wait time, duration, status, product type, attendees, and SMS sent. Figure 8-13 shows the report.

Teams EHR connector virtual appointments report: This report measures things like start time, duration, primary (name of meeting organizer), primary's email (email of meeting organizer), department, attendants, lobby wait time, and whether the appointment is within the allocation limit. Figure 8-13 shows the report.

Audio conferencing dial-out usage report: This essential report gives you an overview of usage and dollars spent on the audio-conferencing dial-out service. This report allows you to consume user-level data regarding communication credits spent and dial-out minutes used. It will help to determine the future communication credits needed going forward from any point in time. See Figure 8-13.

Teams analytics and reporting: There are several reports available from Teams analytics. More reports are being added, so check the Teams analytics and reports documentation. Select the Microsoft Excel symbol to download data from each report.

Using the CQD for Call Quality Troubleshooting

Specific to call quality troubleshooting, you as an admin can use Call Analytics for per-user level troubleshooting and the CQD to find out call-quality problems affecting multiple users. You can access these tools through the Teams admin center.

Call Analytics and the CQD operate in parallel and can be utilized individually or together. For instance, if a communications support specialist decides they need more help troubleshooting a user's call quality or connectivity problem, they can escalate the call to a communications support engineer, who has access to additional information about the call. In turn, the communications support engineer can alert a network engineer to a possible site-related issue they noticed in Call Analytics. The network engineer can check the CQD to see if overall site-related issues could be a contributing cause to the user's call problem.

Using Call Analytics for Call Troubleshooting

This tool displays detailed information about Teams calls and meetings for each user in the tenant. Additionally, you can see the devices, networks, and connectivity-related information for specific calls and meetings for each user in Teams. The Teams admin can use this information to troubleshoot call quality and connection problems in a specific

433

call or meeting. If you upload building, site, and tenant information (as part of the Call Analytics setup), this information will also be shown for each call and meeting. Use Call Analytics to help you determine why a user had a poor call or meeting experience.

Troubleshooting Individual Calls Using Call Analytics

It displays each leg of a call or meeting (every call has two legs, inbound and outbound) for instance, from participant one to participant two. By analyzing this information, you can isolate problem areas and identify the root cause of poor quality.

To open Call Analytics to see a user's call/meeting information, log into Teams admin center ➤ Users. Under Users, select Manage users and then search and select a user to open the user's profile page.

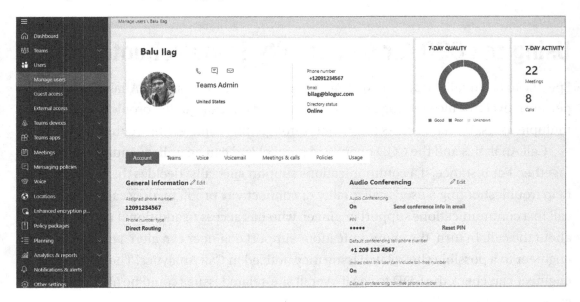

Figure 8-14. *A user's profile with the account*

On the user's profile page (Figure 8-14), you will see valuable information that can be used for troubleshooting purposes. Here is the list of tabs with information:

- **Account tab:** Shows the phone number assigned to the user, audio conferencing information with PIN, default conferencing toll/free phone number, directory status, and last seven days' activity. Refer to Figure 8-14.

- **Teams:** The list of Teams the user is part of

- **Voice:** Outbound calling and call answering rules. See Figure 8-15.

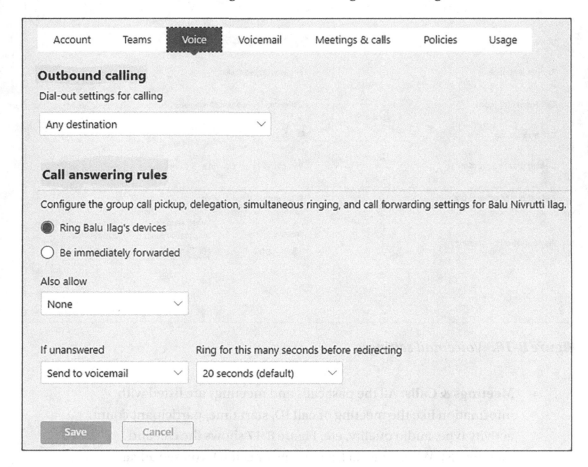

Figure 8-15. *User's Voice settings*

- **Voicemail:** Voicemail settings such as enabling voicemail and changing greeting prompts and out-of-office greetings. See Figure 8-16.

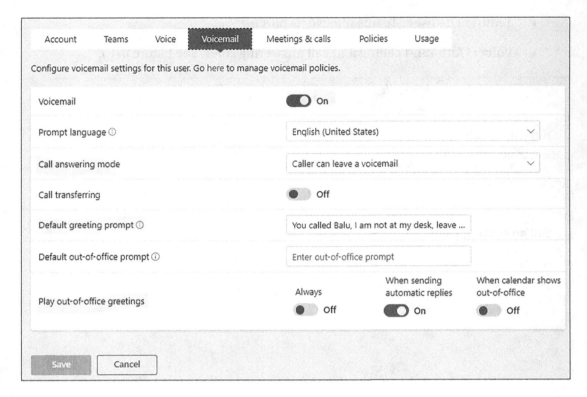

Figure 8-16. *Voicemail settings*

- **Meetings & Calls:** All the past calls and meetings are listed with information like the meeting or call ID, start time, participant count, activity type, audio quality, etc. Figure 8-17 shows the call and meeting list. When you click a meeting or call ID, you see advance information about call quality.

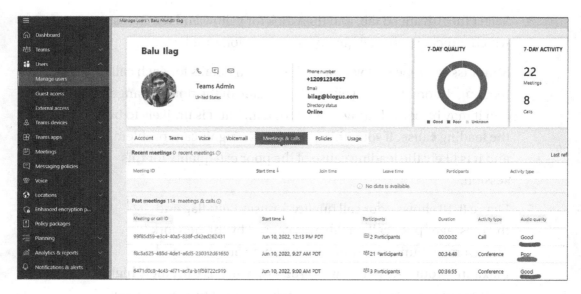

Figure 8-17. *Meeting and calls list*

- **Policies:** This is another important setting you can use for troubleshooting. Policies include the meeting policy, messaging policy, live events policy, app permission policy, app setup policy, call park policy, calling policy, caller ID policy, teams policy, update policy, emergency calling policy, emergency call routing policy, dial plan, enhanced encryption policy, voicemail policy, templates policy, and audio conferencing policy.

- **Usage:** Audio conferencing dial-out usage

For Deep-Dive Troubleshooting

Get more information about a given session, including detailed media and networking statistics.

1. To do so, log into the Teams admin center and on the dashboard, in User Search, start typing either the name or SIP address of the user whose calls you want to troubleshoot, or select View users to see a list of users.

2. Select the user from the list, select Call history, and select the call or meeting that you want to troubleshoot.

3. Select the Advanced tab, and then look for yellow and red items, which indicate poor call quality or connection problems.

4. Minor issues appear in yellow in the session details for each call or meeting. If something is yellow, it is outside of the normal range, and it may be contributing to the problem, but it is unlikely to be the leading cause. If something is red, it is a significant problem, and it is likely the leading cause of the poor call quality for this session.

5. Figure 8-18 shows poor call quality for user Balu Ilag and the message "poor call quality was caused by the network." The average round-trip time was very high at 574 ms and the maximum round-trip time was 1732 ms, which is extremely high. Another parameter, the maximum packet loss rate, was also high (11.21%). Both parameters mark call quality as poor.

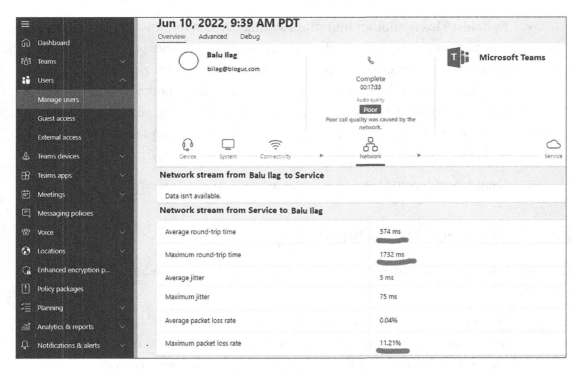

Figure 8-18. *Poor call parameters*

Sometimes you may not see call quality data because Quality of Experience data is not being received for audio sessions. Frequently this is triggered by a dropped call or when the connection with the client terminates. When this occurs, the session rating is unavailable. So, if you do not see Quality of Experience data or it's marked as unknown may occur due to a short session or audio call is dropped instantly.

Main Issues That Mark a Call As a Poor Session

Here is a list of issues that will categorize the session as a poor call.

- **Call setup issue:** If the session shows a call setup issue, then the error code Ms-diag 20-29 indicates the call setup failed. The user could not join the call or meeting.

- **Audio network classified poor call:** If the call session is marked as a poor call, then in that call session, network quality issues like high packet loss, jitter, NMOS degradation, round-trip time (RTT), or concealed ratio were encountered.

- **Device not functioning:** In Quality of Experience, if the device area shows that a device isn't functioning correctly, that call will be marked as poor. Remember, the device-not-functioning ratios are

  DeviceRenderNotFunctioningEventRatio >= 0.005

  DeviceCaptureNotFunctioningEventRatio >= 0.005

Using the CQD for Call Troubleshooting

The CQD gives you a network-wide view of call quality across your organization. Use CQD information to help you identify and fix problems. First, set up the CQD. Then read the "Managing Call and Meeting Quality in Teams" section.

Using Teams Real-Time Analytics for Poor Call Quality Troubleshooting

Like Call Analytics, you can use Real-Time Analytics (RTA) to troubleshoot poor Microsoft Teams' meeting quality for individual users. It's best if you have Teams Administrator, Teams Communications Support Specialist, or Teams Communications Support Engineer roles assigned to access Real-Time Analytics.

RTA allows Teams admins to look at their essential users' scheduled meetings and see audio, video, content sharing, and network-related issues. You, as an admin, can use this telemetry to investigate these issues during meetings and troubleshoot in real-time.

The Call Analytics tool allows for troubleshooting an individual call/meeting but after the call/meeting ends. However, what if you want to troubleshoot scheduled meetings while they are in progress? Well, this is where RTA helps you by allowing you to troubleshoot scheduled meetings while they are in progress. RTA shows detailed information about Teams meetings for each user in the tenant, updated in real time. RTA includes information about devices, network, connectivity, audio, video, and content sharing issues, which will help you troubleshoot call quality more effectively.

Opening Real-Time Analytics

As mentioned, RTA is available for each user in the tenant. To open all meeting information and data for a user, log into the Teams admin center ➤ Users ➤ Manage users, select a user, and open the Meetings & calls tab on the user's profile page. Under Recent meetings, you will see a list of meetings the user has attended within the past 24 hours for which real-time telemetry is available, including any in-progress meetings. If the meeting is not in progress or does not have real-time telemetry data, it will show up in Past meetings.

When you click the in-progress meeting session, it will take some time to open and shows Quality of Experience data. Figure 8-19 shows the recent meeting section in the in-progress meeting session. For instance, in the figure, only one meeting session has a meeting status of in progress.

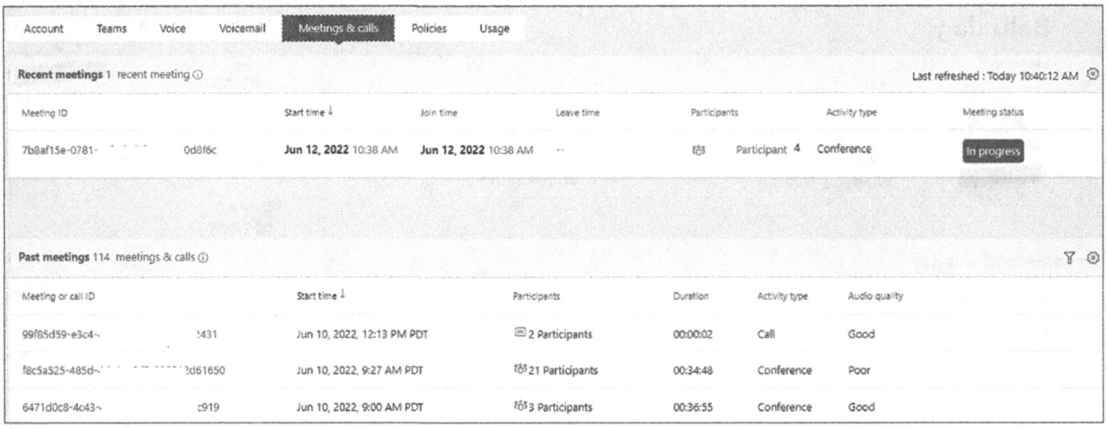

Figure 8-19. RTA in-progress session

Note   RTA takes 1-5 minutes to show in-progress meeting sessions in the Teams admin center.

When you click the meeting session, it will show additional information about participants of a meeting that's in progress, including their devices, networks, and audio statistics. To find the meeting in Recent meetings, select the link under the Participants column to see detailed Quality of Experience information for the participants. Figure 8-20 shows the detailed QoE information of participant Balu Ilag.

Specific to the call quality troubleshooting purpose, you need to look at the telemetry of a given user for an in-progress meeting, including information around device name, network type, audio, video stream details, content sharing details, the Meeting ID, and so on.

Figure 8-20. *Teams RTA stats*

What Is the Teams Client Platform, and Do Teams Devices Support RTA?

There are many Teams' clients and devices that support real-time telemetry. The Teams clients that support RTA are the Teams desktop client (Windows, macOS, and Linux) and Teams mobile apps (Android and iOS). Teams devices that support RTA are Microsoft Teams Room (MTR) - Surface Hub, MTR - Teams Display, MTR - Collaboration bar, and Teams IP Phone devices.

It is essential to understand the limitations of RTA. Here is the list of limitations:

1. Real-time analytics are unavailable for ad-hoc meetings (Meet Now), PSTN calls, Teams 1:1 calls, and group calls. This means RTA is only available for scheduled Teams meetings.

2. Live event-specific limitations and real-time telemetry are only available for presenters of scheduled live events. They are currently not available for live event attendees.

3. Real-time telemetry data is available for a meeting under Recent meetings for 24 hours after the meeting has ended. After 24 hours, you cannot access the data, and the meeting moves to Past meetings. If a meeting is longer than 3 hours, real-time telemetry will only be available for the last 3 hours.

4. Telemetry is not available in real-time when using older versions of Teams. If no telemetry is available, try updating your client.

5. If external participants or anonymous users join a meeting, their display name will show as unavailable to retain cross-tenant privacy.

Summary

It is crucial to know the different telemetry tools that help troubleshoot Microsoft Teams call quality and connectivity issues. In this chapter, you explored the most frequent Teams troubleshooting areas, including the Teams client, Call Analytics, and the CQD to investigate voice issues. You should now be able to explain important aspects of Teams troubleshooting. You should additionally be able to identify call quality issues using Call Analytics, the CQD, and the Direct Routing Health Dashboard.

References

"Evaluate your environment for cloud voice workloads." https://docs.microsoft.com/en-us/MicrosoftTeams/3-envision-evaluate-my-environment

"Upload tenant and building data in Call Quality Dashboard (CQD ...." https://docs.microsoft.com/en-us/microsoftteams/cqd-upload-tenant-building-data

"What is Call Quality Dashboard (CQD)?" https://docs.microsoft.com/en-us/MicrosoftTeams/cqd-what-is-call-quality-dashboard

"Evaluate your environment for cloud voice workloads." https://docs.microsoft.com/en-us/MicrosoftTeams/3-envision-evaluate-my-environment

"Data and reports in Call Quality Dashboard (CQD)." https://docs.microsoft.com/en-us/microsoftteams/cqd-data-and-reports

"Install Power BI Connector to use CQD query templates." https://docs.microsoft.com/en-us/microsoftteams/cqd-power-bi-connector

"Use Power BI to analyze CQD data for Microsoft Teams." https://docs.microsoft.com/en-us/microsoftteams/cqd-power-bi-query-templates

"Health Dashboard for Direct Routing." https://docs.microsoft.com/en-us/microsoftteams/direct-routing-health-dashboard

Kaiser, Alexander, and Florian Kragulj. "Building Intellectual Capital by Generative Listening and Learning From the Future." European Conference on Intellectual Capital, Academic Conferences International Limited, Apr. 2015, p. 165.

"Monitor and improve call quality for Microsoft Teams." https://docs.microsoft.com/en-us/microsoftteams/monitor-call-quality-qos

"Use Call Analytics to troubleshoot poor call quality." https://docs.microsoft.com/en-us/MicrosoftTeams/use-call-analytics-to-troubleshoot-poor-call-quality

"Understanding Microsoft Teams Real-Time Call Quality ..." Tom Talks, https://tomtalks.blog/understanding-microsoft-teams-real-time-telemetry-reporting-analytics/

"Use real-time telemetry to troubleshoot poor meeting quality ...." https://docs.microsoft.com/en-us/microsoftteams/use-real-time-telemetry-to-troubleshoot-poor-meeting-quality

Glossary

AAD: Azure Active Directory

aCDN: Azure Content Delivery Network

AD: Active Directory

AD DS: Active Directory Domain Services

AFD: Azure Font Door

AMS: Azure Media Service

API: Application Programming Interface

B2B: Business-to-B=business

BSSID: Basic Service Set Identifier

CA: Conditional access

CAP: Common area phone

CQD: Call Quality Dashboard

DC: Domain controller

DLP: Data loss prevention

DR: Teams Direct Routing

E164 format: Globally acceptable phone number format

eCDN: Enterprise content delivery network

ELIN: Emergency Location Identification Number

Email: Electronic mail

FQDN: Fully qualified domain name

GPO: Group Policy Object

HD: High definition

HTTPs: Hypertext Transfer Protocol Secure

ICE: Interactive Connectivity Establishment

IP: Internet Protocol Address

KPI: Key performance indicator

KBPS: Kilobytes per second

LBR: Location-based routing

LIS: Location information service

macOS: Macintosh operating system

© Balu N Ilag and Arun M Sabale 2022

B. N. Ilag and A. M. Sabale, *Troubleshooting Microsoft Teams*, https://doi.org/10.1007/978-1-4842-8622-7

MFA: Multifactor authentication

Microsoft 365: Microsoft cloud services formally known as Office 365

MTR: Microsoft Teams Room

NAT: Network address translation

NER: Network Effectiveness Ratio

NOC: Network Operations Centers

PAI: P-Assisted-Identity

PBX: Private branch exchange

PIM: Privileged identity management

PSAP: Public safety answering point

NOC: Network operations centers

PSTN: Public switched telephone network

Proxy server: The proxy server is a server application that acts as an intermediary between a client requesting a resource and the server

QoS: Quality of service

REST API: Representational state transfer application programming interface

RTA: Real-Time Analytics

RTP: Real-time Transport Protocol

RTCP: Real-Time Transport Control Protocol

SBC: Session border controller

SBA: Survivable Branch Appliance

SDN API: Software-defined network API

SDP: Session Description Protocol

SFB: Skype for Business

SIP: Session Initiation Protocol

SLA: Service-level agreement

SRTP: Secure Real-time Transport Protocol

SRTCP: Secure Real-time Transport Control Protocol

STUN: Session Traversal Utilities for NAT

TAC: Teams Admin Center

TCP/IP: Transmission Control Protocol/Internet Protocol

TLS: Transport Layer Security

TR: Transport relays

TURN: Traversal Using Relays around NAT

UCC: Unified communication and collaboration

UDP: User Datagram Protocol

UPN: User Principal Name

URL: Uniform Resource Locator

VoIP: Voice over IP

VPN: Virtual private network

WAP: Wireless Access Point

WebSocket: An event-driven protocol

Index

A

Active Directory Domain Services (AD DS), 174
Active directory users and computers (ADUC), 115
Admin app discovery, 62, 221
Admin center, 221
    analytics and reports, 57
    App setup policies, 63
    dashboard, 58
    devices, 51
    emergency policy option, 54
    home, 49
    interface improvements, 59
    locations, 55, 56
    managing apps, 62
    meetings, 52, 53
    network planner, 57
    notification framework, 69
    notifications and alerts, 57, 58
    options, 60
    policy packages, 56
    teams, 49, 50
    Teams apps, 51, 52
    users, 50
    user search, 61
    voice routing policy, 55
    voice settings configuration, 53, 54
Administrator and Teams functionality, 5
Advanced call analytics, 241
Alert message, 284

Antivirus exclusion, 346
Apple CarPlay, 377
Apps
    block, 222
    custom, 223
    external, 223
    issues, 222
    manage, 222
    permission policies, 223, 224
    tailored, 222
    third-party, 223
Apps and workflows, 4, 21
Audio conferencing
    admin center
        capabilities, 59–63
        management role, 47, 48
    calling into meetings, 45
    configuration
        add-on licenses, 127, 128
        assigning communications credit licenses to users, 130
        communication credits, 130
        conference bridge default number, 129
        toll-free conference bridge numbers, 131
    configuring and troubleshooting, 304–306
    default bridge, 304
    device management (*see* Device management)

© Balu N Ilag and Arun M Sabale 2022
B. N. Ilag and A. M. Sabale, *Troubleshooting Microsoft Teams*, https://doi.org/10.1007/978-1-4842-8622-7

Printed in the United States
by Baker & Taylor Publisher Services